Dorchester Abbey
Oxfordshire

FRONTISPIECE *Dorchester Abbey from the south-east in 1842, immediately prior to the Victorian restoration. Drawn and engraved by William Willis. (Dorchester Abbey Museum)*

DORCHESTER ABBEY OXFORDSHIRE

The Archaeology and Architecture of a Cathedral, Monastery and Parish Church

by

WARWICK RODWELL

Oxbow Books
Oxford and Oakville

Published by
Oxbow Books, Oxford, UK

© Oxbow Books and the individual author, 2009

ISBN 978-1-84217-388-6

This book is available direct from:

Oxbow Books, Oxford, UK
(Phone: 01865-241249; Fax: 01865-794449)

and

The David Brown Book Company
PO Box 511, Oakville, CT 06779, USA
(Phone: 860-945-9329; Fax: 860-945-9468)

or from our website

www.oxbowbooks.com

A CIP record for this book is available from the British library

Library of Congress Cataloging-in-Publication Data
Rodwell, Warwick.
  Dorchester Abbey, Oxfordshire : the archaeology and architecture of a cathedral, monastery, and
parish church / by Warwick Rodwell.
      p. cm.
  Includes bibliographical references and index.
  ISBN 978-1-84217-388-6
  1. Dorchester Abbey. 2. Church architecture--England--Dorchester (Oxfordshire) 3. Dorches-
ter (Oxfordshire, England)--Buildings, structures, etc. 4. Excavations (Archaeology)--England-
-Dorchester (Oxfordshire) 5. Dorchester (Oxfordshire, England)--Antiquities. I. Title. II. Title:
Archaeology and architecture of a cathedral, monastery, and parish church.
  NA5471.D6R63 2009
  726.509425'79--dc22
                              2009039557

Front cover:
14th-century figures in stained glass and stone in the Jesse window in the chancel. (Frank Blackwell, FRPS)

Back cover:
Raking sunlight on the painted reredos in the south nave aisle. Watercolour by Rebecca Hind. (Private collection)

Printed and bound in Great Britain by
Short Run Press, Exeter

For John Metcalfe, who initiated this book project
and
Diane Gibbs-Rodwell, who inspired its completion

CONTENTS

PART 1

ARCHAEOLOGY, ARCHITECTURE AND CONTEXT

PART 2

THE FABRIC AND FITTINGS OF THE CHURCH

PREFACE

Dorchester-on-Thames and its abbey have been subjects of antiquarian interest for more than 450 years, and during that time much has been written about them. They are, however, still far from being comprehensively studied and recorded. Indeed, the most substantial architectural description of the medieval church was written as long ago as 1845, and a thoroughgoing reappraisal has long been overdue. While the focus of this study is the parish church of St Peter and St Paul, I have also briefly discussed the wider topographical and archaeological context in an attempt to demonstrate how the church came to be erected where it is, what influenced its geographic orientation, and how it related to the surrounding settlement pattern. Although I have been keenly interested in Dorchester since the 1960s, it was only in 2001 that an opportunity arose for detailed study, when the Parochial Church Council (PCC) embarked on a major programme of repair, conservation and improvement to the facilities of the church. Consequently, scaffolding was erected throughout the building, both internally and externally, allowing access for close inspection of the historic fabric in nearly all areas. The addition of a pentice structure on the site of the south cloister walk and the installation of new heating apparatus necessitated excavation, which provided the opportunity to record archaeological evidence below ground.

Thus, through a combination of observations during repair and conservation, information derived from archaeological excavation and watching briefs, and prolonged scrutiny of the building, between 2001 and 2007, our knowledge of the fabric of the church, and the archaeology of its site, has been substantially enriched. Assembling all this material, together with a reappraisal of past observations and previous discourses on the architectural development of the building, enables us to offer a fresh and fuller account of the origins, history and architecture of Dorchester Abbey. The present study concentrates principally on the archaeological and architectural evidence, and does not attempt a detailed review of the historical documentation, although that is embraced where relevant. Nor is the topography of the town reassessed, except in the immediate vicinity of the church. This volume is divided into two parts: the first contains an account of the archaeology of the site and the architectural development of the abbey, while the second comprises a series of detailed notes and observations on the present structure, its fittings and furnishings.

An unexpected outcome of this enquiry has been the discovery of a remarkable quantity of previously unstudied and unpublished topographical and architectural material, housed in several archives. While Anthony Wood's mid-17th-century plan and account of the church are well known, other early plans and descriptions held by the British Library and the Bodleian Library are virtually unknown. More remarkable still is the fact that in both libraries there are innumerable 18th- and 19th-century sketches and drawings of Dorchester which have escaped the catalogues. These include works by such notable topographical and architectural artists as Samuel Grimm, John Carter, the Bucklers and Orlando Jewitt.

The total volume of pictorial material held in archives is truly impressive, and there can be very few, if any, other parish churches in Britain which can boast a more voluminous record. The publication of a monograph based on these antiquarian illustrations, with an accompanying commentary, would make a further valuable contribution. The collections of especial significance are listed here in the Appendix. However, against the successes of discovery must be weighed the disappointments: the loss of virtually all pre-Dissolution records relating to the abbey is regrettable, but not entirely surprising. However, it is our failure to discover much documentation, particularly architects' drawings and specifications associated with the Victorian restoration that occasions greater surprise. No less than four architects were involved during the period 1844–83, but little documentary record of their work seems to have survived.

No study of a complex, multi-phase building and its site can be comprehensive or definitive: as knowledge accrues either through the discovery of physical or historical evidence, or through advances in scholarship generally, fresh insights will give rise to new interpretations and hypotheses. This account of Dorchester Abbey, although wide-ranging and more comprehensive than any that has hitherto been attempted, is nevertheless only a stepping-stone in the pursuit of a complete and authentic understanding of one of the most remarkable and historically important parish churches in England.

Acknowledgements

The research upon which this study is based was commissioned by Mike Thrift on behalf of the Dorchester PCC, and I am grateful to the Rector and Churchwardens for their interest and support throughout, particularly the Revd Canon John Crowe and the Revd Canon Susan Booys. I am especially indebted to the former Secretary of the PCC, John Metcalfe, M.B.E., who has been unstinting in his encouragement and practical assistance, especially in providing access and information, including copies of past reports and other documentation. Furthermore, he has been responsible for raising the funds necessary to facilitate this publication: we wish to acknowledge generous donations from the Friends of Dorchester Abbey, Dorchester Abbey Museum, Dorchester Historical Society, Michael and Jill Brookes, and John and Margot Metcalfe.

Martin Ashley and Andrew Harris, of Martin Ashley Architects, have been most helpful at all stages, and have also supplied valuable background material. Other local information was kindly provided by Professor Malcolm Airs, Fr Jerome Bertram, Michael Brookes, Frank and Christiane Norman, and Dr David Sturdy. Some of the photographs reproduced here were generously supplied by Frank Blackwell FRPS, and Rebecca Hind kindly allowed the reproduction of three of her watercolours. Similarly, Dr Kate Tiller and Fr Jerome Bertram willingly gave permission for the use of material derived from their own publications.

I am indebted to Graham Keevill for conducting me around the excavations while they were in progress; Julian Munby and Edmund Simons shared with me the results of the architectural recording works carried out by Oxford Archaeology, and Martin Rush kindly supplied information derived from his geophysical survey of the claustral area. Caroline Atkins assisted with the archaeological recording of the north wall of the nave. For the benefit of fruitful discussion on the medieval wallpaintings I am grateful to Ann Ballantyne; and on the chancel windows to Dr Tim Ayers. The latter also kindly gave permission to cite from his unpublished thesis on the sanctuary. As always, I am grateful for the continuous support and perceptive observations made by my wife, Diane Gibbs-Rodwell, and we are both indebted to Margot Metcalfe for her excellent hospitality.

Finally, I must record my gratitude to the staff of the British Library, Bodleian Library, Oxfordshire Record Office, Centre for Oxfordshire Studies and the National Monuments Record (English Heritage) for assistance with accessing the archival collections in their care. I have also made much use of the Sackler Library, Oxford, the library of the Society of Antiquaries of London, and the archives of Dorchester Abbey Museum.

Warwick Rodwell
Downside, Somerset
New Year's Day, 2009

PART I: ARCHAEOLOGY, ARCHITECTURE AND CONTEXT

CHAPTER 1

The Antiquarian Background

The substantial Oxfordshire village of Dorchester-on-Thames, together with its immediate environs, is one of the archaeologically most complex and interesting areas in Britain. There is not just *something* illustrative of every period in history, but an abundance of material evidence of high-ranking importance.[1] The early prehistoric era is principally represented by the Dorchester cursus, a henge monument and tumuli; and the riverside fortification of Dyke Hills is an important monument of later prehistory. In the early Roman period there was a fort guarding the crossings of the rivers Thames and Thame, and this was later superseded by a small walled town. The area remained densely settled in the early Anglo-Saxon period, and some outstanding finds have been made, particularly from pagan cemeteries. However, Dorchester's greatest claim to fame is arguably in the middle Saxon period, when it became the seat of a huge bishopric, which initially extended from Dorset to the south Midlands; a later redefinition of the diocese retracted its southern territory but took its northern limit to the Humber. The founding bishop (later saint) was Birinus, whose name has been firmly associated with Dorchester since A.D. 635. Unlike many Anglo-Saxon cults which fizzled out and were never rekindled, that of St Birinus not only survived the Norman Conquest, but continued to flourish until the Reformation.

When Dorchester lost its diocesan status to Lincoln in the late 11th century, it remained a local market town, and the former cathedral became a church of secular canons, who, in the mid-12th century, were superseded by Augustinian canons. Although Dorchester Abbey was neither large nor rich, it nevertheless flourished in unexpected ways, and most notable amongst its surviving treasures is the unique suite of windows installed at the east end of the church in the early 14th century. Inevitably, the abbey was suppressed at the Reformation, but the church survived almost in its entirety, and stands today as one of the larger and more remarkable ex-monastic parish churches in England. The town, meanwhile, declined as an urban focus, to be transmuted into an attractive village replete with many fine historic buildings. The history and topography of the Dorchester region has justly attracted much attention from antiquaries. Nevertheless, considerable areas of uncertainty remain, some of which can only be remedied by large-scale archaeological excavations.

The topographical situation of Dorchester is particularly favourable to both settlement and defence. The site lies at the confluence of the Thames and Thame, on a roughly rectangular promontory of

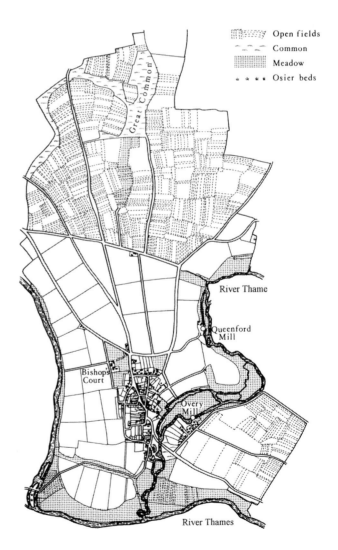

FIGURE 1: The parish of Dorchester and topography of the promontory between the rivers Thames and Thame, c. 1840. (Cook and Rowley, 1985)

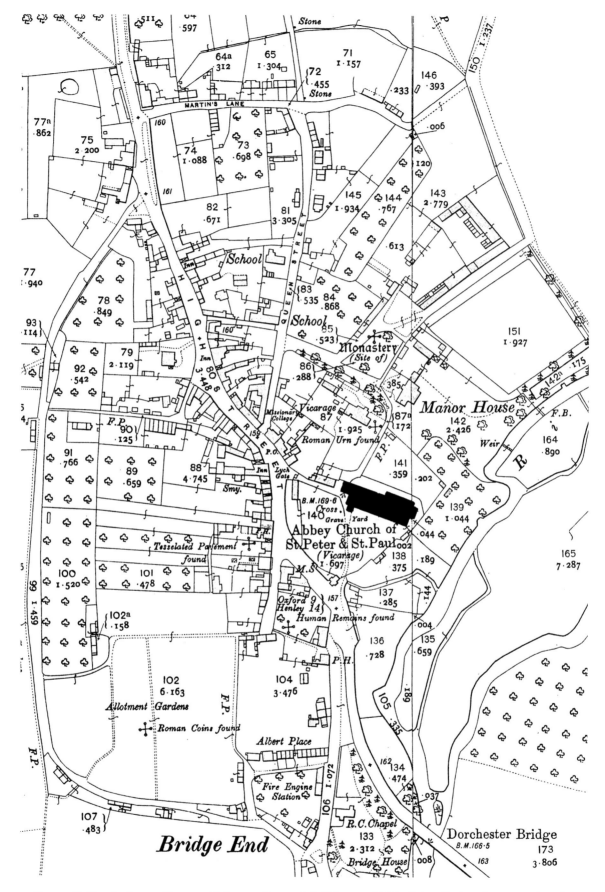

Figure 2. Dorchester-on-Thames: Ordnance Survey 1:2,500 map, 1910 edition. Reduced to 1:3,250 scale.

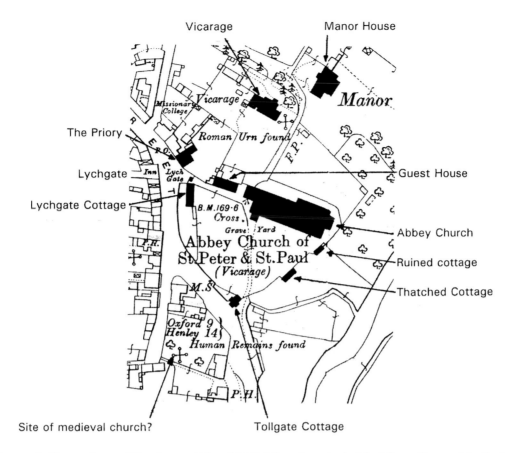

FIGURE 3. The environs of Dorchester Abbey, highlighting the principal buildings discussed in the text.

gravel, over which is a thin capping of brickearth (Fig. 1).[2] The west and south sides of the promontory are formed by a right-angled bend in the Thames, and the east side by the Thame. The Roman and medieval town grew up alongside the latter river, and thus the designation 'Dorchester-on-Thames' is somewhat misleading. However, the Thames was a major artery of communication, and in the Middle Ages it was navigable as far as Oxford. The main overland route through Dorchester runs from north-west (Oxford) to south-east (Wallingford), and there is a bridge over the Thame at the southern end of the town (Figs 2 and 3).

The principal disadvantage of the locality is the lack of good building stone: hence timber and cob have always been the major structural materials, later followed by brick. Chalk was available from the Sinodun Hills (Wittenham Clumps), just south of Dorchester, together with flint nodules that are found in association with the chalk; both materials were pressed into service by builders. For good quality masonry, however, oolitic limestone had to be transported from quarries on the Oxford Heights, several kilometres to the north. The abbey church is built mainly of rough limestone rubble, with finely dressed ashlar reserved for quoins and mouldings.

EARLY DESCRIPTIONS OF DORCHESTER

The earliest recorded description of Dorchester is by the chronicler William of Malmesbury who, in *c*. 1125, referred to the town as 'obscure and unfrequented', but commented on its churches as remarkable for their beauty.[3] In 1340, another chronicler, Ranulf Higden, commented on Dorchester in his *Polychronicon*.[4] Although William Worcestre evidently called at Dorchester whilst on his itineraries in 1480 he did not dally,[5] and the earliest topographical description of the place was not penned until 1542 by John Leland. He described the town briefly:

> The toun of Dorchestre was sore defacid by the Danes. Of old tyme it was much larger in building then it is now toward the south and the Tamise side. There was a paroche chirch a litle by south from the abbay chirch. And another paroch chirch more south above it. There was a 3 paroch chirch by south weste.
> In the closis and feeldes that lye southly on the toun that now standith be founde *numismata Romanorum* of gold, silver and brasse.
> The bisshop's palace, as is saide the[re], was at the toune's end by north west, wher yet appere fundations of old buildings; and there as yet be kept the courtes.
> The abbay of chanons, wher afore the Conquest was a bisshopes sete. Remigius translatid it to Lincoln. Alexander Bisshop of Lincoln erected there an abbay of blak chanons. Yet the chirch berith the name of the

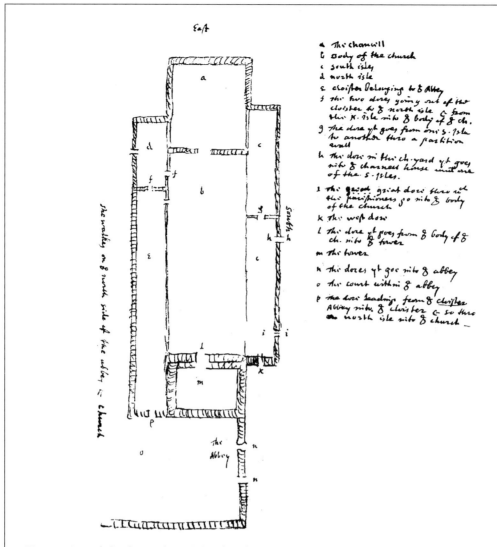

Transcript of the legend on Wood's plan:

a　The chancill
b　Body of the church
c　South isles
d　North isle
e　Cloister belonging to ye Abbey
f　The two doors going out of the cloister to ye north isle & from this N. isle into ye body of ye ch[urch]
g　The door yt goes from one S. isle to another thro[ugh] a partition wall
h　The door in the ch[urch] yard yt goes into ye charnell house under one of the S. isles
i　This [?is the] great door thro[ugh] wh[ich] the parishioners go into ye body of the church
k　The west door
l　This door yt goes from ye body of ye ch[urch] into ye tower
m　The tower
n　This door yt goes into ye abbey
o　The court within ye abbey
p　The door leading from ye cloister
　　Abbey into(?) ye cloister & so thro[ugh] the north isle into ye church –

The legend on the left-hand margin reads: 'The walkes on ye north side of the abbey & church'

FIGURE 4. *Annotated sketch plan of Dorchester church by Anthony Wood, shortly before 1657. East is at the top. (Clark, 1891)*

prebend chirch. There was burid, as it is said, the bodie of S. Birine bisshop there.[6]

Leland went on to list features within the abbey – mostly tombs – that captured his attention.

Visitors who were principally interested in heraldry have left behind their notes, including Richard Lee and Robert Cooke (Clarenceux King of Arms) in 1574,[7] Nicholas Charles (Lancaster Herald) and Francis Thynne, in 1596–97,[8] and Richard Symonds, in 1644.[9] In the 17th century, a remarkably full description of Dorchester Abbey was contained in the manuscript notes of Anthony Wood, the Oxford antiquary (1632–95).[10] He visited the church in August 1657, noting, inter alia:

> The church is larg and antique, and hath contained many monuments of antiquity, which are since spoyled and defaced. Those that remain he took an account of, as also the arms in the windowes, and tricked out with his pen the ichnography of the church and cloyster and buildings adjoyning.[11]

He continued:

> The frontispeice of the abbey of Dorchester stands at the west end of the church, and the rest of the building run behind the north side. The outside of the abbey is all built of free-stone three storey high, but the inside next to the court is built of timber and plaister. The limits of the abbey run mostly on the north side of the church. There be great slatted barns that are supported with buttresses, yet standing ... There be verie pleasant walks in the grounds below the abbey, all shadowed with elmes, and the river Thame running thereby.
> When the schoolhouse was built ... about 3 yeares agoe, at the west end of the church, there were in digging of the foundations discovered certaine little roomes under ground, some pav'd very smoothly with hard white stone, and some brick'd round. In one of the rooms was an hearth in the middle, much like those (but farr less) in College halls. ... in digging at the west end of the church there was discovered a smal vault that would hold 3 or 4 men or more, and at the top was a tonnell, like unto a chimney but somthing larger ....

> There was a cloister on the north side of the church that led from the abbey to a north isle, joyning thereunto. See in the iconography. [See Fig. 4][12]

[Wood next gives a long and minutely detailed account of arms and monuments]

> In the body of the church are no monuments remaining but one which is at the entrance into the choire. 'Tis a flat greyish marble, and thereone hath been the picture of a crosier engraven, now almost worn out. It seems to be verie antient.
> At the upper end of Dorchester chancell on the south side are 4 seates of stone in the wall, witrh canopies over each curiously carved in stone. Over them is a verie antient window, wherin is represented the picture of S. Birine in his episcopall habit, standing on the deck of a ship on the sea, sayling for England, and severall priests with tonsur'd crowns or heads. In another light of the same window he is represented preaching on the sea before certaine people with him. In another he is preaching to king Kenigilsus. In another he is obtaining leave of pope Honorius to goe and venture himself to preach Xt unto the infidells. In another he is baptizing king Kenigilsus, and Oswald king of Northumbria stands there to be his godfather.
> In the north window opposit to the former is the stock of Jesse, with their images, all curiously cut in stone in the pillars of the window. They have each of them a scroule of writing in their hands, of an antient character, but now almost quite obliterated. There are 27 or 28 images, some of which were much defaced by the parliamentary soldiers in the late rebellion.
> The walls of the chancell have been all painted verie gloriously with severall sorts of beasts. There yet remaines a lyon, a griffin, a leopard.
> In my searches about the church I could not find any signe of bishop Aeschwyne's tomb, of free stone, which Leland mentioned.
> The tower that now is, is but of late standing; the staircase old. Upon the great bell is this: 'Protege, Birine, quos convoco, tu sine fine'.[13]

Another Oxford antiquary, Thomas Hearne, frequently commented on Dorchester in his journals during the first quarter of the 18th century.[14] He was friendly with Mr Bannister, a local collector of antiquities, whom he often visited. Consequently, Hearne provides us with a running commentary on discoveries at Dorchester over a period of more than twenty years. Interestingly, he was one of the earliest observers of evidence demonstrating that buried structures could give rise to changes in the colour of growing crops, especially during dry spells.[15]

Interest in Dorchester by antiquaries of national repute was primarily aroused through discoveries of Roman remains, of which there were many in the 18th century. Indeed, they had already been mentioned by Edmund Gibson in his edition of William Camden's Britannia in 1695.[16] John Horsley, who collected Roman inscriptions for his Britannia Romana (1732), excitedly described the recent finding of an altar at Dorchester, and slipped a drawing of it into his publication while it was in press (Fig. 15A). And it is well that he did, for this is the primary record of a most important discovery, the altar itself having long ago disappeared from public view. Hearne, too was much exercised by both the altar's discovery, and the interpretation of its inscription.[17]

Richard Gough, in his augmented edition of Camden's Britannia (1789), quoted Leland and Horsley, and added a good deal of material of his own, mainly topographical.[18] For example, he provided the earliest description of the town's defences: 'the vallum is very bold with a double ditch in the fields on the southwest side of the town and the churchyard'.[19] One of the first antiquaries who attempted to understand the layout of the Roman settlement was the Revd Thomas Barns, in 1881, and others followed.[20]

Serious interest in the architecture of the abbey church began to develop in the first half of the 18th century, and from then on gathered pace. William Stukeley wrote a eulogistic description in 1736: 'I came with an eager view of the most antient of our church antiquities, and my expectation was fully answer'd. I believe no place in England can show such a site of religious antiquity belonging to our Saxon Christian ancestors' (p. 42).[21] An illustrated account of the abbey in the early 19th century, by Joseph Skelton, was included in his *Antiquities of Oxfordshire*.[22]

Towards the end of the 19th century, notes began to appear in the *Gentleman's Magazine*: the Jesse window, font and various tombs all attracted comment.[23] The general upsurge of public interest in matters ecclesiastical in the middle decades of the 19th century led to the publication of a stream of books and pamphlets on the abbey church, and interest was further fuelled by the major restoration which began in 1844–45. Henry Addington and the Oxford-based architect John Henry Parker were responsible for the earliest serious accounts of the building, both published in 1845.[24] Addington's copiously illustrated book was subsequently augmented and reissued by the Revd William Charles Macfarlane (in 1860 and 1882), as the restoration of the church proceeded.[25] A considerable debt is owed to Macfarlane (vicar, 1856–85) not only for his personal and financial contributions to the restoration, but also for recording the history of the period.[26]

In 1850, the Royal Archaeological Institute held its annual meeting at Oxford at which a paper on Dorchester Abbey was read by the historian Edward Augustus Freeman, and a site visit was also made.[27] Freeman's paper was a major contribution to the study of the abbey, and included the first attempt at an architecturally phased plan of the church (Fig. 8).[28] Freeman also made frequent allusion to Dorchester in his important study of the development of English medieval window tracery,[29] as did numerous other 19th-century writers on architectural history, including Thomas Rickman in his seminal *Attempt to Discriminate the Styles of Architecture in England* (1817, *et seq.*) and Parker in his equally influential *A B C of Gothic Architecture* (1881, *et seq.*).[30] In 1881 and 1882 Macfarlane and Parker, respectively, published general histories of Dorchester.[31]

There was not always a consensus of opinion amongst antiquaries as to the age and correct interpretation of various features in the abbey: as Parker wrote in 1882, 'The architectural history of this magnificent church has been a battle-field of the archaeologists for the last half-century'.[32] However, in his own advertisement for the volume that he edited, Parker claimed, 'In collecting together for the use of students in archaeology all the information that is extant respecting Dorchester, I believe that I

have done useful service', concluding that there was 'no need of another essay on the subject, enough has been written about it, and the high reputation that Mr E.A. Freeman has now deservedly obtained would make anyone unwilling to differ in opinion from him, and his essay is well worth reprinting, although written quite in his youth'.[33]

Since the mid-19th century, other learned societies have paid visits to Dorchester and various short, and largely derivative, accounts have been published in journals.[34] Finally, at the close of the 19th century the architect Roland Paul[35] included Dorchester Abbey in his series of studies published in *The Builder*.[36]

Many of the earlier descriptions of the church and its monuments contain inaccuracies, particularly in dating, because architectural history, as an academic discipline, was still in its infancy. For example, the distinction between Anglo-Saxon and Norman work was not defined until well into the 19th century, with the consequence that the Romanesque doorway leading from the north transept to the cloister was described in 1793 by Carter as 'Saxon'. Its true age was appreciated by the time architectural manuals came to be written in the middle years of the 19th century.[37] The 14th-century Decorated architecture of Dorchester figured prominently in those manuals.[38]

ANTIQUARIAN ILLUSTRATIONS
Watercolours, Drawings and Sketches

The number of surviving antiquarian illustrations of Dorchester Abbey and its contents is remarkable for a parish church: over 400 have so far been located, but scarcely more than a handful of these has ever been published.[39] Apart from Wood's plan of the church (Fig. 4, and see below), the earliest published illustrations relating to Dorchester are a drawing of the Roman altar dedicated to Jupiter (Fig. 15A), found in 1731, and the earthworks at Dyke Hills, 1755.[40] A gold and cornelian finger-ring dug up behind the church was illustrated in 1789 (Fig. 15B), and other antiquities were subsequently published.[41]

The abbey church, being both picturesque and replete with rich and interesting architectural detail, commanded the attentions of many artists in the late 18th and 19th centuries. The earliest known view, dating from before 1722, is by John Harris (Fig. 5). Other early drawings include those by Samuel Grimm, made in the late 1770s and 1780s.[42] The architect John Carter, the most prolific of late 18th-century antiquarian artists, visited in 1792 and 1793 and recorded many details, including a sketch plan marked with a key to the positions of all the monuments that were considered to be historically interesting.[43] In association with Gough, Carter began to prepare a portfolio of *Antiquities of Dorchester* in 1793 (Pls 1 and 22),[44] but the project never reached publication.

John Buckler, another architect with a prodigious output of drawings, made excursions to Dorchester in 1802–03, 1812–13 and 1821.[45] On his first visit Buckler prepared sketches covering the entire exterior of the church. These were then used as the basis for working up a series of superbly executed watercolour drawings (Pl. 3). From 1807, Buckler's son, John Chessell Buckler, also visited Dorchester on several occasions and made further drawings. In 1813, he began to turn his sketches into watercolour drawings, for a portfolio of Dorchester antiquities which was never completed.[46] Buckler also recorded the destruction of the late medieval bridge over the Thame in 1815.

John Britton, when preparing his seminal volumes on the history of medieval architecture in England (1820–21), included several fine plates of Dorchester, particularly of the chancel windows (Figs 85, 87 and 98).[47] Skelton similarly published a series of high quality engravings in the mid-1820s (Figs 86, 99, 100 and 191A).[48] In 1845, Addington was the first to publish not only a large number of measured drawings of architectural features in the church, but he also included a plan, views of small details, and moulding profiles. His monograph was published by Parker, and the illustrations were clearly organized by the latter: as usual, his principal artist was Orlando Jewitt.[49] Jewitt was a talented Oxford-based architectural and book artist, and Dorchester featured prominently in his early career.[50] His original drawings and proofs have survived.[51]

The artistic tradition of illustrating Dorchester and its antiquities continues to the present day (Pls 27, 44 and 47).

Early Photographs

Dorchester has not been well served by photographers over the last 150 years, but the record is better than for many parish churches. The earliest surviving photographs were taken by Henry Taunt of Oxford in the 1870s, following the effective completion of the church restoration.[52] It is puzzling why nobody seems to have recorded the church in the 1860s, or even the 1850s, either before restoration or while it was in progress. Such shots would have been immensely helpful.

The extant views, by Taunt and others, record little more than the final stages of re-roofing, changes in the layout of furniture inside the church, and the growth of trees and vegetation in the churchyard. Taunt also recorded aspects of the town and a few details of former abbey buildings (since destroyed) at Manor Farm. He published a detailed guidebook to Dorchester, postcard views, and a portfolio of fifty photographs.[53] Other 20th-century photographs of the church and its environs are restricted in their coverage, very repetitive, and add little to the sum of knowledge.[54]

MAPS AND PLANS OF DORCHESTER ABBEY

Dorchester is poorly served in the cartographic record, and understanding the extent and layout of the Augustinian abbey precinct would be greatly facilitated if estate maps of the 17th or 18th centuries existed, as would changes to the churchyard boundary brought about by the creation of the turnpike road through the town. Nothing antedating the turnpike era is extant apart from general maps of the county which show the town much simplified (e.g. Davis's map, 1797).[55] The earliest map of the parish was surveyed by John Neighbour, 1837–38 (Fig. 1).[56] The first Ordnance Survey 1:2,500 plan was surveyed in 1877 (Fig. 2),[57] and there is a plan of Manor Farm in 1889.[58]

In contrast to the uninspiring history of cartography at Dorchester, the number of historic ground plans that have been produced of the church, over the course of 350 years, is remarkable, although their accuracy varies. Dorchester is exceptional for having a surviving plan drawn in the mid-17th century, one in the early 18th, and another in the middle of the same century. Very few English church plans antedating the late 18th century have survived, and most cathedrals do not possess one earlier than the 1720s.

The principal plans of Dorchester Abbey are worth listing and illustrating:

1. The plan which accompanies notes made by Anthony Wood during a visit in August 1657 had been drawn on an earlier visit, probably in the previous year.[59] The plan is not to scale, but is a careful sketch with useful annotations (Fig. 4).

2. An undated plan, drawn to scale and engraved by John Harris whose *floruit* was in the 1720s. Published in 1722, it shows the layout of the interior, including screens, the monastic return-stalls, pews, pulpit, floor slabs and much other detail (Fig. 6).[60] An omission is the stair-turret in the tower. There is a key to the principal features and monuments, and the ledger-slab of the Revd Philip Keen (d. 1713) is marked, thus providing a *terminus post quem*.

3. In 1768, William Stukeley visited Dorchester and drew a sketch plan which was based on that prepared some years earlier for Stevens (see no. 2, above). Stukeley corrected and annotated the plan.[61]

4. In 1793, John Carter made an annotated and dimensioned sketch plan, which he then worked up into a carefully executed plan with a key.[62] This shows more detail than the last, and is of considerable importance.

5. An unsigned plan dated 1807 is possibly by Henry Hinton, and seems to be derivative from Carter.[63] It is well drawn and appears to be reasonably accurate by the standards of its time. Major furnishings and many monuments are shown; there is a key and annotations.

6. Addington's book (1845) included a poor version of the ground plan of the church, initially drawn in 1844 by Jewitt.[64] It is not notable for its accuracy: *e.g.* a complete pier is shown at the east end of the nave

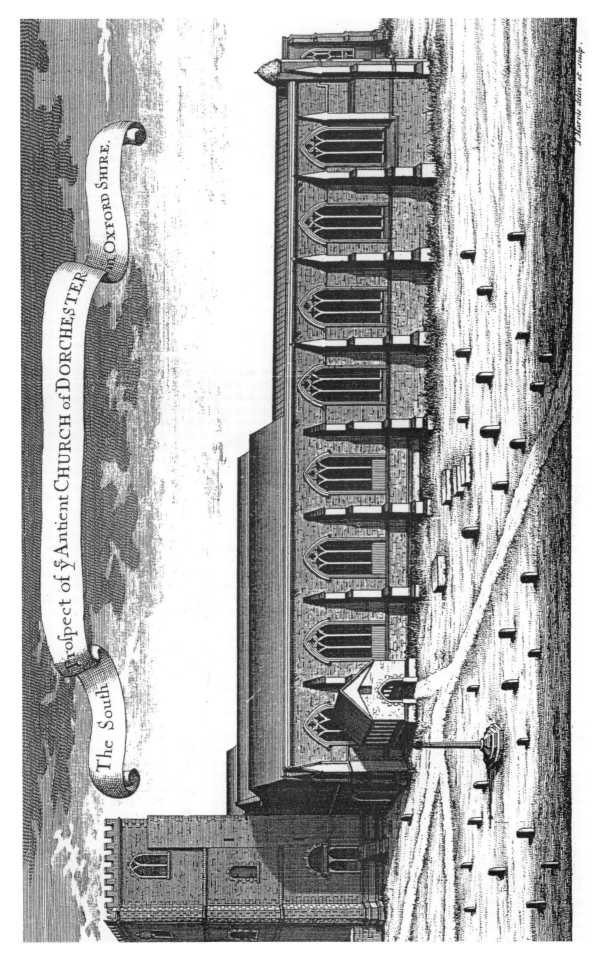

FIGURE 5. *The church from the south by John Harris, c. 1720. (Stevens, 1722)*

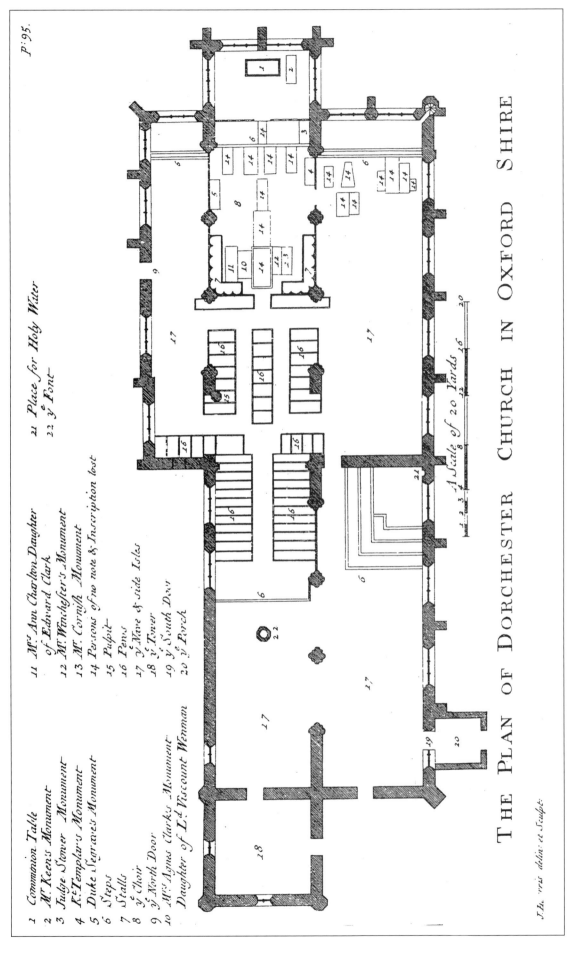

P: 95.

1 Communion Table
2 Mr Keens Monument
3 Judge Stoner Monument
4 Knts Templar's Monument
5 Duke Negrave's Monument
6 Steps
7 Stalls
8 ye Choir
9 ye Quire
10 Mrs Agnes Clarks Monument
Daughter of Ld Viscount Wenman

11 Mrs Ann Charlton Daughter
   of Edward Clark
12 Mr Winchester's Monument
13 Mr Cornish Monument
14 Persons of no note & Inscription lost
15 Pulpit
16 Pews
17 ye Nave & side Isles
18 ye Tower
19 ye South Door
20 ye Porch

21 Place for Holy Water
22 ye Font

A Scale of 20 Yards

J. Harris delin: et Sculpt:

THE PLAN OF DORCHESTER CHURCH IN OXFORD SHIRE

FIGURE 6. Annotated plan of the church by John Harris, c. 1720, showing monuments and the monastic return-stalls in the quire. (Stevens, 1722)

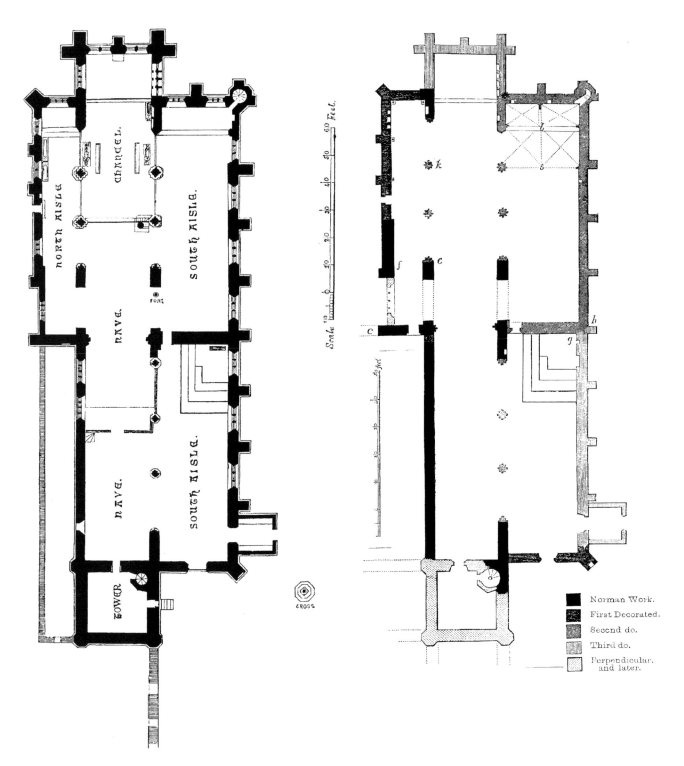

FIGURE 7. *Plan of the church based on a survey by Orlando Jewitt, showing the layout immediately prior to the Victorian restoration. (Addington, 1845)*

FIGURE 8. *Edward Freeman's plan of 1850, the first to attempt an analysis of the structural phasing of the church. (Freeman, 1852)*

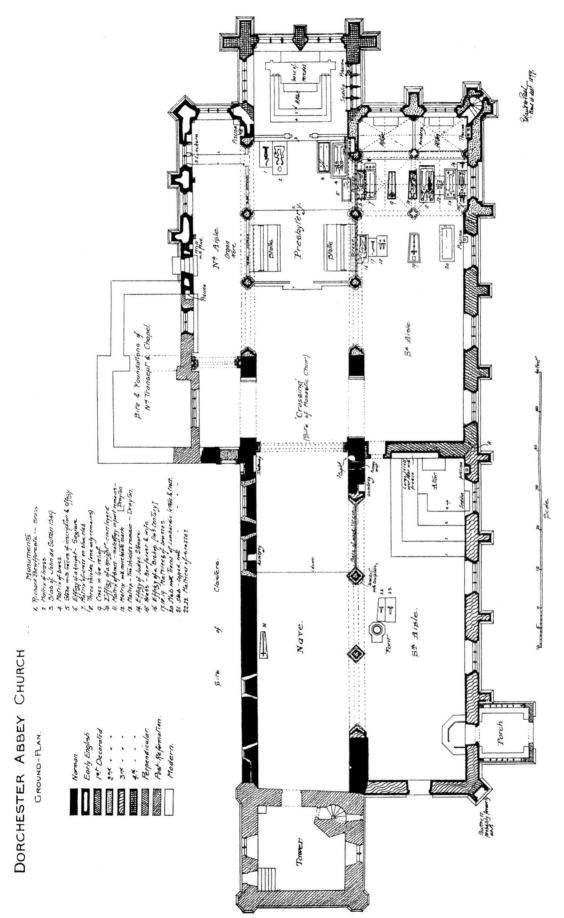

FIGURE 9. Roland Paul's plan of 1899, the first archaeologically annotated plan of the church. (Paul, 1900)

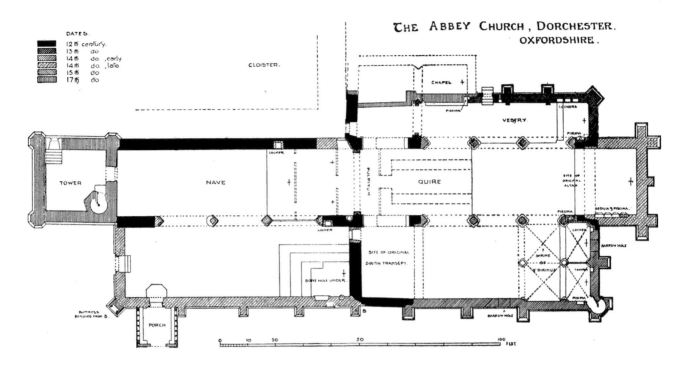

FIGURE 10. William St John Hope's plan of 1910, showing a conjectural reconstruction of the monastic quire. (Anon., 1910)

arcade, instead of a respond.[65] This is not up to Jewitt's standard, and he clearly did not prepare the final plan for publication (Fig. 7).

7. Freeman's study of the church in 1850 was accompanied by a more reliable plan of unknown authorship (Fig. 8).[66] This was the first plan which attempted to analyze the relative ages of the components.

8. A plan by James Johnson, dated 1852, shows the complete reseating scheme implemented by Butterfield.[67]

9. J.M. Bignell, formerly architectural assistant to Sir G.G. Scott, prepared what he called an 'index plan' in 1879, which was coloured to show the structural phasing of the church.[68] A large-scale plan, indicating phasing, is in existence.[69] It is crudely executed, unsigned and undated, but is clearly mid/late 19th century. This item accords with the description contained in Bignell's notes.[70] In detail, the plan is not however reliable.

10. Roland Paul's paper of 1900 was accompanied by the first reasonably accurate ground plan of the abbey, which also differentiated the phases of construction (Fig. 9).

11. Henry Taunt published his own plan of the church in 1906, on which he marked the then-exposed foundations of the demolished north transept and some internal features that do not appear on other plans.[71]

12. Another phased plan was prepared by (Sir) William St John Hope in 1910 (Fig. 10).[72]

13. Francis Bond's seminal study of 1913 contained its own general plan, as well as a series of interpretative plans. Although rather crudely drawn, these represent the first attempt to reconstruct development plans of the church (Figs 11 and 12).[73]

14. A phased plan drawn to modern conventions

accompanied (Sir) Howard Colvin's account of Dorchester Abbey for the *Victoria County History*, published in 1962.[74]

15. A new, accurate plan was prepared by Sterling Surveys in 2001, showing furnishings, floor paving, etc. (Figs 118, 162, 168, 176 and 187). For a new archaeologically phased plan based on this, see Pl. 4.

TWENTIETH-CENTURY SCHOLARSHIP

The proximity of Dorchester to Oxford ensured that it was continually noticed by scholars of classics and archaeology throughout the 20th century. In 1882, Parker had already pronounced: 'there is certainly no place within easy reach of Oxford where [students] can learn so much by merely using their eyes with sufficient care'.[75] Indeed, numerous forays have been conducted by the Oxford University Archaeological Society, as well as individual academics, resulting in a stream of papers published in *Oxoniensia*, and elsewhere.

The defences of the Roman town were first surveyed in detail and archaeologically sectioned in 1935–36 (Fig. 13).[76] During the 1960s and 1970s several sites that were threatened with building development were partially excavated, contributing further to an understanding of the defences and, for the first time, exploring structures and streets within the town.[77] There has also been a miscellany of excavations in gravel-extraction pits and other threatened sites around the periphery of Dorchester, several of which have yielded important evidence for Anglo-Saxon

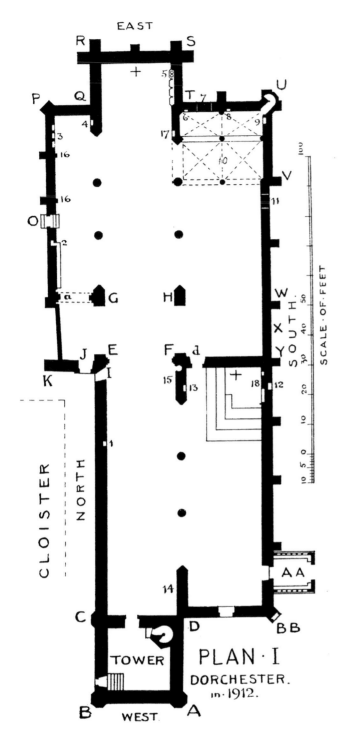

FIGURE 11. Francis Bond's plan of 1912, annotated with numbers and letters which relate to his detailed description and analysis of the church's development. For his analysis, see Fig. 12. (Bond, 1913)

settlements and cemeteries (*e.g.* Bishop's Court and Berinsfield); these have helped to provide a local cultural context for the town and cathedral in the post-Roman period. A steady stream of papers appeared in the second half of the 20th century on Roman Dorchester,[78] and another on the Anglo-Saxon archaeology of the neighbourhood.[79]

As a result of intensive aerial reconnaissance, particularly since the 1920s, the archaeology of the river gravels around Dorchester has been well studied from the air.[80] The Neolithic henge monument was a spectacular discovery as a cropmark in 1927.[81] Aerial photography is of little use in built-up areas and thus cannot assist with elucidating the complex archaeology of the town and abbey. However, it is clear that the palimpsest of archaeological features revealed around the margins of the town continues beneath it, and the alignment of the church coincides with that of a pair of ditches seen from the air immediately west of the built-up area. The archaeology of the town was summarized in a survey of historic towns in Oxfordshire in 1975.[82]

In the first half of the 20th century, little attention was paid by archaeologists to the abbey and its surroundings, but in 1960–62 three trenches were cut in the garden to the north of the church, with a view to establishing the positions of the vanished cloister walks.[83] A small excavation was also made in the south chancel aisle in 1964, prior to the reconstruction of St Birinus's shrine.[84] Architectural historians, however, have revelled unceasingly in the abbey: Britton, Addington, Macfarlane, Parker and Freeman have already been mentioned. In the early years of the 20th century, Francis Bond dominated the field of ecclesiology, and he carried out a masterly analysis of the church, publishing a series of phase-plans to illustrate its development.[85] It was through Bond that Dorchester entered the annals of modern church archaeology: the exercise was well ahead of its time, and has been cited as an exemplar by later scholars.[86] Nevertheless, reconsideration of some aspects of Bond's analysis is overdue.

Bond's structural history and interpretation differed significantly from those of previous writers, and so he concluded, '[the abbey's] history has been eventful and curious, and not easy to decipher: a whole literature has grown round it.' He recognized that the 'divergence of opinion is to be seriously noted, as shewing that any such reconstruction of architectural history from imperfect data, however plausible it may be, cannot be regarded as final, conclusive, or authoritative.' Dorchester also featured in Bond's magisterial studies of the fittings and furnishings of medieval churches.[87] The windows of the chancel are remarkable, and the Jesse window in particular has often been illustrated. A careful study of the chancel, its decoration and fittings was undertaken in 1991 by Dr Timothy Ayers.[88] The window glass, bells, brasses and effigial monuments have featured in scholarly works on these subjects,[89] but few pieces of in-depth research have been carried out on individual items, such as Philip Lankester's masterly study of the cross-legged effigy of a knight.[90] In 1996 a basic list was made of memorial inscriptions inside the church.[91]

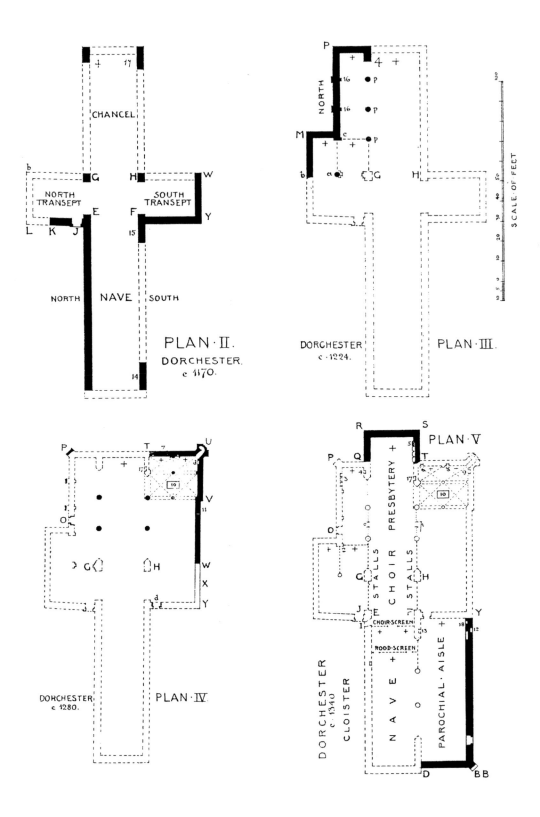

FIGURE 12. *Bond's analytical plans of the church, showing four stages of development. The letters and numbers correlate with his detailed description and general ground plan, Fig. 11. (Bond, 1913)*

The town and abbey have both benefited from substantial researches carried out by modern historians:[92] an introduction to all periods of Dorchester's history was compiled in 1985,[93] and a new general history of the abbey church appeared in 2005.[94] Unfortunately, the quantity of surviving medieval documentation is small, the records of the abbey having been destroyed at the Dissolution: to a large extent the building has to tell its own story. Lists of the major published works relating to Dorchester can be found in Oxfordshire bibliographies,[95] but there is also much unpublished material.[96]

Dorchester has been described, in varying amounts of detail, in innumerable general works on churches, abbeys, architecture, stained glass, and other related subjects.[97] Various guidebooks have also been issued during the course of the 20th century,[98] but they tend to repeat errors and popular misconceptions.[99] Although suffering from the latter defect, Taunt's guide (1906) is the most substantial and contains contemporary observations that are not found elsewhere.

Finally, Dorchester Abbey has been subjected to a range of archaeological investigations in recent years. Surveys by ground-probing radar (GPR) were carried out in 1999 and 2000;[100] excavations and watching briefs were undertaken during developments both inside and outside the church in 2001;[101] fabric recording took place during restoration between 1999 and 2003;[102] there was a geophysical survey of the cloister garden in 2004;[103] and a detailed study of the church and its setting was prepared between 2001 and 2007.[104]

NOTES

1   The breadth of archaeological interest at Dorchester is well illustrated in Briggs, *et al.* 1986.
2   For an introduction to the topography and drift geology, see Cook and Rowley, 1985, 3–7.
3   *Dorcestra est villa in pago Oxenfordensi exilis et infrequens. Majestas tamen ecclesiarum magna, seu veteri opera seu sedulitate nova.* (Hamilton, 1870, 312).
4   Babington, 1865, cap. 47, 52 and 53. For the historical context of the *Polychronicon*, see Gransden, 1982, 43–5.
5   Worcestre mentioned Dorchester only in connection with a book that was in the canons' library (Harvey, 1969, 329).
6   Smith, 1964, **1**, 117–18.
7   Turner, 1871. See also Addington, 1845, 43–8.
8   BL, Lans. Ms 874, f. 144 and Sl. Ms 3836, f. 14. See also Lankester, 1987, 155, n. 37.
9   BL, Harl. Ms 965.
10 Clark, 1891. For details of monumental inscriptions recorded by Wood, see Davies, 1922, 114–23.
11 Clark, 1891, 223. *N.B.* Wood is writing here about himself in the third person.
12 The plan is copied from a drawing in one of Wood's earlier manuscripts.
13 Clark, 1891, 224–5. Wood visited Dorchester again in May 1659, but did not record any further details concerning the church fabric: *ibid.*, 278.
14 OHS [Hearne], *Remarks and Collections of Thomas Hearne,* vols. III, IV, V, VII, VIII and X (1889–1915), *passim*.
15 In 1722, he commented on cropmarks at Dorchester as being 'like Silchester': Hearne, vol. VIII, 354. OHS, **50** (1907).
16 Gibson [Camden], 1695, 263. Two-thirds of Camden's relatively extended entry for Dorchester is taken up with poetry, in Latin and in English, which, he says, 'you may read or pass over as you please'.
17 Hearne, vol. X, *passim*. OHS, **67** (1915).
18 Gough [Camden], 1789, **1**, 306–8. See also Gough, 1786–96; Bertram, 2004, 209.
19 Gough may have mentally elided the defences of Dyke Hills with those of the town when he says that they were 'very bold' and double-ditched. However, evidence for a pair of shallow ditches on the south side of the town, in the post-Roman period, was found in excavations in 1963 (Frere, 1984, 126).
20 Barns, 1881. See also appendix in Parker, 1882, xxxiii ff. For an earlier account, see Parker, 1868.
21 Bodl., Gough Maps, 26, f. 42B(c).
22 Skelton, 1823. A grangerized copy is in Dorchester Abbey Museum.
23 *Gents. Mag.*, 1785, pt. 2, 434 (Jesse window and monuments, as noted in 1749); *ibid.*, 513 (font); 1796, pt. 1, 105 (brass); 1802, pt. 1, 124 (sword hilt?); 1816, pt. 2, 297 (topography and new bridge); 1818, pt. 1, 105 (old bridge); 1823, pt. 1, 297–8 (description of church). Several of these notes were accompanied by engravings. For collected extracts (without the illustrations) relating to Dorchester, see Gomme, 1897, 97–102.
24 Addington, 1845 (reissued 1848); Parker, 1845.
25 Addington, 1845, included a view of the proposed restoration of the chancel east window, whereas the 1882 edition illustrated the actual restoration (which was somewhat different).
26 For accounts of these incumbents, see Tiller, 2005, ch. 6.
27 *Archaeol. J.*, **7** (1850), 310.
28 Freeman, 1852; republished in Parker, 1882, 33–92.
29 Freeman, 1851.
30 Rickman, 1817; Parker, 1881. Rickman's treatise ran to six editions (1862), and Parker's to thirteen editions (1907).
31 Macfarlane, 1881; Parker, 1882. Parker's volume included a republication of two previously published papers: Freeman, 1851, and Addington and Macfarlane, 1860.
32 Parker, 1882, general introduction, ix.
33 *Ibid.*, advertisement, iii.
34 *E.g.* James Parker's lecture to the Oxford Architectural and Historical Society, 1874 (Parker, 1882, 93–102).
35 Paul, 1900.
36 Two other articles published in *The Builder* are of little consequence. The first, a report on the Architectural Association's visit to Oxford (and Dorchester) in 1890 (vol. **59**, 124) includes a drawing of the Segrave

monument by Roland Paul; the second is trivial (Roberts, 1930).

37 Rickman, 1862, 164.

38 *E.g.* Britton, 1835; Rickman, 1848, *passim*.

39 A complete list is contained in Rodwell, 2005a, appendix 2.

40 The earliest known view is by Stukeley, 1755: Bodl., Gough Maps, 26, f. 42B (reproduced in Keevill, 2005, fig. 7. For an illustration of *c.* 1780 by S.H. Grimm, see BL, Add. Ms 15,545, f. 164. A fine view of the earthworks, with the abbey in the distance, was published by Skelton (1823), pl. 6.

41 Horsley, 1732; Gough, 1789, **1**, pl. XV; Skelton, 1823, 10 (Celtic, Roman and Anglo-Saxon coins).

42 Grimm's drawings are in the BL: Add. Ms 15,545.

43 Carter's drawings of Dorchester are mainly to be found in his albums of 'Architectural and Monumental Drawings' in the British Library (Add. Mss 29,931 and 29,943), and in the Gough collection in the Bodleian Library (Gough Maps, 227). One of Carter's drawings was published in Carter and Britton, 1837, pt. 2, pl. 23E.

44 For this, Carter devised an attractive title-page, dated 1793: Bodl., Gough Maps, 227, f. 32.

45 The Buckler Collection is split between the British Library and the Bodleian Library. BL, Add. Ms 36,372, 36,405, 36,432. Bodl., MS Top. Oxon. a.64, a.66, b.24, b.42, c.532; MS Top. Gen. a.11, a.15, c.103.

46 Like Carter, twenty years earlier, Buckler prepared a coloured title-page for his portfolio, *Antiquities of Dorchester, Oxfordshire, 1813*: Bodl., MS Top. Oxon. c.532, f. 44.

47 Britton, 1835, **5**, pls 61–3.

48 Skelton, 1823. Although the title page bears the date 1823, the volume was issued in parts, and the plates illustrating the Dorchester Hundred are variously dated 1824–26. The six plates and several vignettes of Dorchester appear to attain a high level of accuracy in detail, although the artist was selective in what he chose to include in any particular view. Skelton himself engraved the plates, from drawings by F. Mackenzie.

49 Addington, 1845. Some of Jewitt's engravings were also reproduced by later writers.

50 There have been several recent studies of Jewitt (d. 1869): Carter, 1962; Broomhead, 1995, esp. cat. items 91.1 and 110; Broomhead, 1996.

51 His original drawings are preserved in ORO, PAR87/11/Y2/2/6–43 and 11/Y2/3/1–34.

52 Taunt became the official photographer to the OAHS in 1871, thus closely involving him in archaeological and architectural subjects (Graham, 1973). Most of Taunt's surviving photographs are in the COS. Some copies are in the Bodleian Library, NMR and elsewhere.

53 Copies of the guidebook (Taunt, 1906) are held at the COS. It was in this publication that Taunt advertised the availability of his portfolio, copies of which were probably produced only to order. No complete portfolio seems to have survived, and the total number of known photographs of Dorchester by Taunt barely adds up to fifty. The photographs, measuring 7 x 5 ins, were mounted on card, and

captioned. Many of the extant copies are entitled 'Shilling Series', which was published in January 1869.

54 The NMR holds a substantial collection of mainly donated material. It also has good photographs of the abbey guest house, taken by RCHME in the 1980s.

55 The map of Oxfordshire by Richard Davis, surveyed in 1793–94, is useful in showing the setting of the town. The main streets are all delineated, but not very accurately, and without additional detail.

56 ORO, PC/087/H/1. This is just pre-enclosure; land-parcels are numbered, but there is no surviving schedule. It may have been an early draft for the Tithe map, produced by Neighbour in 1845 (ORO, Tithe Map and Award no. 132).

57 OS, Oxfordshire, sheet nos. XLVI.13, 14 (pub. 1881); second edn., 1900; third edn., 1910/1912.

58 Bodl., G.A. Oxon. b.92*/1; another copy in ORO. This relates only to a small part of the manorial complex, and accompanies a sale catalogue of the property; it is taken from the first edition OS map. The catalogue provides a little assistance in understanding some of the buildings that no longer exist.

59 Clark, 1891, pl. II. The ms was originally in the Ashmolean Museum, but is now in the Bodleian Library.

60 Published in the scarce edition of Dugdale's, *Monasticon Anglicanum*, by Stevens, vol. **2** (1722). Accompanying the plan is a view of the church from the south, also by Harris (Fig. 5). Copies are held by COS. Harris produced similar pairs of drawings for Browne Willis, to illustrate his *Survey of the Cathedrals ...* (London, 1727 and 1730).

61 A Victorian ms catalogue of the Gough collection in the Bodleian Library asserts that Richard Gough was responsible for the plan, but it may be Stukeley's. It bears notable similarities to Wood's plan, suggesting that Stukeley consulted that also. The plan has been published in Tiller, 2005, fig. 5.

62 Both versions survive. For the sketch, see BL, Add. Ms 29,931, f. 180, and for the finished plan, see Bodl., Gough Maps, 227, f. 33.

63 Bodl., MS Top. Oxon. b.220, f. 111; b.283, f. 12; c.688, f. 42.

64 For the original, see ORO, PAR87/11/Y2/3/1.

65 Confusingly, details are also shown of the south cloister walk and a wall to the west of the tower; these were on Wood's plan, but had long gone (before 1768).

66 Freeman, 1852, opp. 158.

67 The plan is held by the Incorporated Church Building Society, ref. 04477.

68 This is not in Bignell's finished style, but certain similarities can be observed. For exquisitely detailed drawings by him, including a plan of the north aisle, see ORO, PAR87/11/Y2/1/3.

69 ORO, PAR87/11/Y2/2/60.

70 Extended notes on the plan, and the development of the church in general, are contained in Bignell's letter to the vicar, 17 Jul. 1879. For a full transcript, see Ashley, 2000.

71 Taunt, 1906, 17.

72 Anon., 1910, 333. There are only slight differences between this and Paul's plan.

73 Bond, 1913, 257.
74 VCH, 1962, 71.
75 Parker, 1882, advertisement, iii.
76 Hogg and Stevens, 1937.
77 Bradley, 1978; Rowley and Brown, 1981.
78 Frere, 1962; Aston, 1974; Rowley, 1975; May, 1977; Bradley, 1978; Miles, 1978; Harman, *et al.*, 1978.
79 Kirk and Leeds, 1952–53; Hawkes and Dunning, 1961; Dickinson, 1974; Rowley, 1974; Blair, 1994, 1–6.
80 Some of the earliest air photographs published by British archaeologists included cropmarks around Dorchester: Crawford, 1927; Allen, 1938. See also St Joseph, 1966; Benson and Miles, 1974; Gray, 1977.
81 Atkinson, *et al.*, 1951.
82 Rodwell, 1975, 101–7. For the regional archaeological context, see Briggs, *et al.* 1986, *passim*.
83 Cunningham and Banks, 1972. A similar exercise had taken place in 1882: *Proc. Oxon. Archit. and Hist. Soc.*, n.s. **4** (1882), 78. I am grateful to Dr David Sturdy for supplying copies of brief notes that were made by participants in 1959–62.
84 Unpublished. Dr Sturdy kindly provided copies of his plan, sections and notes.
85 Bond, 1913, **1**, 254–69. See here Figs 11 and 12.
86 *E.g.* Rodwell, 1981, 75–8.
87 *E.g.* see numerous references in his books on chancels (Bond, 1916), and fonts (Bond, 1908a).
88 Ayers, 1991.
89 The principal modern reference works are as follows. Glass: Newton, 1979; Ayers, 2002; Ayre, 2002. Bells: Sharpe, 1950. Brasses: Stephenson, 1926; 1938. Medieval inscriptions: Bertram, 2000; 2003. There is no recent study of the monuments as a whole.
90 Lankester, 1987.
91 Ms held by the PCC (Perks and O'Connell, 1996). This is a list of surviving inscriptions, correlated with the parish registers. It does not record uninscribed slabs, dimensions, stone types, heraldry, decoration, or condition. The document also lists 19th-century stained glass. A separate rudimentary list of the memorials in the churchyard was prepared.
92 VCH, 1907; 1939; 1962. The principal account of the abbey, by (Sir) Howard Colvin, will be found in VCH, 1962, 52–61.
93 Cook and Rowley, 1985.
94 Tiller, 2005. Some of the contributors to this volume drew extensively on the unpublished ms of Rodwell, 2005a.
95 Cordeaux and Merry, 1955, 225–30; 1981, 165–6.
96 The principal archival material located and consulted during the course of this study is listed in the Appendix. Some of these items appear in mss catalogues prepared by, and consultable at, the relevant repositories, but the great majority do not. Inexplicably, the hugely important collections of drawings by Carter and Grimm do not feature in the general catalogues. The Grimm drawings were discovered by Harvey van Sickle, whilst working on the Conservation Plan (Ashley, 2000), and the Carter drawings by the present writer. The mss catalogues in the Bodleian (Duke Humfrey) Library list a mere handful of documents relating to Dorchester. However, a topographical card index for Oxfordshire directs the researcher to many more items. Nevertheless, the existence of the important Carter collection (Gough Maps, 227), and much else, cannot be tracked down by these means.
97 Among the more authoritative are James, 1926; Sherwood and Pevsner, 1974; Sherwood, 1989.
98 Taunt, 1906; Kirkpatrick, 1927 and later edns.; Anon., n.d. and 1964; Best, 1967 and 1970; Jessel and Stedman, n.d.; Bloxham, 1990 and 2002. Copies of these, and other ephemeral documents, are held at COS.
99 *E.g.* Ford and Haywood, 1984, 44–51; superficially, this appears authoritative, but is replete with both errors of fact and unsupported claims.
100 Barker and Brookes, 1999; 2000.
101 Keevill, 2003.
102 Brooke, 2001; Ballantyne, 2003; Simons, 2004.
103 Rush, 2004.
104 Rodwell, 2005a.

CHAPTER 2

Before the Cathedral: Archaeology and Topography

PREHISTORIC SETTLEMENT

Throughout its length, the Thames valley is packed with archaeological sites, many of which enshrine remains spanning several millennia.[1] At the points where early trackways converged on the river even greater concentrations of archaeological evidence for long-term settlement and religious activity are found. Dorchester is one of those focal crossings. Its significance is enhanced yet further by the fact that the river Thame flows into the Thames here from the north, and the promontory coincidentally formed between the two rivers comprises a gravel plateau which is exceptionally well defended by natural features (Fig. 1).

Research in recent years, in many parts of Western Europe, has demonstrated strong links between prehistoric religion and ceremonial, and watery places (rivers, lakes and bogs).[2] Although finds from the rivers around Dorchester are not numerous, records show that several prehistoric bronze weapons (spearheads and shields) have been recovered in the past;[3] also, a magnificent Celtic sword and scabbard were discovered in a pond at nearby Little Wittenham in 1982.[4] The establishment of a major religious and ceremonial centre on the Dorchester promontory certainly occurred in the Neolithic period, when a cursus, a henge monument and settlements were constructed.[5]

During the Neolithic and Bronze Age the gravel plateau became peppered with burial mounds, mortuary enclosures and other features. Overlooking all this from the south is Wittenham Clumps,[6] a low hill with twin peaks: one was defended in the Early Iron Age with earthworks, while the other is rich in prehistoric and Roman remains. By the Late Iron Age, Dorchester was a major regional centre, as demonstrated by the creation of a large, fortified enclosure (*oppidum*) at Dyke Hills, lying at the confluence of the rivers.[7] The very considerable number of finds of Celtic coins, of both precious and base metals, from the Dorchester locality serves to emphasize its importance as a trading centre, and a dense concentration of findspots has been recorded at Dyke Hills. One of the highest-status coins, a gold *stater* of Cunobeline, was found in the cloister excavation at the abbey in 2001.[8]

THE ROMAN TOWN

During the Roman conquest of southern Britain, it was common practice for forts to be established at major river crossings and alongside Celtic tribal centres: these were part of the trappings of military rule. An early Roman fort was constructed just to the north of Dyke Hills, in an area that was later partly covered by the walled town.[9] The plan and full extent of the fort have not been established, since the site is now built-up and not readily susceptible of archaeological exploration.

Forts spawned civilian settlements (*vici*) outside their gates, and Dorchester was no exception.[10] Contrary to fanciful antiquarian claims, the Roman name for Dorchester is unknown, although the first element of the Anglo-Saxon name, *Dorcic*, is British. It is not impossible that the Anglo-Saxon appellation conceals the Roman name.[11]

Enclosure and Defence

In common with other civilian settlements deemed to be of strategic or economic importance, the core of Roman Dorchester was protected in the late 2nd century by an earthen rampart and ditch, probably enclosing only half, or even one-third, of the total occupied area. The defensive capacity was enhanced in the late 3rd century by the addition of a stone wall in front of the rampart.[12]

It now seems certain that the defended area took the form of a narrow rectangle, with the main road running through the centre, and gates in the north and south sides. Although the lines of three of the walls are well established, the fourth – on the east – has given rise to much debate. A survey of the field evidence in 1935 pointed to the eastern defences running on a line which passed under the lychgate of the churchyard (Fig. 13),[13] and the foundation of a large but archaeologically undated wall was seen in 1961, under the High Street south-west of the abbey.[14] There was formerly a hump in the road at this point, which had already been identified in 1935 as indicative of the defensive line.

The foundation, which was intercepted by a pipe-trench, was reported to be 2.5 m (8 ft) thick, and still standing to a height of 0.9 m (3 ft); it was backed by

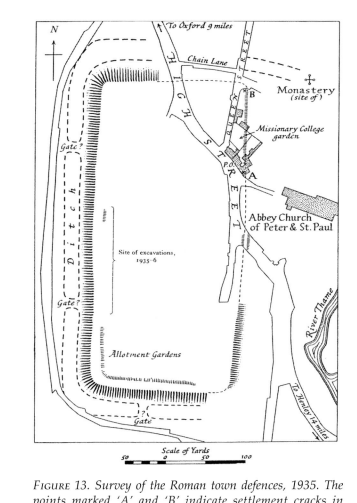

FIGURE 13. Survey of the Roman town defences, 1935. The points marked 'A' and 'B' indicate settlement cracks in buildings. (Hogg and Stevens, 1937)

soil which was interpreted as a rampart.[15] The evidence is compatible with that of the wall and rampart of the western defences, which were archaeologically sectioned in 1962.[16] It has therefore been claimed that the pipe-trench discovery in the High Street marks the site of the eastern town wall, and this is undoubtedly the most plausible explanation, both on account of the thickness of the masonry, and the fact that it is located well away from the abbey. No convincing connection with the latter can be adduced. Early in 2009, a comprehensive new drainage scheme was installed by Thames Water in Dorchester, which involved trenching along the length of High Street, Queen Street, and elsewhere. The line of the eastern town wall was cut twice, as were other putative or known historic boundaries. Incredibly, no provision was made for archaeological recording, and a major opportunity to learn about the Roman and later topography of the town was lost.

Further south, on the putative line of the eastern defences, an excavation in 1972 at the rear of the Old Castle Inn revealed the butt-end of a major Roman ditch, which potentially marks a break in the defensive circuit for an entrance close to the south-east corner.[17] The rampart associated with the corner itself was

located nearby in 2006.[18] Another piece of evidence emerged in 2002, when foundations were dug for a small extension at the rear of 'The Priory' (Figs 3 and 13: the house is labelled 'A' on the latter).[19] The excavation trenches were restricted, but apparently encountered the upper silting of a large ditch. This is precisely where one would expect to find the Roman town ditch if the eastern wall followed the posited line between the High Street and the abbey.

Although fragmentary, there are thus several pieces of evidence for the elusive east side of the walled town, indicating that an area of about 13.5 acres (5.5 hectares) was enclosed. While most modern writers have opted for a rectangular plan with rounded corners ('playing-card' shape), which excludes the site of the abbey,[20] others have felt the need to extend the lines of the northern and southern defences eastwards as far as the Thame, thus embracing the abbey site (Fig. 14).[21] Arguments may be advanced in support of both scenarios. Beginning with the case for the inclusion of the abbey site, two principal issues need to be addressed. First, it is a well established fact that many early Christian churches were founded inside walled enclosures of Roman origin (towns, forts and even courtyard villas), and given that there was such an *enceinte* at Dorchester, it is odd that Birinus should have shunned the protective enclosure and built his church immediately outside, rather than within.[22] Second, the ground upon which the abbey was erected comprises a slight natural eminence, which stands a little higher than the general level of the walled town. The exclusion of such a topographically distinctive feature in the Roman period from the walled *enceinte* is difficult to explain. Leaving unprotected high ground immediately outside a fortification does not make defensive sense.

The alternative – hypothetically extending the defences to the river – and thus embracing the abbey site, would have the effect of increasing the enclosed area by about fifty percent and involve canting the north side: the plan of the town would then have been an irregular polygon, not a rectangle. As Roman small-town plans go, that is unexceptional. The major disadvantage of the larger enclosure would undoubtedly be the weakness of its eastern flank: adopting the river as one side of the town enclosure might have been considered when there was only an earthwork defence, but not when the wall was built. There is no archaeological or topographical evidence to suggest that a masonry wall was constructed alongside the river bank (where there is a broad floodplain today), and it is inconceivable that the river itself would have been deemed a sufficient form of defence on the east.

Another argument often used against the larger enclosure is that it would take in the Vicarage site where a 3rd-century cremation burial was found in

1856, suggesting that this was a Roman cemetery area (Fig. 14). The inclusion of fine glass vessels in the burial indicates the moderately high status of the deceased person.[23] Roman law forbade burial within towns, and cemeteries were confined to the periphery. The general consensus amongst scholars of the Roman period is that the walled *enceinte* was most likely of rectangular plan, with both the abbey site and the cemetery at the Vicarage lying outside to the east, although potentially in an annexe enclosed by earthworks on the north and south.

A second burial, found somewhere just west of the church, is of uncertain date, but may well have been Roman. A massive stone coffin was dug up 'on the west side of Dorchester Church', in or shortly before 1722. In that year it was seen and sketched by Hearne, 'in the back side of one Richard Elton's at Dorchester ... they now call it the horse trough'.[24] It is difficult to see how any burial west of the church could have belonged to the monastic period, and it is therefore plausible that this was a Roman inhumation of fairly high status. The alternative would be an Anglo-Saxon burial, reusing a Roman coffin; this is a well attested practice.

Returning to the defences, in reality the situation may not be as straightforward as has been supposed. First, there is no guarantee that the 3rd-century wall precisely followed the circuit of the 2nd-century earthwork defences. At Verulamium and Silchester,

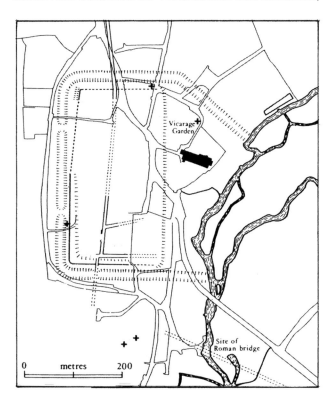

FIGURE 14. *Plan of the town defences, showing a hypothetical extension of the earthworks to the river Thame, thereby enclosing the site of the abbey. Burials are marked by crosses. (adapted from Cook and Rowley, 1985)*

for example, the successive earthen and stone defences were not wholly coincident. The possibility that the earlier enclosure extended as far as the river, perhaps relying upon that as its eastern side, cannot be dismissed. The alignment of existing topographical features north of the abbey, which deviates from that of the main part of the town, could reflect a change of direction in the northern defences.[25] The stone wall at Dorchester may, as elsewhere, have been designed to enclose and protect only the administrative core of the settlement. An ambiguous reference to a major wall, evidently to the west of the church, is preserved in a papal bull of Eugenius III (1146). It mentions property held 'within the wall', and land 'outside the wall' on the west: whether this refers to a precinct boundary erected in the late Saxon or early medieval periods, or to the Roman town wall which was serving the same purpose, is unclear. Circumstantial evidence may point to the latter.[26]

A Temple(?)

What, then, lay on the small eminence between the town wall and the Thame? This topographically distinctive site was perhaps adopted for a special use early in the Roman period: a brickearth and gravel knoll with the river flowing by on the east and the ground sloping away gently in all other directions, this was an ideal location for a temple.[27] All small Roman towns were provided with at least one temple, and Dorchester would have been no exception. Although the temple site has yet to be identified on the ground, an inscribed stone altar which must have come from it was discovered in 1731 when digging a sawpit behind the Red Lion Inn, which lay on the west side of the High Street, a short distance north-west of the church.[28] Although the altar itself is now lost, a drawing of it survives (Fig. 15A). This early 3rd-century altar, dedicated jointly to Jupiter Optimus Maximus and the deities of the emperors, was gifted by Marcus Varius Severus, who was a *beneficiarius consularis*.[29] He was a public official, probably concerned with tax collection and securing supplies for the Roman army.[30] The inscription demonstrates the importance of Dorchester as a place where imperial officials were stationed.

The temple in which this altar was placed is unlikely to have been a classical structure, but was probably of the Romano-Celtic variety which was ubiquitous in southern Britain: they were square, polygonal or circular in plan, and examples of all types are known from the Oxford region (Alchester, Frilford, Silchester, etc.). Sometimes temples were centrally located within the town (as at Alchester), but in the smaller settlements they were often sited towards the edges. The entrance normally faced east or south-east. A sacred precinct (*temenos*) might contain one or more temples, and the area enclosed could vary considerably.[31]

A

I · O · M
ETNMINB·AVG
M·VAR·SEVERVS
· B · CoS ·
ARAM· CVM
CANCELLIS
·D · S · P ·

Jovi Optimo Maximo et numinibus Augusti
Marcus Valerius Severus beneficiarius con-
sulis aram cum cancellis de suo posuit

B

OCXXXVL

FIGURE 15. A. *Lost altar from a Roman temple, dedicated to Jupiter by Marcus Varius Severus, who was a public official* (beneficiarius consularis) *in Dorchester in the early 3rd century. (Horsley, 1732) B. Lost finger-ring of gold, with cornelian intaglio and inscription. (Gough, 1789)*

The temple and its precinct could be set slightly apart from the main settlement area, on a local eminence, as at Great Chesterford or Harlow (Essex); in other instances it was annexed to the outskirts of the town. Chelmsford (Essex) provides a potential analogue for Dorchester: there, the temple precinct lay on a brickearth spur between the earth-and-timber defences of the small town and the river Can.[32] Burials are often found in association with rural and suburban temples, which could also function as mausolea.

Very little archaeological excavation has so far taken place in the vicinity of the church, and thus solid evidence relating to the Roman period is sparse. Three trenches were dug on the cloister site in 1960–62, one inside the south chancel aisle in 1964, and in 2001 a pit to house a new boiler was excavated against the north-west corner of the nave. These excavations yielded numerous artefacts of Roman date, but no masonry structures and, in the case of the boiler-house pit, no minor features were found either; this is not entirely surprising given the amount of post-Roman activity here. Consequently, the interest of the area around the abbey has been

summarily dismissed: 'The large quantities of Roman finds recovered are likely to derive from sub-urban rubbish dumping'.[33] This explanation is weak, being based on the exposure of only a few square metres of the brickearth subsoil in the base of the boiler-house pit.

A markedly different story was revealed by the three trenches of 1960–62, when the excavators reported that on the site of the east cloister range Roman-period layers 'accounted for some 5 ft of the 9 ft depth of soil to the natural sand'.[34] Regrettably, only a brief report was published on the Roman levels, and on some of the artefacts found, but a section drawing of the trench dug on the site of the north claustral range clearly reveals floor levels of what must have been timber buildings (Fig. 25A). Also, a Roman well-shaft of square plan (doubtless once timber-lined) was found close to the north-west corner of the church, only one metre away from the 2001 excavation (Fig. 25B).[35]

That the abbey site was not wholly devoid of Roman masonry structures is to be inferred from the discovery in the 19th century of a tessellated floor beneath the north chancel aisle.[36] In this connection, it is interesting to note that, just outside the north-east corner of the aisle, a fragment of wall (running north-south) was located in a drainage trench in 2002. The masonry incorporated Roman tiles, but it is uncertain whether the wall is of Roman or Anglo-Saxon date.[37] The excavation of 2001 yielded a considerable quantity of Roman brick and tile fragments, all residual in later deposits. More significant, however, is the fact that no fewer than ninety tesserae made from tile, and fifteen more of coloured stone, were recovered too:[38] such a large number points to the former existence of a tessellated pavement in the near vicinity. While the brick and tile could have been brought to the site for reuse as building material in the Anglo-Saxon period, the presence of tesserae cannot be convincingly explained in that way. They are useless as building material, and are seldom found in quantity at any great remove from the location where they were originally used.

In c. 1654, an interesting discovery was made, when digging the foundations for the school-house, only a short distance to the west of the 2001 excavation.[39] Anthony Wood reported the uncovering of 'certaine little roomes under ground, some pav'd very smoothly with hard white stone, and some brick'd round' (p. 5). This description is more suggestive of a Roman building with decorated floors than anything that is likely to have been part of the medieval abbey. The term 'brick'd round' was sometimes used by antiquaries to describe plain red-brick tessellated borders, and the smooth, hard white stone is reminiscent of the ornamental pavement in one of the buildings of the Roman temple complex at Springhead (Kent).[40]

In 1964, a gravel surface – which can only be of Roman date – was located at a depth of 2.8 m, beneath medieval deposits in the south chancel aisle.[41] Finally, the fragment of undated masonry incorporated in the south-east corner of the medieval crypt beneath the nave aisle could potentially be of Roman origin too: it is markedly different in character from all the known Anglo-Saxon and medieval work (Fig. 198; p. 186).

In conclusion, this topographically prime site, less than 150 m from the centre of the Roman town, on an eminence facing towards the river, and having at least one building on it with a tessellated pavement – possibly two – is most unlikely to have been reserved as a rubbish dump for four centuries. More plausibly, what was found on the boiler-house site was a scatter of occupation débris, churned up and spread across an area that had been maintained largely as an open space – arguably a precinct – throughout the Roman period. The gravel metalling reported under the south chancel aisle may have been the surface of that precinct.

A close study of all the prehistoric and Roman artefacts found near the church might be informative. Meanwhile, three items especially evoke interest: first, the late Iron Age gold *stater* found in 2001 recalls to mind the fact that these valuable coins were regularly deposited as votive offerings at major pre-Roman shrines. The Iron Age and Roman temple at Harlow is particularly notable in this respect.[42] Second, a fine Roman bronze brooch with inlaid enamels was found in 1962, stratified in Roman levels on the site of the north cloister range.[43] Third, a plain brooch was found in the excavation of 2001.[44] Brooches regularly feature amongst the votive offerings found at temples.

The evidence for one, or perhaps two, Roman masonry buildings with tessellated floors on the site of the abbey church is compelling, but that does not in itself prove the presence of a Roman temple, mausoleum, or *capella memoriae*, and its *temenos*. For the timebeing, we can only observe that the evidence is wholly consistent with such an explanation. More substantive details are required to confirm or refute the putative religious association. While the foregoing discussion has centred on the hypothesis that a temple lay between the walled town and the river Thame, the Vicarage burial reminds us that there was a cemetery in the area too. Indeed, it was not uncommon for religious and funerary activities to be combined, and the term 'temple-mausoleum' has been coined to cover those structures which apparently fulfilled both functions. In the context of late Roman Christianity, some of these buildings were transmuted into cemetery chapels, or *memoriae*.[45] London, St Albans and Colchester all provide examples.

Roman Christianity

Nothing beyond mere speculation can be said about Christianity in late Roman Dorchester, since no diagnostic artefacts have yet been found. However, not only was Christianity embraced as an acceptable religion in the Empire, following the conversion of the Emperor Constantine in AD 313 (later Christianity became the official religion), but its practice was widespread in Britain: hence, it cannot be seriously doubted that there was a Christian presence in Dorchester in the 4th century. The late Roman, or sub-Roman, inhumation cemeteries encircling the town are likely to include Christian burials, but religious affiliation is notoriously difficult to prove in graves without any diagnostic accoutrements.[46]

However, a beaker found with a burial at Long Wittenham is overtly decorated with biblical scenes and Christian symbols. Hitherto assumed to be of Frankish origin, the beaker is now thought to belong to a local Romano-Christian milieu.[47] Not far south, at Silchester (Hants.), artefacts bearing Christian symbolism and a potential Roman church are known, while from Caversham (Berks.) comes a lead cistern bearing a *Chi-Rho* monogram. These cisterns, of which several have been found in Britain, are now believed to be late Roman baptismal fonts.[48] It is probably only a coincidence that in the 12th century Dorchester acquired a Romanesque lead font, itself something of a rarity (Fig. 191).[49]

One discovery which could be relevant to the Roman-Christian period is the hoard of five silver spoons, deposited just outside Dorchester after AD 395.[50] The hoard was found in a gravel pit in 1872, alongside the Roman road leading south-east from the town.[51] Hoards of late Roman silver-ware, often comprising spoons and sometimes other utensils, are known from a score of sites in Britain.[52] Particularly intriguing is the fact that one or more items in several of these hoards carry Christian monograms (usually the *Chi-Rho*), or inscriptions, showing that they are likely to have had a liturgical use.[53] Unfortunately, none of the Dorchester spoons is decorated or inscribed, and thus it cannot be established whether they had Christian associations.[54]

EARLY ANGLO-SAXON OCCUPATION

The earliest excavated evidence of buildings on the cloister site comes in the form of a timber structure with a sunken floor or shallow cellar.[55] Of Germanic origin, this building type – generally known by the name *Grubenhaus* ('sunken hut') or, more prosaically, 'sunken-featured building' – was introduced into southern Britain in the 5th century. Several other examples have been recorded during excavations at Dorchester, demonstrating that early Saxon settlement was widespread here.[56] The *Grubenhaus* found in 2001 has been dated to the 6th century on the basis of pottery found in it.[57]

The period between the early 5th century and the mid-7th is usually dubbed 'pagan', and a number of early Anglo-Saxon burials discovered in the vicinity of Dorchester were found to be richly furnished with grave goods in the pagan Germanic manner.[58] We remain uncertain to what extent late Roman Christianity lingered on in midland Britain into the 5th century, and even beyond: pagan and Christian beliefs could, and often did, co-exist. The case for seamless continuity and gradual transmutation is as strong at Dorchester as it is anywhere in England. Historical support for this comes from the assertion in the *Anglo-Saxon Chronicle* that the Dorchester area remained under British control until 571.[59] In that year several towns in the Oxford region were overrun, the nearest to Dorchester being Benson. Excavation has demonstrated on the cloister site, at Beech House, and elsewhere in the town, that the 'sunken-hut phase' was succeeded in the 7th or 8th century by settlement characterized by timber-framed buildings, the wall positions of which are evidenced either by lines of postholes or shallow slots for sill-beams. Such structures could be either secular or ecclesiastical.

The widespread distribution in and around Dorchester of both occupation evidence and burials of the Anglo-Saxon period points to the presence of a sizeable and important settlement. A few stray finds of exceptional quality are indicators of the high status of the place: a gold coin (*solidus*) of the Byzantine emperor Mauricius Tiberius (582–602), an Anglo-Saxon runic gold coin (minted *c.* 640–650), and a 7th-century gold pyramidal stud inset with garnets.[60] Other late Roman gold *solidi* have been found at Dorchester, but not properly recorded: it cannot now be determined whether they were casual losses in the Roman period, or had been acquired by Anglo-Saxon jewellers to make pendants (a not uncommon practice).

Finally, an interesting discovery was made in the excavations of 2001, in the form of four sherds of green-glazed pottery of early or middle Saxon date: it has been suggested that these may be of Byzantine origin, and as such are an exceptional rarity in Britain.[61]

Notes

1 Benson and Miles, 1974.
2 Bradley, 1990.
3 VCH, 1939, 263.
4 Cook and Rowley, 1985, 18.
5 Atkinson, *et al.*, 1951.
6 Before the 20th century, Wittenham Clumps was generally known as Sinodun Hill; in the 18th century it also bore the nickname 'Lady Dunche's Buttocks': Hearne, vol. V (1901), 380. (OHS, **42**.)
7 Lane-Fox, 1870. One of the more impressive antiquarian illustrations of Dyke Hills, with the town and abbey in the distance, is in Skelton, 1823, pl. 6. See also Keevill, 2005, fig. 7.

8 See, P. de Jersey, in Keevill, 2003, 338–9.
9 Frere, 1984, 94–106.
10 VCH, 1939, 288–96. The most up-to-date consideration of Roman Dorchester is in Henig and Booth, 2000, 58–63.
11 The oft-mentioned 'Dorocina', which appears on early editions of OS maps, is pure invention. Bede provides the earliest reference (*c.* 730), calling the town *Dorcic* and *Dorcicaestrae*. In the *Anglo-Saxon Chronicle* (compiled *c.* 900, but referring to the years 635/636) the name is written *Dorceceastre* and *Dorcesceastre* (Gelling, 1953, 152). For the Roman perspective, see Rivet and Smith, 1979, 48, 57, 466, 513.
12 For small towns and their fortifications, including Dorchester, see Rowley, 1975; Burnham and Wacher, 1990.
13 Stevens and Keeney, 1935; Hogg and Stevens, 1937, 42–4.
14 The observation was made by Prof. Christopher Hawkes, when mains drainage was laid in Dorchester. At the time, he resided at The Priory, Dorchester. Information derived from Hawkes was included in Aston, 1974, fig. 1.
15 Where the town wall has been archaeologically explored on the south and west, it was found that the masonry was robbed out. Under the road, however, robbing could not readily take place, and consequently the Roman masonry has remained *in situ*. As heavy traffic pounded the road in the early 20th century, slight sinkage occurred to either side of the wall, resulting in the hump that was plotted by Stevens and Keeney (1935, 218).
16 Frere, 1962.
17 Bradley, 1978. An entrance here is compatible with a road leaving the town on the south-east, and heading for a bridge across the Thame.
18 *Britannia*, **38** (2007), 282.
19 Archaeological watching brief by Margaret Henderson of John Moore Heritage Services (ms report, 2002).
20 *Cf.* Hogg and Stevens, 1937, fig. 11; Frere, 1962, fig. 1; Burnham and Wacher, 1990, fig. 32; Henig and Booth, 2000, fig. 3.4.
21 First proposed by Aston, 1974 (who revised his view in a *postscript*); followed by Rodwell, 1975, 106, map 2; and Cook and Rowley, 1985, 24.
22 For early churches inside Roman walled enclosures, see Morris, 1989; Blair, 1992.
23 Two of the vessels are illustrated in Cook and Rowley, 1985, 23, where the date of discovery is given (probably erroneously) as 1866. The findspot is indicated on the OS 1:2,500 map (1st edn., 1877), in the Vicarage garden, immediately east of the house: see here Fig. 3. The Vicarage was built in 1856–57, but there are no records of discoveries being made at the time, or in 1866.
24 Hearne, vol. VIII (1907), 2 (OHS, **50**); vol. X (1915), 6 (OHS, **67**).
25 As suggested in Rodwell, 1975, map 2.
26 Lincoln Rec. Soc., **27**, 286; the relevant extract was also printed as an appendix to Hogg and Stevens, 1937, 73.
27 See Keevill, 2003, 322–3, for a note of the subsoil conditions under the abbey.
28 Horsley, 1732, 339, 352; fig. 76. Collingwood and

Wright, 1965, 76, no. 235. The Red Lion has long since disappeared. However, Hearne, who saw the altar immediately after its discovery, records that the yard in which it was found was known as Court Close, or Bishop's Close. It lay three or four doors north of The George Inn, which is directly opposite the churchyard entrance. Hearne, vol. X (1915), 427 (OHS, **67**).

29 Hearne was also much exercised by the interpretation of the inscription. Hearne, vol. X (1915), *passim* (OHS, **67**).

30 An interesting coincidence was the discovery, during an archaeological excavation at Wittenham Clumps in 2003, of part of the head of a perforated ceremonial spear of the distinctive type carried by a *beneficiarius consularis* (shown on the 'Time Team' programme on Channel 4 television, 29 Feb. 2004).

31 *Cf.* Lewis, 1966, figs 112–29.

32 Wickenden, 1992.

33 Keevill, 2003, 354; 2005, 14–15.

34 Cunningham and Banks, 1972, 158.

35 Frere, 1984, 127–9. The well was mentioned in Cunningham and Banks, 1972, where it was referred to as 'shallow'. However, the section published by Frere (1984, fig. 23), indicates that the excavation was taken to a depth of 13½ ft (4.1 m), below present ground level, and the bottom of the shaft was not found. Pottery recovered from the well shows that it dated from the late 1st century (Frere, 1984, 166–9). Keevill (2003) was evidently unaware of this report.

36 *Oxford Times*, 4 Jun. 1886. Unfortunately, no further details of the structure seem to have been recorded. The finding of charred corn and bones is also mentioned. Another reference, twelve years later, to what was almost certainly the same discovery, mentions the south-east chapel, but this is probably erroneous: *Berks, Bucks and Oxon. Archaeol. J.*, **4** (1898), 80. A well is also said to have been found under the church during the restoration, but no further details are recorded.

37 Keevill, 2003, 327, 354, feature 4592. The wall is not marked on any plan.

38 Keevill, 2003, 344–5.

39 The school-house was an extension on the north side of the abbey guest house.

40 Smith, 2004.

41 Details of the 1964 excavation on the site of the reconstructed shrine were provided by Dr Sturdy.

42 See, A.P. Fitzpatrick, in France and Gobel, 1985, 49–66.

43 Found in cutting III. Details given in Cunningham's ms.

44 Keevill, 2003, 338.

45 The same conclusion is reached in respect of Dorchester by Doggett (1986).

46 Durham and Rowley, 1972; Harman, *et al.*, 1978; Chambers, 1987; Henig and Booth, 2000, 187.

47 Henig and Booth, 2000, 185–6; Petts, 2003, 17.

48 Thomas, 1981, 220–7; Watts, 1991, 158–73; Petts, 2003, 96–9.

49 Zarnecki, 1957.

50 Johns and Potter, 1985, appendix 2; Cook and Rowley, 1985, 23 (illus.).

51 The findspot is marked on the OS 1:2,500 map, first edn. (1877). See also Cook and Rowley, 1985, 22 (map).

52 The Thetford treasure is significant in this context: Johns and Potter, 1983. For an interpretation of its Christian significance, see Watts, 1991, 146–58.

53 Thomas, 1981, 108–21; Watts, 1991; Petts, 2003, 118–22.

54 For a negative view on both the Dorchester hoard and the sub-Roman cemeteries around the town, see Watts, 1991, 216–17. However, hoards of silver spoons seem to have strong Christian associations.

55 Keevill, 2003, 354–7.

56 At Beech House, the Old Castle Inn and the allotments; see Frere, 1962; Rowley and Brown, 1981; Cook and Rowley, 1985, 31–3; Blair, 1994, 1–6.

57 Keevill, 2003, 323–4, 354–7.

58 VCH, 1939, 350, 370; Dickinson, 1974. The best general account of the Anglo-Saxon period is Blair, 1994.

59 Whitelock, 1961, 13, *s.a.* 571; Stenton, 1947, 27.

60 The gold and garnet stud, now lost, was clearly a piece of Anglo-Saxon jewellery of the highest quality. It was found in *c.* 1776 and is known only from a contemporary drawing in the Minute Book of the Society of Antiquaries: see Dickinson, 1974, 29, pl. 4b; Cook and Rowley, 1985, 33.

61 Keevill, 2003, 343–4.

CHAPTER 3

Dorchester Cathedral, *c.* 635–1067

THE MIDDLE SAXON FOUNDATION

Dorchester formally enters English history in A.D. 635, when it is recorded that a church and episcopal see were founded there. The event was reported at some length by Bede in his *Historia Ecclesiastica* (completed in 731).[1] The kingdom of Wessex – otherwise known as the 'Gewissae' – was ruled by Cynegils (probably 611–43), but it is not known where his seat of power lay. His conversion to Christianity in 635 was an important milestone in spreading the faith. Conversion was carried out by Bishop Birinus, who had been consecrated in Genoa and was sent to Britain by Pope Honorius I to continue the Augustinian mission, begun in 597.

When Birinus 'reached Britain and entered the territory of the Gewissae, he found them completely heathen .... He therefore evangelized that province, and when he had instructed its king, he baptized him and his people.' Bede continues, 'It happened at the time that the most holy and victorious Oswald [king of Northumbria] was present, who greeted King Cynegils as he came from the font, and offered him an alliance most acceptable to God .... The two kings gave Bishop Birinus the city of Dorcic [Dorchester] for his episcopal see, and there he built and dedicated several churches, and brought many people to God by his holy labours. He also died and was buried there ....'[2]

King Oswald appears to have come to Wessex to seek the hand of Cynegils's daughter in marriage, at the very time when Birinus was converting and baptizing Cynegils. Where these momentous events took place is not recorded, but almost certainly it was at Dorchester. It is unlikely that Birinus would have been invited to build his cathedral anywhere other than at the place of Cynegils's baptism. Interestingly, Bede refers to Dorchester as a 'city' (*civitas*), the term he reserved for towns of high rank. Clearly, in the 630s the former Roman town was a significant Anglo-Saxon royal centre. Two further details of Bede's narrative are worth reflecting upon. First, his use of the term 'font' potentially suggests that baptism took place in a dedicated receptacle or chamber, rather than merely in the river. Secondly, the slightly ambiguous allusion to Birinus's building 'several

churches' could be taken to imply that they were either in Dorchester itself, or in the see. If the latter, one might have expected the description to be more expansive, saying 'many' rather than 'several'. It may therefore be that Birinus was responsible for the construction of an integrated group or 'family' of two or three churches in Dorchester. Almost invariably, major ecclesiastical foundations of the 7th and 8th centuries did not comprise a single church, but there were at least two (plus other liturgical foci, such as crosses and wells) in axial alignment. Much research has been conducted in this field in recent years.[3]

Thus Birinus became the first bishop of the West Saxons and his cathedral at Dorchester is likely to have comprised a church dedicated to St Peter and St Paul (or, initially, to St Peter alone: see the abbey seal, p. 40), and perhaps another to St Mary the Virgin. Axially aligned 'families' of middle Saxon churches are now known at Winchester, Glastonbury, Wells, Lichfield, Canterbury and elsewhere: there is no reason why Dorchester should not have followed the trend.[4]

While some middle Saxon churches were founded in walled Roman enclosures which are believed to have been ruinous and largely if not wholly deserted (*e.g.* Bishop Cedd's church at Bradwell-on-Sea, in 654), that situation clearly did not obtain at Dorchester. The choice of site for the cathedral, between the town wall and the river, may have been conditioned by contemporary knowledge of its previous history. The fact that a structure identified as Roman lies beneath the eastern arm of the present church is poignant, and almost certainly not coincidental. The possibility that a standing Roman building – perhaps a temple, mausoleum, or *memoria* – was physically incorporated in the fabric of Birinus's church must be seriously entertained. It happened elsewhere: St Martin's, Canterbury, and Stone-by-Faversham church (Kent) both incorporated Roman buildings in their chancels; the early cathedral at Leicester seems to have been built inside the walls of the Roman baths-basilica (now St Nicholas, Jewry Wall); and Paulinus's church at Lincoln stood in the centre of the forum courtyard.[5] In other instances, medieval churches of unrecorded antiquity appear to have had meaningful relationships to Roman buildings, even if nothing of the latter now stands above ground level: thus the parish church of St Mary, Silchester, sits in a *temenos* adjacent to several temples, and there is almost certainly another one beneath it; the chancel of St Helen-on-the-Walls, York, was constructed directly over a mosaic pavement with a central roundel depicting a female head; and at Widford (Oxon.), there is not only a Roman mosaic pavement *in situ* under the church but at least one of the chancel walls stands on Roman foundations.[6] Birinus may well have been mindful of Pope Gregory's instruction to Augustine in 597, to 'build and restore [Roman] churches', and he warned Abbot Mellitus in 601 that 'temples of the idols ... should on no account be destroyed ... [they] are to be aspersed with holy water, altars set up, and relics enclosed in them'.[7]

Bishop Birinus died *c.* 649/650 and was buried in his cathedral church;[8] he was succeeded by Agilbert, who was a Frank by birth and was consecrated bishop in Gaul. At that time, the see of Wessex stretched across much of central southern England and the south Midlands, and Dorchester lay somewhat north of its centre-point. This was to change: by *c.* 648 Cenwalh, who had succeeded his father Cynegils as king of Wessex, caused a minster church to be built in the centre of the former Roman city of Winchester. That church, honouring St Peter, was presumably dedicated by Birinus. In *c.* 662 the church was raised to cathedral status when the new see of Winchester was carved out of Dorchester. All the territory south of the Thames went to Winchester, leaving Dorchester on the southern boundary of a much smaller see. The history of the see is complex and cannot be explored here: even the list of bishops is incomplete and many of their dates are uncertain.[9] However, it can safely be asserted that during the political and ecclesiastical turmoil, between the later 7th century and the beginning of the 10th, Dorchester's status as a see waxed and waned.[10] Many lines of enquiry deserve to be pursued: for example, numismatic evidence suggests that there may have been a Mercian mint in the locality in the 8th century, and Dorchester would have been an obvious candidate to house this.[11]

Birinus's good work was not forgotten, and popular sanctification followed. Presumably his tomb became a shrine within a few years of his death, and his remains were considered sufficiently important as holy relics for Hedda, a later bishop of Winchester (676–703), to remove them from Dorchester to his own cathedral. The presence of Birinus's bones in Winchester is confirmed by the *Secgan* (a list of resting places of Anglo-Saxon saints) in the early 11th century.[12] By what authority the translation took place is not recorded, but it must certainly have marked a diminution in the influence and importance of Dorchester. A shrine to Birinus was now erected in the Old Minster at Winchester, with a further translation to the new Norman cathedral in 1093–94.

Nevertheless, in 1224, the canons of Dorchester still claimed to have the body of Birinus, and wished to translate it to a new shrine within their church (p. 39). Interest in the saint had not lapsed meanwhile at Winchester, since an indulgence of 1254 recorded that those who visited the altar of the Blessed Birinus would be granted an indulgence of ten days.[13]

Thus, the circumstantial evidence points to the likelihood that Dorchester Abbey not only stands on the site of the cathedral church of Wessex, begun in 635, but that in turn perpetuated an already long tradition of religious activity. Some writers in the past have questioned whether Birinus's foundation lay elsewhere, and that the present church marks only the site of the Augustinian abbey. The latter is demonstrably not the case, as will be shown below. Three alternative locations have been suggested. First, several antiquarians opined – although with no firm evidence – that the Anglo-Saxon nucleus lay at Abbey Farm,[14] a short distance to the north of the Manor House (Fig. 2). Second, Bishop's Court Farm, just to the north-west of the Roman town, has long excited attention but, although this is an archaeological site with features of many periods, it has yielded no evidence for a church or high-status settlement of the middle Saxon period (Fig. 1).[15] Third, across the Thame to the east, at Overy, is a cemetery and cropmark complex of enclosures and timber buildings having the superficial appearance of a middle Saxon settlement.[16] However, excavation has shown that the features date mainly from the Roman period.[17] There is still no plausible evidence for an alternative location for Birinus's foundation.

It is impossible to suggest what his church looked like, or precisely where it stood in relation to the present building, since none of its fabric appears to have survived above ground. Historians have sought it for more than three centuries, but only archaeology can find and interpret its remains. As previously observed, there was almost certainly more than one structure involved during the Anglo-Saxon era. If the Old Minster of *c.* 648 at Winchester is anything to go by, we should perhaps expect to find that the main component at Dorchester was transeptal in plan, and was smaller but otherwise not very different from its ultimate Norman successor. Not only has none of the earliest Anglo-Saxon fabric survived above ground, but no pre-Norman grave-slabs, decorative sculpture, or fragments of carved stone crosses have been found either. The absence of these is almost certainly due to the lack of suitable limestone for sculpting in the Dorchester area. To date, the only excavated archaeological evidence comprises traces of several timber structures, a well, and possibly some graves, to the north of the present nave.[18] It has been claimed, on the basis of certain finds made in 2001, that window glass was being manufactured on site in the middle Saxon period: if this can be substantiated, it is an important indicator of status.[19]

Next, the question of the religious precinct must be addressed: where were its bounds? The middle Saxon church was a minster and it would have lain within a defined precinct, bounded by the *vallum monasterii*. Pre-existing boundaries of the Roman period are likely to have been used, at least in part: that would almost certainly have included the eastern component of the Roman town wall. A less likely alternative is that the Roman boundaries were levelled, and the minster was surrounded by a newly constructed earthwork of curvilinear or sub-circular plan. The curving southern boundary of the present churchyard, which partly follows a natural contour line, has been seen by some as indicative of a sub-circular enclosure, but the topographical evidence is unconvincing.[20] Examples of curvilinear *valla* can be found at Bampton and Binsey (Oxon.) and Bisley (Glos.), but they are not associated with major Roman settlements:[21] their origins and morphology are different. The curvilinear boundary at Dorchester is, however, illusory and the existing segment dates only from the early 19th century, when the south and south-west sides of the churchyard were cut back to widen the turnpike road. The northern circuit of the supposed enclosure is wholly conjectural.

Finally, a tantalizing discovery is worthy of mention in the present context: in 1736 a small gold finger-ring, set with a cornelian, was found 'in a garden behind the church', apparently referring to the area of the former cloister (Fig. 15B). The hoop was said to be inscribed with the Roman numerals 'DCXXXVI', which it was claimed represented the date '636', corresponding approximately to the year of Birinus's consecration.[22] The intaglio depicted a pillar-like feature, flanked by sprigs. The description of the ring – gold mounted with a cornelian – suggests that it was of Roman or Byzantine origin, with the Gothic-lettered inscription added later, just possibly in 1536.[23] The ring was in the possession of the Revd John Bilson, Proctor of the University and rector of St Clement's, Oxford; he refused the very substantial offer of twenty guineas for it. Instead, he left it to Jacob Applegarth (d. 1774), master of Dorchester Grammar School: he in turn bequeathed it to his nephew, Mr Day.[24] Regrettably, the object has long been lost, and it is useless to speculate further upon its potential significance. Dr Martin Henig considers the ring to be medieval, but incorporating a Roman gemstone of the early 3rd century; he further suggests that the pillar-like motif represents an altar.[25]

CATHEDRAL AND TOWN IN THE LATE SAXON PERIOD

Morphology and Development of the Town

History is remarkably silent about events at Dorchester during the era of the Danish incursions into central England, and in the centuries that followed. Indeed, we do not even know who followed Agilbert (second bishop) after he left for Gaul in the 660s. The new see of Winchester went its own way, and Dorchester fell under the control of the bishops of Mercia. Lying on the southern boundary of a huge kingdom, Dorchester was ill-suited to house the Mercian bishopstool. The bishopric was therefore divided between Leicester and Lindsey (north Lincolnshire), and Dorchester must have been reduced to the status of a minster church.

In the 870s, Danish raids instigated the break up of the Mercian kingdom, disrupting ecclesiastical life at the same time. The see of Lindsey was expunged and Leicester was abandoned: Dorchester was re-established as the seat of the bishopric of Mercia, and its church once again enjoyed the status of cathedral. It retained that status, despite its inconvenient location, for some two hundred years, until shortly after the Norman conquest. Memory of Dorchester's former glory lingered on, and in 1813 one writer recalled, 'the see was long of gigantic magnificence'.[26]

As the cathedral church of the largest diocese in England, we might expect a late Saxon building of some substance at Dorchester. Consequently, generations of architectural historians have attempted to discover evidence of a pre-Norman church in the fabric of the present abbey, but without convincing results. Hence, some sceptics have questioned whether the Augustinian abbey is on the site of the Anglo-Saxon cathedral.

As already noted, the middle Saxon cathedral is likely to have been a small building, on the scale of the 7th-century Old Minster at Winchester, or the contemporary churches of Kent and Essex, and its precinct may have been confined to the limits of, or only modestly exceeded, those suggested for the Roman-period enclosure between the town wall and the river. The wealth and influence of the re-established cathedral in the late Saxon period, however, almost certainly caused boundaries to be pushed out, and the precinct substantially enlarged. Although Dorchester was, by contemporary standards, only a small town, it is unlikely to have escaped at least a modest level of episcopal development. The creation of a market and laying out of small blocks of burgages may well have been instigated by bishops in the 10th or early 11th century. Clearly, Dorchester did not prosper commercially to the extent that its neighbour Wallingford did, but there are sufficient clues in the historical topography of the town to show that post-Roman replanning of the site was attempted. No satisfactory explanation has been found as to why Dorchester was not refortified in the early 10th century and accorded the status of *burh*.[27] Wallingford took on that mantle.

It is commonly observable that the outlines of Roman towns with stone walls and gates tended to survive Anglo-Saxon replanning, even though nearly all evidence of the layout within the *enceinte* may have been obliterated. Internally, the commonest survivals are the streets which run directly from one gate to another. In other words, it is the physical constraint of enclosure, the ready access provided by gates, and the principal thoroughfares that have survived the longest in the history of urban development. Eradicating or repositioning any of these topographic fixed-points required considerable funding, planning and collective effort, all driven by a controlling power. When that happened, the driving force was often the Church.

A model for the post-Roman development of Dorchester may be offered, based on analogy with other small towns. The late Roman town had a single north–south thoroughfare with gates in the respective sides; it is also likely that there were two openings in the east wall, one giving access to the suggested temple precinct, and the other to a bridge over the Thame. The loss of the eastern side of the Roman defences is almost certainly due to encroachment either by the late Saxon cathedral, or subsequently by the abbey: the religious precinct expanded into the north-east quarter of the old town *enceinte*, potentially extending as far west as the Roman axial street. Secular development around the southern periphery of the cathedral eventually overran the defences of the south-eastern corner. Comparable processes are witnessed in many urban centres, as at Gloucester: there, St Peter's abbey was founded *c.* 679 inside the north-west angle of the Roman walled town, but in the late Saxon period the need to expand the monastic precinct caused part of the defences to be levelled. Commercial growth outside the abbey, towards the river, was then responsible for the levelling of the remainder of the town wall on the north-west.[28] Lincoln provides another example where, in the early 13th century, the cathedral outgrew its precinct, resulting in the demolition of a section of the Roman city wall.

A market place was established at Dorchester, immediately to the west of the religious precinct, occupying the north-east corner of the Roman walled enclosure. Whether the market was of late Saxon or Norman foundation is debatable, although the former seems more probable, especially in view of the lack of medieval documentation. Indeed, no charter mentioning a market or fair at Dorchester has survived, which points to both an early origin and demise for the market.[29] The original rectangular market place is still clearly discernible in the landscape today, despite being almost entirely built over (Figs 2, 13 and 28). At its north-west corner lay the Roman north gate (on High Street), while diagonally opposite, at the south-east corner, was the entrance to the cathedral precinct (another Roman gate?). Remains of what appear to be small-scale, loosely planned blocks of properties may be detected in the post-medieval topography south-west of the present abbey, and flanking the northern leg of the High Street outside the town wall.

The subsequent demise of the market, and its encroachment by building led to the formation of the present middle section of High Street, the snaking course of which is the result of traffic establishing a through-route from the Roman north gate, diagonally across the market to the main entrance to the cathedral precinct, then around the south-west corner of the precinct to a possible south gate, and thence to the bridge over the Thame. The present Dorchester Bridge was built on a new site in 1815: the medieval bridge – and probably the Roman – lay a little further downstream (Fig. 14). In summary, the development of the cathedral led to the establishment of a market and new blocks of tenements adjacent to the ecclesiastical precinct, at the same time drawing settlement away from the western and southern sectors of the old town. The Roman main street no longer served as an axial route, with the consequence that the latter was literally pulled over towards the church and river, where it remains today. Encroachment on the market place had occurred by the later medieval period, as evidenced by the age of some of the existing houses.

Without extensive archaeological excavation, it is impossible accurately to date the evolutionary stages of the late Saxon and medieval periods. However, there is one strong indicator that the developments just discussed began in the pre-Conquest period and that the present abbey church was not established on a cleared site by Augustinian canons in the mid-12th century. The orientation of the church, and of the boundary alignment which runs westwards from it for 140 m, is skewed by twenty degrees from true east–west (Fig. 3). This is not an insignificant departure from the liturgically 'correct' east–west orientation. In the Anglo-Saxon period, prevailing landscape features commonly dictated church orientation, and deviations of up to forty-five degrees from the notionally correct alignment were tolerated. It is additionally relevant to note that the axis of the Norman church is perpetuated further west, not only by a boundary in the centre of the town (south side of the market place: Fig. 28), but also by a pair of ditches recorded as cropmarks which run for a considerable distance across the fields beyond the town. Hence, the church apparently took its alignment from a linear feature which was fossilized in the landscape and was even older than the fortifications of the Roman town.[30]

In most instances where a wholesale rebuild of an Anglo-Saxon church took place in the Norman period, an attempt was made to improve the liturgical orientation, if that was seriously flawed. In some cases, however, piecemeal reconstruction or insurmountable topographical constraints caused old alignments to be retained: Lichfield and Rochester cathedrals rank amongst the extreme examples that survived throughout the Middle Ages. On the other hand, at both York and Exeter the Norman builders undertook major realignment exercises in order to expunge the Roman-influenced orientations of the Anglo-Saxon churches. At Wells, the new cathedral of the late 12th century was turned by twelve degrees from the Anglo-Saxon axis, to improve liturgical orientation,[31] while at Winchester the adjustment was more modest but nevertheless noticeable.

Anglo-Saxon Church Fabric

In the absence of an identifiable Norman realignment at Dorchester, we should take a closer look for any hint of pre-Conquest masonry that might fortuitously have become encapsulated in the present fabric. Attention in the past has been especially directed towards the north wall of the nave, and that is undoubtedly the most likely candidate for enshrining pre-Augustinian fabric, although the transepts might also hold clues. For an unaisled Norman church, the narrowness of the nave in relation to its great height is noteworthy, being a characteristic that often betrays Anglo-Saxon origins. However, the problem with accepting this is that the upper half of the north wall is most certainly Norman; and the same applies to the upper parts of the surviving stubs of the south wall. The tall windows are integral with the

surrounding masonry, and they cannot be earlier than the mid-12th century (Fig. 172). Consequently, conclusions based on present wall height are inadmissible.

The principal argument for a pre-Augustinian structural phase hinges on the demonstrable difference in character between the externally exposed rubble masonry in the upper and lower halves of the north nave wall, respectively. This is the only part of the church where a sizeable area of early walling can be inspected, although it has been repointed and rebuilt in part (especially in the upper region). Nevertheless, the readily discernible difference in the masoncraft above and below the Norman string-course strongly suggests that the two areas are not coeval, although without raking the masonry joints to expose and study original mortars, it is impossible to be certain whether the building-break occurs precisely at string-course level. When the north wall was first stripped of fragmentary external plaster in the 19th century, the different character of the masonry in the lower half was noted, and a cogent argument advanced for its being 11th century, and therefore pre-monastic at the very least.[32] That argument is still valid, but the situation is more complex.

There is yet another area of interest in the north wall, at its east end, where a large round-arched opening has been blocked (but pierced again by a small 14th-century doorway: Pl. 33). Inexplicably, this blocked feature has attracted very little comment in the past, yet it is of seminal importance and was first illustrated by Grimm, *c*. 1780.[33] It is readily apparent

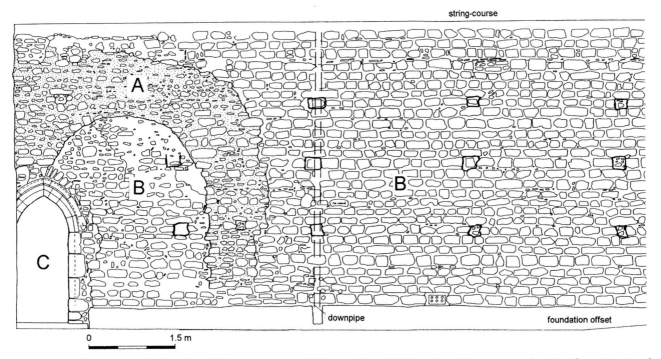

FIGURE 16. *Nave: external elevation of the eastern part of the north wall, below the string-course, showing three structural phases. A. Anglo-Saxon rubblework containing the semicircular arch (stippled); B. Regularly coursed masonry with rows of putlog holes, including the infilling of the arch, early Norman (11th century); C. Small pointed doorway inserted in the 14th century. (Caroline Atkins)*

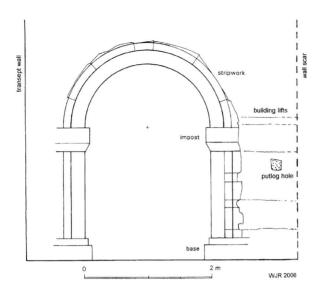

FIGURE 17. *Nave: reconstruction of the lost ashlar lining of the Anglo-Saxon* porticus *arch in the north wall. The impost and base mouldings are notional, but the joints in the stripwork are ghosted in the surviving fabric. (Warwick Rodwell)*

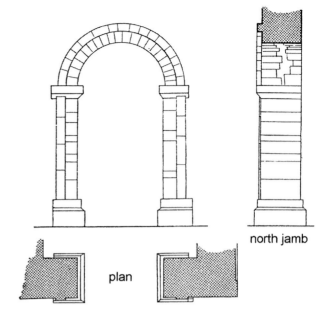

FIGURE 18. *St Matthew, Langford (Oxon.): the surviving Anglo-Saxon west tower arch. Not to scale. (Taylor and Taylor, 1965)*

from a close examination of the masoncraft and mortar types used, that the rubblework containing the arch is not of one build with the rest of the north wall, but is stratigraphically earlier (p. 164). Thus, the north nave wall consists not of two structural phases, but three. In the lower part of its eastern end is preserved a sizeable fragment of uncoursed rubble masonry, different from anything else in the church (except possibly the remaining fragment of the north transept) and retaining the ghosted outline of a large arch that has been robbed of its dressings. Moreover, the infilled opening is too large to have been a normal doorway, and the edges of the masonry defining it are ragged rubble, indicating that stone dressings were removed before the aperture was infilled (Fig. 16).

This is stratigraphically the oldest masonry in the abbey, and there can be no reasonable doubt that it is a fragment of the Anglo-Saxon cathedral. The dimensions of the ragged scar, *c.* 2.75 m wide by 3.5 m high (9 x 11½ ft), indicate the loss of a substantial arch, almost certainly not a doorway. Since the dressings have been removed, and the scale of these is unknown, it is not possible to determine precisely the dimensions of the original aperture, but certain deductions can be made. First, the outline of the arch is not a continuous curve, but exhibits clear 'flats'; this indicates that the voussoirs did not engage directly with the surrounding rubble masonry but were circumscribed by an outer order that was cut on long slabs of stone, placed tangentially. This must have been a hood-moulding in the form of 'stripwork'. Second, the profile of the rubble that abutted the western jamb shows hints of toothing, related to

coursing in the masonry. The toothing pattern is indicative of the presence of tall and short blocks, alternately. This points to the opening being flanked by pilaster-strips, arranged as 'long-and-short' work (Fig. 17).

The scar evidence is wholly consistent with the removal of a typical Anglo-Saxon dressed stone arch and its jambs, both outlined by stripwork. For an arch of the scale implied here, the width of the strips would *c.* 13 cm (5 ins), and the voussoirs *c.* 23–30 cm (9–12 ins) in length. Consequently, it is possible to reconstruct the aperture with a width of about 2 m (6½ ft) and a height of 3 m (10 ft).[34] There would doubtless have been projecting imposts and bases, either plain or moulded. The scale and type of construction is evidenced in many Anglo-Saxon churches, *e.g.* the west crossing arch at Langford (Oxon.) (Fig. 18).[35]

Unfortunately, there is nothing diagnostic to suggest a date within the Anglo-Saxon period, although the posited stripwork would put it relatively late. Deductions may possibly be made from the thickness of the wall, which measures 1.3 m (4¼ ft). Anglo-Saxon walls, even in tall churches, were seldom more than 0.9 m (3 ft) thick, except where there was a need for above-average strength: that usually signifies the presence of a tower, and towers generally occur late in the period. Dunham Magna (Norf.) is a case in point, where the external faces of the nave and axial tower are aligned, but internally the masonry was thickened to 1.2 m (4 ft) to support the tower.[36] In the instance of the massive late Saxon crossing towers at Stow (Lincs.), and Milborne Port (Som.) the walls were thickened to 1.37 m (4½ ft) and 1.5 m (5 ft), respectively.[37]

At Dorchester, the extant masonry to the west of the arch scar terminates in a stepped vertical line, which provides a strong pointer to the position of the lost west wall of the *porticus*: we see here the ghost of block-bonding. That suggests an internal width for the *porticus* of *c.* 4.2 m (14 ft), the same as at St Mary-in-Castro, Dover.[38] If there was a nave-crossing, that is likely to have been square, and the *porticus* of similar or slightly less width. In sum, the principal surviving fragment of early masonry at Dorchester may be interpreted as an east–west wall, pierced by a tall lateral arch, which separated either the crossing or the nave from a north *porticus* in a late Saxon cruciform church. Only excavation could eventually prove whether this analysis is correct. The footprint of the later 11th-century church closely matches that at Dover (Fig. 21), and it would therefore occasion no surprise if the Anglo-Saxon building at Dorchester was on a similar scale too.

Potentially associated with the nave wall, is at least part of the fragmentary west wall of the present north transept (which would have formed the east side of the suggested *porticus*). This too is constructed of random rubble and, although it embodies a 12th-century doorway, it is markedly dissimilar to the Norman masonry of the nave (Pl. 32). Unhelpfully, the transept wall has long ago been heavily repointed using Portland cement, and thus its archaeology cannot be properly studied at present. There is, however, a serious possibility that the wall is Anglo-Saxon in origin, with a Norman doorway inserted to serve the monastic cloister.

Mention must be made here of the two tall, rather crude, round-headed arches flanking the former crossing of the Norman church (Figs 57 and 58). These features have intrigued generations of antiquaries, and some have argued for an Anglo-Saxon date. The debate was started by Stukeley in 1736, when he wrote: 'there are 2 semicircular arches on the N. and on the S. of the middle isle in that part wh may be calld the nave or cross isle of the original work of Birinus'.[39] The arches are certainly not pre-Conquest, and in their present form they are a late medieval adaptation of Norman work (pp. 95 and 160).

Next, it is relevant to inquire how far west the late Saxon nave wall ran, but insufficient evidence is currently available to resolve that issue. In so far as could be seen in 2001, most of the early Norman north wall rises off its own contemporaneous foundation. However, a striking irregularity was noted in the style of construction and alignment of the lower courses of the westernmost two or three metres of foundation. A plausible explanation can be offered for this: a fragment of Anglo-Saxon foundation may have been incorporated when the present nave was laid out.[40] A similar conclusion might be drawn in respect of the foundations of the south wall of the nave, which also exhibit anomalies towards the west

end.[41] However, much uncertainty remains since the foundations have been insufficiently explored. Also, it must be borne in mind that some late Saxon features excavated outside the nave may be stratigraphically earlier than the foundations. The claim by the excavators that the construction pit for a late Saxon stone-lined well, close to the north-west corner of the nave, was cut by the foundation trench must be queried.[42] It may be argued that the well was a liturgical feature, deliberately sited at the corner of the late Saxon church, and there may have been similar features at other corners. The siting of wells and cisterns within and immediately around early churches, doubtless as liturgical features, is a recognized phenomenon: *cf.* the late Saxon cathedral at Wells.[43]

Two further features may be noted, which could possibly have a bearing on the late Saxon cathedral. These were discovered during the shallow excavation for the foundation slab of the pentice, towards its east end. Both features run northwards, at right-angles to the nave, for an unknown distance. First, a narrow wall stub (58 cm wide) was revealed 4 m west of the transept and just beyond the blocked arch already described; it was reported to be bonded to the nave foundation.[44] Its location coincides with the posited site of the west wall of the north *porticus*. Second, a conjoined pair of rectangular features with a thick mortar lining around the rim was exposed (but not excavated) 8 m west of the transept; these may have been medieval mortar-mixing troughs, but could they have been formed within the robber-trench of a major north–south wall?[45] It is difficult to see how either of these transverse features could have existed within the later monastic cloister walk. This raises the possibility that the Anglo-Saxon cathedral had multiple lateral chambers, as at other great churches such as Winchester, Deerhurst (Glos.) and Brixworth (Northants.).

Finally, it should be mentioned that almost nothing is known about the Anglo-Saxon cemetery associated with the church. In the excavations of 1960–62 several burials were encountered beneath the west cloister walk:[46] two of these were evidently monastic-period interments, while others were assigned to an earlier cemetery. Close by, the excavation of 2001 revealed further monastic burials within the cloister, as well as deeper graves which are likely to be Anglo-Saxon. There are thus grounds for believing that a pre-monastic cemetery lay to the north of the present church.

NOTES

1   *Hist. Eccles.*, bk III.7 (Sherley-Price, 1965).
2   For recent general assessments of the Anglo-Saxon diocesan geography, see Doggett, 1986; Blair, 1994; Bond and Tiller, 2005.

3 *E.g.* Rodwell, 1984; Blair, 1992 and 2005.

4 For a useful discussion of the subject, and the historical context of Dorchester, see Doggett, 1986.

5 For relationships between middle Saxon churches and Roman buildings, see Rodwell, 1984.

6 Neal, 1967; Ford and Haywood, 1984, 101–2.

7 *Hist. Eccles.*, bks I.25 and I.30, respectively (Sherley-Price, 1965).

8 *Hist. Eccles.*, bk III.7 (Sherley-Price, 1965). William of Malmesbury, writing in the 1120s, also asserts that Birinus was interred in the church built by him (Hamilton, 1870).

9 For a list of all recorded Dorchester clergy, see Tiller, 2005, 110.

10 Hassall, 1986; Blair, 1994.

11 Hassall, 1986, 110.

12 Rollason, 1978.

13 Crook, 2000, 218–19. I am grateful to Dr John Crook for discussing this subject with me.

14 *E.g.* Skelton, 1823.

15 May, 1977.

16 St Joseph, 1966; Benson and Miles, 1974, 91.

17 Harman, *et al.*, 1978.

18 Keevill, 2003, 326–9; 357–8.

19 *Ibid.*, 346, 357. It is not always easy on a multi-period site to determine whether débris resulting from glass working, found in an Anglo-Saxon context, is of that date, or is residual from Roman activity.

20 Cook and Rowley, 1985, 33; Keevill, 2003, fig. 24; 2005, fig. 8.

21 Blair, 1994, figs 44 and 47; 2005, fig. 23.

22 Gough [Camden], 1789, **I**, 307, pl. XV. The *intaglio* was also illustrated in Skelton, 1823, pl. 3 (where it was incorporated as a border motif).

23 Discussed in Bertram, 2000, 34 (no. 35). He suggests that the inscription read *[m]vcxxxvi* (1536), although the published drawing omits the letter *m*, and seems unambiguous in its depiction of *d* rather than *v*.

24 In 1781 the ring was in the possession of Mr Day's brother (Gough, 1789, **1**, 307), and in 1823 it was in the hands of a carpenter at Wallingford by the name of Phillips (Skelton, 1823, 3).

25 I am grateful to Dr Henig for his comments based, necessarily, on the antiquarian drawing.

26 Brewer, 1813, 369.

27 Hassall, 1986, 111.

28 Heighway and Bryant, 1999, fig. 1.3.

29 A *Gazetteer of Markets and Fairs in England and Wales to 1516*: www.history.ac.uk.cmh/gaz

30 Whether the ditched feature is prehistoric or early Roman cannot be ascertained, but it was undoubtedly severed by the town defences. For a plan of the cropmarks, see Benson and Miles, 1974, fig. 17 (two roughly parallel lines can be seen running diagonally across the centre of grid square 5794); also Gray, 1977, folding plan.

31 Rodwell, 2001, fig. 110.

32 Barns's letter in Parker, 1882, xliii.

33 BL, Add. Ms 15,545, f. 145. Part of the arch also appears on the edge of a drawing of the transept doorway by Stukeley in 1736: Bodl., MS Top. Eccles. d.6, f. 11r. The arch is indicated in Keevill, 2003, fig. 4, but its significance is not discussed.

34 The height is measured from the offset at the base of the north wall, which is likely to represent contemporary floor level. However, the present nave floor is 35 cm lower (at its east end).

35 Taylor and Taylor, 1965, 370–1, fig. 168.

36 *Ibid.*, 217–21.

37 *Ibid.*, 584–93 and 424–8, respectively. The foundations of a possible Saxon axial tower, 4 ft thick, were uncovered in Lichfield Cathedral in 2003 (Rodwell, 2004).

38 Taylor and Taylor, 1965, 214–17.

39 Bodl., Gough Maps, 26, f. 42B. For a full transcript of Stukeley's notes, see Rodwell, 2005a, **2**, 200.

40 I observed this discrepancy on a visit to the excavation, but it is not discussed or illustrated in the published report. Unfortunately, I did not have the opportunity to inspect any of the other trenching operations that exposed the nave foundations, internally or externally.

41 Keevill, 2003, 334–5, fig. 18.

42 *Ibid.*, 326–8, figs 12 and 13. A more plausible interpretation of the published evidence is that the construction pit for the well was dug so close to the corner of the nave that the sliver of soil remaining against the face of the foundation fell away. This is a common phenomenon of digging holes close to foundations, especially in wet conditions, when some undermining of the foundation may occur. When the hole has been backfilled (in this instance around a stone-built well-shaft), the stratigraphic sequence will *appear* to be the reverse of what it actually is.

43 Rodwell, 2001, fig. 43, F1436; fig. 64, F1523; fig. 87, F1533.

44 Keevill, 2003, 333, fig. 17 (feature 4555).

45 *Ibid.*, 333, fig. 17 (feature 4546/4548).

46 Cunningham and Banks, 1972, 161.

CHAPTER 4

From Cathedral to Abbey: the Transition

THE COLLEGE OF SECULAR CANONS
c. 1067–1140

The last Anglo-Saxon bishop of Dorchester was Wulfwig, who died in 1067, thus creating a vacancy. It was filled by Remigius, one of the followers of William the Conqueror, who had been almoner at the abbey of Fécamp in Normandy, and was consecrated bishop by Stigand, Archbishop of Canterbury. In a submission to Lanfranc (archbishop from 1070), Remigius styled himself as bishop of Dorchester, Leicester and Lincoln, thus acknowledging that he presided over an amalgamation of dioceses.

William of Malmesbury visited Dorchester, *c.* 1125, in the critical period between cathedral and abbey. Although he described the place as 'obscure and unfrequented', he added 'yet the beauty and state of its churches [is] very remarkable'.[1] The reference to 'churches' is significant because it confirms that the former cathedral was not the only ecclesiastical structure in Dorchester; indeed, Leland, writing in *c.* 1542, mentioned the ruins of three parish churches (p. 3).[2] These had presumably been erected in the late Saxon years of prosperity.[3] The locations of two of the churches may be approximately deduced. One lay just south of the abbey churchyard, probably where burials were discovered in the 19th century on the site of the Old Castle Inn (Fig. 3).[4] In the late 18th century, the foundations of the second (which Leland reported was 'more south' than the first) were said to be visible, 'as you turn up to the bridge in the gardens of the clerk's house':[5] that implies that the chapel was at Bridge End, probably where the road turned towards the old bridge at the corner of the green.[6] There was also a medieval preaching cross at the approach to the bridge.[7] The site of the third church cannot presently be pinned down, but was somewhere south-west of the abbey.

William of Malmesbury also records that Remigius began to build a new cathedral at Dorchester, but this activity was thwarted by a tide of change which was sweeping through the corridors of ecclesiastical power, at the instigation of Archbishop Lanfranc: in 1072 a council at Windsor decreed that bishops' seats were to be removed from small towns to large ones.[8]

That decree was confirmed by a council in London in 1075, by which time Remigius had already instigated the move from Dorchester to Lincoln. At the 1072 council the bishop was 'of Dorchester', whereas in 1075 he was 'of Lincoln'. The move can be dated historically to 1072–73.[9] Hence, Remigius had no more than five years (1067–72) of building at Dorchester before the bishopric was taken away. But much could have been achieved in that time, certainly sufficient to shape the future structural form of the church. If the foundations and parts of the upstanding walls of the pre-Conquest church were reused, as was indisputably the case, then progress would have been accelerated.

Once the bishopstool had been removed, Dorchester church, like others in the same predicament, would have become a college of secular canons. The original canons would have remained in post, and are likely to have been ruled by a provost elected from amongst their number. History does not record whether the canons accepted their new role gracefully, or whether they clamoured for the reversion to the *status quo ante*, as happened at Wells.[10] For some seventy years the college continued in its modified role, until Augustinian canons arrived on the scene, around 1140, and introduced, for the first time at Dorchester, life under monastic rule.

Apart from the anomaly already noted in the nave foundation, the excavations carried out in 2001 exposed reasonably consistent foundation offsets at the base of the west wall, both internally and externally, and it has hitherto been argued that the whole is of a single 12th-century build.[11] Homogeneity of construction is a powerful argument, but that does not provide evidence of absolute age. It is an unsupported assumption on the part of the excavators that the nave was constructed by the Augustinian canons, and must therefore date from the mid-12th century. Architecturally, the upper part of the nave, with its windows, accords well with that period but, as already demonstrated, below the string-course the masonry is older and lacks diagnostic Romanesque features. *Prima facie*, there is nothing to prevent the lower parts of these walls from being 11th century, and thus associated with the final years of the cathedral, or with the collegiate church that succeeded it. This could be Remigius's work: almost certainly, it is no later.

Of course, one might argue that a major rebuild would be unlikely to take place on a church that had just been demoted from cathedral to collegiate status. However, that is precisely what happened at Wells in the 1170s: when under threat, reconstruction on a grand scale was apparently viewed as a means of proclaiming historical supremacy.[12] In any case, if Remigius had pulled down part of the Anglo-Saxon church in preparation to rebuild it, the canons had little option but to continue what had been started, even if that turned out to be a protracted process. It is not difficult to appreciate why a newly appointed Norman bishop would begin a rebuilding programme: events took the same course in many dioceses. Anglo-Saxon cathedrals were complex multi-cellular structures, lacking large naves and processional aisles: they were alien to Norman culture and liturgical practice, and rebuilding programmes were speedily initiated by most incoming bishops.

Arguably, almost the entire plan of Remigius's church is preserved in the present building, although little of its superstructure remains, apart from the nave walls up to string-course level. The church that Remigius sought to construct at Dorchester was large by contemporary standards, but probably fairly plain: it had transepts but no aisles.[13] This kind of unelaborate cruciform layout has been dubbed the 'austere' plan.[14] It is found in some of the latest Anglo-Saxon churches and, more widely, in early Norman work.

Thus, to a large extent, the conundrum of the nave has been solved, and explanations which comfortably accommodate all the physical evidence are within grasp (see further, p. 66). In summary, the following sequence is now posited:

(i)   Broadly speaking, the body of the Anglo-Saxon church lay on the site of the present Norman nave.

(ii) A short length of wall containing what may have been the north crossing arch (or, alternatively, a lesser *porticus* arch) of the late Saxon cathedral still stands, and fragments of pre-Conquest foundations are probably incorporated in the north and west walls of the nave. Part of the west wall of the present north transept may also be pre-Conquest, and is potentially the east side of a *porticus*.

(iii) Much of the ground plan (probably including the crossing), the lower half of the nave walls, and parts of the south transept date from the Saxo-Norman era, and are potentially assignable to Remigius's rebuild commenced in or soon after 1067. The 11th-century chancel has entirely vanished, although the foundation of its north side has been exposed.

(iv) The upper halves of the nave walls, with their tall windows, are stylistically mid-to-late 12th century and must therefore be associated with the Augustinian abbey. The upper parts of the crossing and the Norman doorway in the west wall of the north transept also belong to this phase.

Finally, it should be mentioned that, despite being built on the site of a small Roman town, the fabric of Dorchester Abbey is remarkably devoid of recycled materials that are obviously of Roman date. Brick and tile, in particular, were reused in great quantities in many Anglo-Saxon and medieval churches, yet, even in the earliest extant masonry of the north nave wall, there is no visible Roman material. This absence remains an enigma. It has been claimed that there is Roman brick in the south nave wall, which was formerly exposed to view (high up in bay 5, opposite the south door), but that area has subsequently been replastered.[15] The identification of this material as Roman is almost certainly erroneous: a photograph shows parts of four rows of very thin tiles laid on edge, closely packed and slightly pitched.[16] They appear to be medieval roof tiles, filling the former Norman window opening.

Nevertheless, the occasional small fragment of pre-medieval brick/tile has been noted in the fabric of the church. The extent to which stone rubble was recycled cannot be ascertained: only the adherence of Roman mortar could demonstrate reuse. However, it is tempting to interpret the occurrence of small, neatly squared blocks of limestone (*e.g.* in the west wall of the south nave aisle, just above plinth level) as recycled Roman *opus quadratum* (Fig. 19).

ARCHITECTURE OF THE COLLEGIATE CHURCH

It has been established in the previous chapter that the north wall of the present nave incorporates fabric of pre-Norman date, and preserved in that rubble masonry is the outline of a large arch. In the next constructional phase, most of the remainder of the church to which that arch belonged was demolished and replaced by a new building, which may also have made limited use of existing foundations. While admitting that diagnostic art-historical dating

FIGURE 19. *South nave aisle: reused blocks of squared masonry* (opus quadratum) *in the west wall, above the plinth.* (*Warwick Rodwell*)

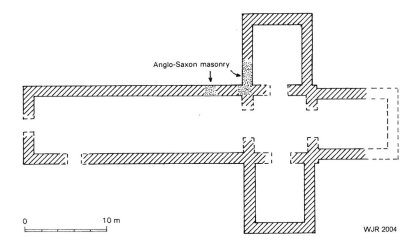

Anglo-Saxon masonry

0   10 m

WJR 2004

FIGURE 20. Reconstructed plan of the early Norman collegiate church at Dorchester, incorporating a fragment of the Anglo-Saxon cathedral. (Warwick Rodwell)

evidence is lacking, it has been argued, primarily on the basis of historical sequence, that the new church was begun c. 1067 by Remigius, bishop of Dorchester, Leicester and Lincoln.

To a large extent, the ghost of Remigius's new church is preserved in the present building, although the only 11th-century masonry that remains accessible to view is in the north wall of the nave (up to string-course level) and in the south wall of the south transept. Nevertheless, with the help of archaeological evidence, the plan may be reconstructed (Fig. 20).

The nave was a long, narrow vessel, of typical proportions for the 11th century: externally it measured 26.5 m by 9.7 m (87 x 32 ft). It was unaisled and had walls averaging 1.3 m (4¼ ft) thick. Since there are no signs of pilasters on the north side of the nave, it seems clear that the walls were unbuttressed. Nothing can be said about the doors or windows, except that there was definitely no entrance on the north: there were probably doors in the south and west walls. The transepts were almost a matched pair,[17] but their western sides were not quite in line; this seems to have been due to a setting-out error in the crossing, probably as a result of the residual influence of earlier structures on the footprint. Externally, the transepts were square in plan, which gave a slightly elongated internal space. It is unlikely that there were apses or other eastward projections, although they cannot be entirely ruled out.

The positions of the east and west sides of the crossing can be deduced from the evidence of later alterations, and it seems clear that the central space must have been notionally square in plan: in reality, it was very slightly rhomboidal, accounting for the misalignment of the transepts. It has previously been assumed that the crossing was rectangular, like some others of the same era, but that is challengeable.[18] The crossing was presumably defined by arches on all

four sides, although nothing of these now remains. However, it may be noted that some crossings of the period were unenclosed by masonry on the west. There is no evidence for any thickening of the walls to carry a substantial crossing tower, but the masonry was adequate to support a low central tower, or timber lantern. This must remain a tentative suggestion until the issue of a structural division between crossing and nave is resolved: if there was no arch in this position, there could be no masonry tower.

The only piece of solid evidence we have concerning the chancel is the inner edge of its north wall, which was revealed when the new base for the pulpit was installed in 1999. This confirms that the chancel was narrower than the nave and crossing by about half a wall's thickness on either side. Hence, there would have been salient angles projecting between the chancel and transepts. There is nothing to indicate the length of the chancel, or to confirm that it terminated in a square (as opposed to apsidal) east end, but it would undoubtedly have been much shorter than its late 12th-century successor. In the 19th century, historians were obsessed with the notion that the early Norman chancel was apsidal, and it was argued that there were transeptal chapels with apses too. While cruciform churches in the 11th century could have one or more eastern apses, these were not prescriptive: most were non-apsidal in their initial build. Some of the grandest churches in this class certainly did not have them: *e.g.* Breamore (Hants.), and St Mary-in-Castro, Dover (Fig. 21).

The plan and proportions of this church point to an 11th-century date, as does the wide-jointed, semi-squared masonry in the nave and south transept, and the absence of pilaster-buttresses (Figs 16 and 147). It is not difficult to find analogues for the plan, in both late Saxon and early Norman milieux. Dorchester

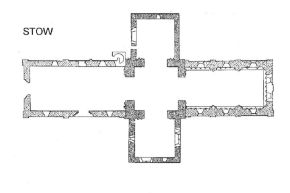

STOW

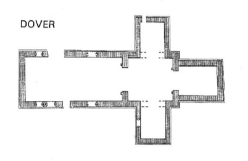

DOVER

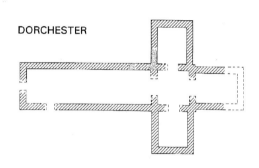

DORCHESTER

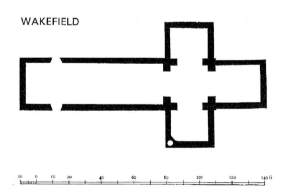

WAKEFIELD

FIGURE 21. *Comparative plans of 11th-century churches at Dorchester, Dover (Taylor and Taylor, 1965), Stow (Taylor and Taylor, 1965) and Wakefield (Bond, 1913). The long chancel at Stow is 12th century, and the plan of the original eastern arm is unknown.*

may be compared favourably with Dover, which is one of the largest and latest Anglo-Saxon cruciform churches (but the latter is slightly smaller).[19] A close parallel, but a little bigger than Dorchester, is All Saints, Wakefield (now the cathedral), the earliest phase of which dates from *c*. 1100.[20] However, that had squatter transepts (Fig. 21). In a paper on 'minor cruciform churches' Malcolm Thurlby has discussed the wider architectural context of 11th-century churches of this type, observing that some were associated with cenotaphs and shrines to Anglo-Saxon saints, and others with bishops.[21] It is particularly relevant to note that the major aisleless cruciform church at Stow (Lincs.) is also in part associated with Bishop Remigius, but its crossing and transepts are on a more monumental scale (Fig. 21).[22]

NOTES

1   Hamilton, 1870, 312.
2   Smith, 1964, **1**, 117. Leland may have assumed that these churches were once parochial, when they were only of chapel status. See also Doggett, 1986, 60–1.
3   Wallingford was a late Saxon foundation and was always larger than Dorchester: by the early 13th century it had no fewer than eleven churches, in addition to a priory (Rodwell, 1975, 155). Doggett (1986) put the total of medieval churches in Wallingford at fifteen.
4   See also Cook and Rowley, 1985, 48.
5   Gough [Camden], 1789, 308. The 'clerk' was presumably the toll-bridge clerk, and his house is likely to have been the cottage at the extreme south-east corner of the green at Bridge End.
6   For Bridge End, see Fig. 2. The front wall of the cottage on the right-hand (south) side of the road that formerly led from the green to the bridge contains various blocks of reused limestone, one of them very large; this may be the site of the church. I am indebted to Prof. Malcolm Airs for drawing my attention to this masonry.
7   Gough [Camden], 1789, 308; VCH, 1962, 40.
8   *Ille primis annis egregia apud Dorcestram meditatus, et aliqua facere ingressus, novissime curam omnem et sedem transtulit ad Lindocolinam civitatem, unam ex populosioribus Angliae* (Hamilton, 1870, 312).
9   Hill, 1965, 64–5.
10   Rodwell, 2001, 123–6.
11   Keevill, 2003, 359–60.
12   Rodwell, 2001, 127–30.
13   Evidence that the church was transeptal comes from the surviving, low-level masonry of the south transept (now incorporated in the 14th-century aisle) which is identical to that of the lower north wall of the nave.
14   Blair, 1996.
15   Kirkpatrick, 1927, 7.
16   Photograph by H.W. Taunt, *c*. 1890, in COS (neg. no. 4051); copy in NMR.
17   The supposed plan of the north transept has taken

various forms in previous publications. Addington (1845) reconstructed it as slightly deeper than the south transept; Paul (1900) made it deeper still, and that version was copied by the VCH (1962), and reproduced in later publications (*e.g.* Bloxham, 1990; Keevill, 2003, fig. 1). However, what I believe to be the correct plan had already been worked out by Hope (Anon., 1910) and Bond (1913, 264). At most, the north transept was *c.* 30 cm deeper than the south.

18 Bond, 1913; Thurlby, 2003, 123. While the position of the east side of the north transept can be deduced from the evidence of a later pier, which was inserted when chapels were added, it does not necessarily follow that the east wall of the crossing was also on the same line. If it lay slightly further east, by the equivalent of a wall's thickness, then the crossing would have been square: scars in the plaster on the side walls of the chancel seem to confirm that that was indeed the case. Final proof will only be established by excavating the foundations of the east and west crossing walls.

19 Taylor and Taylor, 1965, fig. 94.
20 Bond, 1913, 272.
21 Thurlby, 2002, 245–7; 2003, 120–4.
22 Fernie, 1983, 124–7.

CHAPTER 5

Dorchester Abbey: A Historical Summary, *c.* 1140–2007

THE MONASTIC ERA

There is no surviving foundation charter for the Augustinian abbey, no later cartulary and very few extant documents that refer to it.[1] The foundation date of 1140, although often cited, has no firm historical basis. The abbey was certainly in existence by 1142, and is mentioned in a papal confirmation (bull) of its possessions in 1146: they included five chapels which had been part of the endowment of the former cathedral. A second confirmatory charter was issued in 1163.[2]

The foundation of the abbey – and with it the beginning of a new building programme – could have occurred at any time during the second quarter of the twelfth century, but is unlikely to have been much before *c.* 1140. The replacement of secular canons with a group of thirteen Augustinians in Dorchester has generally been associated with Bishop Alexander of Lincoln (1123–48), on the basis of Leland's assertion.[3] The peak decades for the foundation of English Augustinian houses were the 1120s and 1130s. Dorchester, however, was not an Augustinian abbey of the most common type, but was one of twenty-four sites settled by a rarer and independent branch of the order known as the Arrouaisians.[4] None of their foundations was certainly earlier than 1130. Arrouaisians were canons who followed the order of St Nicholas of Arrouaise, a house at Bapaume in Artois. They were noted for their austerity and strict observance of the rule, and for this they drew inspiration from the Cistercian order. While many Augustinian houses were founded in secluded locations, a few were decidedly urban (*e.g.* Oxford and Bristol).

Owing to the loss of all Dorchester's documents at the Dissolution, very little is known about the history of the abbey, and what there is has to be gleaned from external sources. For example, William Worcestre chanced to record in his *Itineraries* in 1480 that the canons' library contained a treatise on the *Hexaemeron* (Six Days of Creation), written in the early 13th century by Robert Grosseteste, Bishop of Lincoln.[5]

A locally important issue concerned the relics of St Birinus and their veneration. According to Bede, Birinus had been exhumed in the late 7th century, and his remains taken to Winchester, where the saint continued to be venerated (p. 26). However, in 1224, the canons of Dorchester petitioned the Pope for consent to move the relics to a more worthy setting than they currently enjoyed. Honorius III faced a dilemma, and asked the Archbishop of Canterbury to investigate whether Birinus was still interred at Dorchester: it was reported that, inspired by a canon's dream, a tomb in front of the altar of the Holy Cross[6] had been opened some fifty years earlier and the body of a bishop conveniently found. This is reminiscent of Glastonbury, where in 1191 the monks excavated and reportedly found the bodies of King Arthur and Guinevere.[7] Whoever was revealed at Dorchester in

Canonicus Regularis S.ᵗ Auguſtini

FIGURE 22. Seventeenth-century depiction of an Augustinian canon, by Daniel King. (King, 1672)

the later 12th century, may have been a bishop, but it is extremely doubtful that he was Birinus.[8] Nevertheless, in 1224 the tomb was opened again for the benefit of the Archbishop of Canterbury, who pronounced himself satisfied. An implausible tale was concocted that the bones taken to Winchester, centuries earlier, were those of one Bertinus, not Birinus. Bertinus is otherwise not known to history.

Rival claims by two or more monasteries to possess the corporeal remains of the same saint were not uncommon, and once again Glastonbury provides an analogue: St Dunstan died at Canterbury in 988 and was interred there, but when funds were suddenly needed by the abbey of Glastonbury in 1184, following a disastrous fire, the monks there announced that they held the relics of Dunstan. When challenged, Glastonbury claimed to have stolen the relics from Canterbury in 1012, and kept them in concealment thereafter: an implausible story.[9]

The fact that in the early 13th century there was no shrine to Birinus at Dorchester points to the saint's devotional focus having been lost and his cult all-but forgotten. The flurry of activity in 1224 was plainly an attempt to reinstate a lapsed cult, and give it credibility, as well as generating revenue from pilgrims. The weight of evidence militates against the likelihood that any shrine constructed in 1224 contained the corporeal remains of Birinus. The same applies to the 14th-century shrine that followed it. Nevertheless, a devotional focus was undoubtedly created, perhaps containing some small relic associated with the saint, and that was what mattered to the medieval pilgrim. With this in mind, one wonders about items that were in the possession of Thomas Smith in the 18th century. He kept the George Inn, was an avid collector of local antiquities, and his family were ancestral to Dorchester. His collection included 'part of the shoes and cope of gilt leather of a bishop, falsely supposed [to be] St Birinus'.[10] These items must have been exhumed from a high-status burial in the church. Not inconceivably, they might have been taken from the tomb opened in 1224, and thereafter regarded as relics associated with the saint; they would have been dispersed at the Reformation, and perhaps saved from destruction by a local resident.

In the virtual absence of records, little can be said about the size and management of the abbey, although it is known that the initial foundation comprised thirteen canons. A bishop's visitation in 1441 reported that there were eleven, and in 1455 the number was twelve.[11] Occasional acquisitions of property by the abbey are recorded, as are failures to provide priests for some of the local parishes for which the canons had responsibility. The usual complaints are recorded in episcopal visitations about lax behaviour and sexual misdemeanours (including the abbot's alleged five mistresses); buildings were also in a run-down condition. Particularly revealing is the visitation of 1441, when it was found that the abbey was heavily in debt, the treasures were pawned (but, by arrangement, were temporarily returned to the abbey for the day of the visitation), and the canons went hunting, hawking and fishing when they should have been in the cloister.[12] The situation was so bad that the bishop adjourned the visitation, and by the time it was resumed two canons had taken flight, and by 1445 the abbot had resigned office.

In 1459 behaviour was still far from seemly: the younger canons were disobedient, and went out at night to eat, drink and generally fraternize with women and layfolk in the town; they even broke doors and windows to effect their escape. When the abbot imprisoned the ringleader, a group of sympathetic scholars from Oxford turned up and enforced his release.

A visitation in 1517 found little amiss except that the dormitory was out of repair, but another in 1530 could hardly have painted a blacker picture of both the buildings and the brethren. The dormitory, cloister and other buildings were out of repair; a public thoroughfare had become established through the cloister. It was used both by men and women, day and night; the cloister gates were never closed, and doors not locked. The abbot was charged with putting matters right, especially to fit new locks to the gates between the parochial nave and monastic quire.[13] The house had shrunk to comprise only the abbot, prior, six canons and two novices. The prior and others found difficulty in rising in time for mattins (often only two managed to attend); one canon was mentally unstable, tried to fight with the prior, and daily went out hunting and fishing; and there had long been no instruction given in grammar because the teacher was usually drunk after midday.[14] And so the catalogue of misdeeds went on. Eventually, the bishop suspended the abbot for open negligence, abuse and disobedience, and also suspended the prior and one canon for sexual misdemeanours.

Mentions of the shrine of St Birinus are rare, and it is difficult to decide whether there was any recognizable trace of one in 1224, or merely a marked grave. However in 1292 Oliver Sutton, bishop of Lincoln, granted an indulgence to all who visited Dorchester abbey, implying that there was then a shrine;[15] the following year he issued a second indulgence, and in 1301 yet another indulgence of forty days was granted by Bishop Dalderby to all those who visited Birinus's bones. Soon afterwards, Higden tells us that a new shrine was completed by c. 1320.[16] At the Dissolution, the offerings at the shrine were worth £5 per annum, and the net income of the abbey was £190.

The dedication of the abbey is usually cited as being to St Peter and St Paul, although St Birinus is also sometimes mentioned as a third joint dedicatee.[17] However, the last seems to be no more than a relatively recent antiquarian addition, for which there is no

FIGURE 23. *Twelfth-century impression of the seal of Dorchester Abbey, showing St Peter. (VCH, 1907)*

ancient evidence. It is quite likely that the primary dedication was to St Peter alone, with St Paul perhaps being added in the 12th century. The abbey's earliest surviving seal impression – which is 12th century – depicts St Peter, full length, robed in episcopal vestments and holding two keys in one hand and a book in the other (Fig. 23).[18] The legend reads:

SIGILLVM · CONVENTVS · SANTI · PETRI · [D]ORCES.

Although only a hypothesis, the addition of St Birinus to the dedication could have occurred in the early 14th century, when a new shrine was erected. His name is not currently part of the dedication at Dorchester, and nor is it found elsewhere, except in the local Roman Catholic church (consecrated in 1849).[19]

Another seal impression, which survives on a document of 1248, belongs to abbot Richard de Wurthe (1236–59). This depicts the seated Virgin and Child, with the abbot below in an adoration pose.[20] The legend reads:

SIGILL RICARDI ABBATIS DE DORCECESTRIA

Although somewhat speculative, the possibility is worth mentioning that a Norman manuscript from the abbey's library has survived, and is now in the Bodleian Library. It comprises a collection of meditations and prayers, written in the second half of the 12th century, bound with two other manuscripts relating to Winchester (one of which mentions Birinus). The third manuscript, which has fine illuminated capitals, was compiled for use in an abbey of regular canons dedicated to St Peter.[21] Dorchester has long been accepted as a likely candidate for that abbey. Two other books that are likely to have

belonged to the monastic library remained in the church until modern times, but are sadly now lost.[22]

A very incomplete record of the abbots has been preserved, from the first mentioned, Alfred in 1146, to John March who signed the deed acknowledging the supremacy of the king in 1534,[23] and who surrendered the abbey to Henry VIII's commissioners in 1536.[24]

In addition to its being a house of Augustinian canons, Dorchester abbey was also a parish church: hence the provision of a Norman font. Moreover, the canons were responsible for the spiritual needs of a number of other parishes in the region, from which the abbey derived income. There has been a tendency in previous histories to imply that the parishioners were permitted to use only the south nave aisle (which is today called the People's Chapel), but that is not the case. The south aisle was the last part of the medieval building to be erected (*c.* 1350–60), and was an adjunct to the nave. The east end of the aisle also served as an ante-chapel to the shrine chapel beyond. Historically, the body of the church was primarily for the people of the locality, and not the preserve of a monastic community. When the canons arrived they took over the chancel and eastern parts, while the parish always retained the nave. The division is made explicit in the visitation of 1530, when the bishop ordered that the gates between the nave and quire should be locked at night, because the former was always open to the outside world and the latter to the monastery.[25] Leland, writing in 1542, confirmed that the 'body of the abbay chirch' (*i.e.* the nave) lately served the lay community, and that Beauforest purchased 'the est part' (*i.e.* the chancel) and 'gave it to augment the paroch chirch'.[26]

AFTER THE REFORMATION

Later Sixteenth Century

Following the suppression of the abbey in 1536, the monastic buildings and precinct were granted by the Crown in 1544 to Sir Edmund Ashfield of Ewelme (Oxon.), along with the prebend and rectory of the parish church.[27] The church itself was not, however, conveyed to Ashfield, who was presumably responsible for demolishing the monastic buildings, or appropriating them to other uses. The nave was already in the hands of the parish, and the monastic quire and chapels were sold for £140 to Richard Beauforest, described by Leland as 'a great riche man, dwelling in the toun of Dorchestre'.[28] The stone altars and shrine of St Birinus would have been dismantled, and images removed. However, there is no evidence for wholesale iconoclasm, and it is clear that the stained glass largely survived the Reformation. The same applies to the small sculptures attached to the chancel windows, the tabernacle work of the sedilia, and the multiple piscinae (all of which retained their bowls intact). Clearly, these redundant liturgical features did not have their projecting parts hacked away; nor were they infilled and plastered over. The fabric of the church survived remarkably intact.

Beauforest allowed the parish to use the whole of the church for parochial services. He also permitted the burial of the last abbot, John March, in the north chancel aisle in 1553.[29] In his will dated 13 July 1554, Beauforest bequeathed the eastern part of the 'Abbey Churche of Dorchester' and 'the implements thereof' to the parish, on condition that they should not be sold or alienated without the consent of his heirs.[30] He also gave twenty shillings 'to the reparations of my parishe church', and ordered that his body should be buried in 'our Lady Ile' (presumed to be the north chancel aisle). It was unusual for a post-Dissolution parish to acquire the entire monastic church, instead of only one component, leaving the remainder to be demolished.[31] Doggett has suggested that the whole church was spared because it was briefly considered a potential candidate for the new cathedral to serve the Oxford diocese. He has also argued convincingly that Beauforest stepped in to purchase the eastern arm because he was a descendent of Abbot Richard Beauforest (d. 1510), whose fine memorial brass still lies in the floor of the chancel (Fig. 122).[32] A second brass commemorates Margaret Beauforest and her two husbands, William Tanner and Richard Beauforest (the benefactor).

The medieval Peculiar of Dorchester (comprising ten parishes) also survived the Dissolution and remained under the control of the Ashfields until 1578, when it passed to the Fettiplace family. The Peculiar Jurisdiction remained intact until the 1830s.

When the Chantry Certificates for Oxfordshire were drawn up, in the reign of Edward VI, Dorchester was described as a parish of eighty householders. There were no chantries in the church, and no chantry priests attached to it: there was only a light and lands with a yearly value of 9*d.* which provided for 'the maytenance of a lampe to brene within the said parishe churche for ever more'.[33] This is unimpressive, and clearly the parishioners were no longer opulent. In 1551/2 an inventory of goods in Dorchester church was drawn up, again by order of Edward VI. The property belonging to the church was listed as follows (paraphrased):[34]

8 brass 'sockettes' [candle sconces]
2 brass candlesticks and 2 lead [pewter?] candlesticks
2 holy water pots and a latten basin[35]
1 'legeh' bell [lych, or funeral bell]
1 iron fire-pan and a brass pot
39 pewter plates
44 lead [pewter?] spoons
1 pair of censers
2 copper crosses

3 cruets and a brass ship
1 parcel-gilt chalice and a latten pyx
2 surplices
3 copes, 5 vestments and their albs
1 canape and 1 altar cloth
2 pawls and a sepulchre cloth
10 towels and a hearse cloth
2 bells [entry altered, from 3]
1 'saunce' bell [calling bell]

This list does not suggest a wealthy parish; nor does the recorded history of the church after the Reformation. Even before the abbey was dissolved, the canons had ceased to minister directly to the parishioners of Dorchester, and had installed a curate to do so on their behalf. No vicarage was endowed then, or by the lay proprietor of the rectory after 1536. Instead, for the next four hundred years, the parishioners of Dorchester were variously served by a series of curates and ministers, until 1868, when the living finally became a titular vicarage.[36] Many of the incumbents did not even reside in Dorchester.

Seventeenth Century

The history of the church in the 17th century is ill documented, and it is difficult to reconcile the two major stands of evidence. On the one hand, a new tower was built at the west end in 1602: it is substantial in scale, decorative to behold, and must have been very costly (Fig. 204; Pl. 2). It is highly improbable that this was funded by the parish, and a private benefactor must surely have been responsible, the Fettiplace family being the most plausible candidate. On the other hand, the surviving Churchwardens' Presentments (sporadic, between 1620 and 1806) confirm that the church was not flourishing, but was in decay. In 1623, two farmers were presented for failing to pay their tithe dues, 'suffering the chancell to goe to ruine'.[37] Also, the body of the church was 'not sufficiently repayred in glazeing, tileing, seiling, paveing, timber worke in the roofe, nor beautified with scripture sentences'. The church moreover lacked the two requisite volumes of homilies and 'Bp. Jewel's works'.[38] Other entries in the 1620s refer to the chancel having 'fallen into decay', to the clock and chimes being out of order,[39] the churchyard railings being broken, and the inhabitants of several outlying parishes refusing to contribute their share to the maintenance of Dorchester.

There are no surviving presentations between 1626 and 1666, and those thereafter were preoccupied with behavioural matters, rather than fabric. However, the reconstruction of the south nave aisle roof in 1633 was recorded by a date cut into the timber, and dendrochronology has confirmed that reused timbers in the present nave roof are likely to date from the 1630s. In 1669 Timothy Smith was presented 'for building upon ye churchyard and opening a doore into ye churchyard': this presumably refers to one of the cottages on the boundaries.[40] In 1674 the churchwardens claimed that 'our church [is] in good repair and ye churchyard mounds [are] all up', but two years later the chancel was again 'out of repair',[41] which suggests that little if anything had actually been done.

Potential encroachments upon the churchyard are indicated by the two timber-framed and thatched cottages on the east, and the stone-built Lychgate Cottage on west (frontispiece; Figs 3 and 211–13). All three are likely to date from the 17th century. The tithe map shows a second building, fronting High Street, in the garden to the south of Lychgate Cottage. On the eastern boundary, the more southerly cottage was a double unit, and there were thus three occupations here, each with a separate garden attached. Although built against the churchyard boundary, the cottages were on manorial land, and they did not come into the possession of the Church until 1930.[42]

There was a parsonage house in Dorchester at least from the 17th century, which was latterly described as 'very small'. It was not directly on the site of the present vicarage (built 1856–57; Fig. 3), but may have been the little house that stood at the southern tip of its considerable garden, adjoining the Grammar School in the former guest house.

Eighteenth Century

Records in the 18th century are slightly more numerous. In 1716 the chancel was again 'much out of repair', and three parishioners were presented for installing pews without a licence.[43] The chancel was still unrepaired two years later, but interest in the creation and appropriation of pews was gaining pace. In 1734 Mr Bush was presented 'for putting a lock upon a seat' and excluding other parishioners from it, while John Almond was at the same time presented 'for cutting the seats' in the church.[44]

Estimates for major repairs costing £2,500 were obtained in 1737, presaging a long drawn-out programme of works. Although it covers only the period 1739–66, the *Dorchester Brief Book* is wonderfully detailed in respect of roof repairs.[45] In 1739 the south chancel aisle roof was completely reconstructed, and the specification provided for reusing old oak, as well as introducing new oak, and deal boards.[46] The old lead was all weighed as it was taken down: it was then recast and reweighed as it was taken back up. The eastern part of the nave roof was reconstructed in 1747, also in lead; this work took place east of the arch, in the area of the former crossing and western part of the original chancel.[47] The work in this area must have followed on from a full refurbishment of the chancel that was funded by the Fettiplace family in the previous year.[48]

In 1754, the roof of the south (nave?) aisle was reported to be defective,[49] and in 1760 reroofing

the nave continued, working from the chancel arch towards the tower, 'so far as the money in hand will repair'.[50] In 1765, it was the turn of the 'north aisle' to be re-tiled,[51] and the following year more work was carried out on the nave roof. Truncation of the north transept and the installation of the crude Gothick window (Fig. 97), are likely to have taken place in the previous century.

After this long haul on roof repairs, in 1787 the churchwardens presented 'that [all] is well: the church is whitewashed and all the windows are glazed', implying that repairs had recently been completed.[52] The Vestry Minutes (sporadic, from 1733 onwards) shed further light on repairs, as well as the perennial strife over pews. The last may have been settled by the comprehensive re-pewing which was authorized in 1792.[53] There are many references to levying rates for church repairs, from 1½d. to 7d. in the pound. The higher rates-charges indicate that serious money was being spent on the fabric in the early 1800s; after 1812 there was a lull, until 1836, when 'alterations and necessary repairs' were again in hand.[54]

Finally, the earliest archaeologically-orientated description of Dorchester Abbey was written by Stukeley on his visit in 1736;[55] it has not hitherto been published in full:

1 Sep. 1736.
I visited Dorchester in company with my old fr[d.] M[r] Becket, Surgeon of Abingdon. I came with an eager view of the most antient of our church antiquities, and my expectation was fully answer'd. I believe no place in England can show such a sight of religious Antiquity belonging to our Saxon christian Ancestors. The Episcopal palace begun by Birinus is on the north and west of the church. Some of it now remaining and inhabited. I cannot say here is much of the first and original church of Birinus remaining. ~~The only part~~ [*struck through*] What I can with certainty pronounce to be such is the door I have drawn on the N. and W.
The whole cathedral seems to consist of two churches at least, joined together. The older part on the S. and W. with the high altar over the p[r]sent charnel house, which probably in its original imitated, the limina aptorii of S[t.] Pet[r]s at Rome, and the subterraneous vaults of Hexham and Rippon cathedrals, Grantha[m] ch andc. A door to this part of the ch to the W. and another on the S. as parish chhs. The rest of the ch has a cathedral form and venerable aspect. 3 large isles. The altar not made with a semicircle but square projecting beyond the east end of the building. There are 2 semicircular arches on the N. and on the S. of the middle isle in that part wh may be calld the nave or cross isle of the original work of Birinus.
On the W. end of the ch is the most antient and only font of its sort (perhaps in the christian world) large and of cast lead, eleven figures of saints sitting in the old Saxon style of drawing, such as we see in the oldest Mss and pretty elegant. There are many ancient monuments of bishops and religious and some of ~~great knights~~ [*struck through*] antient nobility andc. Most flat on the

ground. The brasses mostly taken away and defac'd. This one with a crozier on it:

+ABBATIS:CESSIT:VIRRES:HIC:QVI:REQVES ....
[transcription continues]

Another begins and goes on just in the same manner, with a crozier too and words as far as pfect IOHANNES DE VT.

A monumental effigies of a judg with his coif on and this coat. *[sketch of Stonor arms]*

Much of the oldest small paving tyles colored with figures and laid mosaic with wh the whole quire was pavd., some of the altar part within railes yet undisturbd and in little triangular bits with borders. Much painted glass extremely antient of Saxon times and letters in the window. S. of high altar St Petr crucifyd with head downward. St Paul beheaded. The window N. of altar is the most particular one I ever saw. The mullion work is branchd out into a genealogical scheme or two of David, I suppose, who lyes at bottom. All the rest of the ancestors of our Sav^r in stone carvd or glass painted figures each having labels in their hands, with their names in Saxon capitals. In the E. window many coats of vast antiq. *[sketches of 19 arms in shields, some identified and annotated, others explained with colours]*

Nineteenth Century

The principal manor of Dorchester was effectively broken up in 1806–08, when its possessions were auctioned in fifty-nine lots. Not only were numerous tenements and lands sold, but so too were the greater and lesser tithes for the whole parish, along with the advowson of the church.[56] From the early Middle Ages until c. 1837, Dorchester was the head of a Peculiar Jurisdiction, comprising ten surrounding parishes.[57] The parish of Dorchester included the hamlets of Overy and Burcot, but the latter was provided with its own chapel in 1869.[58]

Meanwhile, turnpiking the road from Henley to Abingdon began in 1736, probably resulting in improvements to the streets of Dorchester. The major change to the topography of the southern part of the town occurred with the construction of a new bridge over the Thame in 1813–16. This brought the Henley road into the town directly opposite the southern churchyard gate, and in order to effect a smooth link between the new bridge and the High Street, a swathe for a wide road was cut both through properties and through the lower end of the churchyard (Fig. 2). A new boundary wall to the latter was erected, apparently using materials reclaimed from the demolition of the old bridge (Fig. 219). At about the same time, the red brick Toll Cottage was built (Fig. 214).

The urge for church 'restoration' erupted in Dorchester in 1844 but, curiously, was not instigated by the vicar and churchwardens. In that year the Committee of the Oxford Architectural Society issued a circular, calling for restoration,[59] and appointed James Cranston, an Oxford architect,[60] to draw up a report on the state of the fabric.[61] In May 1845, the Society issued a second statement, announcing that sufficient funds had been gathered to make a start on the restoration of the south window in the chancel, together with the piscina and sedilia below it. The cost was estimated at £160. Dorchester saw a novel development in the history of Victorian church restoration: the Oxford Architectural Society not only instigated the project, but also amended its constitution so that it could enter into contracts and carry out the work itself. The first building contract was issued in the spring of 1845.[62]

The Committee, which wished to see the abbey 'entirely rescued from its present state of neglect', further announced its intention to proceed with the full restoration of the chancel, including raising the pitch of the roof and reconstructing the head of the east window: that, it was estimated, would cost £380. Third on the Committee's list were the two south aisles and porch (£225), followed by modest work on the north aisle (£25). Re-seating the church and providing a new pulpit was to cost £650 and, finally, complete reroofing of the nave and aisles required £2,500. The total anticipated cost of restoration was thus £3,940.[63] The external appearance of the church on the eve of restoration was recorded by several topographical artists (frontispiece[64]), but unfortunately the interior was not.

Over a period of some forty years, restoration was carried out on an intermittent basis, successively under the direction of four architects: James Cranston, William Butterfield, (Sir) George Gilbert Scott and Joseph Maltby Bignell. Scott had earlier employed his pupil, Bignell, as clerk of works at Dorchester. Disappointingly, little documentation has survived from the restoration period in the way of architects' drawings and specifications, and faculties were seldom applied for.

Although the monastic church has survived almost in its entirety, the medieval fixtures and fittings have steadily been eroded over the ensuing centuries. From today's perspective, it is difficult to understand why this occurred on such a scale, but numerous losses since the mid-17th century can be charted from surviving records. The stained glass was one of the church's most significant assets in terms of medieval decoration, yet that has been massively depleted, and not as a consequence of the Reformation or Civil War.[65] Thus the twenty-six extant shields of armorial glass constitute less than half the number recorded in 1574, 1622 and 1657.[66] A few other items – most notably the font – have also survived, although why the panelled medieval base upon which it stood was destroyed in the mid-19th century, only to be replaced with a very poor pedestal (by Butterfield; Fig. 190), defies comprehension.

Considerable components of the medieval furnishing were also intact until the first half of the 19th century: the monastic return-stalls, pulpitum and side screens were all still in place in 1807, but disappeared soon after. Similarly, the entire complement of pre-Victorian liturgical vessels has vanished: 'This remarkable church has been denuded of all its ancient vessels, and now possesses only a poor silver chalice and paten of modern-medieval fashion, hallmarked 1866 and 1865, respectively'.[67] There are also several undistinguished pieces of 20th-century plate, and a fine new altar cross commissioned in 2004.[68]

Twentieth Century

The history of Dorchester in the twentieth century has recently been discussed.[69] As so often happened, the century following completion of the major 19th-century restoration was characterized by the piecemeal dismantling of the Victorian ideal. The sense of completeness, unity and single-mindedness that was so notable in Scott's work has been lost.[70] Worse still, throughout England, for most of the 20th century, there was a reaction against Victoriana, just as, a century earlier, the high Victorians had denigrated work of the Georgian era. Dorchester has not escaped the changing liturgical practices and fickleness of fashion that have been responsible for a string of architectural and historical losses.

A new chapter in Dorchester's ecclesiastical history opened in 1939, when the office of Suffragan Bishop of Dorchester was created, but this had little practical impact on the abbey. The 20th-century urge to reorder manifested itself in the north aisle in 1958,[71] and henceforth this became known as St Birinus's Chapel. An appeal for £30,000 was launched in 1961 to fund a substantial repair and refurbishment programme. Edith Stedman, an American with a passion for Dorchester, set up the American Friends of Dorchester Abbey, to help raise money for the restoration.[72] The appeal remained open until 1970, when Queen Elizabeth the Queen Mother attended the service marking the completion of the restoration.[73] As part of this campaign, the south chancel aisle was reordered in 1964, when a new shrine to St Birinus was constructed, reusing some of the 14th-century masonry (Pls 24 and 25).[74] The great east window was also restored then, and again in 1989–90.

In 1978, the tower underwent a major restoration,[75] and in the 1980s reordering in the chancel and north aisle led to the organ being resited on a gallery, and the removal of the pulpit, low screen and pews. In the 1960s a museum had been set up at the instigation of Miss Stedman in the then-redundant abbey guest house (which was no longer used as a school), with the caretaker living in a flat above.[76] In 1989, an appeal was launched to fund the restoration of the guest house and to convert the flat into a large meeting room, the function it still serves today.[77]

The east end of the chancel and the south-east chapels underwent major repair in 1995, which included works on masonry and glazing.[78] Finally, a fresh appeal was launched in 2000, to carry out major repairs to the roofs, install new heating, construct the Cloister Gallery (a pentice on the site of the south cloister walk), conserve the wallpaintings, reorder some parts of the interior, and other works, all under the supervision of Martin Ashley Architects.[79] This ambitious scheme was successfully completed in 2008.

NOTES

1   VCH, 1907, 87–90.
2   For the recorded history of the abbey, see generally VCH, 1962, and Bond and Tiller, 2005.
3   Smith, 1964, **1**, 117.
4   The Arrouaisian houses are listed in Robinson, 1980, appendix 2; see also Bond and Tiller, 2005, 29, fig. 19.
5   Harvey, 1969, 193.
6   An altar with this dedication is likely to have lain in front of the rood screen, which would imply that it was in the late 12th-century nave. If our deduction concerning the morphology of the late Saxon church is correct (see above), this would place the tomb in question west of the putative crossing. A saintly tomb in this position is reminiscent of the newly discovered evidence relating to the early medieval shrine of St Chad at Lichfield (Rodwell, 2004; Rodwell, et al., 2008).
7   Crick, 1991, 218.
8   The church had certainly been rebuilt on more than one occasion since Birinus's death, and his remains are therefore likely to have been previously exhumed, and probably not reinterred in the floor. If Birinus's relics stayed at Dorchester, they would have been housed in or under a shrine, rather than in the primary grave.
9   Sharpe, 1991, 205–8.
10 Gough, 1789, **1**, 308.
11 VCH, 1907, 88.
12 Ibid., 88.
13 VCH, 1907, 89.
14 Ibid., 89
15 Hill, 1954, 206. Attention was first drawn to this reference by Ayers.
16 Babington, 1865.
17 VCH, 1907, 89.
18 Ibid., pl. 2.
19 Only one Anglican church bears a dedication to Birinus – Morgan's Vale, Downton, Wilts. – and that is a wholly Victorian foundation. However, it has been argued that two Scottish churches, at Kilbirnie and Dumbarney, derive their dedications from Birinus, but it is hard to see a connection (Arnold-Forster, 1899, **1**, 394–6).
20 Gough, 1789, 308. VCH, 1907, 90.
21 Bodl., MS Auct. D.2.6(c); the identifying details are on f. 184.
22 They were first noted by Taunt (1906, 34) who stated that there was a case in the sacristy containing 'a couple of old English books': Higden's Polychronicon, printed by Caxton, 1482, and 'Sequences in the Sarum

Missal', printed by Wynkin de Worde, at the sign of the Sun in Fleet Street, 1515.

23 The deed is transcribed in Addington, 1845, 96–8.

24 For the list of abbots, see VCH, 1907, 89–90; this omits Abbot Beauforest (d. 1510). For an updated list, see Tiller, 2005, 210.

25 VCH, 1907, 89.

26 Smith, 1964, **1**, 117.

27 Addington and Macfarlane, 1860, 170–1.

28 Smith, 1964, **1**, 117.

29 He was interred under a slab of 'playne marble', which was noted in the 17th century, but is no longer extant: Davis, 1922, 121.

30 Bodl., MS Wills Oxon. 180, f. 261b; transcript printed in Addington, 1845, 98–9.

31 Doggett, 2005, 42.

32 *Ibid.*, 42–3.

33 Graham, 1919, 26.

34 For a full transcript, see Graham, 1919, 101–2, 119.

35 Latten is a metal similar to brass, but softer.

36 VCH, 1962, 54; Pearce, 1918, 182–3.

37 Peyton, 1928, 116.

38 John Jewel was Bishop of Salisbury, 1560–71, and a former Fellow of Corpus Christi, Oxford. The most celebrated of his writings was *Apology for the Church of England* (London, 1562).

39 Nothing appears to be known about this clock, which presumably survived in the tower until 1868 (Beeson, 1989, 37). It presumably dated to sometime after 1602, when the present tower was built. However, a yet earlier clock is referred to in Bishop Alnwick's visitation of 1441, when the abbot was reported for not keeping it in working order, and for appropriating the clock-ropes for the bells (VCH, 1907, 88).

40 Peyton, 1928, 113.

41 *Ibid.*, 127.

42 ORO, MS Oxf. Dioc. pps. c.1796/4.

43 Peyton, 1928, 133.

44 *Ibid.*, 135.

45 ORO, PAR87/11/A1/1.

46 *Ibid.*, ff. 1–7.

47 ORO, PAR87/11/A1/1, ff. 22–4.

48 Bodl., MS Top. Oxon., d.795, ff. 210–11.

49 Peyton, 1928, 136.

50 Reported in the Churchwardens' Accounts: ORO, PAR87/4/F1/1. Obviously, the money ran out since the west end of the nave roof retained its old high pitch until Scott's restoration, whereas the rest was lowered.

51 ORO, PAR87/11/A1/1, f. 25; and PAR87/4/F1/2. Only the first of these references specifically names the north aisle. However, several early 19th-century views confirm that the north aisle was lead-covered, not tiled. This may be a mistake for retiling the south aisle. The reference in 1754 to the defective south aisle roof may also be relevant.

52 Peyton, 1928, 138.

53 ORO, MS Oxf, Archd, Oxon. c.159, ff. 55–8.

54 ORO, PAR87/2/A1.

55 Bodl., Gough Maps, 26, f. 42v. Minimal punctuation has been added, for easier comprehension.

56 Addington, 1845, 102.

57 Wood, 1982.

58 For the exceptionally complex manorial and parochial history, see VCH, 1963, 39–63, *passim*; also Tiller, 2005, 61–83.

59 Pantin, 1939, 178. The records of the Society (now the OAHS) are deposited in the Bodleian Library, and they provide a considerable amount of information on progress during the early years of the restoration.

60 Little is known about Cranston (or Cranstoun). He later transferred his practice to Birmingham.

61 Bodl., MS Don. d.540.

62 C. Miele, in Webster and Elliott, 2000, 282–3.

63 Details published as a supplement to Addington, 1845.

64 *Cf.* Jewitt's similar view (Addington, 1845, frontis.)

65 Some damage to windows is alleged to have been caused by Parliamentary troops who stabled their horses in the church.

66 Bouchier, 1918; Lambourn, 1949, 120.

67 Evans, 1928, 57.

68 Dudley, 2005, fig. 72.

69 Tiller, 2005; Dudley, 2005.

70 Although it is fair to say that since Scott had inherited Butterfield's reordered and refurnished chancel, he never achieved the unified interior at Dorchester that he did elsewhere, *e.g.* at St John's, Cirencester.

71 ORO, PAR87/11/L1/1–2: faculty for works, 1958–59.

72 Stedman is commemorated in a carved corbel at the south-west corner of the nave aisle (Dudley, 2005, fig. 65).

73 The PCC holds a considerable bundle of files relating to this appeal and the works carried out. For a personal account of the event, see Stedman, 1971, ch. 8.

74 The intention to recreate the shrine was publicized several years earlier: *Oxford Times*, 20 May 1960.

75 Account given in the local *Evening Post*, 7 Dec. 1978.

76 For the inception of the museum, see Stedman, 1971, 12.

77 The PCC holds a file of correspondence concerning this appeal.

78 The PCC holds a file of correspondence relating to this work.

79 For accounts of the most recent works, see: 'The Abbey Church of St Peter and St Paul, Dorchester on Thames', *Church Building*, no. 77 (2002), 22–5; 'Preserving our Past', *Building Engineer*, **78**, (2003), 12–23.

Chapter 6

Topography of the Augustinian Abbey, *c.* 1140–1536

When the Augustinian canons arrived in Dorchester, they took over the existing collegiate church, which may have been in an incomplete state. For expediency, the new abbey was designed to incorporate that church, and the requisite claustral buildings had to be fitted around it. The fact that the cloister at Dorchester lies to the north of the church has often been remarked upon, and it has generally been assumed that its placement was in some way determined by the Anglo-Saxon and early Norman ecclesiastical topography: it was. Indeed, there is a possibility that the church, which we have argued was built by Remigius, incorporated – or was intended to incorporate – a cloister, but there is no convincing evidence to determine the matter either way.

Major cathedral and collegiate churches were sometimes provided with cloisters, even though they were non-monastic: their purpose is not fully understood.[1] The late Saxon cathedral at Wells had a cloister, as did the collegiate church that succeeded it in the 1180s. Old Sarum (Wilts.) was cloistered in the early 12th century; St Paul's, London, also acquired a cloister in the same century; and Lincoln and Salisbury in the 13th century. At Dorchester, the most significant pointer to the existence of an 11th-century cloister, or at least to the intention of building one, is the absence of a primary doorway in the north wall of the nave. One would have expected north and south doors in an uncloistered plan, although this is not an inalienable rule.

A northern cloister was not ideal, but there are reasons why this was sometimes inevitable when a monastic order adopted an existing church, such as the exigencies of local topography. Augustinian houses had their share of northern cloisters, as at Bradenstoke Priory (Wilts.), Lacock Abbey (Wilts.), St Osyth's Priory (Essex), and Holy Trinity Priory, London. It is not difficult to appreciate why the cloister was sited north of the nave at Dorchester, since the ground falls away rapidly to the south and east in the present southern churchyard. While there was just sufficient space for a southern cloister *per se*, the terrain could not have accommodated the courts and ancillary structures that invariably lay between the claustral ranges and the precinct boundary.

Conventual Buildings

The thoroughness with which the conventual buildings have been destroyed since the Reformation at Dorchester is remarkable. This makes authentic reconstruction of the layout of the abbey difficult. It is curious that the plan of the cloister has not been perpetuated by features in the modern landscape, implying that the area north of the church was comprehensively cleared of buildings and levelled. Wood's description of 1657, together with later evidence, indicates that clearance did not take place before the 18th century, and possibly as late as the beginning of the 19th. In the mid-17th century, the south cloister walk was still recognizable, having been encapsulated in a narrow pentice flanking the nave and tower (Fig. 4),[2] and in the 1780s Gough observed, 'traces of the cloister may be seen on the north side of the church'.[3] Later still, Dugdale's editors referred to 'the foundations of walls forming a quadrangle … to the northward of the church'.[4]

While a detailed plan of the conventual buildings can only be recovered through extensive archaeological excavation, a generalized idea of their layout may be reconstructed, based on other Augustinian houses. No two monastic plans are identical, but the disposition of the core buildings and the functions they served more-or-less followed a common pattern. In outline, the plan of the cloister garth is known from three exploratory trenches dug in 1960–62, which located the west and north walks, and from excavations in 2001 which were mainly confined to the south walk.[5] Also, in 2004, a geophysical survey was carried out by Martin Rush, revealing shadowy traces of the east, west and north ranges (Fig. 24).[6]

Cloister Garth and Walks

It has been established that the overall east–west dimension of the cloister, including the walks, was 25 m (82 ft). The outer walls were 1.2 m (4 ft) in thickness, and their foundations a little more. The position of the inner, or garth, wall on the west was located in 1961 (Fig. 25B).[7] The masonry had been completely robbed, and the full width of the foundation trench was not exposed, but it is likely that the garth wall had a thickness of *c.* 60 cm (2 ft).

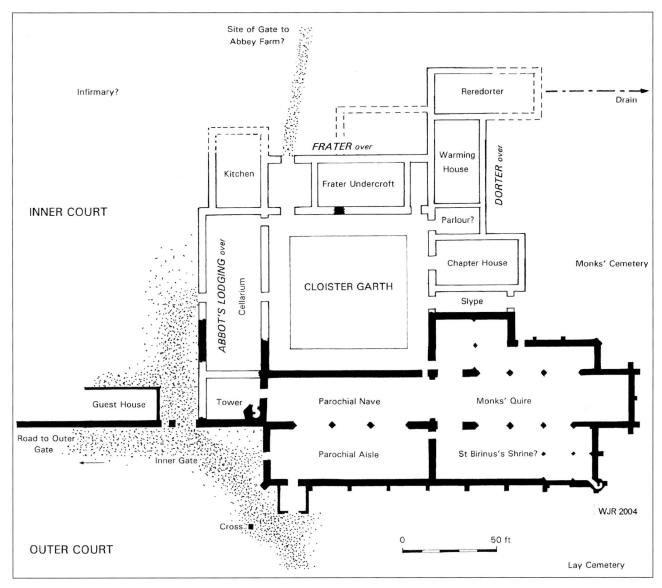

FIGURE 24. Reconstructed plan of Dorchester Abbey in the 15th century, based on archaeological and geophysical evidence. The claustral ranges are interpreted by reference to Lacock Abbey and other Augustinian houses. Walls shown in solid black are certain. (Warwick Rodwell)

The width of the west walk was established as *c.* 2.5 m (8 ft). Since the inner foundation had only to carry a screen wall and roof, it was not as substantial as that of the outer wall which, of course, supported the two-storied west range. The same would have been applicable to the other ranges. It is possible that the garth screen was timber-framed, set on a low wall.

The excavations of 2001 embraced the site of the south walk, but ground level here had been drastically lowered in the 19th century, with the result that the foundation trench for the garth wall was not recovered. Likewise, the return of the east walk should have been encountered, and features possibly associated with it are mentioned in the report.[8] Unsupported suggestions that the south walk was only 1.7 m wide, while the east was over 3.0 m, carry little conviction, and the incompletely recorded pattern of burials provides no help.[9]

Understanding the north walk is no less problematic, since the section excavated across it in 1962 encountered what were considered to be the inner and outer wall trenches, but they were less than 1.8 m (6 ft) apart.[10] That interpretation is clearly not sustainable. Re-examination of the evidence shows that the published site plan is inaccurate, and the position of the trench across the west walk is wrongly plotted. Consequently, the east–west dimension of the cloister was thought to be 88 ft, rather than the 82 ft that it is in reality. On the assumption that the cloister would be square in plan, the 1962 trench was sited too far north to intercept the line of the north walk. Instead, it provided a transect across the north range, missing the walk altogether. Moreover, the excavators admitted that the archaeology was so complex that they were unable to reconcile the different stratigraphic evidence revealed in the east and west sides of their trench.

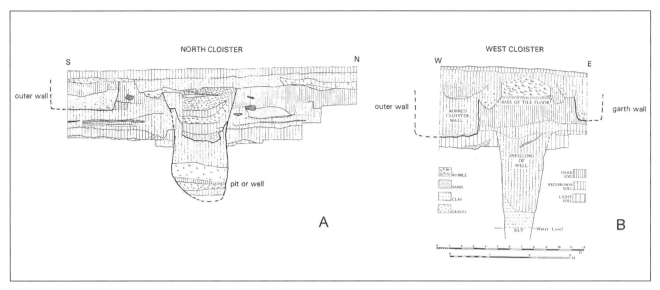

FIGURE 25. Excavated sections in the cloister, 1960–62. A. North cloister range (reinterpreted); B. West cloister walk. (Cunningham and Banks, 1972; Frere, 1984)

In retrospect, we can identify the robbed foundation encountered at the southern end of the trench with the outer wall of the north cloister walk, not the inner wall (Fig. 25A). The feature in the middle of the trench, which was interpreted in 1962 as the robbed outer wall, was only the upper filling of a well or deep pit within the undercroft of the north range.[11]

Thus, the square plan of the cloister can be confirmed, and the apparent variations in the widths of the walks are illusory. Notwithstanding, it would occasion no surprise if future excavations were to demonstrate that the walks had been subject to change over time. Norman cloister walks could be narrow – even as little as 2.0–2.5 m (7–8 ft) – and later medieval rebuilding could have been accompanied by widening to 2.5–3.0 m (8–10 ft). However, given the generally small scale of the cloister, and the certain evidence of a 2.5 m width in the west walk, it is just as likely that this represents the original dimension, which was maintained until the end of the Middle Ages. One or more of the screens surrounding the garth may have been timber-framed, but it should also be noted that some extant Romanesque capitals are likely to be derived from a cloister screen.

At least part of the cloister was paved in the 14th century with ceramic floor tiles, the mortar bed for which was found in the west walk (Fig. 25B). This is interesting since funds were not often directed towards tiling cloisters. The south walk, at least, was also used for monastic burial.

Layout of the Claustral Ranges (Fig. 24)

Turning now to the claustral layout, the nave of the church occupied the whole of the south range, while the principal functional spaces opened off the other three ranges; these would all have been two-storied. The first part of the east walk was taken up with the

north transept, half of which has been demolished since the Dissolution (Fig. 136). The foundations of the destroyed north wall and the transeptal chapel were exposed in the 19th century, and the position of the northern respond of the transept arcade was plotted (Fig. 10).[12]

However, the north side of the transept has been incorrectly plotted on many 20th-century plans (*e.g.* Fig. 9).[13] Unfortunately, the trench cut in 1960 encountered much disturbance and failed to locate the north wall. Inside the transept would have lain the night stair, leading from the church to the dormitory (dorter) on the upper floor over the east range. A bed of flint and gravel, encountered in the 1960 trench, may have been the foundation for the night stair.[14]

North of the transept lay the chapter house where the daily business of the abbey was conducted; it would have been rectangular, probably without a vestibule (vestibules were more common in larger monasteries). Convincing evidence for the outline of the chapter house was revealed through geophysics in 2004. While precise measurements cannot be taken, its east–west length was in the region of 15 m (50 ft). There would have been a slype running alongside the chapter house, either to its north or south, providing access from the cloister to the eastern part of the precinct, and any buildings therein. It is also likely that the main monastic cemetery lay between the cloister and the river. Geophysics suggests that the slype was situated between the transept and the chapter house.

Beyond the chapter house would have been the warming house and perhaps a separate parlour: geophysics indicates a small room and a large one. Somewhere in this area too must have been the day-stair leading from the cloister to the dorter on the upper floor: at St Augustine's, Bristol, the slype and day stair lay side-by-side, between the chapter house and the warming house.[15] The dorter would have been a long room, extending over the chapter house, slype and warming house. Projecting from the north-east corner of the cloister, and accessed from the dorter, would have been the two-storied reredorter containing the washing and lavatory facilities. A drain from this must have discharged eastwards into the Thame. The reredorter would have lain in an area where there is now shrubbery, although its west end seems to have been located by geophysics.

The north cloister range was invariably taken up by the refectory (frater), a long hall which would have been on the upper floor, with store-rooms and other service accommodation in an undercroft below. Geophysical evidence hints at the frater range being *c.* 9 m (30 ft) wide. Structural remains to the north are also discernible, and another stair leading up from the cloister would have been required for access to the frater. In addition, there is likely to have been a ground-level passage passing through the undercroft to a northern court beyond. Topography suggests that the passage lay at the west end of the range, approximately where there is still a footpath today (Fig. 38). Adjoining the frater, at the north-west angle of the cloister, would have been the kitchen. Part of this may have been detected by geophysics in the vicarage garden, where masonry structures lie beneath the lawn. However, the picture here is confusing.

Finally, the west range would have comprised the cellarer's rooms (*cellarium*) at ground level, where the abbey's supplies of food and drink were stored, and the abbot's lodgings were probably on the first floor above. Alternatively, he may have lived in a separate block projecting from the north-west angle of the cloister. That, however, seems less likely given the Augustinians' predilection for placing abbots' lodgings within the west range.[16] There would also have been an entrance into the cloister through the base of the range. Wood's description of the post-Dissolution house on this site, known as 'The Abbey', indicates that the internal elevation of the west cloister range was timber framed (p. 5).

Extending into one, or probably more, courtyards to the west and north of the cloister would have been further service buildings. Somewhere close to the main complex, but detached from it, must have been the infirmary: that could have lain to the north-east of the cloister, towards the river, where it was sheltered from the noise of the town. However, that may not have been a tranquil location on account of the proximity of watermills. Alternatively, the infirmary could have been to the north-west, where the Victorian vicarage now stands. Finally, the possibility that the present Manor House occupies the site of the infirmary should be considered. Indeed,

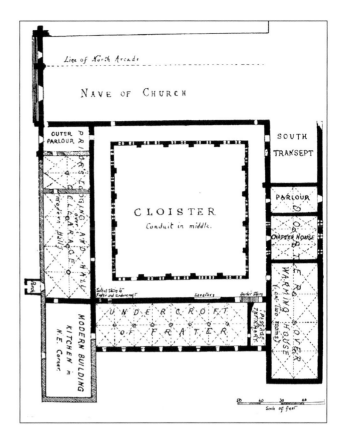

FIGURE 26. *Newstead Abbey (Notts.): plan, showing a typical Augustinian layout of the cloister to the south of the church, which was transeptal and had one (original?) aisle. After the Dissolution, the west and south ranges became a residence. (Thompson, 1919)*

the location, orientation and date of the property prompt the suggestion that the Manor House not only occupies the footprint of a major monastic building, but also incorporates some of its fabric (Figs 3 and 216).[17]

Confirmation of the suggested layout of the claustral ranges may be gained from comparison with other Augustinian houses in Britain. First, it is worth noting that the smaller and medium-sized houses tended to have churches with naves that were initially unaisled and to which the cloister was attached, either on the north or the south. Many, but not all, canons' churches had transepts and eastern chapels. Comparisons with houses on a slightly larger scale may be made with Bradenstoke Priory (Wilts.) (Fig. 39),[18] Hexham Abbey (Northumb.),[19] and St Osyth's Priory (Essex);[20] or, on a smaller scale, with Newstead Abbey (Notts.) (Fig. 26),[21] Brinkburn Priory (Northumb.) and Lanercost Priory (Cumbria).[22]

One of the closest parallels for Dorchester is, however, the house of Augustinian canonesses at Lacock (Wilts.) (Fig. 27). Both had northern cloisters which were of almost identical dimensions, and although the church at Lacock was not transeptal, it had a projecting sacristy/chapel of two bays on the site where Dorchester had its north transept.[23]

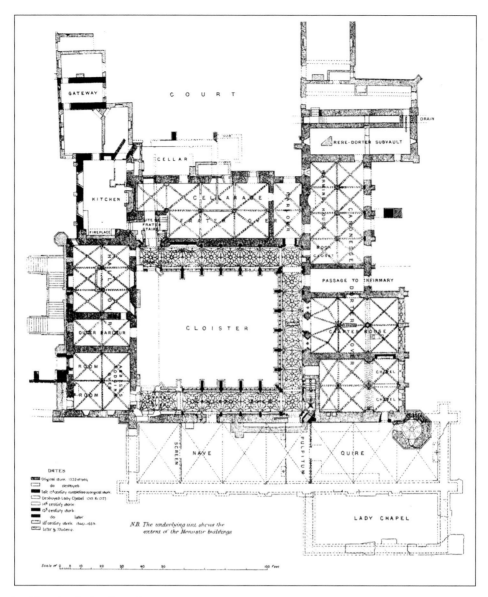

FIGURE 27. Lacock Abbey (Wilts.): plan, showing a typical Augustinian layout with the cloister to the north of the church, which had neither transepts nor aisles. After the Dissolution, the west and north ranges became a residence. (Brakspear, 1900a).

Comparisons between Dorchester and the larger Augustinian foundations – generally with double-aisled churches, as at Oxford and Bristol – are not very meaningful. Nevertheless, one of the smallest Augustinian houses was Ivychurch (Wilts.), which had a fully aisled church with the claustral buildings on the north.[24]

Thus, although we can reconstruct in broad outline the footprint of the conventual buildings, not a trace of their superstructure survives to indicate architectural style. The initial claustral buildings would obviously have been Romanesque, but it is unlikely that these remained unchanged throughout the life of the abbey. The chapter house would have been one of the first claustral appendages to be erected, and probably the most embellished. Given the shortage of local building stone, particularly for dressings and decorative work, timber-framing was almost certainly employed, at

least for the upper storey of the frater and dorter ranges: that may help to explain why there is relatively little carved stonework lying loose, or incorporated in post-medieval structures in the village. The cloister was evidently not vaulted, but had a monopitched roof, covered with either lead or clay tiles: several potential sockets for the half-trusses of the south walk are discernible in the wall of the nave.[25] Likewise, the surviving wall confirms that the internal face of this cloister walk, at least, was not decorated with blind arcading: the east walk may have been more lavishly treated.

The lapidary collection, now displayed in the Cloister Gallery (Pl. 46), includes many items which almost certainly derived from the cloister and its ranges (Fig. 222).[26] However, it is impossible to associate these with confidence with specific structures. The Romanesque fragments include medium-scale capitals which have probably come from wall-arcading of the type that might have embellished the interior of the chapter house, as at St Augustine's Abbey, Bristol.[27] Capitals, bases and chevron-decorated voussoirs of the kind associated with the architecture of doorways could also be derived from the entrance to the chapter house, frater, etc. The beak-head voussoirs point to at least one mid-12th-century doorway of high quality (Fig. 49; Pl. 47):[28] such decoration might be expected on one of the principal entrances to the church. Fragments of ribs from large Romanesque vaults could come from the chapter house, or from the various undercrofts of the dorter and frater ranges.[29]

A second group of medium-sized architectural fragments includes early 13th-century capitals and bases, some of which are double-units and at least one is from a cluster-capital. These items are perhaps derived from an Early English cloister arcade.

PRECINCT

Very little is known concerning the topography of the monastic precinct, or of the structures that lay within it. There are likely to have been several separate but linked precincts with different levels of security. Broadly, there are three areas to consider (Fig. 28):

(i) South and south-east of the church, including the present churchyard. This would have comprised the outer court, and was accessible from the town. Here lay the parochial graveyard and the principal preaching cross (Fig. 34).[30] Next to the cross was an ancient yew tree.

(ii) North and north-west of the church, as far as Manor Farm Road, alongside which there is a marked change in ground level. This comprised the inner court, containing the cloister and its adjuncts, and the whole of this area would have been reserved for the use of the canons. The monastic cemetery would have lain either within the cloister garth, or between it and the river to the east.

(iii) The large area formerly occupied by the buildings, yards and closes of Manor Farm, north of Manor Farm Road. Here lay the demesne farm. The present day Manor House, which has medieval origins, is situated at the interface between this zone and the previous one: the function of the building in the late Middle Ages remains unclear (p. 49).

Boundaries (Fig. 28)

The boundary of the monastic precinct is unconfirmed throughout its entire course, there being no enclosing wall or gatehouses still standing. Some writers have suggested that the *enceinte* was compact,[31] while others have argued for a much larger area.[32] Inevitably, the extent of the precinct will have altered over time, expanding when additional land was acquired and perhaps contracting if street frontages were given

over to speculative development. However, one might have expected the footprint of the precinct at the Dissolution to be indelibly preserved in the later townscape. Perhaps the evidence is still there, and we are simply not recognizing it on account of a heavy overlay of later building. A major opportunity to search for precinct boundaries was lost in 2009, when a new drainage scheme was implemented (p. 19).

Possible hints of precinct boundaries may be gleaned from the large-scale Ordnance Survey map of 1877 (Fig. 2), but there is little cartographic evidence of earlier date.[33] Moreover, the local placename evidence within and around Dorchester is unhelpful, and one would be hard-pressed to deduce from it that there had ever been a monastic house here.[34] The only name with even marginal relevance is Bishop's Court, to the north-west of the town (Fig. 1).[35]

It may reasonably be assumed that the precinct was defined on the east and south-east by the floodplain of the Thame, where minor subsidiary channels, artificially created, indicate that there was a mill which appears to be undocumented (Fig. 28).[36] South of the church, it is tempting to interpret the present curvilinear churchyard boundary as following the line of the precinct fairly closely, but this is misleading and the wall here is of no great antiquity (p. 201). It was probably created in the early 19th century, when the new bridge was built and the road entering Dorchester from the south-east was realigned. Another, straighter, boundary a little farther south (cut through by the new road) must be considered a better alternative for the monastic precinct.

The west side is likely to have been defined, at least in part, by the Roman town wall, to which the papal bull of 1146 seems to make reference (p. 20). The present main entrance to the churchyard, the lychgate, may well be on the site of an original opening in the Roman wall (Figs 3, 14, 28 and 29). North of that gate, the precinct is likely to have followed the edge of the medieval market place (to the beginning of Queen Street), where a junction of boundaries occurs. Here lies the interface between two components of the precinct: early maps and present-day topography confirm that there was a major division between the abbey farm to the north, and the conventual buildings to the south. The first part of Manor Farm Road – the lane running east from Queen Street to the Manor House – appears to follow the ditch of an earthwork which constitutes a clear break in the landscape topography, and may be a legacy from a very early period.[37] The north side of the inner court must surely be coincident with this earthwork and the boundary that extends its line eastwards to the river.

It is argued that the boundaries just described form a coherent quadrangular enclosure which comprised the outer and inner courts of the medieval abbey,

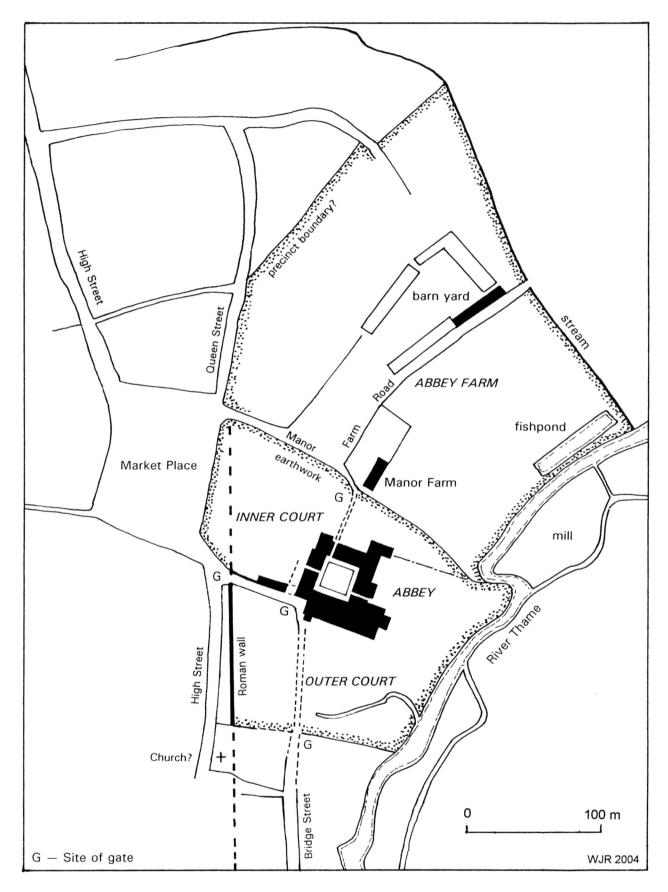

FIGURE 28. *Reconstruction of the precinct of Dorchester Abbey in the early 16th century. (Warwick Rodwell)*

FIGURE 29. *The lychgate and path leading from High Street to the church. Lychgate Cottage is on the right. (Warwick Rodwell)*

with defined access points on the south, west and north. As previously discussed, the Anglo-Saxon cathedral precinct is likely to have extended even further west, potentially including the site of the later market (p. 28).

Outside this *enceinte*, to the north, lay the abbey demesne farm, later known as Manor Farm. Surviving boundaries suggest that this occupied an even larger quadrangular area, naturally defined on the east by the Thame, on the north by a side-stream flowing into the river, and on the west by Queen Street and other extant land boundaries.[38] Inside this enclosure lay a great complex of farm buildings until the mid-20th century: some of those structures were medieval, but they have been lost to a housing development. Also within the enclosure, lying parallel to the river, is a long narrow pond which was almost certainly a monastic fishpond.

Gateways

The main monastic precinct will have been defined by a high wall of stone or cob, pierced at several points by gateways.[39] Internally, the enclosure will have been subdivided into at least two courts, interconnected by further gateways. The present main entrance to the churchyard is from High Street via the lychgate, and this is likely to perpetuate the principal monastic gate (Fig. 29). Contrary to this, it has been suggested that the site of the main gate is now occupied either by the house known as 'The Priory', or the adjacent Post Office, both of which lie just north of the lychgate (Fig. 3; Pl. 44).[40]

A broad path passes through the lychgate and runs directly up to the west end of the church. Indeed, the axis of the road, which also follows the alignment of the church itself, has already been commented upon as being one of the oldest topographical features in the town (p. 28). Rights of way into churchyards are seldom changed, and a compelling argument, with supporting physical evidence, would need to be advanced to explain why this should not have been the medieval entrance.

In 2001, a shallow trench was dug from the lychgate to the church, to install a new gas main.[41] During a watching brief on this work, a flint cobbled surface was found just within the gate, extending eastwards for 6.5 m (21 ft).[42] This was not road metalling, but a discrete area of paving; unfortunately, no dating evidence was found. While the cobbling could have belonged to an enclosed building, given its significant position it is more likely to represent paving within the carriageway ('gate-hall') of a gatehouse, or it could be a hard-standing behind the gate. Cobbled pavements within and to the rear of gatehouses were common, even into the 19th century.

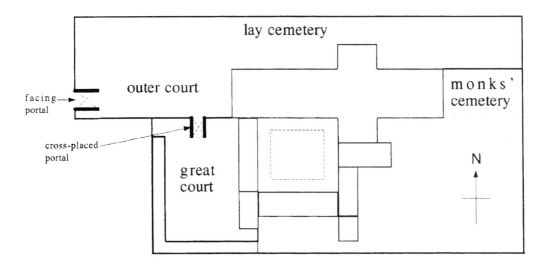

FIGURE 30. *Diagram illustrating a generalized precinct layout for a Benedictine or Augustinian monastery with twin portals placed at right-angles to one another, providing access to the outer and inner courts, respectively. This plan (if reversed, to place the cloister on the north) accords closely with the reconstructible evidence at Dorchester. (Morant, 1995)*

If the present entrance marks the site of the principal abbey gate, it would imply that the churchyard (and perhaps some adjoining land around its margins) constituted an outer monastic court, from which entry to the inner court would be obtained via a second gate. Since the lay public had access to the nave and south aisle of the church, and the southern churchyard was used as the parochial burial ground, there had to be clearcut separation between these areas and everything to the north, where the inner court lay. The latter would have encompassed the cloister, ancillary structures, and some land to the west and north.

The siting of monastic portals was governed by a protocol, and the Augustinian arrangement was often similar to the Benedictine (Fig. 30).[43] It was usual for access to the inner court to be through the outer court, and not directly from the town, which would imply that the second gateway was within the churchyard, somewhere between the present lychgate and the west end of the church. Commonly, the first and second gates were designed to be at right-angles to one-another, and at Bristol's Augustinian abbey, for example, both the Norman portals are still in existence. Logically, at Dorchester, the entrance to the inner court should be alongside, and at right-angles to, the present path from the lychgate to the church. The north side of that path is bounded by a medieval stone wall, now partly rebuilt in brick (Fig. 31); attached to the back of that wall is a building thought to be the guest house (see further below). Although the wall aligns precisely with the south side of the tower, there is a gap through which another path runs northwards (Fig. 32). Topographical evidence points strongly to this being the site of the gateway between the outer and inner precincts.

FIGURE 31. *Remains of the medieval precinct wall between the outer and inner courts, with the timber-framed guest house attached to the north side. (Warwick Rodwell)*

FIGURE 32. *The gap between the guest house (left) and the tower marks the site of the medieval gate leading from the outer to the inner court. (Warwick Rodwell)*

FIGURE 33. *Guest house: fragmentary western jamb of the medieval pedestrian gate arch. (Warwick Rodwell)*

At the point where the wall is broken, are the remains of the western jamb and arch-springing of a doorway or small gate of the 14th or 15th centuries (Fig. 33). There can be little doubt that we see here the last vestiges of an entrance through the precinct wall: this must be part of the inner gatehouse (Fig. 28). The arch fragment is not tall enough to have been a vehicular entrance, and that would imply a twin portal of which the surviving element belongs to the pedestrian opening. The vehicular arch would have lain, appropriately, where the path passes by the west side of the church tower. Realization of this not only explains why the path turns through a right-angle alongside the tower, but also provides the clue as to why the tower itself was almost completely reconstructed in 1602. The previous tower may not have had a presentable west face because it was integrated with the gatehouse range; and it would not have had a finished north face either, because that was adjoined by the west cloister range.

A drawing by J.C. Buckler, 1827, not only shows the extant jamb and arch-springing in much better condition than they are today, but also indicates part of the late medieval window in the wall directly above it (Figs 34 and 35). An earlier drawing by John Buckler, senior, provides confirmation. Of further interest is a drawing of 1807, which shows a fragment of the vehicular gate arch still attached to the west side of the tower.[44] The same detail had been noted by Stukeley in 1736: on his plan, adjacent to the tower, he wrote 'the spring of the abbey gate arch'.[45] The masonry of the tower has been restored and there is no sign of that feature today.

Monastic gatehouses sometimes incorporated towers (usually above the vehicular carriageway) and could have multi-storied wings to one or both flanks, as well as various stair-turrets and other elaborations. The surviving 14th-century stair-turret at Dorchester, which is hexagonal in plan and sits oddly in the

FIGURE 34. *Guest house and churchyard cross from the south-east, in 1827, by J.C. Buckler. Note the fragmentary remains of a gate arch at the right-hand end of the guest house. (Dorchester Abbey Museum)*

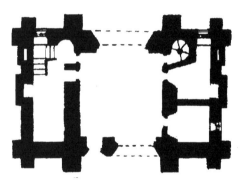

GROUND FLOOR

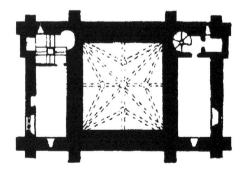

SECOND FLOOR

FIGURE 35. *Guest house: fragmentary jamb of a medieval window above the former pedestrian gate-arch. (Warwick Rodwell)*

FIGURE 36. *Bridlington Priory (Yorks.): plans of the ground and second floors of the Augustinian gatehouse-tower (1388) with separate vehicular and pedestrian arches. (after Morant, 1995)*

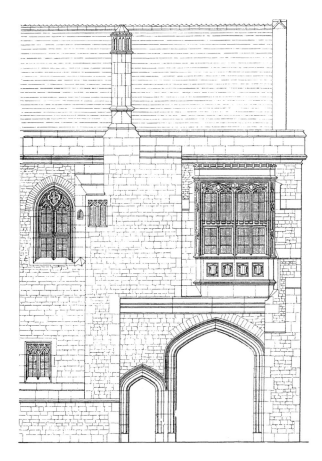

FIGURE 37 *Wells (Som.), College of Vicars Choral: twin-portalled gatehouse to the Vicars' Close, with adjoining hall-block (left). (Pugin and Walker, 1836)*

FIGURE 38. *Cloister garden. This footpath is approximately on the site of the west cloister range, perpetuating a medieval north–south route through the precinct. View south. (Warwick Rodwell)*

corner of the present church tower, is easier comprehended as a survival from a complex gate-tower structure. The Augustinian gatehouse of 1382 at Thornton Abbey (Lincs.) is one of the most elaborate known,[46] while relatively plain examples with twin portals occur at Bridlington's Augustinian priory (Fig. 36), St Albans Abbey, Ely Cathedral and elsewhere.[47] These are all large gatehouses, whereas the 15th-century twin-portalled gate to the Vicars' Close at Wells is on a similar scale to what must once have existed at Dorchester; a two-storied hall-block adjoins the gateway (Fig. 37).[48]

The complaint raised in the bishop's visitation of 1530 that the gates were never closed and that the lay public used the cloister as a thoroughfare (p. 39), is almost certainly a reference, *inter alia*, to this gate. When it was open this gave access to the inner court, from which there would have been an entrance into the west cloister range. That in turn would have facilitated a short-cut through the west and north ranges, via the garth. By implication, there was a second gate, leading out of the inner court, somewhere to the north of the claustral ranges, and it was also carelessly left open, thereby creating a thoroughfare.

The approximate route is reconstructible with the aid of surviving topographical evidence, including the modern footpath leading from the church towards the Manor House and Manor Farm (Fig. 38).

Guest House and 'The Abbey' House (Figs 34 and 41)

Apart from the church itself, and possibly part of the Manor House, the only structure at Dorchester surviving from the monastic era is the two-storied building range west of the tower: it conforms to the axis of the church and is attached to the north side of the wall between the outer and inner precincts. This structure is generally referred to as the guest house, although there is no confirmatory evidence that it fulfilled such a function. It now serves as a museum and tea room. The range, which has been truncated at both its east and west ends, was probably constructed in 1445.[49] In order to understand the late medieval topography of this part of the precinct, it is necessary to look ahead to the later 16th century. The guest house was adapted in or soon after 1544 to form part of a new post-Dissolution residence, and was converted into a grammar school in 1652.[50] Wood's plan shows the range directly abutting the church tower, and he labelled it 'The Abbey' (Fig. 4). This provides an important clue to the post-Dissolution history of the site: the name was given to a substantial house occupying the former west cloister range and adjacent structures.[51] Comparison with Bradenstoke Priory is instructive: there, the west range stood long after the Dissolution because the prior's lodging could be readily adapted to a secular residence (Figs 39 and 40).

It was common for entire cloisters, or single ranges, to be converted into dwellings in the mid-16th century, and many of these survive as residences today: for example, the cloisters at Newstead and Lacock (Figs 26 and 27), elements of the north range at St Osyth, and the complete west range of Bradenstoke.[52] In 1657, Wood described the 'frontispiece' or main elevation of the post-Dissolution house, which faced west. He noted that it stood 'at the west end of the church, and the rest of the building run behind the north side' (*i.e.* the cloister ranges). He observed that the external elevation of 'The Abbey' was three storeys high and built of freestone, while the back was 'built of timber and plaster' (p. 5). Almost certainly, what Wood saw

was the timber-framed abbot's lodging, on to which a stone-built façade had been grafted in the mid or late 16th century. As already observed, the lodging would have been of two storeys, comprising a lofty open-hall above an undercroft. By inserting a floor in the hall at about eaves level, a series of ceiled chambers would be created, with attic rooms above, a common form of conversion in the 16th century. Sometimes, as here at Dorchester, the nature of the parent building was disguised by erecting a domestic façade of stone or brick. It was an economical means of creating what superficially appeared to be a grand new house.

In front of the range just described (*i.e.* to the west) would doubtless have been a courtyard, flanked on the north and south by subsidiary ranges. The southern range included the former guest house. We may suspect that The Abbey was falling into decline by the mid-17th century, when the guest house was adapted for use as the new grammar school and the remainder of the building was then, or subsequently, demolished. The surviving structure deserves detailed archaeological analysis.[53] There was another range at right-angles to the existing one, set back in the gap between the guest house and tower; this was probably the master's residence (school-house), built *c.* 1654.

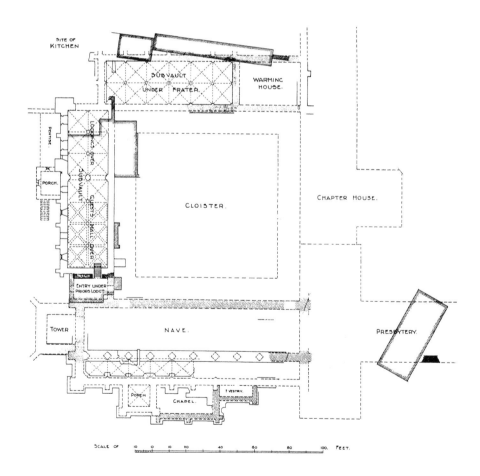

FIGURE 39. *Bradenstoke Priory (Wilts.): plan. The west cloister range survived as a house after the Dissolution. (Brakspear, 1923)*

FIGURE 40 (above). Bradenstoke Priory: the west cloister range, converted into a three-storey house. The timber shed is on the site of the porch shown on plan, Figure 39. (Brakspear, 1923)

FIGURE 41 (left). Guest house: jettied north side, formerly facing into the medieval inner court. (Warwick Rodwell)

It was demolished in 1857.[54]

The south side of the guest house was integral with the abbey precinct wall, which dated from the 15th century or earlier, and on to which a timber-framed building was attached in 1445 (p. 57; Figs 31 and 41). The wall contains a great variety of materials, including some reused ashlars, burnt stone, and fragments of medieval roof tile. There is a chamfered plinth on the south face, and it is clear that the level of the road entering the churchyard from the west has been reduced, thereby exposing foundation rubble (Fig. 31). The wall is pierced by a miscellany of openings, some subsequently altered or blocked. The present windows and doorways were mostly inserted in the 16th and 17th centuries.

Built on to the back of the wall is a timber-framed structure of three bays (Fig. 42). The ground floor appears to have comprised a hall of two bays and a parlour. It had three square-headed windows, each of two lights, with moulded labels and stops, facing south. The first floor had three trefoil-headed windows, each of two lights. The easternmost of these is now only a fragment, above the surviving jamb of the gate arch (Fig. 35). The timber-framed north wall of the guest house rests on a masonry foundation, topped with a chamfered limestone plinth. On the ground floor there is a blocked doorway with a four-centred head, and five-light timber-mullioned window. The north elevation is jettied and incorporates a first-floor gallery that gave independent access to three chambers (Fig. 41). The gallery was originally open to the outside, but is now enclosed: the arrangement is similar to that still surviving in the courtyard of the George Hotel, on the opposite side

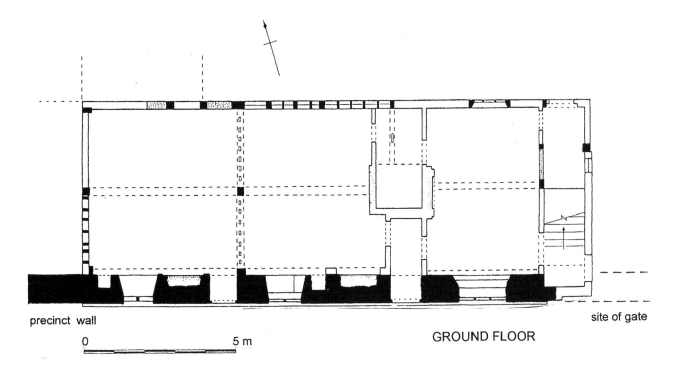

precinct wall   site of gate

0   5 m   GROUND FLOOR

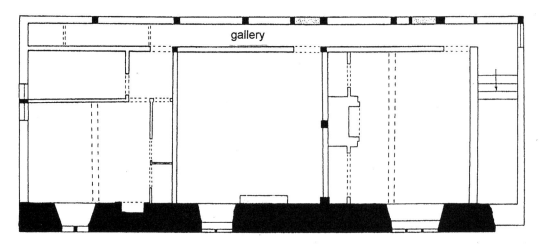

gallery

FIRST FLOOR

FIGURE 42. *Guest house: plans of the ground and first floors. The southern side of the range is formed by the stone precinct wall, to which the medieval timber-framed building was attached; parts of the framing have been replaced with later brickwork. (after RCHME)*

of High Street.[55] The provision of chambers accessed from a gallery is consistent with the building's interpretation as the monastic guest house.

Barns

Finally, another feature of the monastic precinct survived until relatively recently. It was the barnyard complex to which Wood referred as comprising 'great slatted barns that are supported with buttresses' (Fig. 28).[56] Skelton asserted, 'the chief remains of the priory are at a short distance northward of the church. They consist of the foundations of massive walls, which are so entire as to distinctly mark the form of a

large quadrangle ... These walls were strengthened formerly with buttresses; and upon them are now standing a range of wooden barns, of large dimensions, which enclose a farm-yard'.[57] A drawing by Buckler in the early 19th century showed one of these to be of aisled construction, with the outer walls built up to half-height in masonry (Fig. 43).[58] This barn, which probably dated from the early 14th century, was destroyed by fire in the later 19th century. Another substantial weather-boarded barn, with a lean-to cart-shed alongside, survived until the mid-20th century: that may originally have been a granary. It had a cupola, which seems to have been

FIGURE 43. Detail of the cruck construction of one of the great barns belonging to the abbey, drawn by J.C. Buckler in the early nineteenth century; now demolished. (Cook and Rowley, 1985)

the entrance to a dove-house within the roof (Fig. 44).[59] The barn appears in several photographs by Taunt and others.[60]

All that now remains of the barnyard is a considerable length of masonry, forming a wall on the west flank of Manor Farm Road. This was the southeast side of the barnyard complex, and the wall incorporates parts of two major buildings. A photograph by Taunt, *c.* 1899, shows a section of barn or farmyard wall built of reused medieval ashlar and containing a large cross formed in flint flushwork: this was known locally as the 'Monks' Cross'.[61] The location of this wall is now uncertain: it was undoubtedly medieval, probably 15th century.

The 1877 map provides further clues to what has been lost (Fig. 2). As previously noted, the buildings of the post-Dissolution manor lay within their own precinct to the north of the former inner court of the abbey (p. 51). There was the Manor House itself, and north of that a large double courtyard edged by barns and agricultural buildings. The barns (and probably the house; p. 49) were survivals from the monastic era; doubtless the nearby fishpond was also medieval. The tithe map supplies further details of the complex, including a small square building which stood on its own to the north: this was potentially the medieval dovecote.

In sum, more research is needed into the minutiae of the historical topography of Dorchester to clarify the monastic layout and, in particular, the evolution of the religious precinct. Attention has already been drawn to the way that the longitudinal axis of the church is extended westwards not only by the guest house and adjacent road, but is also picked up on the west side of the High Street by property

FIGURE 44. One of the medieval barns (probably a granary) surviving on the abbey demesne farm in the early 19th century; now demolished. (Skelton, 1823)

boundaries and building alignments. The cranked course of the present High Street clearly cuts across much older land divisions within the settlement. This in turn may provide clues to the Roman street pattern in the northern part of the town.

NOTES

1   Montague, 2006.
2   Although the passage constructed on the site of the south cloister had apparently been cleared away before *c*. 1780, when Grimm sketched the angle between nave and transept, the structure indicated by Wood nevertheless still appears on much later plans, *e.g.* Addington, 1845. It does not feature on Harris's plan of *c*. 1720. However, 18th-century topographical artists commonly omitted features that they regarded as 'modern'.
3   Gough, 1789, **1**, 307.
4   Caley, *et al.*, 1846, **6**, 324. This description, which owes much to Skelton (1823, 6), possibly does not refer to the cloister, but to the farmyard further north: see p. 53.
5   Cunningham and Banks, 1972; Keevill, 2003.
6   Rush, 2004. In his dissertation, Rush reproduced a draft plan prepared by the present writer in 2003, showing a hypothetical layout for the claustral ranges. In the event, this prediction proved to be substantially accurate, except that I had placed the slype to the north of the chapter house, whereas it now appears more likely that it was to the south.
7   In addition to the information contained in Cunningham and Banks, 1972, a useful section through the archaeological deposits under the west cloister is published in Frere, 1984, fig. 23.
8   Keevill, 2003, 333. Discussion of the cloister is vague and difficult to interpret; correlation between text and illustrations is poor.
9   Some of the burials were monastic, while others were almost certainly earlier. Partial excavation of the burials in the south cloister area meant that a full picture was not obtained.
10 The site of the 1962 trench is potentially identifiable as a dark rectangle on Martin Rush's geophysical survey (2004).
11 The filling of the pit was of two phases, the upper having had a timber lining (one side of which shows in the published section: it was commented on in the report, but misunderstood). In the published section drawing, the upper filling alone was emphasized in an attempt to make it look like a wall trench.
12 See Addington, 1845, plan; Hope, 1910, fig. 6.
13 Also in Keevill, 2003, fig. 1, where the wall is shown 2 m north of its true location. See Chap. 4, note 17.
14 Cunningham and Banks, 1972, 159–60.
15 Paul, 1912.
16 For a list of known examples, see Thompson, 2001, appendix I.
17 Behind the Gothick façade of the Manor House is an early 16th-century building with moulded ceiling beams (Sherwood and Pevsner, 1974, 583).

18 Brakspear, 1923.
19 Hodges, 1888, pl. 8.
20 RCHME, 1922, 198–202.
21 Thompson, 1919; *J. Brit. Archaeol. Assoc.*, new ser. **39** (1934), 29–33.
22 Moorman, 1994. The dimensions of the respective cloisters (east to west) were: Brinkburn, 70 ft; Lanercost, 75 ft; Newstead, 78 ft; Hexham, 100 ft; St Osyth, 108 ft; Bradenstoke, 110 ft.
23 Brakspear, 1900a; 1900b. The overall cloister width at Lacock is 80 ft.
24 RCHME, 1987, 148–53. The cloister measured only 55 ft across.
25 The pockets for the medieval timbers are infilled with masonry. The three sawn-off ends of roof timbers embedded in the nave wall are not medieval: they belong to the pentice that occupied this site in the 17th century.
26 See the unpublished catalogue of the lapidary collection (Kendrick, 2002).
27 Now Bristol Cathedral. The chapter house and principal gatehouse, both of *c*. 1140–50, are heavily embellished with wall-arcading: Rogan, 2000, pl. 3.
28 Keevill, 2003, 345–6; 2005, 18–19.
29 Given the shortage of good stone, and the absence of vaulting in the Romanesque church, it is considered highly improbable that the undercrofts were vaulted. Only the chapter house is a likely candidate for vaulting.
30 There were apparently other standing crosses in medieval Dorchester, and Skelton (1823, 4) refers to finding 'the bases of ancient crosses'.
31 *E.g.* Rodwell, 1974, 102.
32 *E.g.* Cook and Rowley, 1985, 49.
33 The earliest available maps are by Richard Davis (1797), a parish map of 1837–38, and the Dorchester Tithe map, 1845. For a possible topographical reconstruction based on these, see VCH, 1962, 49.
34 Gelling (1953, 152–3) provides no tell-tale evidence in the local names. Similarly, examination of the Dorchester Tithe Award of 1846 (ORO, no. 132) yielded no topographically significant names in the area of the presumed abbey precinct.
35 This is *le Byshoppes Courte* in a survey of 1551–52 (Gelling, 1953, 153). It is presumably the site of the Bishop of Lincoln's house in Dorchester. Antiquarian descriptions in the 16th to 18th centuries frequently allude to ruined buildings and foundations being unearthed there.
36 North of Dorchester Bridge, the Thame divides into two channels (Figs 1 and 2), and the more easterly still houses Overy Mill. The abbey mill was evidently on the western channel, where the accompanying leat is still intact (Fig. 28).
37 The putative boundary line also continues west of Queen Street, being marked by a narrow track. There is a visible dip in the tarmac of Queen Street where it runs over the ditch, and in wet weather this area floods. John Metcalfe informs me that there is an ancient storm-water drain following the ditch line; it runs underneath the Manor House, and heads for the river.
38 *Cf.* Cook and Rowley, 1985, 49, map.

39 Owing to the shortage of natural building stone, cob has traditionally been used for walling in the Dorchester area. If the precinct wall was made of this somewhat unstable material, and was not kept in good repair, collapse would quickly ensue: surely this is the explanation why there is no sign of a medieval precinct wall surviving in the town.

40 Keevill (2003, 361). Without offering any supporting evidence, he asserts: 'the current access to the abbey through the lychgate and past the south front of the guest house is misleading, as it can now be shown that the medieval entrance would have been to the north of the guest house'.

41 The line of the trench is visible in the tarmac in Fig. 29.

42 Keevill, 2003, 334.

43 Morant, 1995, 37–41.

44 Bodl., MS Top. Oxon. b.220, f. 110v. Harris's view of *c.* 1720 shows only a low wall abutting the south-west buttress of the tower.

45 Bodl., Gough Maps, 26, f. 42B.

46 Morant, 1995, 165.

47 Illustrated in Thompson, 2001, figs 67, 57 and 60, respectively.

48 Pugin and Walker, 1836, pl. 14; Rodwell, 2005b, 122–8.

49 Two primary roof timbers were dated by dendrochronology, yielding felling-dates of spring 1444 and winter 1444/45. A stud from the east gable-end relating to a repair, when the building was truncated, was dated to winter 1543/44: *Vernacular Archit.*, **38** (2007), 129.

50 Anon., 1976; VCH, 1939, 468–9.

51 Conceivably, the nearby house known as The Priory is for all practical purposes its successor as a residence.

However, The Priory incorporates timber framing behind a Georgian façade, and is not chronologically later than the demise of The Abbey.

52 Brakspear, 1923. The west range at Bradenstoke stood in remarkably complete and original condition until the 1930s, when it was taken down by William Randolph Hearst and shipped to America.

53 Abbey Guest House is Listed Grade II*. A brief report on it was prepared by the RCHME in April 1991 (unpublished).

54 This secondary range appears on the tithe map and is glimpsed in several topographical illustrations of the 18th and 19th centuries. Bodl., Top. Oxon. b.283, f. 11. The school-house was demolished when the new Vicarage was built and the present drive between it and the church created.

55 Cook and Rowley, 1987, 63; Tiller, 2005, fig. 46.

56 Clark, 1891.

57 Skelton, 1923, 6. From his discussion, it is apparent that Skelton believed the monastery was centred on this barnyard, rather than on the present church. Nevertheless, he goes on to describe the south nave aisle as the 'chapter house'.

58 Cook and Rowley, 1985, 47.

59 Skelton, 1823, 3; Bond and Tiller, 2005, fig. 29. Other illustrations showing lost barns occur in Roberts, 1930, figs 1 and 3. Taunt (1906, 10) confirms that there was a dovecot in the farm yard.

60 The demise of this building can be charted from a series of photographs held by the NMR and COS.

61 NMR, Taunt photo no. 10692. The diagonally tooled ashlar blocks evidently dated from the 12th or early 13th century.

CHAPTER 7

The Abbey Church and its Architectural Evolution, *c.* 1140–1536

In 1913, Francis Bond made a valiant attempt to decipher the architectural development of the abbey church, working his way systematically through the various clues in the fabric. His method of analysis was inspirational and subsequently emulated by innumerable scholars (Figs 11 and 12).[1] However, Bond was neither in possession of an accurate ground plan, nor did he have the luxury of a prolonged period of intensive study of the church. The new plan (2001) has revealed relationships between parts of the building that were not previously clear, as well as highlighting varying wall thicknesses and slight changes of alignment. Similarly, a fresh examination of the fabric *in extenso* has focused attention on subtle details that had hitherto been overlooked. Consequently, it is now possible to augment and refine Bond's analysis, and to move several steps closer to understanding the complex architectural development of the church. Nevertheless, there are still gaps in the evidence and alternative interpretations of some aspects of the building's development are possible (Fig. 45; Pl. 4).

NOMENCLATURE

In describing the church and discussing its architectural history, it is impossible to adopt a consistent nomenclature that suits all periods. The present-day naming of parts has no profound historical basis. The only chapel and the only altar expressly named in early documents are the Lady Chapel and altar of the Holy Rood, respectively, and we cannot be certain where they were. However, it is argued here that the Lady Chapel was in the north chancel aisle, and the altar of the Holy Rood was at the east end of the nave, in front of the rood screen. The present Lady Chapel in the south chancel aisle was designated thus in 1873. St Birinus's Chapel, Requiem Chapel, Shrine Chapel and the People's Chapel are all 20th-century namings.

Architecturally, transmutations have occurred which demand changes in terminology. While today the chancel is simply flanked by north and south aisles, in the 12th century there was a crossing and transepts, which have since been expunged as identifiable spaces. In the 13th century, there were

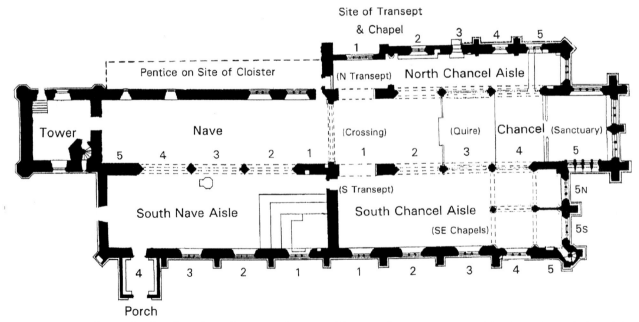

FIGURE 45. *Key plan of the church to show the nomenclature and bay-numbering system used in this volume. (adapted from VCH, 1962)*

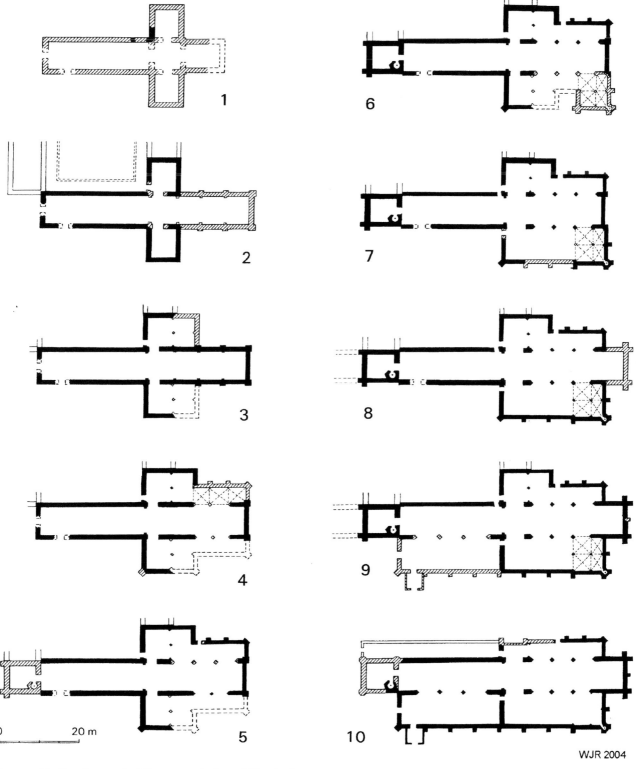

Figure 46. *Development of the ground plan of Dorchester Abbey, from the 11th to the 17th century. Shading indicates new work at each phase, and black denotes masonry retained from a previous phase. (Warwick Rodwell)*

WJR 2004

Key:		6.	c. 1290–1300
1.	c. 1067–1140	7.	c. 1310–1320
2.	c. 1170–1200	8.	c. 1330–1340
3.	c. 1230–1250	9.	c. 1350–1360 and
4.	c. 1250–1260		c. 1450–1500 (porch)
5.	c. 1280–1300	10.	c. 1600–1650

separate transeptal chapels and chancel-aisle chapels, which in the 14th century were combined to create continuous aisles. In the following discussion, architectural nomenclature appropriate to the era is employed, as far as possible. For convenience, the three chapels occupying the south chancel aisle are referred to collectively as the 'south-east chapels' (Fig. 45).

Liturgically, too, changes have occurred: when in monastic use, the eastern arm was divided into a quire and presbytery, but under parochial use these were merged to form a chancel. The Victorian restoration, however, sought to reintroduce physical and liturgical divisions, and so the quire (or choir) reappeared. To add further to the confusion, lines of demarcation have changed over time. What most commentators would naturally call the 'chancel arch' is actually the west crossing arch, the eastern one having disappeared in the 14th century. Moreover, neither position accurately reflects the division between nave and chancel. At least since the mid-17th century, the nave has extended so far eastwards that it not only takes in the former crossing but also the first bay of what should be architecturally described as the chancel.

For ease of description, bay numbering has been assigned conventionally, working eastwards and westwards, respectively, from the existing 'chancel arch' (*i.e.* west side of the former crossing). This chapter attempts to provide a general overview of the development of the church, and detailed descriptions of features and further discussion will be found in Part 2.

TWELFTH CENTURY

All the architectural evidence points to the Augustinian canons making use of the existing collegiate church (Fig. 46.1) for several decades, before embarking on a major reconstruction programme. Most likely, from *c.* 1140 to 1170/1180, effort was concentrated on the erection of claustral buildings, and only when they had reached a satisfactory state of completeness were funds directed towards remodelling the church. The surviving architectural evidence bears this out: the chancel arch – the principal decorative component – is Transitional in style and can hardly be earlier than *c.* 1175. The tall nave windows with their very regular spacing are also likely to be late 12th century, and may represent the completion of Remigius's unfinished reconstruction of the nave.

The form of the Augustinian church in the later 12th century was thus largely determined by its 11th-century predecessor, the western parts of which may have lain in an uncompleted state for decades. The chancel was, however, entirely rebuilt to suit the monastic liturgy: the 11th-century eastern arm was demolished and its successor made slightly wider. Henceforth, the walls of the nave, crossing and chancel were in continuous alignment (Figs 46.2 and 47).

Nave

The nave is the easiest part to understand: internally, it was divided into five bays with regular fenestration. Evidence survives for four of the tall, round-headed windows on the north, and two on the south (Fig. 172). The windows rise from a continuous string-

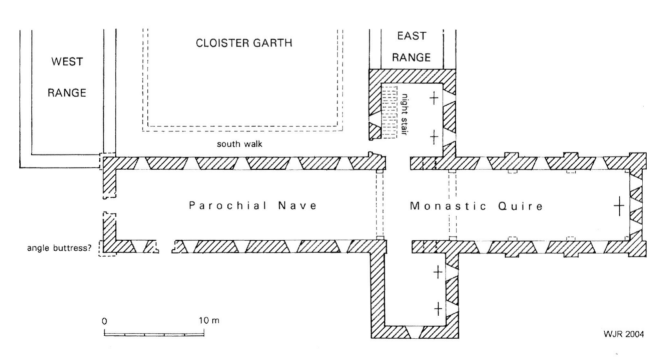

FIGURE 47. Reconstructed plan of the Augustinian church at Dorchester in the late 12th century. (Warwick Rodwell)

FIGURE 48. Nun Monkton Priory (Yorks.): west front. (Parker, 1881)

course, and their spacing reveals that a system of mensuration was employed: centre-to-centre, the openings were one rod (or pole) apart (*i.e.* 16½ statute feet, or 15 'Northern' feet: 5.03 m).[2]

There is no surviving evidence to suggest how the west end was treated. Had there been an axial tower, it is likely that some of its masonry would have been incorporated in the subsequent towers and still survive in the west wall of the nave, there being no necessity to remove it in order to facilitate later work. It has been suggested that there were twin west towers,[3] or twin stair-turrets projecting from the corners,[4] but the scale of the nave, and in particular its lack of aisles, renders reconstructions along these lines improbable. Stair-turrets, projecting either externally or internally, were only necessary for churches with aisles, triforia and westworks.[5] Dorchester is unlikely to have had anything more elaborate than flat angle-buttresses at its western corners, mirroring those at the east end of the church (see below).

Nevertheless, monastic churches generally had western entrances, and the likelihood that there was a modestly elaborated doorway or even a shallow porch in the centre of the façade cannot be ruled out. Whatever the arrangement, it was destroyed in the

14th century to build the tower that preceded the present one.[6] Dorchester may not have appeared very different from the small, unaisled Benedictine church at Nun Monkton (Yorks.), although the latter had a low tower supported on arches within the nave (Fig. 48). Keevill has plausibly suggested that there was an ornate western portal, as at Iffley (Oxon.), since several well-cut voussoirs with zig-zag decoration and beak-heads have been found at Dorchester (Fig. 49; Pl. 47).[7] There was probably also a doorway in the south wall of the nave, symmetrically placed between the windows in bays 4 and 5,[8] but there was demonstrably no door in the north wall.

Eastern Arm and Presbytery

Interpreting the eastern arm is fraught with difficulty, since there have been so many subsequent changes. There was a crossing, the west side of which is marked by the present, rather ephemeral arch of Transitional style (now the 'chancel' arch) (Figs 50, 51, 58 and 170).[9] Whether the 11th-century church had a major transverse wall and arch here, which were later removed in order to create more space, cannot be determined at present. The Romanesque string-course in the north and south walls, connecting nave and crossing, provides critical evidence that the two spaces were united at the time of building the present arch. Thus, all indications point to the crossing having been suppressed as a formal space by the late 12th century.

The truncation of the string-course also indicates where the eastern crossing arch must have lain (Fig. 170). In the 11th century there would have been a substantial chancel arch here, but in the late 12th century that may have been replaced by another relatively ephemeral arch, similar to the existing Transitional one to the west. Beyond that, a new, long chancel was erected, the eastern angle-buttresses of which remain embedded in later masonry (Figs 52–54). Hence, we can reconstruct the chancel as a three-bay structure, probably with as many windows in either side. The east wall may have been pierced by three closely set windows, or perhaps it followed the less common arrangement seen at St Frideswide's, Oxford, where there are only two eastern lights.

A length of the internal string-course that ran around the walls of the chancel has survived, although not *in situ*: it was reset as the sill moulding beneath the east window in the 14th-century extension of the sanctuary. The moulding is slightly larger and more elaborate than that used in the nave and crossing, having a quirk between the square-section above and the roll below.

The height of the eastern buttresses is noteworthy, particularly the south-eastern one which retains, at the very top, the truncated remains of a pair of angle-shafts. This implies a lofty chancel, with decorative turrets at the corners. The turret-tops may have been

FIGURE 49 (right). St Mary, Iffley (Oxon.): Norman west doorway with prolific beak-head and zig-zag ornament, drawn in 1814. (Britton, 1835)

FIGURE 50 (below left). Chancel arch: south respond and string-course, with the transept arch (left) and upper rood-loft doorway (right). (Warwick Rodwell)

FIGURE 51 (below right). Chancel arch: Transitional impost on the north side. (Addington, 1845)

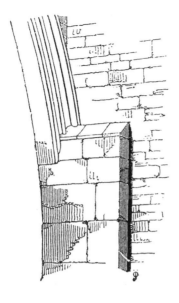

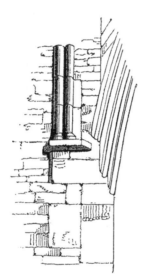

FIGURE 52 (top left). Remains of the north-east angle-buttress of the Norman chancel, seen externally. The moulded arch springing from it belongs to the later north chancel window. (Freeman, 1852)

FIGURE 53 (above). North aisle: fragment of the Norman north-east angle-buttress surviving internally, and now supported by a corbel. (Warwick Rodwell)

FIGURE 54 (left). Remains of the Norman south-east angle-buttress of the chancel, seen externally (cf. Figure 153). The moulded arch springing from it (right) belongs to the later south chancel window. (Freeman, 1852)

similar to those at St Cross, Winchester (Fig. 55).[10] It is unlikely that these were the only buttresses on the chancel, and they were probably complemented by pilaster-buttresses on the north and south walls. Internally, the bay divisions may have been punctuated by wall-shafts, but no evidence remains.

Crossing and Transepts

Continuity of string-courses, both internally and externally on the north side of the church, together with vestigial scarring on the south, confirms that there were transepts in the late 12th century, just as there had been in the 11th century. The west sides of both transepts survive, and the ornate cloister doorway in the north transept is contemporary with the chancel arch (Fig. 56; Pl. 32).[11] The tympanum is modestly decorated and capitals of the nook-shafts are well carved (Fig. 137). The south wall of the south transept is partly extant (Fig. 147), while archaeological

and circumstantial evidence reveal that the depth of the north transept was almost certainly the same as its southern counterpart (p. 35). Whether there was a doorway in the west side of the south transept, where the 14th-century opening now is, cannot be determined.

Nothing is known about the eastern sides of the transepts, although the wall position in the north transept is ghosted by later features, and in the south transept a foundation stub was recorded in a trench dug for a heating pipe. It is assumed that the transepts were initially plain on the east, and did not have projecting chapels: those seem to have been additions of the 13th century.[12] The fenestration has all been lost, except for part of a high-level window in the west wall of the north transept. There is likely to have been a pair of windows in the east side of both transepts, and one in the south wall of the south transept.

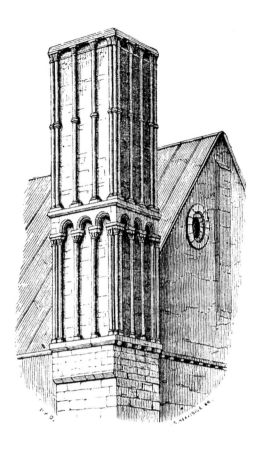

FIGURE 55 (above). St Cross, Winchester (Hants.): the top of
a Norman angle-buttress embellished with blind arcading.
(Parker, 1881)

FIGURE 56 (top right). Blocked Norman doorway leading into
the north transept from the cloister. The large stones at the
base of the filling are canopy fragments from St Birinus's
shrine. The 14th-century doorway to the nave is seen on the
right. (Addington, 1845)

Finally, the problem of the transept arches must
be addressed, the present form of the tall, round-
headed openings being a much later adaptation (Figs
57, 58 and 170). The surviving evidence confirms that
there were no tall lateral arches in the late 12th
century, and many writers have commented on the
fact that the present openings are cut through the
Norman string-course. Like the nave, the north and
south walls of the crossing were divided into two
stories by a moulded string-course, above which was
a wide round arch that was not on the axis of the
crossing, but slightly to the west; this arch arguably
contained two, or possibly three, recessed sub-arches.
Today, only the square-edged voussoirs of the outer
order survive, but originally the openings must have
resembled a tribune gallery (Fig. 59). Below the string-
course was an off-centre arched opening of uncertain
width leading into the transept. In each case, only
the western respond of that arch now survives.

While the individual elements can readily be
understood, the composition as a whole is more
difficult to parallel. St John's Chapel in the Tower of
London provides an example of the plain, open-arched
upper register,[13] while the crossing of St Albans Abbey
has pairs of recessed sub-arches.[14] Many examples
occur in smaller Norman churches too, such as
Bucknell (Oxon.) (Fig. 60). At Melton Constable (Norf.)
the east wall of the Romanesque nave is pierced by
two semicircular arches of similar size, located one
above the other, with a string-course between (Fig.
61). The lower opening comprises a plain chancel
arch, and the upper contains a pair of sub-arches with
a plain tympanum, all supported by a heavy columnar
pier.[15] Christ Church, Oxford, has a particularly
unusual arrangement of triforium and clerestory
openings in the nave (Fig. 62),[16] and although this
does not provide a direct analogue for Dorchester, it
demonstrates a local affinity for complex arrangements
of arches contained within several registers.

While the western responds and plinths of the
ground-level openings into both transepts survive
up to springing-level, the eastern responds and the
arched heads were destroyed when the present tall
openings were created in the later Middle Ages. The
transept arches in the lower register were clearly
narrower than those in the upper storey and were
asymmetrically positioned beneath them (Fig. 58A).[17]

FIGURE 57. *South crossing arch: view from the south-east. (Warwick Rodwell)*

FIGURE 59. *South crossing arch: view from the organ loft, showing also the respond of the chancel arch (right). (Warwick Rodwell)*

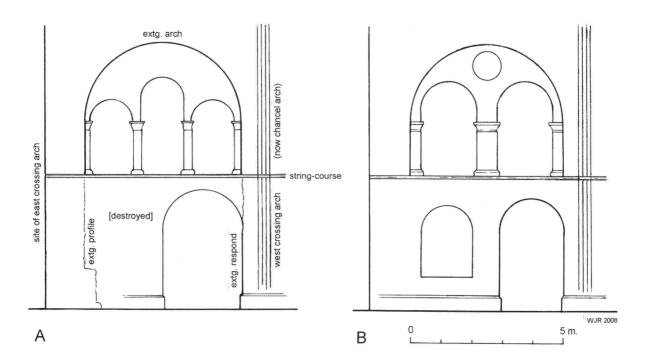

FIGURE 58. *Alternative reconstructions of the Norman south crossing arch and arcaded opening above. (Warwick Rodwell)*

FIGURE 60 (above left). St Peter, Bucknell (Oxon.): twin-arched belfry opening. (Parker, 1881)

FIGURE 61 (left). St Peter, Melton Constable (Norf.): two-storied east wall of the nave. (Bond, 1908b)

FIGURE 62 (above right). St Frideswide, Oxford: reconstruction of the nave arcade and gallery openings. (Halsey, 1988)

at Dorchester: a reconstruction of the suggested arrangement is offered in Fig. 58B.

In 1910, Hope attempted to reconstruct the 14th-century liturgical plan of the church (Fig. 10), hypothesizing that the pulpitum lay under the west crossing arch, and the rood screen was well into the nave.[19] It is difficult to see how this would have worked in practice, and it does not accord with the plan of c. 1720, which shows the remnants of the monastic layout (Fig. 6). The rood screen position in the 14th century is not in doubt since the loft doorway is preserved in the wall on the south (Figs 50 and 183); it is unlikely that the screen was ever further to the west.

Hence, although the canons' church was un-doubtedly cruciform, it did not have a regular crossing, and there was probably a constriction in plan under the eastern arch caused by the presence of a pulpitum screen. However, it is uncertain whether the pulpitum initially occupied that location: later, it was one bay further east. The Augustinian community at Dorchester was always small, and it had no need of a spacious quire and presbytery.

The reason for this can only be surmised, but one possible explanation is that the eastern part of the crossing was substantially encumbered by a pulpitum screen with flanking altars: Augustinian pulpita survive on the east side of the crossing at Christchurch Priory (Hants.), and Carlisle Cathedral. Alternatively, instead of there being an area of solid masonry immediately to the east of each transept arch, there could have been a second, smaller opening (perhaps with a grille) that served as a window onto the transeptal altars. In this context, one is reminded of the east wall of the nave at Eartham (Suss.), where the Norman chancel arch is flanked by a pair of sizeable semicircular-headed openings (Fig. 63).[18] A combination of the features seen at Melton Constable and Eartham would explain the surviving evidence

FIGURE 63. St Margaret, Eartham (Suss.): chancel arch and flanking openings. (Bond, 1908b)

The existing west crossing arch is a lightweight structure, and if there was a second one matching it on the east, we can be fairly certain that the late 12th-century arrangement did not support a stone tower, although the possibility that the crossing was surmounted by a timber-framed, lantern-type of structure holding bells might be entertained, especially if there was no tower or bell-cote at the west end of the nave. The form of the church at Dorchester in the later 12th century may have been closely similar to that of Leonard Stanley priory (Glos.), a small Augustinian house that subsequently became a Benedictine cell.[20]

Two further points emerge from reconstructing the medieval crossing. First, the relatively narrow openings into the transepts, and their asymmetrical siting, meant that the latter were more enclosed and chapel-like than usual. This is reminiscent of Lacock, where there was a pair of chapels instead of a north transept. Second, the emphatic horizontal division in the elevation of the crossing implies that the transepts were storied, and that there were either upper chapels or galleries. Although little is known in detail about upper-level features in transepts, they were not uncommon. It should also be noted that the night stair leading to the dorter range would have risen inside the north transept. Indeed, the asymmetrical reveals of the cloister doorway point to the first step lying immediately alongside.

More could perhaps be teased out about the architecture of the Norman abbey through a detailed study of the loose masonry fragments (Fig. 222). It is apparent, and not altogether surprising, that close architectural connections seem to have been maintained between Dorchester and Lincoln. Thus, a Greek-key motif which is found on a voussoir at Dorchester is matched on the main west portal at Lincoln.[21] Later stylistic links are evident too.

Font

The only furnishing surviving from the 12th-century church is the magnificent cast lead font bowl, which is a relic of the parochial component of Dorchester Abbey (Figs 190–192; Pl. 38). Its original position is most likely to have been at the west end of the nave, close to the south door. The bowl has been illustrated and mentioned by numerous writers[22] (for further discussion, see p. 181).

It is not certain what is represented on the bowl, which is decorated with eleven nimbed figures under arcades. This is a curious number, unless they are intended to represent the Apostles without Judas. Another view expressed, albeit highly implausible, is that they are all representations of Christ in different attitudes.[23] The circular lead font (now damaged) at Walton-on-the-Hill (Surr.) had twelve arcaded figures, as does the hexagonal bowl at Wareham (Dor.), but there is no consistent formula and the numbers on other fonts vary.[24]

THIRTEENTH CENTURY

A long and complex sequence of works began in the second quarter of the 13th century, and continued until the middle of the following century.

Phase 1: Addition of Transeptal Chapels, c. 1230–1250 (Fig. 46.3)

An arcade of two bays was inserted into the east wall of the north transept, opening into a new pair of lateral chapels. Only the southern bay of this arcade survives, and the arch falls at bay 1/2, the division between the present sacristy (with organ chamber above) and the north aisle (St Birinus's Chapel) (Fig. 64). The northern arch and its associated chapel were lost when the transept was truncated and a post-Dissolution blocking wall was erected across the middle of it (p. 101).

The capitals carry stiff-leaf foliage typical of the early-to-mid 13th century, and the bases are characteristically of the 'water-holding' type, probably dating from *c.* 1220–50. What appears today to be a respond supporting the northern flank of the surviving arch was once a freestanding pier separating the two arches of the arcade: this feature was revealed behind plaster in 1858 (Figs 138 and 139).

The position of the new east wall to those chapels has been fossilized in the north aisle, at the junction between bays 2 and 3. Externally, the vertical scar is visible where the chapel's east wall was abutted by the slightly later aisle (Figs 133–135). Internally, not only can the inner face of the chapel wall be glimpsed, but so too can an *in situ* fragment of a piscina with a cusped head: it belonged to the northern transeptal chapel.[25] The addition of the transeptal chapels could

FIGURE 64. *North chancel aisle: transverse arch, formerly part of the arcade between the north transept and its eastern chapels. View east. (Warwick Rodwell)*

be related to a general aggrandizement of the church when the shrine to St Birinus was re-established, following papal approval for the veneration of his relics in 1225.

Another noteworthy feature, found in the spandrels above the arcade (facing west) between the transept and its chapels, are the unenclosed trefoils (Figs 64, 138 and 140). Moulded in stone, they are blind and are purely ornamental.[26] Foiled motifs, with or without enclosing circles, applied to plain ashlar, tend to be

FIGURE 65. *Westminster Abbey Chapter House: the inner entrance arch with large trefoils filling the spandrels. (Warwick Rodwell)*

FIGURE 66. Lichfield Cathedral: cinquefoiled circles in the spandrels of the nave arcade. (Britton, 1836)

found in churches of high status. Most apposite are the blind trefoils in the spandrels flanking the entrance to the chapter house at Westminster Abbey, *c.* 1250 (Fig. 65).[27] There are pierced trefoils in the spandrels of the north transept screen at Gloucester Cathedral, *c.* 1230;[28] encircled trefoils and split cinquefoils in the spandrels of the nave at Lichfield Cathedral, *c.* 1265 (Fig. 66);[29] trefoils in the Angel Choir at Lincoln Cathedral (*c.* 1270);[30] and enclosed demi-quatrefoils above the late 13th-century aumbry in the former south transept chapel at Pershore Abbey.[31]

Nothing remains on the south side of the church to confirm whether a matching pair of chapels was added to the transept there at the same time, albeit that was very likely. However, a piece of circumstantial evidence may be noted. When the south chancel aisle was constructed in its present form in the 14th

century, the builders were clearly influenced by pre-existing fabric which caused the south wall to be slightly misaligned: the evidence is consistent with the proposition that earlier chapels were attached to the transept.[32]

Phase 2: Narrow North Chancel Aisle, *c.* 1250–1260 (Fig. 46.4; Pl. 6)

The next phase of 13th-century work relates to the addition of the narrow north chancel aisle of three bays, which is itself a two-stage construction.[33] Initially, it was much squatter than it is today and only three bays in length. It was separate from the transept, and had an eastern gable and a low arcade communicating with the chancel. The arcade was almost certainly of two bays, rather than three, as now. The present traceries in the east window and the two windows in the north wall belong to this phase (bays 4 and 5; Figs 126–128, 131 and 132).[34] Attached to the north and east walls are four slender shafts with ring-bases and capitals decorated with dogtooth: they now serve no function (Figs 67 and 68). It has sometimes been claimed that they provide evidence that the chapel was intended to be roofed with a stone vault which was never built. However, the small scale of the capitals, coupled with the absence of springers and wall-ribs above them, leaves little room for doubt that no stone vault was ever intended. The capitals may only have carried the feet of roof trusses, but more plausibly their function was to support a quadripartite timber vault.

In recent years, there has been a growing appreciation that timber vaults, simulating stone, were relatively common in Britain, although most have subsequently been lost.[35] They became popular in the 13th century, and in 1243 Henry III, after admiring one at Lichfield Cathedral, ordered a similar timber vault to be constructed at St George's Chapel, Windsor.[36] The tell-tale evidence usually takes the form of masonry wall-shafts and respond capitals defining structural bays, but with no evidence of their ever having supported contemporaneous stone vaulting.[37] That is precisely the situation at Dorchester, and we may wonder whether the new, vaulted north-east chapel was conceived to enhance the setting of the shrine of St Birinus.[38] If so, the modern appellation – St Birinus's Chapel – is indeed fortuitous. At St Augustine's Abbey, Bristol, the outer north aisle (Elder Lady Chapel) exhibits both the support structure for a primary timber vault (*c.* 1220), and the later addition of a stone vault (*c.* 1300).[39]

The interior of the aisle contains several liturgical features, potentially signifying a special purpose for the chapel. South of the altar, which was always raised on at least one step, is a piscina with a Geometrical head. Opposite this, in the north wall, is a row of three identical rectangular lockers, internally plain and now fitted with 19th-century oak doors (Figs 69

FIGURE 67. *North aisle: wall-shaft and capital to support a timber vault, bay 3/4. (Warwick Rodwell)*

FIGURE 68. *North chancel aisle: string-course and wall-shaft at the north-east angle, bay 5. The base of the shaft is largely buried in the Victorian dais. (Warwick Rodwell)*

FIGURE 69. *North chancel aisle: three medieval lockers in the north wall of bay 5. The doors are Victorian. (Warwick Rodwell)*

FIGURE 70. North chancel aisle: close-up view of two of the lockers. (Warwick Rodwell)

FIGURE 71. Lichfield Cathedral: three 13th-century lockers in the wall of the treasury forming part of the St Chad's Head Chapel complex. (Warwick Rodwell)

and 70). A side-altar did not require three large aumbries, and it is likely that these were specially designed to house reliquaries or other treasures. Multiple lockers are sometimes found in sacristies and treasuries: *e.g.* Lichfield Cathedral, where there are three in the treasury adjacent to St Chad's Head Chapel (Fig. 71).[40] A unique arrangement of two tiers of three 'aumbries' occurs at Langford (Oxon.), which must also have been provided to serve a special function.[41]

Finally, low down in the north wall of the chapel is a small, rectangular recess with a pointed head; it is plain and not embellished with mouldings. In the back is a circular opening, forming a flue which passes through the external wall (Fig. 143). The feature is apparently an oven, and it has been suggested that this is the place where Eucharistic wafers were baked. Bristol Cathedral, another former house of Augustinian canons, has a slightly larger oven in the vestibule of the 14th-century Berkeley chapel.

Again, the question arises as to whether there was a corresponding south chancel aisle at Dorchester in the 13th century. While no specific evidence survives in the fabric, the sequence of events in the 14th century is easier to explain if there had formerly been a narrow south aisle. If so, the plan now superficially resembled that of the Augustinian Merton priory (Surr.).[42]

Phase 3: North Chancel Aisle Rebuilt, *c. 1280–1300 (Fig. 46.5)*

The second aisle-phase involved removing the timber vault and raising the walls in height; at the same time, the north-east chapel and the transeptal chapels were modified, being united to form an aisle of four bays, opening eastwards from the transept: that effectively created an ambulatory of five bays in total (Fig. 129). This modification was accompanied by the reconstruction of the chancel arcade, creating the present

A

FIGURE 72 (left). A. North chancel aisle: repositioned window in bay 2. (Addington, 1845) B. St Albans Abbey: traceried roundel. (Freeman, 1851).

FIGURE 73 (above). Chancel: detail of a reticulated band on one of the buttresses of the sedilia. (Warwick Rodwell)

B

arrangement, which does not synchronize with the earlier buttressing provision. At the same time, the eastern arch of the Norman crossing must have been removed, thus throwing it in with the presbytery. The inner of the two transeptal chapels was expunged in the rearrangement, while the outer one was provided with a fine new Geometrical east window: that survives, although now reset in bay 2 of the post-Dissolution aisle (Fig. 72A). The unusual cusped roundel in the tracery is identical to one in a window at St Albans Abbey (Fig. 72B),[43] and presaged the reticulated bands on the buttresses of the sedilia in the chancel (Fig. 73).

In order to install the lofty north arcade in the chancel, the old low aisle had first to be heightened

(Fig. 64). The traceried heads of the east window and two adjacent north windows were dismantled, their jambs increased in height, and the heads replaced (Figs 126 and 131). The disjuncture in the internal reveals of all three windows is clearly marked, and coincides with the capital level of the wall-shafts that supported the posited timber vault. Externally, the hood-mouldings over the window arches were initially linked by a string-course at springing-level, and the remnants of this abandoned detail are still present. The north door and the window above it (bay 3, Fig. 133) are associated with this phase, as may be the wafer oven alongside. Potentially, this aggrandizement of the aisle belongs to the years around 1290, when interest in the shrine was increasing.[44]

Other 13th-Century Features and Decoration

Two unconnected features in the south nave aisle belong to the 13th century, but both were reset in their present positions in the later 14th century. These are the west window, and the diagonal buttress with its integral statue niches at the south-west angle (Fig. 74; Pls 1 and 2). The origin of the relocated buttress was established with near-certainty during Scott's restoration. It was observed that a vertical cutaway strip of masonry, at a high level on what had once

FIGURE 74. *South nave aisle: view from the south-west, showing the repositioned buttress with statue niches, the porch and churchyard cross. (Addington, 1845)*

been the external corner of the south transept (but is now visible inside the south-east corner of the aisle), matches the profile of the buttress. What we see in this corner today is a negative image of the mouldings of the removed buttress.[45]

The buttress was designed to hold statuary in two registers which would be seen by the lay public as they arrived at the south door, via the churchyard (Figs 74, 179 and 180). The buttress is no later than the mid-13th century, and the statues it housed were doubtless of similar date. When the new aisle was added there was obviously a strong desire to retain the display of statuary (which probably included Birinus), and the simplest way of achieving this was to dismantle the buttress and rebuild it at the new south-west corner.

Buttresses incorporating statue niches on one or more faces are found in 13th-century buildings of high status, as on the west fronts of Wells and Salisbury cathedrals, and on the tower of St Mary Redcliffe, Bristol. Some of the smaller monastic churches also had low-level statue niches, particularly

flanking doorways, as at Nun Monkton priory (Fig. 48). The extent to which significant architectural features of the 12th and 13th centuries were dismantled and reconstructed at later periods is often underestimated: doorways were the most commonly repositioned elements. In the 14th century there was a predilection for statuary placed in ornate niches on the fronts of buttresses: *e.g.* on the south aisle of St Mary Magdalen, Oxford. Thus, the planned retention of a niched buttress at Dorchester, more than a century after it was built, is not surprising. It is interesting to note that the niches occur on only two of the three faces of the buttress, which is entirely plain on the south-east side. Superficially, that would appear incongruous because this is the face visible to parishioners as they enter the south door. However, when the buttress was attached to the transept, the entrance to the church would have been west of it, and not to the east as now. The plain side would have faced the river.

Determining the likely origin of the west window in the south aisle is more problematic (Fig. 75). The

FIGURE 75. *South nave aisle: west elevation, showing the repositioned window and buttress. Note also the fragmentary string-course to either side of the door. (Warwick Rodwell)*

engaged shafts of the rear-arch have water-holding bases, pointing to a date not later than the middle of the 13th century. The large scale of the window suggests the possibility that it came from a gable-end (transept or aisle), but it is difficult to achieve a chronological match. It is unlikely to have come from the gable of the south transept (which it would have fitted very well), since that was refenestrated when the chancel aisle was built, which occurred several decades before the nave aisle was added (p. 83). There seem to be only two viable options. First, the window may have derived from the south wall of the nave, being released when the arcade was built. The window would have appeared out of scale, but dimensionally could just have fitted. The second alternative must envisage a previous aisle, or chapel, to the south of the nave, but again it must have been substantial if it accommodated this large window.

The first option is not very plausible, but there is evidence to support the second in the form of wallpainting.[46] The remains of a Crucifixion painted on the back of the high-level recess at the east end of the present aisle, and the contemporary scrollwork in the reveals, are late 13th century (preceding the large painted cross, Pl. 39). The discovery of these details during recent conservation work confirms that there must have been a structure on this site before the present aisle. Whether that was a full-length aisle,

or a chapel adjoining the west side of the transept, can only be established by further archaeological investigation. The position is too far east for it to have been a porch. The discovery raises questions concerning both the small 'external' door in the same wall (Fig. 184), and how the niched buttress at the south-west angle of the transept was accommodated. The hood-moulding does not fit the door-arch, indicating that this is another reconstructed feature.

Turning to decorative materials, the roundel bearing the name *Bernivs* [*sic*] is the oldest piece of stained glass in the church, dating from the mid-13th century (Pls 22 and 23).[47] It has been cut down in size since the 18th century (losing the recorded prefix *Sanctvs* in the process),[48] and repositioned several times: although its original setting cannot now be determined, there is every likelihood that the roundel adorned the shrine chapel. There was probably a commissioned series of lights depicting the life of Birinus, and a fragment of another inscription (now in the north chancel window) was part of that suite: it reads, *Baptizat conversos ad fidem*.

Some of the other extant fragments of medieval glass may date from the late 13th century, but nothing is of particular note. There are also traces of wallpainting, above the south crossing arch, dating from the late 12th or 13th century: they depict a false-ashlar pattern, the lines being drawn in red.[49] A few of the extant fragments of glazed floor tiling are also likely to date from the late 13th century, although most are later.

Very little survives of the church's complement of early funerary monuments, the notable exception being the cross-legged effigy of a knight in armour (Fig. 164A, M.10).[50] The monument, which was once a piece of sculpture of the first rank, has been studied *in extenso*, and identification of the knight as William de Valence the younger (d. 1282) is currently favoured.[51] Also of late 13th- or early 14th-century date is the limestone effigy of a bishop, with polychrome decoration. Almost certainly, this is the monument described by Leland in 1542 as bearing an inscription to an Anglo-Saxon bishop named Aeschwyn (Fig. 165, M.16). The effigy then disappeared from view, and was probably turned face-down and let into the floor of the nave to serve as paving, or as a step. It was rediscovered under the south arcade in the mid-18th century.[52] This effigy was perhaps one of several that adorned the quire or shrine chapel, being commissioned as retrospective memorials which provided a tangible reminder of Dorchester's episcopal past. Similar series of retrospective effigies were commissioned at Worcester and Wells cathedrals.[53]

Several coffin lids decorated with floriated crosses are recorded (some now lost): these belong to the 13th and 14th centuries (*e.g.* Fig. 164C, M.9). Middle-

FIGURE 76. *South chancel arcade: view from the north-west, showing the south aisle, chapels and shrine beyond. (Warwick Rodwell)*

ranking memorials of this kind are to be expected in a monastic church. Finally, the oak chest is the oldest item of wooden furniture in the church, and dates from the 13th century (Fig. 194).

LATE THIRTEENTH AND FOURTEENTH CENTURIES

Dorchester's era of pre-eminent architectural glory lay in the early years of the 14th century. Five constructional phases can be identified, and building works must have been in progress almost continuously for more than half a century. In addition, a magnificent new shrine to St Birinus, in limestone and Purbeck marble, was constructed: Higden, in his *Polychronicon*, records its completion in *c.* 1320. Where that shrine stood is a matter for debate, but it seems unlikely to have been in the north chancel aisle which, by 1320, was a distinctly old-fashioned space, as well as being cramped. Alternatively, the shrine could have been in the south transept, or an early chapel attached to it. We shall examine the new works one-by-one.

Phase 4: West Tower, c. 1270–1300+ (Fig. 46.5)

The construction of a west tower probably took place around the beginning of the 14th century, although where it came in the sequence of events is unclear, there being no diagnostic dating evidence. The tower may not therefore be correctly sequenced here in relation to other parts of the church, but one fact is certain: it was erected before the south aisle was added to the nave. Nothing is known about the medieval tower, except its newel staircase which survives and was incorporated in the south-east corner of its successor in 1602 (Figs 74 and 94). The tower was probably not of the conventional type found at the west end of a parish church, but was part of a gatehouse structure that gave access to the monastic inner court (p. 55).

The type of construction employed in the staircase, namely placing the treads on a helical vault, argues for an early date. This was a rare form of construction by the mid-13th century, but there is no possibility of such an early date in this instance.[54]

FIGURE 77. *Chancel: south arcade and double piscina in bay 4, with a view of the south-east chapels beyond (lacking vaulting). (Addington, 1845)*

Phase 5: South-East Chancel Chapel, c. 1290–1300 (Fig. 46.6)

The first phase of alteration at the east end involved the construction of the south chancel arcade of three bays (Fig. 76). This was made to appear superficially similar to the existing north arcade, but with one major and several minor differences. The major difference is the unequal spacing of the bays, the easternmost being markedly shorter on account of the need to leave sufficient space beyond, in which to set a piscina for the high altar. The elaborate double-basined piscina is integral with the arcade's eastern respond (Fig. 77). Also integrated with that respond, and with the next column to the west, are the springers of the vaulting for the south-east chapel (Fig. 157).

These details confirm that not only was a south aisle constructed, but that a stone-vaulted chapel of two bays was also part of the design.[55] Although the chapel is now architecturally integrated with the wide south aisle, there are reasons for believing that the two are not of contemporary build. The south side of the chapel does not align, either internally or externally, with the wall of the present aisle. The offset is plainly visible inside, but is partly masked by a buttress outside. Nor do the buttresses of the south aisle synchronize with the columns of the arcade, which would be expected if they were contemporaneous. Also, the window tracery in bay 4 is set deeper behind the wall-face than in the other bays. An even clearer indication that the chapel and aisle were erected in separate phases is provided by the two temporary 'barrow doors' used by the builders and infilled upon completion of the work: one in the east side of the chapel and another in bay 3 of the aisle (Figs 10, 148 and 154). If the two components had been erected together, only one builders' door would have been required.

Thus, there can be little doubt that, initially, the south-east chapel projected from the side of the chancel as a squarish, buttressed structure, and was entered from a narrow aisle that has subsequently disappeared. The chapel accommodated two altars and had a double-bowled piscina in its south wall (Fig. 158). In the east wall, on the northern flank of each altar, was a simple aumbry (Fig. 106). The twin chapels were lit from the east by a pair of Decorated windows with a 'split-cusp' tracery design: visually, it combines a spherical triangle with a trefoil and a three-pointed star (Figs 78 and 153).[56] The stair-turret contained within the buttresses at the south-east angle led to an upper chamber, lit by two lancet windows in the east wall (Figs 155 and 159). The purpose of the upper chamber can only be surmised, but it may have combined the functions of chapel and treasury, also with a sacristy at ground level to serve the high altar. This two-storied chapel and sacristy complex is closely mirrored by the Berkeley Chapel (built before 1309) at St Augustine's Abbey, Bristol, and at other major churches in the 13th and 14th centuries (*e.g.* Lichfield Cathedral: see below).

Phase 6: Wide South Chancel Aisle, c. 1310–1320 (Fig. 46.7)

The arrangement just described did not obtain for long, before the south aisle was reconstructed, expunging the former transept and the transeptal chapel that was almost certainly still attached to its east side (Fig. 76). The width of the enlarged aisle was determined by the Norman transept, and some of its masonry was incorporated in the new south wall. Sets of matching windows and equally spaced buttresses were provided (Fig 144 and 146). The tops of the buttresses were enlivened with carved creatures: human, animal and imaginary. They appear to have no religious significance, but recall medieval secular entertainment (Figs 149–152).

The motivation for enlarging the aisle is likely to have been the provision of an aggrandized setting for

the shrine of St Birinus, and that was partly achieved through the use of stone vaulting, a relatively rare feature in parish churches and small monasteries in the 13th and 14th centuries.[57] The shrine needed to attract pilgrims, and to be accessible without disrupting the *opus dei* in the quire. One small detail provides a strong argument for a link between the south-east chapel and the shrine, namely the detailing of the tracery in the blind panels of the latter: they mirror the chapel's eastern fenestration.[58] The modern reconstruction of the shrine is therefore sited in the correct part of the church. Additional supporting evidence may come to light when more is known about the medieval wallpaintings underlying the limewash in this chapel. Whether the shrine was hitherto in the north chancel aisle, as suggested (p. 75), or had already been moved to the south transept since the 1220s, can only be a matter of speculation.

While the chapels occupying the two easternmost bays were already stone vaulted, with a chamber above, the remainder of the aisle was not similarly treated. Consequently, the upper chamber must have been converted into a gallery at the east end of the enlarged aisle. Most likely, this gallery carried a chapel, the interior of which was visible from below, as at Compton (Surr.): there, an open-sided, upper-level chapel is present over the vaulted Romanesque chancel (Fig. 80).[59] While the original arcaded timber screen enclosing the gallery on the west still survives at Compton, the present balustrade at Dorchester dates from 1874. The gallery would also have served as a convenient watching loft over the shrine, and possibly a place from which relics could be displayed to pilgrims on the floor below. Such a gallery, carried on vaulting and projecting into the south aisle, survives at Lichfield Cathedral (Fig. 81). It too dates from the 14th century.

Finally, the small 14th-century doorway tucked into the angle between the west wall of the aisle and the nave gives the appearance of having once been external because it has a hood-moulding (Figs 57, 183 and 184). Although this could have allowed public access to the shrine chapel, or previously to the transept, without impinging upon the monastic quire, it is a disconcertingly plain and ignominious entrance for any 14th-century chapel, let alone one where a regionally important saint was venerated. The doorway has been resited and reduced in size, thus accounting for the fact that the arcature of the hood-moulding does not fit the opening (p. 175). This was probably an external door in the south chancel aisle or chapels.

The shrine itself comprised a limestone pedestal that was presumably solid at the base, and above which lay a series of recesses, each with an intricately vaulted canopy and blind-traceried sides (Fig. 76; Pls 24 and 25). Polychromy and gilding were lavishly applied, and considerable traces of these remain

FIGURE 78. *South chancel aisle: east window of chapel, bay 5 north. Note the aumbry below the window sill. (Addington, 1845)*

FIGURE 80. *St Nicholas, Compton (Surr.): vaulted Norman chancel with a galleried chapel above. (Mervyn Blatch)*

FIGURE 79. *St Mary, Cheltenham (Glos.): detail of window tracery, drawn by Carter, 1801. (Carter and Britton, 1837)*

beneath an excess of modern paint.[60] The survival of the canopies, built into the blocking of the former west doorway of the north transept, is remarkable, although how and when they were placed there is problematic (p. 138). Above the canopied stage would have been the shrine chest (probably coped, or 'house-shaped') which, nominally at least, should have contained the corporeal relics of the saint. Nothing of this top stage seems to have survived and thus the form of the chest remains conjectural. Two pieces of Purbeck marble cornice, now used as paving in the nave floor, probably capped the pedestal (Fig. 176).

Thus, it is clear that St Birinus's shrine was not of the openwork type, as seen in St Edburg's shrine at Stanton Harcourt (Oxon.), but a solid, niched and tabernacled base akin to that of St Alban.[61] The latter, constructed *c.* 1302–08, was a near-contemporary of Dorchester's shrine, which was completed by *c.* 1320.[62]

Phase 7: Eastward Extension of the Presbytery, *c. 1330–1340 (Fig. 46.8)*

In the next phase, the monastic presbytery was extended eastwards by one bay, taking the church to

FIGURE 81. Lichfield Cathedral: gallery projecting over the south quire aisle, in front of St Chad's Head Chapel. (Warwick Rodwell)

FIGURE 82. The east end of the church before restoration. (Addington, 1845)

FIGURE 83. Merton College, Oxford. East window of the chapel, drawn by Carter, 1794. (Carter and Britton, 1837)

The basic design belongs to a group of grand windows found in the Oxford area, around the beginning of the 14th century: the most intricate is probably the east window of Merton College chapel, dating from *c.* 1290 (Fig. 83). What sets the Dorchester window apart from all others is the fact that the main lights do not have continuous mullions but are filled with reticulated tracery (Pl. 5). Such a structure is inherently weak and unable to resist wind pressure without bowing. Consequently, it would have been built with a wrought iron tying-bar, running across the entire window from side to side, at the springing-level of the arched head.[65] The bar would have sufficed to stiffen the tracery under normal circumstances, but the chancel extension suffered from structural instability caused by ground movement. The walls became distressed and both the east and south windows required support, probably within a few decades of being built. Hence, the inelegant central buttress was added to the east window, completely destroying the middle light.

the very edge of the floodplain. This new bay has built before the old east wall was demolished, and consequently another builders' temporary doorway was required for access; this is now partly concealed by the later central buttress (Fig. 111). Much has been written about the magnificence and unconventional designs of the three new windows that light the presbytery from the east, north and south.[63] The east window is vertically divided by a buttress into two sections, each of three lights, but that division only occurred late in the 14th century when the buttress was added as a matter of structural necessity. When built, the extended sanctuary had clasping buttresses at the outer corners, and the east wall was entirely filled by a seven-light window with a traceried circle or 'rose' (Fig. 82). The latter element was largely destroyed when the pitch of the chancel gable was lowered, but has subsequently been reconstructed. It is debatable whether the asymmetrical tracery of the rose was a correct restoration by Butterfield, and some commentators have argued that it should have been symmetrical. All that can be said now is that the small amount of archaeological evidence surviving in the lower part of the circle accords with the arrangement as reconstructed (Figs 101 and 102; Pl. 10).[64]

FIGURE 84. Chancel: north (Jesse) window. Outline drawing by Carter, 1793. The preparatory sketches for this are in the Bodleian Library. (Carter and Britton, 1837)

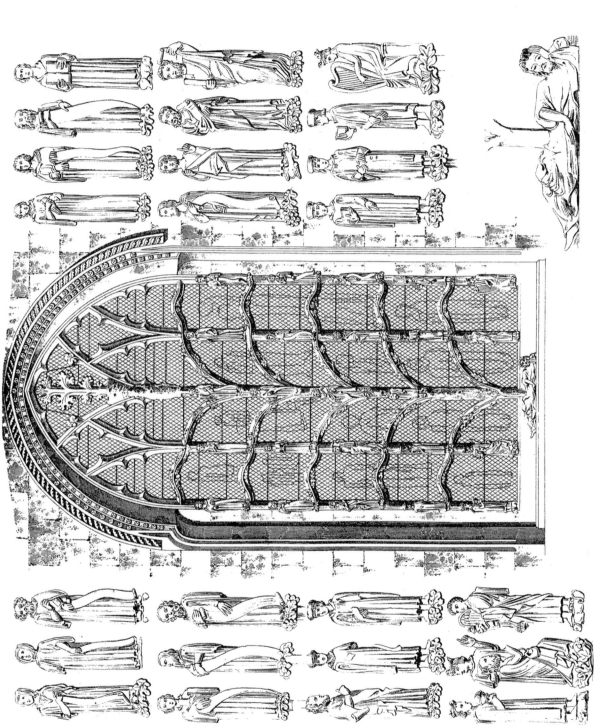

Figure 85. Chancel: north (Jesse) window. Britton's archaeological drawing of 1820, with separate details of the figures carved on the jambs and mullions. (Britton, 1835)

FIGURE 86. Chancel: north (Jesse) window. Skelton's atmospheric drawing showing figures in sculpture and stained glass. (Skelton, 1823)

Figure 87. Chancel: south window and sedilia. Britton's view of 1820, with details of the six figures carved on the jambs and mullions. The triangular window has been omitted from the piscina recess on the left (then blocked). (Britton, 1835)

FIGURE 88. *St Peter, Barton-upon-Humber (Lincs.): rood window in the north aisle, with figures sculpted on the mullions. (Simon Hayfield)*

On the north side of the sanctuary is an equally remarkable window in which the tracery of the four lights is arranged in the form of the Tree of Jesse: many artists have illustrated this, in varying levels of detail (Figs 84–86). Finally, on the south side is a third window of exceptional design, although less flamboyant than the others (Figs 87 and 110). Moreover, all three windows are highly unusual for another reason: they have small figure-sculptures on the mullions. Although on a much humbler scale, the nearest analogue for this treatment is the early 14th-century rood window at St Peter's, Barton-upon-Humber (Lincs.): there, the figures of the crucified Christ, together with St Mary and St John are sculpted on the three mullions (Fig. 88).[66]

The three sanctuary windows at Dorchester form a contemporary ensemble, and they are all heavily decorated with ballflower ornament. The small stone sculptures on the mullions and tracery were complemented by figures and inscriptions in the stained glass (Pl. 9). The east window served as a huge reredos to the high altar,[67] and it was further emphasized by having its rear-arch framed by freestanding shafts. These have annulets at the mid-point, a feature so characteristic of the 13th century that it is surprising to see it here: elements of an earlier east window have surely been reused? The sills of the north and south windows rest on string-courses which are not at the same height. Moreover,

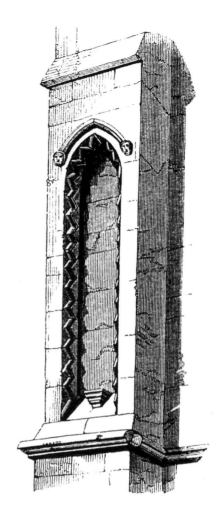

FIGURE 89. *Chancel: remodelled Romanesque niche in the north-east buttress. (Addington, 1845)*

in the case of the south side the sill and string have been hacked away to accommodate an ornately canopied sedilia and piscina. This is unique in having a single light – in the form of a modified spherical triangle – in the back of each of the four recesses (Fig. 117; Pl. 7). Reticulated bands around the buttresses that mark the bay divisions are reminiscent of detail in one of the north aisle windows (Figs 72 and 73). Despite the hacked string-course, it is difficult to envisage how this feature could be other than part of the original design: it cannot be secondary. However, while the niches would have been formed as the walling masonry went up, the delicate canopy work would not have been installed until after the completion and roofing of the shell. An error, or slight modification to the design of the canopy work, would explain the need to cut back the window sill at a late stage.

One curious anomaly requires comment, namely the late Norman, chevron-ornamented recess in the face of one of the clasping buttresses at the north-east angle (Figs 89 and 113). Although a diminutive pedestal to carry a statuette has been installed in the

FIGURE 90. *St Mary, Iffley (Oxon.). Chevron-ornamented window of the mid-12th century. (Parker, 1881)*

base of the recess, it was not originally a statue niche, merely a decorative feature. The niche is fully integrated with the construction of the early 14th-century buttress, and is not an antiquarian confection of later date. It is a complete late 12th-century feature which was presumably taken from the old east end and carefully rebuilt as part of the new buttress. Arched openings edged by chevron ornament, without imposts, are found in other churches in the Oxford region, *e.g.* on the chapter house entrance at Christ Church, Oxford, and at Iffley church (Fig. 90).

Phase 8: South Nave Aisle, c. 1350–1360 (Fig. 46.9; Pls 34 and 38)

The final phase of 14th-century building comprised the addition of the south nave aisle and its arcade of three bays. This was not a straightforward parish-church aisle, and it exhibits several anomalies. First, there is a stone-vaulted crypt beneath the south-east corner, which it has often been asserted was merely a bone-hole constructed to receive human remains that were displaced from the churchyard as a result of digging the foundations for the south aisle. That

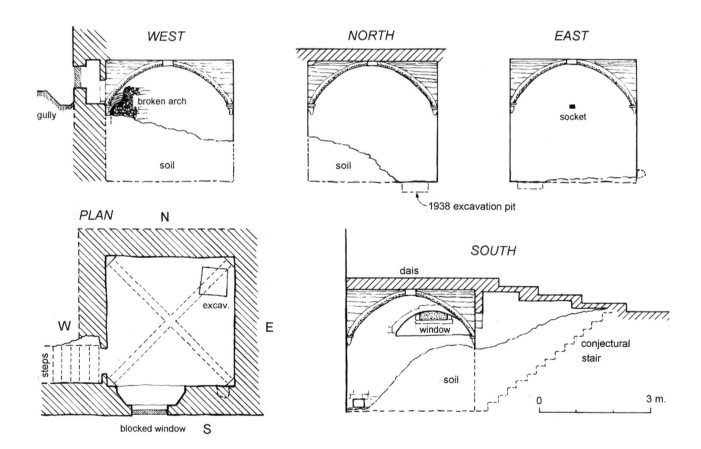

FIGURE 91. *South nave aisle: sketch plan and elevations of the crypt under bay 1. (adapted from a survey by Martin Ashley Architects)*

is implausible, a myth doubtless fuelled by the crypt's condition in the 19th century: 'the staircase is nearly filled with rubbish, and the whole place is a receptacle for bones and filth'.[68] The crypt was a significant structure with a liturgical or mortuary purpose. It was lit by an external window and accessed by a narrow flight of steps leading down from the aisle above (Figs 91, 196 and 197; Pl. 41). In this last respect it is reminiscent of the much larger crypt under the north transept of St Mary Redcliffe, Bristol.

It has already been observed that the crypt embodies a fragment of earlier chalk walling in its south side (p. 22; Fig. 198). It is also readily apparent that the structure is only semi-subterranean, and that the crown of its vault projects dramatically through the aisle floor, raising the altar on a prominent dais. A similar situation is found at Burford (Oxon.), where the floor of the south aisle chapel of St Thomas is elevated above a 14th-century vaulted crypt of similar design to that at Dorchester, although of four bays (Pl. 42).

The altar dais at Dorchester does not extend across the full width of the aisle, but leaves a clear passage alongside the nave arcade, allowing access to the small doorway leading into the south-east chapel complex, and hence to the shrine (Fig. 183). The 14th-century wallpainting of the Crucifixion forming a reredos to the aisle altar was also centred on the dais, and not on the axis of the aisle (Pl. 38). Moreover, high above the reredos – and entirely separate from it – is a large but shallow, flat-backed recess of pointed form in the east wall of the aisle; it dates from the 13th century. This is a purpose-built feature, not a partially infilled window, as has sometimes been supposed. The recess is axial to the aisle and has no connection with the off-centre chapel below. Furthermore, it is evident that there must once have been a timber floor, coincident with the base of the recess, and this also corresponds to the threshold of the doorway that led on to the rood loft in the nave. There was thus a gallery, or upper room, at the east end of the aisle. The recess itself contains wallpaintings of two periods, the earlier depicting a 13th-century Crucifixion (p. 176). Hence, there were two levels of chapels at this end of the aisle.

In the 14th century, the lower part (85 cm) of the recess was infilled with masonry – apparently to form an altar – and a new painting was applied to the wall above. This principally comprised a large, plain cross with blocked ends (cross potent), painted in red (Pl. 39). There is no sign of the crucified Christ upon it, and it is clear that there never has been a painted figure here. Instead, it would appear that the cross was a background for either a suspended figure of Christ under the arch, or for a rood figure mounted in front. A similar painted cross occurs at Bengeo (Herts.), but it carries the figure of Christ.[69]

The geography of the south aisle makes it clear that this space alone did not serve as the parochial nave, as some previous commentators have supposed. Instead, it simultaneously fulfilled at least three functions: first, it housed a screened chapel with the altar raised on a dais and a vaulted crypt beneath. In all probability, this was a privately constructed and endowed family chapel, possibly with an associated chantry, although no record of one has survived. Secondly, the inner part of the aisle, adjacent to the nave arcade, served as a passage to reach the south-east chapels and the shrine.[70] Thirdly, there was an upper chapel on a timber gallery at the east end of the aisle, with a direct connection to the rood loft in the nave. The former existence of a second gallery chapel at Dorchester, in addition to that already noted in the south chancel aisle (p. 83), is of great interest, and one wonders whether its purpose was primarily as a place from which relics could be displayed to pilgrims below, particularly at times when the shrine was not publicly accessible. One is again reminded of the St Chad's Head Chapel complex in the south quire aisle at Lichfield Cathedral. Although early 13th century in origin, Lichfield displays the same three-storey construction: crypt, aisle-level chapel (St Peter's), and upper chapel (St Chad's Head) to which a relic-display gallery was added in the 14th century (Fig. 81).[71]

The disposition of features at Dorchester is also reminiscent of an arrangement found in the south nave aisle at St John's, Cirencester (Glos.): there, at ground level, an arch in the east wall opens into a large chapel beyond, while to one side of the arch is a small private chapel enclosed by oak screens. Above, and extending across the full width of the aisle, was the timber floor of an upper chapel that has disappeared. Its east wall bore a painted reredos, now largely obliterated with limewash.[72]

Summary of Dating

Having outlined the structural evidence, we must review the dating of the various late 13th- and 14th-century works. The heraldic glass is pivotal to any consideration, but is bedevilled by the fact that not only has much been lost since the 17th century, but it has also been moved around the church. Several historians have examined the tangled history of the medieval glass and its peregrinations, and it is not necessary to embark on a lengthy discussion here.[73]

Equally relevant are the architectural similarities between Merton College chapel, of c. 1290, and the east end of the south chancel aisle at Dorchester; these have been discussed by Ayers.[74] In essence, a date around 1290–1300 seems certain for the south-east chapel, south chancel arcade and associated details such as the chancel piscina. The alterations to the chancel, as opposed to the erection of the chapel, must surely have been completed by 1292 for Bishop

Sutton to have consecrated the high altar in that year.

Ayers also argues that the new sanctuary was designed and begun at about the same time, but demonstrates convincingly that it could not have been completed before the 1330s. This needs re-examining in the light of archaeological issues that have now arisen. It seems unlikely that the sanctuary would have been refitted in the 1290s, if there was an intention to demolish the east wall and extend it almost immediately. More plausibly, that idea developed in the 1320s, as the new south-east chapel complex was erected and the chancel lost all direct light from the south. One of the most striking features about the added sanctuary bay is the way that its three great windows fill their respective walls entirely, flooding the high altar with light. A *terminus ante quem* of 1354 for the chancel extension is provided by the tomb of Judge Stonor, which obstructed access to the piscina of the previous phase (Figs 77 and 98).

None of the previous commentators appears to have recognized that the buttress in the middle of the east wall is an addition, and that it caused the destruction of the central lights of the window: the evidence, for this was clearly seen when the chancel was scaffolded in 2003.[75] In his brilliant discussion of the iconography of the sanctuary windows, Ayers concluded that there should have been a Crucifixion sculpture in the central section of the east window (in the second tier of lights), with a martyrdom of St Eustace in the tier above.[76] He was forced to hypothesize that, on account of the central buttress, these two critically important scenes had to be omitted from the sculptural programme, and were represented, off-centre, in stained glass alone. Now that we know the buttress is secondary, it can be appreciated that the original iconographic scheme reconstructed by Ayers could have been accommodated with complete symmetry.

The close similarity in detail between the south-east chapel and the rest of the present south chancel aisle, argues for the rebuilding of the latter to have followed soon after, and almost certainly before the sanctuary was extended. That just leaves the west tower, which had to fit somewhere relatively early in the sequence, and the south nave aisle which was undoubtedly the last addition. A date not earlier than *c.* 1350 for the latter seems likely.

The suggested sequence of reconstruction in 13th and 14th centuries may be summarized as follows:

c. 1230–50	Addition of two eastern chapels to the north transept. The south transept is likely to have been similarly treated.
c. 1250–60	Erection of a low, north-east aisle/chapel to the chancel. A similar addition may also have been made to the south.
c. 1280–1300	Raising the height of the north-east aisle/chapel, and uniting it with the inner transeptal chapel, to form a continuous aisle; new north arcade built.
c. 1280–1300	West tower built?
c. 1290–1300	Construction of the south-east chapel to the chancel and a (new or refurbished?) narrow south aisle; new south arcade built.
c. 1310–20	Remodelling of south chancel aisle and chapels to create the present wide aisle, as an enhanced setting for St Birinus's shrine (completed by *c.* 1320).
c. 1330–40	Eastward extension of the chancel, creating a new sanctuary; sedilia and piscina constructed last.
c. 1350–60	Addition of south nave aisle, replacing an earlier structure of unknown form (aisle or chapel).

The masons working at Dorchester in the last decade or two of the 13th century, and in the early part of the 14th, were both innovative and in touch with mainstream developments elsewhere in central southern England. The close connections with Oxford are obvious and not unexpected, but direct parallels may also be drawn with contemporary developments at Gloucester, Cheltenham and St Albans.[77]

Furnishings

The eastern arm of the abbey church would have been compartmented by screens, and much of the evidence for these survived until the early 19th century.[78] The entrance to the quire was marked by the pulpitum screen, a deep structure with a narrow central doorway. The pulpitum, which is shown on several early plans, survived until the mid-19th century, although it was dismantled and rebuilt in 1809.[79] It stood one bay east of the crossing, which may not have been its original position: the primary pulpitum is likely to have lain under the east crossing arch, being moved eastwards, either when the chancel was extended in the early 14th century, or perhaps after the Dissolution when the internal layout of the church contracted. Unfortunately, no record of the form of the pulpitum has been preserved, but it was constructed of timber and is most likely to have dated from the early 14th century. It may have served as the base for mounting an organ.[80] Stone pulpitum screens of this period remain in their original locations at Exeter and Wells cathedrals, but few timber pulpita have survived. At Hexham Abbey (Northumb.) a fine Tudor oak pulpitum occupies the eastern arch of the crossing, and at St Mary's Hospital, Chichester, a lightweight screen (without canopy) stands behind the return-stalls.[81]

Although no illustration of them has yet come to light, the return-stalls in the monastic quire were still *in situ* in the early 19th century, and are shown on several early plans (Fig. 6). Most likely the stalls were contemporary with the pulpitum screen. One bay (comprising five stalls, plus three on the return against the pulpitum) remained on each side, giving a total of sixteen stalls. The recorded number of canons did not exceed this (p. 38), and thus the stalls may never have occupied two bays. However, we cannot be certain.

Under the western crossing arch lay the rood screen, another timber structure carrying a loft. This screen separated the parochial nave from the monastic eastern arm. There would have been two doorways through this screen, with a nave altar (Holy Rood) placed centrally between them. The rood loft was accessed by a timber stair which was perhaps in the south aisle, being somehow integrated with the upper chapel or gallery there (p. 92); alternatively, the stair could have been in the crossing. The high-level doorway connecting the loft in the nave with the upper level in the aisle has already been noted (Figs 50 and 183).

The rood screen is likely to have been highly decorated with 'popish' imagery, and may therefore have been destroyed at the Reformation. Certainly, it had gone by the mid-17th century. The medieval oak screens that filled the arcade bays (3 and 4) on both sides of the quire were of two designs: there was quatrefoiled tracery on the north[82] and cinquefoiled tracery on the south (Figs 103 and 104).[83] The lower register of a different kind of screen also survives in its original position in the nave, under the arcade in bay 2.

The provision of stained glass, at least in the eastern arm of the church, seems to have been lavish in the 14th century, and included much heraldry. Of particular interest is the very rare combination of figurative glazing, labelling and related stone sculpture in the tracery (Pl. 9).[84] The remaining fragments of glass have been well described and discussed.[85]

The quire and sanctuary were paved with glazed tiles, some of which survived until the end of the 18th century.[86] Almost certainly, the dais in the south nave aisle would have been tiled too, and so may have other areas of the church: *e.g.* the threshold of the small doorway leading from the nave into the cloister was tiled, as were at least some parts of the cloister walks. For the rest of the church, all that survives today are a few complete and many broken pieces of inlaid tiles, all reset in the 19th century (Pl. 36).[87] Many of the tiles came from the prolific factory at Penn (Bucks.), others from Wiltshire.[88] No detailed study of medieval floor tiles in Oxfordshire has yet been published.[89]

The interior of the church was decorated with wallpaintings, of which traces survive in many parts.[90] The Crucifixion scene and the large cross in the recess, both in the south nave aisle, have long been known, and were the subject of considerable retouching by Clayton and Bell in 1863.[91] Indeed, two-thirds of the lower painting and the wallplaster behind it is Victorian.[92] The side walls of the sanctuary were once painted with 'lions, griffins and various fantastical effigies' which, in the 18th and early 19th centuries were observable beneath peeling limewash.[93] Traces of diapering were also noted in the back of the chancel sedilia, and in the south chancel aisle indications of other paintings were said to be visible. Recent investigations have confirmed that there is extensive medieval polychromy on the walls of the aisle, and a large figure of St Christopher holding the Christ Child has been uncovered between the windows of bays 1 and 2 (Pls 26 and 27).[94]

There were doubtless some very fine tombs of the period in the eastern arm, but only the Segrave and Stonor monuments (M.6 and M.14, respectively) survive today, together with other fragments in the lapidary collection. The Segrave monument (probably 1387), which was formerly in bay 4 of the chancel, against the north arcade screen, comprises two elements which do not necessarily go together (Figs 99 and 163). The highly ornate and once brilliantly coloured tomb chest is of clunch and dates from the end of the 14th century. Its identification with the Segrave family seems certain from the painted heraldry that it originally bore, and which was recorded in the 17th and 18th centuries. The knight's effigy, however, is of alabaster and does not fit comfortably on top of the chest, leading to the suggestion that the two are possibly a marriage. Nevertheless, they could perhaps have belonged together if the effigy had been partly encompassed in a shallow wall-recess behind the chest. Although the Segrave tomb was already in the chancel in the early 18th century, it must have been moved there, plausibly from the north transept chapel when that was demolished in the 17th century.

The monument to Judge Stonor (d. 1354) is, by contrast, very plain.[95] His recumbent effigy, with a canopy, lies on a low chest bearing the family arms. The tomb was originally located against the south side of the quire, where it obstructed the double piscina that had become redundant following the eastward extension of the sanctuary (Figs 77, 98 and 164B). The church was also graced with some fine brasses in the 14th century.[96]

Finally, two of the surviving bells date from the middle and latter part of the 14th century. The inscription on the tenor, which was given by Ralph Rastwold, invokes the protection of Birinus. There must have been a clock installed by this time too, because it was reported as being out of order in 1441.[97]

FIFTEENTH AND EARLY SIXTEENTH CENTURIES

This was a period when there was very little impact on the fabric of the church: the only surviving addition is a partly timber-framed porch, erected at the south doorway (Figs 46.9, 74 and 199). It dates

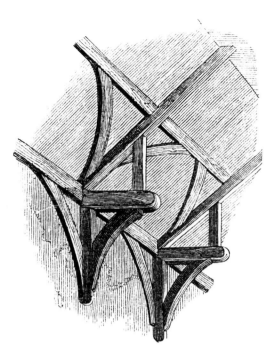

FIGURE 92. North chancel aisle: hammerbeam roof, destroyed in 1858. (Addington, 1845)

FIGURE 93. Crossing: south-east pier. The Norman masonry has been crudely cut back to form a ledge for a side-altar; view north-east. The limewash above the ledge conceals a fragmentary late medieval painting. (Warwick Rodwell)

from *c.* 1450–1500 and has a low pitched roof. In the north wall of the nave there is a small Tudor window set in a recess (Figs 173 and 174). Although no other architectural features in the Perpendicular style survive, there is a strong possibility that parts of the church were reroofed in lead in the 15th or early 16th century. Thus, the low-pitched roof over the chancel and part of the nave, seen in the earliest illustrations, was probably of that period (although it was renewed in the 18th century).[98] A fragment of low-pitched gable coping survives externally (p. 121), and there are stone corbels inside the western part of the chancel that must have supported wall-posts (p. 126). Until it was destroyed in 1858, a late medieval hammerbeam roof survived over the north aisle (Fig. 92). Other new works may have been carried out on the monastic buildings, as late medieval fragments in the lapidary collection attest.

Inside the church, it seems clear that the two great arches flanking the crossing were created in their present form during this period, although close dating is impossible. The ledges created in the eastern responds of both arches accommodated small side-altars or settings for devotional objects, and in the case of the southern arch there are the remains of a 15th-century reredos wallpainting on the plaster above (Fig. 93). Although very fragmentary, it appears to have depicted the Virgin and Child.[99] Moreover, the painting had been deliberately attacked and gouged, but was subsequently patched and repaired. This suggests reinstatement under Queen Mary of a previously mutilated image.

The presence of the altar setting expressly confirms a pre-Reformation date for the enlargement of the arches. Small side-altars were often placed against heavy masonry piers of this kind (*cf.* St Albans Abbey).[100] Had the modification of the crossing arches taken place in the 14th century, when funds were being lavished on the fabric, we should have expected the openings to be embellished with mouldings. Instead, the work was crudely executed, at minimum expense.

We also know a little about the furnishings and monuments of the period. Abbot Richard Beauforest (d. 1510) gave a new pair of benches for the quire (Fig. 119), and his memorial brass remains there too (Fig. 122).[101] The lead font bowl was placed on an octagonal stone base (now destroyed). This had simple trefoil-headed blind panels around its sides, and an embattled cornice moulding (Fig. 191).[102] More sepulchral brasses were installed in the chancel and chapels,[103] giving Dorchester one of the finest assemblages of brasses in any parish church, dating between the early 14th and the early 16th centuries. Antiquarian descriptions provide a depressing roll-call of what has been lost over the last two centuries.[104]

At least nineteen indents containing brass figures and inscriptions are known to have existed (Figs 122, 124 and 166; Pl. 20), and there were also several incised and inscribed medieval tomb-slabs. Finally, a pre-Reformation parcel-gilt chalice was still in the church in the 1540s, but its fate is not recorded.

NOTES

1 Bond, 1913, 254–69; Rodwell, 1989, 81–4.
2 In recent years, it has been demonstrated that the 'Northern' or 'long' Roman foot (33.5 cm) was extensively used in building construction in the Anglo-Saxon and early medieval periods. Units of 5 Nft (one-third of a rod) are commonly encountered (Huggins, *et al.*, 1982).
3 The suggestion of a pair of west towers is unsupported by evidence (Keevill, 2003, 360). The scale of the nave is too narrow to have carried a twin-towered façade. Had there been aisles, as at St German's, Cornwall (which has a nave of the same width as Dorchester), then externally flanking towers would have been feasible.
4 A recent suggestion that the Norman west end included a great ceremonial entrance flanked by a pair of buttress-like projections, *c.* 2.5 m square, containing staircases is fanciful, and is unsupported both by archaeological evidence and architectural precedent. A plan showing a twin-turreted west end, purporting to be based on evidence gathered in 2001–02, was included as an 'archaeological update' in the church guide-book (Bloxham, 2002).
5 The existing structure provides confirmation that there can never have been a pair of stair-turrets projecting into the nave, as at Bishop's Cleeve (Glos.), or Redcliffe, Bristol. Similarly, externally projecting turrets, as at Blythe Priory (Notts.), were only possible when aisles were present.
6 The usual reason for removing a west wall when constructing a tower was on account of its being too thin to support the intended new structure. This provides another hint that there was no monumental Romanesque west front at Dorchester.
7 Keevill, 2003, 346, fig. 22; 2005, 18, fig. 12; Britton, 1835, **5**, pl. 10.
8 When an aisle was added to a nave, the approach to the original doorway was commonly respected, and the new aisle door placed in a corresponding position; this was done for purely practical reasons relating to paths, access, etc. In this instance it is also likely that the west jamb of the Norman nave doorway was taken as a convenient point to site the respond of the 14th-century arcade.
9 References to this arch in the 18th and 19th centuries simply describe it as being 'in the nave'.
10 Parker, 1907, 63.
11 The west sides of the two transepts are not aligned, the wall of the north transept being offset westwards by 40–50 cm: this is presumably a residual anomaly from the 11th-century church.
12 The possibility that the transeptal chapels had 12th-century predecessors, as at Ewenny Priory (Glam.), cannot be entirely ruled out.
13 Clapham, 1934, pl. 11; Impey, 2008.
14 Clapham, 1934, pl. 9. Both the examples cited date from the late 11th century, but the type continues throughout the 12th century, although frequently embellished with mouldings and other decorative detail.
15 Bond, 1908b, 6. If the masonry between the upper and lower arches at Melton Constable were to be removed, the result would be remarkably similar to what we see at Dorchester.
16 Halsey, 1988, figs 55–7. Thurlby (2002, 242) also independently came to the conclusion that the openings from the crossing to the transepts at Dorchester were originally in two registers.
17 On the evidence of the surviving responds, and the level of the string-course, the maximum possible width for the transept arches can be estimated as *c.* 3 m (10 ft); *i.e.* equal to two-thirds of the width of the arch in the upper register (4.5 m). If, however, the transept arch was only 2.25 m wide, and the arch in the upper register was filled with two sub-arches, then a degree of symmetry between the upper and lower elements would have obtained.
18 Bond, 1908b, 27. The openings at Eartham are far too large to be classed as squints.
19 Anon. 1910, 333. Hope's plan reveals that he recognized that the transept arches at ground level were narrow and sited towards the west side of the crossing.
20 For its plan, see Blair, 1996, fig. 1.8.
21 Previously noticed by Richard Riddell and David Kendrick. The motif also occurs on the north doorway at Faringdon (Berks.): Keyser, 1911, pl. 17.
22 *E.g.* Skelton, 1823, 3–4; Addington, 1845, 32–4; Fryer, 1900, 44; Bond, 1908a; Clapham, 1934, 156, pl. 41; Druce, 1934; Zarnecki, 1957; Drake, 2002, 171, pl. 370.
23 Fryer, 1900, 44.
24 The font bowl at Brundall (Norf.) depicts the Crucifixion ten times; Childrey (Berks.) has twelve figures of bishops; Burghill (Herefs.) has thirteen arcaded figures; and Ashover (Derbys.) has an arcade with twenty un-nimbed figures.
25 The southern jamb and part of the arch of the piscina are visible in a viewing-pocket that was formed in the aisle wall during the Victorian restoration.
26 The Manor House at Dorchester has small pierced trefoils in the spandrels of the Gothick porch, its builder doubtless inspired by the abbey (Fig. 216).
27 RCHME, 1924, pl. 158.
28 Pevsner and Metcalf, 1985b, fig. 63.
29 Britton, 1836, pls 7 and 9; Pevsner and Metcalf, 1985b, fig. 93.
30 Dean, 1986, pl. 3.
31 Andrews, 1901, 22.
32 The deformity in the aisle wall is best appreciated from the parapet gutter, looking west from the stair-turret at the south-east corner. Bays 1 and 2 of the aisle (*i.e.* those on the site of the former transept and putative chapel) enjoy the same alignment; at the junction with bay 3 there is a slight kink, and another at the junction with bays 4–5. This strongly suggests that the 14th-

century aisle superseded a series of earlier structures on the same site.

33 Observations by Oxford Archaeology, when plaster was stripped from the north wall indicated that the masonry in the lowest 90 cm of wall is of markedly different construction from that above (Simons, 2004, 14). There may thus be an aisle-phase yet earlier than the two described here.

34 *Cf.* The north window in the tower of St Mary the Virgin, Oxford.

35 Hearn and Thurlby, 1997.

36 *Cal. Close Rolls, 1242–1247*, 39.

37 A few medieval timber vaults survive, as at Ely Cathedral, St Albans Abbey, York Minster and Warmington church (Northants.).

38 Ayers (1991, 12) also argues for the shrine having first been established in the north aisle, but soon after moved to the south, where it was more conveniently accessible to pilgrims without intruding upon the monastic quire.

39 Hearn and Thurlby, 1997, 53, pl. 15d.

40 W. Rodwell, 'St Chad's Head Chapel and Related Structures at Lichfield Cathedral: An Archaeological Survey', 38–9 (unpubl. ms, 1985; Lichfield Cathedral Library).

41 Bond, 1916, 207.

42 Miller and Saxby, 2007. At Merton, the aisles did not extend for the full length of the chancel.

43 This detail was first observed by Sharpe (1849, 80).

44 Bishop Oliver Sutton of Lincoln, who had recently consecrated an altar at Dorchester, issued an indulgence on 16 May 1292 to all who visited the shrine of St Birinus (Hill, 1954). I am grateful to Dr Ayers for drawing my attention to this previously overlooked reference (Ayers, 1991, 12).

45 This was explained by J.O. Scott in his ms notes on the architectural history of the church (*c.* 1885). The original position of the buttress is marked on several published plans: *cf.* for example Fig. 9.

46 Ballantyne, 2006.

47 Newton, 1979, 84.

48 The letters 'C' and 'T' of *Sanctvs* were ligatured, as shown in Carter's drawing of 1793: Bodl., Gough Maps, 227, f. 47. Bertram, 2003, fig. 21; Bond and Tiller, 2005, fig. 16.

49 Ballantyne, 2003.

50 The medieval monuments are numbered M.1 to M.24, following Paul's plan (1900). For further notes on individual monuments, see here the relevant sections of chapters 10, 12, 14 and 15.

51 Lankester, 1987.

52 Skelton, 1823, 4–5, pl. 1.

53 Robinson, 1914.

54 The wave-moulded doorway at the base of the tower must be 14th century, and no hint can be detected that it is a later insertion.

55 It has not been possible to determine whether there was an existing 13th-century aisle here, as on the north.

56 *Cf.* The 'spiked' quatrefoil windows at Cowley (Oxon.) and Billingborough (Lincs.) churches (Freeman, 1851, pl. 22.4; Sharpe, 1871, pl. 34); also at Cheltenham (Fig. 79). For further examples, see Sharpe, 1849.

57 Although the vaulted chapel had been erected in Phase 2, it was very small, and its enlargement westwards provided a more spacious setting for the shrine. For a discussion of stone vaulting in lesser churches, see Hoey, 1994.

58 This association was first pointed out by Ayers (1991).

59 Blatch, 1997, 94, fig. 15.

60 See the report on the preliminary examination of the shrine polychromy by Martin O'Connor of Nimbus Conservation, 'Polychrome Investigation on the Memorial to Gerald Allen at Dorchester Abbey, Oxon.' (January 2000).

61 Pevsner and Metcalf, 1985a, fig. 131.

62 Roberts, 1993a, fig. 47. For 14th-century shrine bases generally, see Coldstream, 1976.

63 The windows were also a favourite subject for antiquarian illustrators, and examples by Carter, Britton and Skelton are included here. They reveal significant changes to the stained glass.

64 When Cranston was architect, before Butterfield, he intended to reconstruct a symmetrical rose, as shown in a drawing prepared by Jewitt (Fig. 101A).

65 There is a modern replacement for the bar. Remains of medieval tying-bars spanning large traceried openings can be seen in the cloister at Salisbury Cathedral. A complete set of tying-bars dating from the 13th century survives in the triforium openings at Westminster Abbey.

66 Rodwell, forthcoming [2010], chapter 8.

67 For a discussion of the relationship between the stone and glass elements, see Ayers, 2002.

68 Addington, 1845, 39. For an unpublished view of the interior of the crypt by Jewitt, see: ORO, DD. Par. 6.12, 1.

69 Rosewell, 2008, fig. 62.

70 Freeman (1852, 277) first commented on this unusual arrangement of a passage and small doorway providing a low-key link between the two southern aisles. He further drew an analogy with St David's Cathedral, which has small doorways instead of the usual open arches between the transepts and the nave aisles.

71 Rodwell, 1993.

72 An unpublished study of the archaeological evidence was carried out by the writer in 2000–01.

73 See principally: Addington, 1845; Newton, 1979; Ayers, 1991; Ayre, 2002.

74 Ayers, 1991.

75 However, Ayers recognized that the lower part of the buttress was not bonded to the masonry beneath the east window, and suggested that it represented a modification whilst building was in progress.

76 Ayers, 1991, 50–1.

77 Ayers, 1991.

78 Vallance, 1947, 100–1; Howard, 1910.

79 Skelton, 1823, 8. The screen, which was referred to as the 'gallery', was rebuilt in the nave, where it is shown but not labelled on Jewitt's plan of 1845: see here Fig. 7.

80 There was an organ of unknown age mounted on this screen until the early 19th century, when it was moved to the west end of the nave.

81 Tracy, 1987, pl. 28.

82 Seen in one of Carter's drawings of 1792, behind the Segrave tomb.

83 Measured drawings were made by Jewitt in 1844 (Addington, 1845, 28–9). The Victorian replacement screens are similar to these, but the buttresses and sill have been modified.

84 See especially Ayers, 1991.

85 Newton, 1979.

86 Mentioned by Stukeley in 1736 (Bodl., Gough Maps, 26, f. 42B(c)), and published in Gough, 1789, 307. Stukeley refers to both patterned tiles and 'little triangular bits with borders'. Whether he was describing conventional paving using bands of diagonally-cut half-tiles (*i.e.* triangles), or to true mosaic work, is unclear. In the early 19th century, the chancel was still 'paved with glazed tiles, within the rails' (Brewer, 1813, 376).

87 Most of the pieces are assembled in a strip under the arcade in bay 2 of the south nave aisle; a few others are scattered in the floor of the nave.

88 Two complete tiles from Dorchester are in the British Museum: Eames, 1980, cat. nos 11,419 and 11,420. One tile is from the Penn factory, the other from a Wessex source.

89 For the earliest study of medieval floor tiles in Oxfordshire, see Church, 1845 (Dorchester, pls 18 and 19). For a fuller listing of the Dorchester tiles, see Haberly, 1937, pls 1, 3, 15, 20, 22, 26, 29, 31, 32, 42, 43, 44, 51, 54, 57, 77, 188, 238, 242, and fragment 'X' on p. 304.

90 Keyser, 1883, 87–8; Tristram, 1955, 165–6; Long, 1972, 95; Ballantyne, 2003.

91 Addington, 1845, 12; Keyser, 1883, 87–8; Tristram, 1955, 165–6.

92 Ballantyne, 2006.

93 Brewer, 1813, 376; *The Ecclesiologist*, **5** (1846), 24.

94 Ballantyne, 2003; 2006

95 Stonor, 1952.

96 Bertram, 2000, nos 2, 8, 9, 11, 12, 15, 16. See here monuments M.3, M.7, M.13, M.19, M.20 and M.21.

97 VCH, 1907, 88.

98 Steeply pitched roofs on many churches were lowered in the late Middle Ages and covered with sheet lead, and it was not uncommon for the apices of large windows to be truncated in the process, as is the case with the rose in the east window at Dorchester. The fact that some internal illustrations show 18th-century trusses over the chancel (Fig. 102) does not prove that the pitch of the roof was not lowered at a much earlier date.

99 Ballantyne, 2006.

100 Roberts, 1993b; Rosewell, 2008, fig. 188.

101 Field, 1909.

102 Bond and Tiller, 2005, fig. 21.

103 Bertram, 2000, nos 17–19, 21–25, 28, 29, 31–33. See here monuments M.1, M.2, M.4, M.8, M.11, M.12, M.15, M.15a, M.17, M.18, M.22 and M.23.

104 For a summary catalogue of the extant and lost monuments, see Bertram, 2000.

CHAPTER 8

After the Dissolution: Architectural History of the Parish Church, 1536–1844

LATER SIXTEENTH CENTURY

The Augustinian abbey was dissolved in 1536, and its properties appropriated by the Crown. The monastic buildings, excluding the church, were sold to Sir Edmund Ashfield of Ewelme (Oxon.) in 1544. The eastern arm of the church was purchased by Richard Beauforest for £140. In an act of great public spiritedness, Beauforest bequeathed his part of the church to the townspeople, who were already in possession of the nave. In so far as we know, SS Peter and Paul henceforth became the only parish church of Dorchester, and the fate of the other three to which Leland made reference is not known (and their parochial status may be questionable): they were probably converted to domestic use. In his will, dated 13 July 1554, Beauforest desired to be buried in the Lady Aisle, but whether that was on the north or the south side of the chancel is unspecified, although the former is more likely.

No records have survived to show how and when the claustral buildings of the abbey were destroyed. Almost certainly the abbot's lodging occupied the west range, and was converted by Ashfield into a residence known as 'The Abbey' (p. 40). The north range is likely to have been adapted for ancillary use, and the east range demolished; gardens would have been laid out on its site, stretching down to the river. The former inner monastic court to the west would have become an entrance courtyard and yards associated with the house, and a new access from High Street or Queen Street was probably created.

The footprint of the cloister survived down to the 18th century, or even later, as a formal garden. The geophysical survey revealed a miscellany of features, including walls running diagonally across two of the corners of the cloister, which are easier explained as post-Dissolution than as monastic. A prominent pit-like feature revealed in the centre of the garth may have been a fountain, or just a tree. The new post-monastic residence survived at least until the mid-17th century,[1] and in 1657 the gardens on the site of the cloister were described as 'the walkes on ye north side of the abbey and church'.[2] In 1736, Stukeley confirmed that part of the claustral range, north-west of the church, was still occupied as a residence (p. 42).

Little can be discovered regarding works carried out on the church in the early years of its life as a purely parochial building. Judging by the dilapidated state of the structure in the next century, little if anything was done. In 1591 another bell (now the sixth) was added to the medieval tower, seemingly opening a new phase of care and concern for the building.

It may be appropriate to notice here that, with the exception of the north aisle, and possibly the westernmost bay of the nave, none of the medieval roofs of Dorchester Abbey survived beyond the mid-18th century, and at least one (south nave aisle) was gone by 1633. Either this betokens wholesale neglect in the 16th and 17th centuries, or a catastrophe, or a combination of both. The great majority of medieval churches retained at least some of their ancient roofs until 'restorers' replaced them the mid-19th century: today, all the roofs at Dorchester are Victorian, but their predecessors were mainly 17th and 18th century, not medieval. The loss of the stone vaulting at the east end of the south chancel aisle is likely to have occurred in the 16th century, and the many moulded timbers in the present 19th-century roof were probably reused from a compartmented ceiling of Tudor date that formerly covered this aisle (Fig. 161).

The possibility that a fire or lightning strike caused serious damage to the tower and roofs may be considered, but no firm conclusions can be drawn. Certainly, there is a modest amount of evidence for fire, but not for a serious conflagration. First, a large limestone slab on the floor of the south nave aisle is patchily burnt, although that is more likely the result of a brazier having stood here, either for heating the church or for plumbers' works. Secondly, there is some burning on the internal masonry at the top of the tower stair, which can hardly be explained other than by a fire in the roof. The evidence is consistent with burning timbers falling into the stairwell, scorching the steps and lining. If the stairwell masonry at this high level is 14th century, then the fire could be of any subsequent date. On the other hand, if the top of the stair was rebuilt in 1602, a *terminus post quem* for any fire is indicated.[3] Thirdly, several patches of fire reddening occur on the effigy of Judge Stonor, and these can only be the result of

FIGURE 94. *Tower: south face, showing the incorporation of an earlier stair-turret at the south-east angle. (Warwick Rodwell)*

FIGURE 95. *Tower: the hexagonal stair-turret inside the ringing chamber. (Warwick Rodwell)*

burning débris falling on the tomb. The fire must either have occurred in the chancel roof above, or in the stalls. However, since sixteen return-stalls and several timber screens survived into the 19th century, and two medieval benches are extant today, there cannot have been a devastating, low-level fire in the chancel. Hence, it would seem unlikely that the main medieval roofs were lost through fire, and the enigma remains.

SEVENTEENTH CENTURY

The 17th century was a time when consolidation of the church fabric took place, separating what was required for parochial worship from the residue of the dissolved monastery. The process probably began with the tower at the west end in 1602 (Figs 38 and 204; Pls 1 and 2). Here, the church was linked to a range of late medieval buildings that included the inner monastic gatehouse and adjoining guest house. Embodied in this complex was a tower, but it was not a discrete structure that could stand alone when the gatehouse was demolished; nor is it likely to have been feasible to adapt the existing masonry to form a bell tower. Consequently, only the 14th-century newel stair in its irregular hexagonal turret was retained and incorporated in a new tower (Figs 94 and 95). Why the west wall of the nave was not also retained is unclear, but it was not, and the north wall

was also cut back to some extent: the new tower with octagonal buttresses on three corners, was erected almost as a free-standing unit. The north wall of the nave was then reinstated as an abutment to it, at the same time creating the unexplained high-level recess that incorporates the window in bay 5.[4]

The new tower was a costly undertaking, especially since its buttresses were decorated with flint flushwork in the late Gothic tradition (Figs 206 and 207). Indeed, the tower almost appears to have been a conscious display of antiquarianism: the windows of the ringing chamber have a Romanesque appearance (Fig. 209) but are not recycled features from the Norman abbey; and the belfry openings could be mistaken for 13th-century work (Fig. 94). However, the Oxford region is renowned for the local retention and adaptation of the Gothic style throughout the 16th and 17th centuries, and down to the onset of the Gothick Revival in the mid-18th. The person responsible for rebuilding the tower is recorded only by his initials and date, 'J.W. 1602'. Not surprisingly, the new tower attracted additional bells: the fourth and fifth are dated 1603 and 1606, respectively, and they were joined by the third in 1651. The remaining, and now entirely separate, element of the gatehouse complex (the monastic guest house), was converted into a school by John Fettiplace in 1652.

Sometime, presumably in the early 17th century (if not the late 16th), the part-ruined north transept,

FIGURE 96. *North chancel aisle: reset transeptal chapel window in bay 2. Note the disjuncture with the medieval string-course in the adjoining bay to the left (cf. Figure 135). (Warwick Rodwell)*

FIGURE 97. *North chancel aisle: 'Churchwarden Gothick' window in the blocking wall of the truncated north transept, bay 1. (Warwick Rodwell)*

together with the more northerly of the two transeptal chapels, was remodelled (Fig. 136). The remaining half of the transept and one surviving chapel were incorporated in the north chancel aisle, increasing it from three bays to five (Fig. 46.10). The north wall of the aisle had to be extended westwards, and that was done partly using salvaged materials. The fine 14th-century east window from the northern chapel was carefully dismantled and reconstructed in the new north aisle wall in bay 2 (Fig. 96). It was even provided with a string-course below the sill, although this did not connect properly with the string in the adjacent bay to the east (Fig. 135).

This stands in marked contrast to the new wall and window installed in bay 1 (Fig. 97). There, the blocking wall is thinner, the masoncraft cruder, and there is no string-course. The window itself is in essence a 'domestic' four-light mullioned and transomed window, which has been conflated with a pointed head and Y-tracery: it could date from any time in the 17th century. It is difficult to envisage the alterations to bays 1 and 2 both being of the same date; hence, two phases are probably represented. Although the two tall arches marking the former entrances to the transepts have sometimes been attributed to the 17th century, on account of their unconventional form, they are demonstrably earlier (p. 70).[5]

The condition of the church during the Commonwealth is unrecorded, and there is no substantive evidence that it suffered much damage during the Civil War. The only record is Wood's assertion that some of the glass figures in the Jesse window were broken by Parliamentarian soldiers.[6]

As noted above, almost the entire church was reroofed in the 17th and 18th centuries: while there may have been a localized roof fire, the need for most of this work can only be put down to neglect, allowing the timberwork to decay beyond repair. The steeply pitched roof of the south nave aisle was removed and replaced with a parallel pair of gabled roofs of much smaller scale; they were tiled. One of the beams bore the date 1633. In order to form the central valley gutter to this roof, the west window of the aisle had to be destroyed: the top of the arch was removed and the entire aperture was infilled with masonry (Fig. 74).[7] It is likely that the porch roof was raised in pitch and tiled at the same time.[8]

Prior to its Victorian reconstruction, the nave roof presented an odd spectacle: three-quarters of it had been reduced to a very low pitch, and was lead covered, while the westernmost one-quarter, abutting the tower, was steeply pitched, half-hipped, and covered with clay tiles (frontispiece; Pl. 3). Whether that was a surviving medieval fragment cannot now be determined, but it seems very likely.[9] Some of the timber reused by Scott in his new roof came from a 17th-century roof, and dendrochronology revealed that one of the trees had been felled in the second quarter of the 17th century.[10]

Dorchester is exceptional in possessing Wood's sketch plan and description of the church in 1657.[11] Although the proportions are awry,[12] the major components are identifiable on his plan, and are listed in the accompanying key (Fig. 4). Several interesting points emerge. First, the nave and chancel are shown as separated by a solid wall with a central doorway: if this was the medieval pulpitum screen, it was one bay further east than would be expected (at chancel bay 2/3). However, a timber screen appears in the same position on Harris's plan of *c.* 1720 and Carter's plan of 1793 (see further, p. 105). Second, the chancel seems to have been separated from its aisles by substantial partitions, rather than openwork screens (a not uncommon occurrence at this period).[13] Wood's plan does not mark furnishings, but Harris shows a pulpit against the north-east crossing pier, and the font in the centre of the nave (Fig. 6). Whether the pulpit was Jacobean, or a medieval one that had been resited from the parochial nave, cannot be determined: either way, it was superseded in 1745. Third, Wood was at pains to mark and list all the doorways. Thus, while the south porch is inexplicably omitted from the plan, the entrance was described as 'the great door thro[ugh] wh[ich] the parishioners go into ye body of the church'. The adjacent west door was noted and, surprisingly, so too was the tiny external opening into the crypt: 'the door in the ch[urch] yard yt goes into ye charnell house under one of the S. isles'.

On the north side of the church, Wood depicted and described a succession of doors leading out of the nave and crossing, into the north chancel aisle and thence into the south cloister walk. Although doubtless incorporating elements of the monastic cloister, the latter was now apparently an enclosed passage, the purpose of which was to provide covered access from 'The Abbey' house,[14] to what was almost certainly a private pew established in the former north aisle[15] (Fig. 46.10). The passage had a pitched roof, and the pockets for its rafters are discernible in the north wall of the nave; three still retain the ends of the timbers.

It was probably Ashfield who created this arrangement, after purchasing the dissolved abbey and establishing a manorial seat in the buildings of the inner court.[16] The layout recorded by Wood has an incidental but important corollary: the Norman doorway in the west wall of the aisle was not blocked at this time, and therefore the fragments of Birinus's shrine that were recovered from its filling in 1858

could not have been put there at the Dissolution.

On his plan, Wood labelled the chancel, the nave ('body of the church'), the north aisle and two south aisles, supplying further details in his commentary.[17] Thus, when speaking of the chancel he was referring to bays 4 and 5 only, while the 'quier' evidently occupied bay 3. The Communion table stood in the middle of the quire. Wood also referred to 'the tower that now is, is but of late standing; the staircase old', thus independently confirming the 17th-century rebuild.[18]

Wood listed and discussed all the historic memorials in the church, from which it is readily apparent that the interior had changed little since Leland's day. Only three effigial tombs were present, the fourth having disappeared (it was rediscovered in the 18th century: pp. 154–5). No mention of Birinus's shrine occurs, but steps up to former altar daises at the ends of the north and south aisles were noted. The surviving monuments, mostly floor slabs, were concentrated in the chancel (including the quire) and south aisle; there was a defaced slab reported to be in the north aisle, and only one in the nave (and that was at the quire door).

EIGHTEENTH CENTURY

The Fettiplace manor (one of two Dorchester manors) fell into demise in the 17th century. Part of 'The Abbey' had become the grammar school in 1652, the enclosed 'cloister' passage along the north side of the church disappeared during the 18th century, and the doorways that opened from it into the nave and transept were blocked.[19] The blocking had occurred before *c.* 1780, when Grimm illustrated the doorways, and Buckler's sketch of the north side of the church in 1801 shows no encumbrances, although we should be mindful that artists frequently omitted what they considered to be irrelevant.

The interior layout of the church in the 18th century is reconstructible from contemporary illustrations and descriptions, and there is no reason to believe that it had changed greatly since the Reformation, until the chancel was refurnished in 1745. There was of course only one altar, and that was sited in the sanctuary, where it was raised by two steps and enclosed by a low oak rail with turned balusters. Against the east wall stood a classical timber reredos with a broken pediment, in the centre of which was an open book on a pedestalled book-rest. The top of the 1745 reredos appears in one of Grimm's drawings, *c.* 1780: it was tripartite, and was doubtless painted with the usual texts (*Lord's Prayer*, *Decalogue* and *Creed*). The reredos is similarly glimpsed in Neale's drawing of 1824.[20] It obstructed the lower part of the east window, which was partly infilled, as shown by Skelton in 1823 (Fig. 99). The flanking walls were panelled too, causing the sedilia in the south wall of

FIGURE 98. Chancel: Britton's view of the interior in 1821. The majority of the furniture has been omitted, including the Georgian reredos. (Britton, 1835)

the chancel to be obstructed.[21] Moreover, the fronts of the stone seats, and the bases of the shafts of the sedilia, had been 'entirely cut away to make room for the woodwork'.[22]

The chancel pavement was relaid as part of the refurbishment, and a ceiling was supposedly installed, but this does not appear to have been accomplished

until much later. The low-pitched chancel roof shown in Buckler's view of 1812–13 depicts an unembellished tie-beam construction with king-posts and raking struts, dating from the mid-18th century.[23] However, views of the chancel between 1821 and 1824 confirm that a plain ceiling was then in place (Figs 98 and 99).[24]

FIGURE 99. *Chancel and aisles: Skelton's view before restoration. The screens and all furnishings have been omitted, except the three major medieval tombs. Note the font on the dais in the south aisle.* (Skelton, 1823)

The quire was still furnished with monastic stalls and medieval tombs (Fig. 99), and there was a screen located one bay east of the presumed original site of the medieval pulpitum (*i.e.* at bay 2/3 junction). The screen marked the liturgical division between nave and chancel. The easternmost one-third of the old (architectural) nave, together with the former crossing, sufficed to house the congregation, and this area was completely enclosed with partitions. The screen and partitions were already in place by 1657. Part of the former north transept was brought back into use for seating, which obstructed the now-blocked doorway in the west wall. The arrangement is shown in Harris's plan of *c.* 1720 (Fig. 6). While the sizeable gothick window in bay 1 of the re-formed aisle could belong to this phase, it is more likely to be earlier (p. 101).[25] A vestry was created at the east end of the north aisle, in what had probably been the Ashfield/Fettiplace private pew. A three-decker pulpit was erected against the north-east crossing pier, and is captured in Neale's view of 1824. The Georgian pulpit must have replaced the medieval or Jacobean one that was there in c. 1720.

The seating for the congregation consisted of box-pews with high panelled sides and doors to keep draughts at bay: 18th-century plans show three rows of pews occupying the crossing and part of the chancel (bays 1–2) west of the pulpit, and also continuing into the west end of the north aisle; two blocks of pews filled the eastern part of the old nave (Fig. 6).

The two south aisles and the west end of the nave appear to have been almost devoid of furnishings, and in 1845 it was reported that they were still partitioned off with walls of lath-and-plaster, and were 'either wholly unoccupied or used for the reception of the parish engines'.[26] It was common for fire engines to be kept in churches at this period, and the double doors in the west wall of the nave aisle provided ready access.

It is noticeable that most if not all of the windows in the north and south sides of the church had their lowest sections infilled with brick, a detail that is consistently indicated on 18th- and early 19th-century illustrations (Pl. 3).[27] Infilling the bottoms of windows was a common occurrence where box-pews and wainscoting provided obstructions; it also helped to reduce draughts from broken and ill-fitting glazing. With the exception of part of the north aisle, there is no suggestion that the aisles at Dorchester were ever pewed before the mid-19th century: the lower parts of the windows were nevertheless infilled.

The nave and aisles were repaved in 1757, and that is likely to have been the occasion when the effigy attributed to Bishop Aeschwyn was rediscovered, and placed on the dais at the end of the south nave aisle (M.16: Fig. 165). The font stood axially in the west part of the nave (bay 3),[28] where it must have been when Grimm drew it. At that time it had a tall, pointed octagonal cover.[29]

The ground-stage of the tower was subdivided into two levels before *c.* 1720. A floor was inserted at about window sill level, and access to the mezzanine room thus created was through an external doorway which was formed by enlarging one of the lights in the south window. The doorway was approached via a short flight of steps in the churchyard (Figs 5 and 7).[30] The mezzanine floor was a large but ill-lit space with unplastered walls; there is no indication as to the use it served.

It is noteworthy that there are no grand tombs or even important wall monuments of the 17th or 18th centuries, and nor have they been lost.[31] The families that held the two manors in Dorchester were not long-term residents, and hence have not left a legacy of memorials.[32] However, there were some middle-ranking monuments of the Georgian era: one was mentioned as being of black marble, and having columns (Francis Dandridge, d. 1714). The remains only of its inscription panel are now in the floor of the nave, against the north wall.

EARLY NINETEENTH CENTURY

After 1807, but prior to the great Victorian restoration, various minor changes and improvements occurred. They are mostly undocumented. In 1806–07 the remaining medieval glass in the church was collected together and arranged in the chancel windows.[33] In 1809, the font was moved from the nave to the dais at the east end of the south chancel aisle (Figs 99 and 191A).[34] The pulpitum was removed and made into a gallery at the back of the nave, and the medieval return-stalls were also probably ejected at the same time. Certainly, all had been swept away by 1824, when Neale produced the only known drawing of the furnished chancel in its pre-Victorian state.[35] Other antiquarian views of the same era contain a good deal of artistic licence where furnishings are concerned. Thus, Britton's drawing of 1821, does not show the classical reredos, but only a simple draped table, flanked by a pair of sanctuary chairs (Fig. 98).[36] Skelton shows an entirely empty chancel (Fig. 99).[37] Addington supplies a cryptic observation: 'The Communion-table is *ingeniously* contrived to serve likewise for a chest'.[38] Two Communion tables have survived at Dorchester – one early Georgian, the other late Georgian Gothick (p. 127) – but neither fits this description. It may be that a separate chest was installed underneath one of these tables.

Unspecified 'alterations and repairs' were carried out in 1836, which may have included erecting a chancel screen at the junction of bays 2 and 3. Adjoining this was a three-decker pulpit with steps against the south arcade pier: the pulpit must have been moved from its former location against the

FIGURE 100. *Chancel and south-east chapels, before restoration. One of the thatched cottages on the edge of the churchyard is also shown.* (Skelton, 1823)

north-east crossing pier. The choir stalls were shunted further east, being placed in front of the two major medieval tombs flanking the chancel. Jewitt's pre-restoration plan of 1844 captured the final Georgian layout (Fig. 7). The east end of the nave (bay 2, and one-quarter of bay 3) was enclosed by screens, and against the north wall was a flight of steps leading to an organ gallery over the west end of this enclosure.

Despite the various works carried out in the preceding two centuries, the fabric of the church was clearly not in good condition, if Skelton's exterior view of the east end in 1823 is to be believed (Fig. 100), and there were calls for restoration. They were heeded in 1844.

NOTES

1 It is clear that Wood's several mentions of 'The Abbey' in 1657 refer to a post-Dissolution residence immediately to the north-west of the church, and not to the former monastery in general. More recently, a house on the High Street frontage, adjoining the lychgate, has been named 'The Priory'; there is no connection between the two.

2 Again, this emphasizes that 'The Abbey' was an existing and separate structure from the church.

3 Archaeological investigation could resolve this matter.

4 The cutting back applies only to the nave wall above string-course level; below it, the Norman masonry is intact right up to the tower buttress. This was visible both externally (before the pentice was erected) and internally, when the wallplaster was renewed in 2002.

5 Cf. Taunt, 1906, 18.

6 Davis, 1922, 118.

7 The outline of the window is faintly indicated on Carter's sketch of 1792; there were also putlog holes shown in the blocking masonry: BL, Add. Ms 29,931, f. 179. Other artists omitted to record this critical evidence.

8 Raising the porch roof substantially obstructed the aisle window above. The aisle and porch roofs appear in several views, from c. 1780 onwards: e.g. BL, Add. Ms 15,545, f. 135; Ms 36,405, ff. 50, 51.

9 In the 19th century it was reported that Scott had found evidence for the 'Norman' roof, but no details were given.

10 See chap. 14, note 38.

11 Clark, 1891.

12 The north and south aisles are shown as being of similar width, when the latter is actually twice the width of the former; also the north aisle has been made too short, and with it the division between nave and chancel has been pushed eastwards.

13 The medieval timber screens may well have been covered on both faces with lath-and-plaster; when planned, they could then give the appearance of being substantial walls.

14 The Abbey was evidently the seat of the Fettiplace manor.

15 At the east end of the cloister passage are labelled 'the two doors going out of the cloister to ye north isle and from this N. isle into ye body of ye ch[urch]'. To the west, the passage had been extended beyond the nave, and along the north side of the tower, where we find 'the door leading from ye Abbey into ye cloister and so thro[ugh] the north isle into ye church'.

16 The Fettiplaces were descendants of the Ashfields.

17 Wood's detailed description of monuments and stained glass was not included in Clark, 1891, but was separately published in Davies, 1922, 114–23.

18 Clark, 1891, 225.

19 Addington's plan of 1845 is thoroughly misleading in showing the cloister passage, which had long gone: he copied that from Wood's plan.

20 Bodl., MS Top. Oxon. b.283, f. 12; reproduced in Doggett, 2005, fig. 35.

21 'The sedilia are now boarded up as high as the piscina with the modern panelling which surrounds the chancel.' (Addington, 1845, 11).

22 Addington, 1845, 11, 12.

23 The roof is of a distinctive kind championed by Francis Price, surveyor to Salisbury Cathedral and author of The British Carpenter (London, 1733, et seq.). The construction uses multiple, closely spaced purlins, with the boarding for the lead laid in vertical lines rather than horizontal.

24 Britton's view is dated 1821 (Britton, 1835, 5, pl. 63). Skelton also shows a ceiling in or before 1823, and Neale in 1824 (Doggett, 2005, fig. 35).

25 The window was certainly in existence by c. 1720. Buckler's sketch of 1801 shows that the lower part had by then been infilled with brick.

26 Addington, 1845, 2, 6, 35.

27 By 1720 the windows in the south nave aisle had been partly infilled (Fig. 5), and in 1823 Skelton indicated blocking in two windows of the north aisle (Fig. 99). Confirmation of the latter is provided by Buckler in 1809 (Doggett, 2005, fig. 33) and Jewitt in 1845 (Fig. 130).

28 Shown first on Harris's plan of c. 1720 (Stevens, 1722, 95); then on Stukeley's plan of 1768 (Bodl., Gough Maps, 26, f. 42B); also on Carter's plan of 1792, and in his sketch (BL, Add. Ms 29,931, f. 181).

29 BL, Add. Ms 15,545, f. 149.

30 The entrance and steps are shown on Harris's plan and view of c. 1720, and on many later illustrations. The steps were omitted from Grimm's watercolour drawing of c. 1780.

31 Details of all the significant monuments inside the church, including their full inscriptions, seem to have been noted in the 1807 account of the church: Bodl., MS Top. Oxon. b.220.

32 The Fettiplaces are commemorated by fine monuments, but they are in Swinbrook church (Sherwood and Pevsner, 1974, 800), and the Daveys of Overy were recusants (Davey, 1897). The latter maintained their own chapel, initially in a barn, until they built the Roman Catholic church of St Birinus in Dorchester in 1848 (Tiller, 2005, 68–70).

33 Skelton, 1823, 4n.

34 Ibid., 8, pl. 1.

35 Doggett, 2005, fig. 35.

36 Britton, 1835, 5, pl. 63.

37 Skelton, 1823, pl. 5.

38 Addington, 1845, 12 (his italics).

CHAPTER 9

Dorchester Abbey Restored, 1844–2007

VICTORIAN RESTORATION, 1844–1883

Four architects successively made their mark on Dorchester Abbey during the forty-year restoration (see also Chapter 5). Following a survey in 1844, work began on site in 1845 under James Cranston, a little-known architect.[1] He was superseded in 1847 by William Butterfield, one of the most prominent architects of the mid-Victorian era, who was elected an honorary member of the Oxford Architectural Society in 1848. His involvement at Dorchester seems to have petered out in 1853–54,[2] followed by a hiatus until 1858, when (Sir) George Gilbert Scott was appointed, and he continued in office until the restoration reached semi-completion in 1874.[3] There was then another period of inactivity (during which Scott died), before James Maltby Bignell supervised some relatively minor works in the early 1880s.

Cranston restored the north and south windows of the chancel, but within two years he was dismissed because his proposals were too costly to be fully enacted.[4] His builder was John Castle of Oxford. In 1846, the Society asked another of its members, James Park Harrison, to prepare designs for the restoration of the east window.[5] The tracery in the central light and apex had been mutilated, first by the erection of the medieval medial buttress, and secondly by the lowering of the roof sometime between the 16th and early 18th centuries. Harrison investigated the largely destroyed circle at the apex and discovered evidence for the form of the tracery that had filled it. He was about to restore it when an extraordinary dispute arose over payment, and Harrison resigned before anything was done: he wished to give his architectural services *gratis*, but the offer was declined by the restoration committee of the OAS.[6]

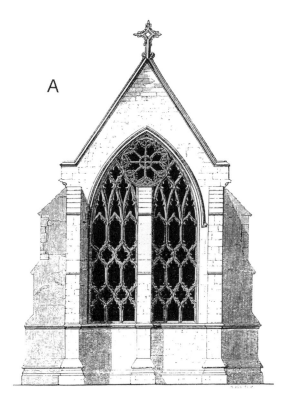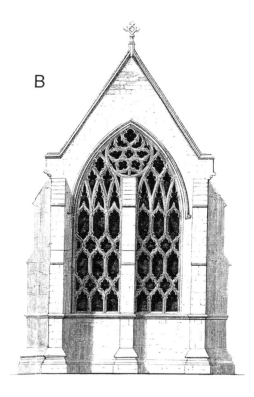

FIGURE 101. *Chancel: east window. A. Cranston's proposed restoration, 1845. B. Butterfield's restoration, 1847. Cf. Figure 82. (Addington, 1845; 1882)*

FIGURE 102. Chancel: interior before 1858, looking east, showing Butterfield's restoration. (Dorchester Abbey Museum)

Butterfield was then engaged, and restoration assumed a new direction, which itself led to local tensions. His principal task was to restore the remainder of the chancel.[7] In 1847, he replaced the low-pitched roof of the eastern part with the present steeply pitched one. For repairing the delicate stonework, Butterfield employed the reputable London carvers, G.P. White of Pimlico and John Thomas.[8] His asymmetrical restoration of the tracery of the 'rose' was controversial (Fig. 101B), and Freeman inveighed against it: 'Mr Butterfield's completion of the window appears to me to be open to very great doubt and criticism; he has made the circle not complete, but flowing into the lines of the arch. I do not remember the remaining fragments gave any grounds for supposing that so unusual and unpleasing an arrangement ... formed part of the original design. I strongly opposed this freak – for it is nothing more – at the time'.[9]

Thus the present form of the rose tracery may owe more to Butterfield's arrogance than to archaeological evidence. Moreover, for some reason that is hard to fathom, the idea of intruding a massive and ugly buttress into the centre light of an east window appealed to Butterfield to the extent that he copied the arrangement at Dorchester in his new church of St Matthias, Stoke Newington (1850).[10] This is an exemplar of what Sir John Summerson aptly described as Butterfield's 'glory of ugliness'.[11]

Butterfield's waggon roof over the eastern part of the chancel is a magnificent, if expensive, construction which in his repertoire is matched only at Amesbury Abbey (1852–53). He also fitted the chancel with new oak screens under the arcades, designed the pulpit, and installed the nave benches (Fig. 102). Here, the Incorporated Church Building Society became involved, making a grant towards the work on condition that the majority of the seating was free and unreserved for all parishioners.[12] A plan showing work completed down to 1854 has survived,[13] and a rare cast iron plaque in the south nave aisle records the basic details (Fig. 195). The design for the arcade screens was based on the existing 14th-century one on the south side, which was described as 'a very good wooden screen, of the Decorated style'.[14] Regrettably, Butterfield destroyed the original, but incorporated some of the medieval traceried heads in his new work in one bay (Figs 76, 103 and 104).

He was also responsible for reflooring the chancel and ejecting the medieval sepulchral effigies from their original locations. The east wall was garishly decorated with polychromatic tiling and panels of marble (Pl. 16), while the north and south walls of the sanctuary were painted in imitation of tiling. All three walls carried inscriptions, but they may have been added in 1863. The altar was raised on a tiled step, and had a dossal behind. A plain, 'ranch-type'

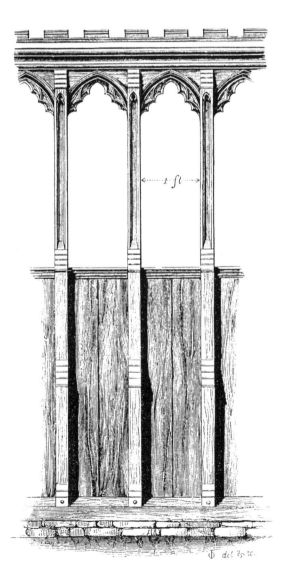

FIGURE 103 (left). Chancel: medieval screen under the south arcade, before its reconstruction by Butterfield. (Addington, 1845)

FIGURE 104 (below). Chancel: medieval screen under the south arcade, as rebuilt by Butterfield. View from the south-east. (Warwick Rodwell)

FIGURE 105. Chancel: Butterfield's oak pulpit, 1853. (Warwick Rodwell)

communion rail was erected on the sanctuary step. Butterfield's oak pulpit was typically Spartan, and attracted contemporary criticism (Fig. 105).[15] The plain iron handrail has a newel with a curious metal finial.

Butterfield had a hand in some of the glazing and first commissioned Michael O'Connor to produce work for the chancel (1847–48), but he did not like the result, describing it as 'very bad'. This was presumably the glazing for the rose in the east window (Pls 10 and 11). For the remainder of that window Butterfield thankfully decided to restore the medieval glass, rather than introduce new work.[16] In 1853–54, he commissioned John Hardman to make new east windows for the south-east chapels, but it is doubtful whether the work was ever carried out.[17] The fabric of the chapels was not restored for another twenty years, and in 1874 Hardman produced the present windows for Scott.[18]

Although Butterfield drew up abortive plans for restoring the remainder of the church, these have not survived. His other work included installing the font on its present plain stone base (Fig. 190),[19] which suggests that he was responsible for moving the font from the east end of the south aisle to the position that it briefly occupied under the south crossing arch. That cannot, however, be the case because the font was already in its new position in 1845.[20] Claims that Butterfield designed the lychgate are unfounded: that was Scott's.[21]

It is not recorded why Scott was brought in to restore the north aisle in 1858, seemingly working in tandem with Butterfield for a very short period, before taking over completely. By January 1857, Scott had already been approached with a view to taking on the north aisle, to which he responded enthusiastically,

at the same time enquiring whether this would cause problems with Butterfield.[22] The change of architects was plainly linked to the arrival of a new incumbent: in 1856 William Addison was succeeded by William Macfarlane, as vicar. The latter was well-off and personally paid for some of the works, such as the installation of new quire stalls in 1862. The chancel and nave were lit by iron and brass candelabra, attached to stalls and benches, and by wall-mounted brackets (Pl. 19). Four of the latter survive more-or-less intact, along with some dismembered components of candelabra. They were all made to support oil lamps, there being no gas supply to the church.

Having gained a foothold, Scott worked his way around the church, restoring roofs and masonry, which also included complete underpinning of the east end in 1860. He rebuilt the south nave aisle roof in 1861, reconstructing the west gable, but not the window in it; he completed the western part of the chancel roof (*i.e.* over the crossing) in 1863 and started work on the tower. However, it was not until 1868 that the tower was fully restored, the present pyramidal roof added, and the bells rehung.[23] Scott restored the south chancel aisle in 1872–74. That not only involved rebuilding the east gable and the roof, but also included the reconstruction of the four demolished bays of stone vaulting to the eastern chapels (Figs 106 and 107).[24] The more northerly – henceforth designated as the Lady Chapel – was furnished with a stone altar and its walls were decorated with polychromy by Clayton and Bell in 1894. That decoration, which included the Annunciation and other Marian detail, had not only deteriorated but was also partly obliterated with emulsion paint in the mid-20th century. It has now been fully exposed and conserved (Pls 28–31). The more southerly chapel is designated as the Requiem Chapel.

Scott did not make a big impact on the interior, but he was responsible for several pieces of furniture, and adjustments which included reinstating the Georgian altar rails in place of Butterfield's plain rail (Pl. 18). His masterpiece would have been the new high altar and towering reredos that his pupil John Medland designed in 1873.[25] The limestone base of the reredos, with its panelled wings, was built in 1874, but the two capitals in the re-entrant angles were never carved. They are still rough-hewn blocks today (Pl. 16).

The sanctuary was repaved with tiled steps and predella, and in front of the central section of the reredos, which incorporates a stone gradine (ledge for candlesticks), is an oak-framed altar, carrying a stone *mensa*. History does not record why work on the reredos was abandoned, and the intended superstructure never built: the surviving design drawing shows that if it had been completed, much of the east window would have been obscured (as is

FIGURE 106. *South chancel aisle: Scott's proposed restoration of the chapels, although not precisely as executed in 1872–74. (Dorchester Abbey Museum)*

FIGURE 107. *Interior of the church in 1878, looking north-east, showing Scott's restored vaulting in the south-east chapels, and the organ in the north chancel aisle. (Dorchester Abbey Museum)*

the base of Butterfield's reredos, which survives behind Scott's). Instead, a dossal was erected.

Of the various reports and drawings known to have been produced by Scott, nothing seems to have survived except the design for the uncompleted reredos. There is even some confusion about what Scott did, and when: for example, there are conflicting reports concerning the restoration of the tower. Macfarlane's unpublished notes on expenditure during the period 1840–74 record work on the tower, bells and new clock in 1864–65. In his published account, however, he states that this work was carried out in 1868–69. The latter would appear to be correct, since the quotation from Moore's of Clerkenwell 'to make a superior church clock' is dated 1867, while Mears and Stainbank of Whitechapel quoted for rehanging the bells in a new oak frame in 1868 (Fig. 210). Two additional bells themselves bear the date 1867. So how does one interpret a detailed quotation and agreement, signed by the vicar and contractor in 1863, for amendments to work that appears to have been in progress on the restoration of the tower? Almost certainly, two incompletely documented phases of activity are represented here. A new organ, by Walker, was installed in bay 3 of the north aisle in 1871 (Fig. 107).[26] Nothing is known about its predecessor.

Outside the church, Scott was responsible for the oak-framed lychgate in 1867 (Fig. 29), and for restoring the churchyard cross in *c.* 1872. He placed an excessively elaborate new head on the medieval shaft, which has subsequently been removed (Pl. 45). When Scott died in 1878, most of his commissions were carried on by his sons. However, his former assistant at Dorchester, J.M. Bignell, evidently appropriated the completion of the restoration at the abbey to himself, and continued in post at least until 1883.[27] But the drive for restoration was effectively over by 1874, and few additional works were carried out under Bignell's supervision. These were, principally, opening up and restoring the tall, late Norman window in the north wall of the nave (1882) (Fig. 172), and reinstating the west window in the south aisle (1883) (Fig. 75); it is odd that this had not been tackled by Scott in 1861, when he restored the rest of the aisle.

In 1879 Bignell drew up a scheme to reconstruct the destroyed parts of the north transept in a late 12th-century style, and the northern transeptal chapel in the Decorated style; the latter involved resetting the displaced 14th-century east window, which is now in aisle bay 2 (Figs 108 and 109).[28] Windows were also designed for the north side of both transept and chapel, although there may not have been any here originally, owing to the abutment of the east cloister range. The proposal,[29] costings, and detailed drawings survive;[30] also artistic views of the completed scheme were published.[31] Either funding or enthusiasm ran out, and the project was never executed. This proposal,

FIGURE 108. *North transept: Bignell's proposed restoration of the transept and its eastern chapel, 1879; not executed. View from the north-east. (Dorchester Abbey Museum)*

and Bignell's work under Scott, were subsequently alluded to in a short manuscript history written by Scott's younger son, John Oldrid.[32]

Evidently Sir George Gilbert Scott did not regard his work at Dorchester as memorable, since he failed to mention it in both his autobiography and his lectures delivered to the Royal Academy.[33] This is probably because he never really had the chance to make his mark on Dorchester through comprehensive restoration and re-ordering in the same way that he did, for example, at St John's, Cirencester, or at Bath Abbey.

REPAIRS AND ALTERATIONS SINCE 1883

The chancel in particular has witnessed many changes in the name of fashion, both liturgical and popular (Pl. 5). Some of Butterfield's work has been eradicated, and Scott's painted designs flanking the high altar, on the north and south walls, have been obliterated. The chancel rails and gates have been removed, as have some rows of benches in the nave, and all of

them in the two south aisles. Works carried out in the earlier part of the 20th century were of a minor nature, and need not be detailed here. They included repairs to the Jesse window in 1925–26, and routine works to the roofs and walls in 1949–55.[34]

The north aisle was reordered in 1959, when the organ was moved from bay 2 to bay 1, and at the same time raised on a gallery, underneath which a clergy vestry was created. This project necessitated the removal of the pulpit from its Victorian position on the north side of the nave (Fig. 102): it was deposited in the south aisle, where it remained unused. In 1999, the pulpit was moved back to the chancel (Fig. 105).[35]

Following an appeal in 1961, restoration began anew: external masonry repairs were undertaken, particularly to the buttresses and plinth of the south aisle; also the south-west buttress with its statue niches was at last tackled. It had awaited restoration since it was first mentioned in Cranston's report of 1844. The blocked Norman doorway in the west end of the north aisle was opened in 1962, and a new

FIGURE 109. *North transept: internal view of Bignell's proposed restoration of the transept and its chapel, 1879; not executed.*
(Dorchester Abbey Museum)

electric heating system was installed in 1964. Another project was the re-creation of a shrine to St Birinus in 1964, using the surviving sections of vaulting from the 14th-century shrine pedestal. The new shrine, designed by Russell Cox, was erected in the centre of the south chancel aisle, as a memorial to the first Suffragan Bishop of Dorchester (Fig. 76);[36] it was heavily painted and gilded, imparting a garish appearance (Pl. 25). Henceforth, the unvaulted part of the aisle became known as the Shrine Chapel.

Considerable stone replacement occurred on the tower in 1978, including rebuilding all the parapets. The chancel roof was retiled in 1989, using Stonesfield slates, and in 1995 major work was carried out on the masonry and glazing of the east end. The four medieval effigial tombs were dismantled and rebuilt in 1999, removing cementitious mortars; integral sheet-lead membranes were installed, to prevent further deterioration of the monuments through rising dampness.[37] In 2001, the south chancel aisle was cleared of its pews and timber platforms, and was paved.

The appeal launched in 2000 funded a wide range of repairs and improvements, carried out under the supervision of Martin Ashley Architects, and costing in excess of £3 million. In 2001, an oak-framed pentice (now known as the Cloister Gallery) was constructed by Peter McCurdy against the north wall of the nave, on the site of the former cloister walk (Fig. 171; Pl. 46). As well as containing plant and services, this houses a display of the church's important lapidary collection. A new gas-fired boiler was installed in the pentice, with fan-assisted heat-emitters in the church. Access to the pentice was created by reopening the small medieval doorway at the east end of the nave; this work revealed fragments of medieval floor tiling *in situ* in the threshold.[38]

Extensive roof repairs were carried out in 2001–03, which included renewing decayed ends of tie-beams, retiling, re-leading the valley and parapet gutters, installing anti-freeze tape and a comprehensive system of lightning conductors. Internally, cementitious plaster was removed from the lower parts of the walls, and replaced with lime plaster; and the church was redecorated with limewash. At the same time, preliminary investigations into the survival of medieval murals were carried out, subsequently leading to the conservation of the paintings in the south nave aisle, and the uncovering of the large figure of St Christopher in the south chancel aisle (Pl. 26).

Scott's heavy and forbidding timber draught lobby inside the south door was taken down in 2002 and replaced with one of glass and metal, to a design by Martin Ashley.[39] Finally, in 2006–07, the organ gallery and sacristy in the north aisle were re-configured (Fig. 170). The restoration of Dorchester Abbey was complete.

SUMMARY OF POST-REFORMATION REPAIRS

The following summary list is based on documented evidence for repairs and alterations to the church since the beginning of the 17th century.

1602	Present west tower built.
1603/1606	Two new bells hung.
1633	South nave aisle double roof built.
1651	Another new bell hung Guest house adapted for use as a grammar school.
1736	Alterations to churchyard wall resulting from turnpiking the road through Dorchester.
1739	South chancel aisle roof rebuilt.
1743–44	Roof work; reflooring (nave?).
1745–46	Chancel refurnished and repaved; new altar-piece installed.
1747	Nave roof rebuilt (east of arch).
1757	South aisles repaved.
1760	Nave roof rebuilt (west of arch).
1764	Roof retiled (probably nave aisle).
1792	Abbey re-pewed.
1803	'Repairs done'.
1806–07	Medieval glazing rearranged.
1809	Pulpitum screen dismantled and rebuilt in nave; font moved to south-east chapel.
1836	'Alterations and repairs'.

J. Cranston, architect, 1844–46

1845	South chancel window and sedilia restored.
1846	North chancel window restored. New font cover(?).

J.P. Harrison, architect, 1846

1846	Designs for restoration of the east window: not executed.

W. Butterfield, architect, 1847–58

1847	New chancel roof (east part); east window masonry restored; old glazing restored and new work by O'Connor installed; Minton tile floor laid in sanctuary.
1848	New high altar with stone top. New plain glazing, and re-leading old glass, in chancel by Powell and Sons.
1853–54	New stalls in chancel; new benches in nave; new pulpit; font moved to south crossing arch.

Sir G.G. Scott, architect, 1858–78

1858	North aisle restored. West doorway unblocked and reblocked again (shrine fragments recovered).
1860	East end underpinned.
1861	South nave aisle roof rebuilt; aisle restored; porch restored. New chancel screen and gates.
1862	Nave roof rebuilt (from arch to tower).
1863	Nave roof rebuilt (east of arch, to chancel). Tower repairs begun. Decoration of chancel and restoration of medieval painting in south nave aisle, by Clayton and Bell.

1867–68	Floor of south nave aisle relaid; Godwin tiles laid on steps and dais.
	New heating scheme.
	Tower and belfry restored.
	Two new bells and frame installed; new tower clock.
	Lychgate constructed.
1870	New Clayton and Bell glass installed in the east window (two of the lower lights).
1871	New organ.
1872–73	South chancel aisle and roof restored.
	New head fitted to the churchyard cross.
1874	Chapels and vaulting in the south aisle restored; new glass for the east windows by Hardman. Steps for high altar; new reredos begun; polychromy and new glass for east window by Clayton and Bell.

J.M. Bignell, architect, 1878–83 (clerk of works from 1858)

1879	Proposal to rebuild north transept: not enacted.
1882	Norman window in nave restored.
1883	West window of the south aisle reinstated.
1888	Repairs to tenor bell.
1893–94	New wallpaintings in Lady Chapel.
1900	Two new stained glass windows in the south-east chapel.
	Chiming train added to tower clock.

F.E. Howard, architect

| 1925–26 | Repairs to Jesse window. |
| 1936 | Bells rehung. |

Thomas Dale, followed by W.H. Godfrey and R.R. Cox, architects

| 1949–55 | Various repairs, including roofs and parapets. |

Carden and Godfrey, architects

1958	North aisle reordered.
1961–70	Appeal for major repair programme.
	Museum created in the guest house.
1964	St Birinus's shrine reconstructed as a memorial.
1966	Restoration of the chancel east window.
1980–81	Organ overhauled and raised on a gallery.
1986–89	Pulpit moved; repairs to chancel; bells restored.
1989–93	Appeal for restoration of the guest house.
1994–95	Repairs to the chancel and south-eastern chapels.

Martin Ashley, architect

1999	Conservation of medieval funerary monuments.
2000–06	Appeal for a major restoration and reordering of the church.
	Erection of the timber-framed pentice (Cloister Gallery) against north wall of nave; new boiler house and heating system; new service rooms constructed in the base of the tower; roofs overhauled; partial reordering (pews removed from south chancel aisle and pulpit reinstated in chancel).
2007	New organ gallery and sacristy built in the north transept.

NOTES

1 Sherwood, 1989, 82, 188. See also *Directory of British Architects, 1834–1914*, 458 (RIBA, London, 2001).

2 Reports on Butterfield's work were published in *The Ecclesiologist*, **4** (1845), 219; **5** (1846), 24, 161, 193, 259; **6** (1846), 38, 228; **7** (1847), 145; **8** (1848), 43; **12** (1851), 61; **15** (1854), 145, 180; and in *The Builder*, **4** (1846), 250, 273; **10** (1852), 141, 407; **11** (1853), 408.

3 *Building News*, **6** (1860), 418.

4 Apparently Cranston's design for the east window was considered too elaborate: *The Ecclesiologist*, **5** (1846), 161, 259. See here Fig. 101A.

5 Harrison is even more obscure, and there is no entry for him in *Directory of British Architects, 1834–1914*.

6 Freeman, 1852, 332.

7 Tyack, 2005, 53–5. Correspondence and accounts held by OAHS. See also Butterfield's notebook no. 11 in the archive now held by Caroe and Partners, architects, London.

8 Thompson, 1971, 454.

9 Freeman, 1852, 332.

10 Thompson, 1971, 88, pl. 7.

11 *Archit. Rev.*, **98** (1949), 166–75.

12 Webster and Elliott, 2000, 282, n. 117. Tyack, 2005, 55–6.

13 LPL, ICBS 04477. The plan is signed by James Johnson, an otherwise unknown associate or draughtsman. The work is recorded in the ICBS Minute Books, vol. 14, p. 155 and vol. 15, p. 12.

14 Addington, 1845, 28.

15 Thompson, 1971, 479, 501, pl. 362.

16 *Ibid.*, 462, 469 n. 1 and 472 n. 2, n. 3. Freeman (1852, 333) was critical of spending 'a large sum … on the luxury of modern stained glass for the head of the east window', even though funds were gifted for the purpose.

17 However, a standing figure is indicated in the glazing of one of the east windows in a careful sketch antedating 1858 (Fig. 102). So perhaps the windows were glazed in the mid-1850s, and replaced twenty years later.

18 *Ibid.*, 470. Sherwood and Pevsner (1974, 583) incorrectly claimed that the two Hardman windows date from 1830 (a misreading for 1838) and 1842, respectively. This dating seems to have been based on the commemorative inscriptions in the glass of the southern window only. But these are dates of death, not of glazing.

19 *The Ecclesiologist*, **15** (1854), 145–6.

20 The font is shown in both locations in Addington, 1845, suggesting that it was moved in 1844/45. When Jewitt first drew the font, probably in 1844, it stood on the brick dais at the east end of the south chancel aisle (Addington, 1845, opp. 33; here Fig. 191B), but when he later sketched the small doorway between the chancel and nave aisles the font had already been moved to its new position under the crossing arch (Fig. 184). Addington's plan (1845, opp. 1), which

was adapted early in 1845 from a survey by Jewitt, also locates the font under the transept arch (Fig. 7).

21 Sherwood and Pevsner, 1974, 583. They assign the lychgate to *c.* 1852–53, but it is dated by an inscription to 1867 and is in any case unrepresentative of Butterfield's style.

22 Scott's letter of acceptance (1 Feb. 1857) is in the possession of the PCC, which also holds a series of other letters and financial documents relating to the restoration of the aisle. The clerk of works seems to have been John Burlison.

23 Several letters and other papers referring to this are kept in the Abbey Museum.

24 Previous writers have variously speculated on the date at which the vaulting was removed, or whether it was ever constructed. Archaeological evidence suggests that the vault came down in the 16th century, potentially as a result of serious structural movement in the east end, which was the same as caused the east window of the chancel to be buttressed. Scott arrested that movement by underpinning the walls, buttresses and stair-turret.

25 Fisher, *et al.,* 1981.

26 ORO, PAR87/11/F1.

27 Little is known about Bignell, except that he was a pupil of Scott's and was in practice in Brixton, London, by 1868, when his name appeared in the *Architect's, Engineer's and Building Trades' Directory* (London, 1868). No further details were discovered by the compilers of the *Directory of British Architects, 1834–1914* (RIBA, London, 2001), 179.

28 An excavation took place in 1858, to locate the northern corners of the transept and chapel; this was reported in J.O. Scott's memorandum of the mid-1880s (see below, n. 32). See also Taunt, 1906, 18.

29 Bignell's proposal was set out in a long, rambling and semi-illiterate letter to the vicar, 17 Jul. 1879 (transcript in Ashley, 2000). An estimate of £1,920 for the work was submitted on 12 Aug., and was followed by a revised version for £1,670 on 2 Sept. 1879 (correspondence held by PCC).

30 ORO, PAR87/11/Y2/1. The undated drawings are all signed by Bignell, who styled himself 'Architect'.

31 The views, which were printed by Sprague and Co., London, are undated but were clearly drawn to accompany the proposals of 1879. One is an external view from the north-east; the other an internal view looking north. The latter is signed 'Harold Oakley del.' Both bear Bignell's name too. Copies are held by the PCC.

32 J.O. Scott, *Dorchester Abbey Church.* Undated ms; transcribed in Ashley, 2000. This document must have been written after 1885, since Scott refers to Macfarlane as 'the late vicar': he died in 1885. I have not traced the source of the original ms.

33 Scott, 1879; Stamp, 1995.

34 Both phases of work were supported by the ICBS, and notes and photographs survive: LPL, ICBS Minutes, vol. 33, p. 294, vol. 35, pp. 174, 210.

35 An investigation carried out by Oxford Archaeology revealed the foundation of the north wall of the early Norman chancel.

36 Gerald Allen, Suffragan Bishop, 1939–64.

37 This project cost £30,000, and reports were prepared by Nimbus Conservation: C. Jackel, 'Report on the Conservation Work to the John Stonor Monument ...' (May 1999); E. Simpson, 'Report on the Conservation of three Monuments in Dorchester Abbey, Oxon.' (January 2000).

38 Keevill, 2003, fig. 14.

39 Dudley, 2005, fig. 71.

CHAPTER 10

Chancel

EXTERIOR (PLANS, FIGS 45 AND 118)

East wall

Only the easternmost bay (no. 5) of the chancel is visible externally. The eastern corners are supported with pairs of clasping buttresses, entirely of ashlar (Figs 82 and 110). A chamfered plinth and a string-course at window sill level run around the walls and buttresses. The walling masonry up to string-course level is of well squared limestone rubble, neatly laid to courses. The east-facing buttress at the south-east corner projects less than the others, perhaps pointing to the need for access around a restricted corner, where the ground falls away to the flood plain.[1]

The central buttress is smaller in plan and differently constructed from the others: it is an addition, and the plinth moulding suggests a late 14th-century date (Fig. 111). This buttress has partly masked a blocked opening which was not quite central to the east wall. It has a segmental arch and an ill-defined north jamb, all built of squared rubble: there are no dressings. This was never a permanent entrance, but a builders' door, or 'barrow hole', used by workmen and then infilled upon completion of the chancel extension. By leaving the sides of the opening as toothed rubblework – and not constructing regular jambs – it was possible more effectively to tie together the masonry courses on either side when the opening was infilled (see south chancel aisle for two further examples of builders' doors: Figs 148 and 154; p. 143). The present blocking seems to be associated with tying-in the buttress.

FIGURE 110. Chancel: south window, clasping buttress and stair-turret to the south-east chapels. (Warwick Rodwell)

FIGURE 111. Chancel: lower part of the central buttress on the east wall, with the blocked 'barrow door' behind. (Warwick Rodwell)

The east window is now of six lights, arranged in two groups of three with a plain, buttressed pier in between; they are united under a single arch, in the apex of which is a circular window (Fig. 101).[2] When built, the window had seven main lights, but it was presumably found to be inherently weak and the central light was replaced by a column of masonry, expressed internally as a pier and externally as a buttress. The mouldings of the window arch die into plain chamfered jambs; the mullions are plain too, and the hood-moulding is without label-stops. The masonry to either side of the window is ashlar, bonded into the corner buttresses, and there are filled putlog holes in both this ashlar and the rubble below the window (Fig. 82).[3]

Externally, the decorative details of this window are rudimentary, whereas their internal counterparts are exquisitely carved. Much of the external detail may have been renewed in the 19th century. While the east gable is entirely of 1847, the gable-cross is well weathered and has the appearance of possibly being medieval; if it is, it has been reset.[4] Several of the coping stones are possibly Tudor, reused.

North wall

The construction of the projecting bay (no. 5) is similar to that of the east wall, with plinth and string-course, and preserved putlog holes. The four-light Jesse window with cusped Y-tracery has a moulded arch and plain chamfered jambs; the hood-moulding has a simple stop to its eastern end (Fig. 112). The mullions and tracery, by contrast with other windows at the east end, have roll-mouldings on their outer faces, although the branches of the Jesse tree are plain chamfered. The west jamb does not match the east, since it incorporates a pre-existing pilaster-like feature relict from the earlier east end of the church. This plain ashlar feature rises without any offsets or mouldings: it is the eastern flank of one of the pilaster-buttresses clasping the north-east angle of the Norman chancel (p. 67; Fig. 52).

Built into the middle register of the north-facing buttress at the eastern corner of the chancel is a tall, shallow, flat-backed niche, pointed at the head and having a steeply chamfered base. A Norman chevron moulding runs continuously around the sides and arch, and there is a separate hood-moulding with small stops of 14th-century type (Figs 89 and 113). The niche is unquestionably part of the 14th-century build, but the moulding is reused Norman work. However, the chevrons are cut on the ashlars that form the buttress, and they are thus not casually recycled fragments. It would appear that this feature is a late 12th-century blind arch, the blocks of which have been carefully trimmed and incorporated in the 14th-century buttress. The purpose of the feature is unclear, and its proportions are too attenuated for it to have held a sizeable statue. Nevertheless, a small figure has stood here because a diminutive, moulded bracket of uncertain age

FIGURE 112. Chancel: north (Jesse) window. (Warwick Rodwell)

FIGURE 113. Chancel: north-east buttress incorporating a reused Romanesque niche. (Warwick Rodwell)

(Tudor?) has been inserted into the sloping base of the niche.

Although only bay 5 of the chancel projects, the topmost courses of the north wall, in bays 1–4, are visible above the roof of the north aisle. The wall is capped throughout its length by a plain parapet resting on a hollow-moulded cornice embellished with ballflowers interwoven with a continuous running scroll in the form of a thick stem. Although badly eroded for much of its length, preservation is best in bay 5. Here, much of the ballflower is in good condition, perhaps as a result of being sheltered from the elements by a belt of trees. Several short lengths of cornice have been renewed, but the ballflower has either been very poorly modelled or, in some cases, omitted altogether.

South wall

This is constructed of squared rubble laid to courses, above a plain chamfered plinth. The masoncraft is closely similar to that of the south chancel aisle and chapels (*q.v.*). However, a chronological relationship between the two components cannot be demonstrated stratigraphically. An exposed rubble offset and footing, *c.* 50 cm high, is the result of 19th-century underpinning.

The wall is mostly taken up with the four-light reticulated window, which is constructed in three registers (Figs 100 and 110). The moulded arch dies into plain chamfered jambs (as in the east window). The lights have cinquefoiled ogival heads and there is a hood-moulding terminating with simple stops. The mullions are plain chamfered. An odd feature is the thin transom which runs across the inverted cusping at the bottom on the middle register: this must surely be a secondary insertion, added to impart strength and rigidity in what was inherently a weak structure.[5] The masonry above the window arch sags markedly towards the centre, as a result of structural movement in the past (Fig. 114). The moulded cornice and parapet are, however, level and must have been added (or reconstructed) after the sagging took place.

Directly beneath the main window is a line of four squat, two-centred lights for the piscina and sedilia. These openings have no external mouldings and the glazing is deeply recessed: superficially, the feature resembles a short run of 13th-century blind arcading. However, deeply set within each arch is a trefoil light with reversed cusping. The whole ensemble is framed on three sides by a string-course, which is unconnected to the string that runs around the chancel. Unlike the north wall, only bay 5 on the south has a parapet, which still has a medieval roll-topped coping. At its west end, this abuts a fragment of masonry that appears to be part of a former chancel gable running north–south.[6] It has a low-angled coping as might be

FIGURE 114. *Chancel: distorted coursing in the masonry over the south window. (Warwick Rodwell*

expected on a Tudor roof, of which it is probably a remnant.

INTERIOR

Chancel arch

The present late 12th-century arch occupies the west side of the former crossing. It is two-centred and moulded on both faces: see crossing (p. 160).

East wall

The end of the chancel is dominated by the east window, now of six lights but originally seven (Figs 102; Pl. 5). The tracery is complex and the mullions are interrupted by a reticulated zone which occupies more than half the total height of the main lights. Filling the centre-top of the window is a traceried circle or 'rose' which is actually pear-shaped. Although there are basically six divisions, or petals, to the rose the layout is irregular (Pl. 10), and the authenticity of the reconstruction has been questioned. While the majority of the rose window is Butterfield's reconstruction of 1847, the lower half of the frame-moulding, complete with some rather 'squashed' ballflower ornament, is almost entirely 14th century. The inner margin preserves several cusps and the stoolings for bar tracery. Consequently, the reconstruction of the two lower petals is geometrically possible. The two reticulations flanking the rose are original, and they also carry small, misshapen ballflowers.

The window is so wide that there was no space for an elaborate rear-arch to flank it; instead, the reveals are defined by a single keeled shaft set into a hollow moulding, rising from the high sill and dying into the soffit of the rear-arch. There are shaft-rings midway, but no capitals. The rear-arch is elaborated with two orders of ballflower separated by a filleted roll, and a hood-moulding also carrying ballflower. At least two carvers were employed

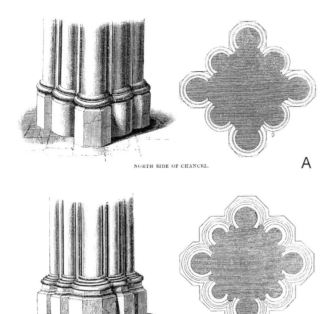

NORTH SIDE OF CHANCEL.

A

SOUTH SIDE OF CHANCEL.

B

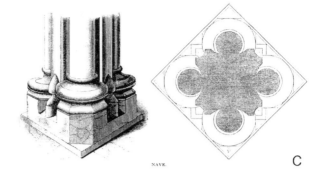

NAVE.

C

FIGURE 115. *Comparative drawings by Jewitt of the arcade bases and their shafts. A. North chancel aisle; B. South chancel aisle; C. South nave aisle. (Addington, 1845)*

on the production of the ballflower on the rear-arch, one of whom used deep drilling to enhance the shadow effects. The same dichotomy is seen on the north window.

The ends of the rear-arch moulding are supported on a pair of curious brackets. They have the appearance of flattened capitals, with a beaked abacus and recessed seating on the underside as though they were designed to rise from shafts, but there are no shafts now, and it is difficult to envisage how there could ever have been any. The keeled shafts described above are set further back in the reveals, and have no capitals. An error or change in design is suggested by this mismatch of detail. The southern bracket is plain, but the northern is decorated with flat, semi-naturalistic foliage. These incongruous elements were perhaps recycled from the previous east window. The internal edge of the sill consists of a quirked roll-moulding, and is evidently a length of late Norman string-course, presumably reused from the previous east wall.

The inserted central pier is splayed (almost pointed) in plan, is of plain ashlar throughout its height, and is finished with a pyramidal cap around the base of which is a slim moulding comprising a keeled roll and hollow. Attached to the west-facing nose of the cap is a 14th-century, semi-grotesque carved head (Pl. 12). It represents a male who appears to be laughing. He has flowing hair and the mouth hangs open, revealing rows of squarish teeth. The head is crudely carved on a separate rectangular block which seems to be jointed to the cap with resin. The ends of the hair are carved on the cap itself, indicating that the head was designed to be part of the buttress and is not a subsequent addition.

The main lights have cinquefoiled ogee-heads with crockets and poppyhead finials, and the west faces of the mullions are decorated to resemble diminutive buttresses of the kind found on tabernacle work of the 14th century. Hence on each mullion, at springing level, there is a three-dimensional crocketed gablet with its own finials. All of this, together with the springing of the ogee-headed lights to either side, is carved on a single block, as would be expected. When the buttress was intruded into the central light – necessitating the removal of its tracery – the springer-blocks on either side had to be sliced vertically in order to leave *in situ* those elements which belonged to the two adjacent lights. However, in doing this a small part of the tabernacle work that formerly decorated the face of the mullions was not removed. The evidence that the central pier was inserted after the window was constructed is thus clearcut.

Stability of this huge window remains a problem. A new iron tie-rod running right across the window has been introduced at springing level in recent years. This must replace an original, continuous wrought iron bar which would have been leaded into the mullions when the window was constructed. There are also individual iron bars of heavy, rectangular section set into each light.

North wall and arcade

Bay 1 will be described as part of the crossing (p. 160). Bays 2–4 are taken up with an arcade (Figs. 99 and 107; Pl. 5).[7] Above the tops of the arches the wall reduces in thickness, which may reflect a heightening. The arcade, although superficially similar to that on the south, differs significantly in detail.

The piers are compound, consisting of a quartet of circular shafts, with smaller ones flanked by hollow mouldings placed in between, on the diagonals. The shaft-bases are triple-ringed and supported by, alternately, octagonal and circular plinths (Fig. 115A). This arrangement is found on the bases of the east and west responds of the arcade, and on the pier of bay 2/3. The base of the pier in bay 3/4 is different, and does not match anything else in the chancel.

Here, the individual shaft bases have only two rings, separated by a quirk. The upper ring verges on being of waterholding type; this may have been reused from an arcade of mid-13th-century date.

The capitals are a unified set, well moulded with double abaci. The arches are very richly moulded, and enclosed by a label which includes four head-stops. From west to east, they represent: a tonsured monk, a king, a hooded monk, and possibly another tonsured monk (Pls 13–15): all are14th century. The wallplaster above the arcade is medieval, and investigations have revealed crude vertical stripes of black paint in the spandrels between bays 3/4 and 4/5.[8] This appears to be post-medieval decoration.

The Jesse window is located in bay 5 (Figs 85, 86 and 112; Pl. 9). The rear-arch is decorated with two orders of ballflower, like the east window, but the hood-moulding carries small, slightly curled leaves.

South wall and arcade

Bay 1 will be described as part of the crossing (p. 160). Bays 2–4 are taken up with an arcade.[9] Above the tops of the arches the wall reduces in thickness, again suggesting that it has been heightened. The scar where the arch in bay 2 was cut through the 12th/13th-century wallplaster which extends into the crossing, and was subsequently made good, is clearly visible. Traces of an imitation masonry pattern, painted with double lines in red, have been found on the earlier plaster in the spandrel between bays 1 and 2.[10] The arcade in bays 2–4 is all of a piece, but does not match its counterpart on the north (Figs 76 and 77; Pl. 5). The heights of the masonry courses in

the piers are, for example, markedly different: on the south they measure 45–80 cm, while on the north they are consistently in the region of 40–45 cm. Also, the plinths of the piers are taller on the south than on the north.

The piers comprise a cluster of shafts and rolls, and they have ring-bases resting on compound octagonal plinths (Fig. 115B). The capitals of the shafts are well moulded and have double abaci; they match the north arcade. The arches are richly moulded and enclosed by a hood-moulding that incorporates four head-stops. The arch mouldings are not the same as those on the north, which has more filleted rolls, whereas on the south some are unfilleted. From west to east, the head-stops represent: a hooded monk, a king, a bishop and a tonsured monk. They are much bolder than the head-stops on the north arcade and it is uncertain whether they are all medieval: the bishop in particular is suspect. In bay 2, the pier bases under the arcade have been cut back to accommodate tombs or furnishings, but no certain evidence of a screen is present.

Damage incurred during construction is evidenced on the pier of bays 2/3: here, sections of the east- and north-facing shafts were fractured and had to be repaired with hot resin-mastic (cf. Pl. 35). The fragment which broke off the east shaft was glued in position, but on the north shaft the fracture was cut back to a neat line and a new stone pieced-in. Both exhibit the classic signs of hot mastic repairs: a brown line (resin) in the fracture, between pink-tinged edges to the stone on either side. The discolouration is the result of heating the stone to effect a bond. A further

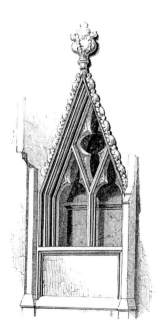

FIGURE 116A (left) and 116B (right). Chancel: double piscina in bay 4/5. (Warwick Rodwell; Addington, 1845)

mastic repair may be seen in the base of the north-facing shaft.

Adjoining the arcade respond of bay 4, to the east, is an ornate double piscina, the construction of which is integral with the arcade (Figs 77 and 116; Pl. 18). In bay 5, immediately beyond the piscina, is the scar where the primary east wall joined the south wall, before the chancel was extended. In bay 5, the lower register of the wall is occupied by a monumentally elaborate piscina and triple sedilia, installed when the chancel was extended (Figs 87 and 117; Pl. 7). The four bays have octopartite vaulting surmounted by intricate canopy work which incorporates figurative carvings. These include representations of the Seven Deadly Sins. The canopies are supported by slender, freestanding shafts and buttresses. These have bands of decoration around the square shafts, comprising panels of reticulated tracery (Fig. 73). In the back of each recess is a curiously shaped window, edged with ballflower and fitted with a medieval glass roundel (Pl. 8).

Above the sedilia is a major window, the masonry of which appears to be almost entirely 14th century, apart from the occasional replaced cusp. The rear-arch of the window is decorated with two orders of ballflower, with a third on the hood-moulding; the

arcature goes slightly astray towards the apex. The tracery was entirely taken down and rebuilt in the 1840s, and much work was carried out at the same time on the sedilia.

Vertical stripes of black paint or stain have been recorded on the wall plaster in the spandrels between bays 2/3 and 3/4.[11] These are likely to be post-medieval decoration. There was formerly a stencilled scheme – imitating wall-tiling – painted by Butterfield on the few available areas of low-level plaster at the east end. This work has been obliterated, but is known from photographs: on the north wall, immediately below window sill level, was the inscription, + *Sanctus Sanctus Sanctus Dominus Deus Sabaoth*, and on the south wall, *Gloria in Excelsis +*. There was also an inscription on the east wall. A trial was carried out in bay 4/5, on the south side, to expose some of Butterfield's decoration,[12] but nothing has been found of the medieval wallpainting mentioned in antiquarian sources (p. 94).

Floor

The floor is on three levels, with steps running across the chancel in line with the piers between bays 2/3, 3/4 and 4/5 (plan, Fig. 118). The present arrangement is late 19th century, and incorporates relocated

FIGURE 117. Chancel: sedilia in the south wall, bay 5, before restoration. (Skelton, 1823)

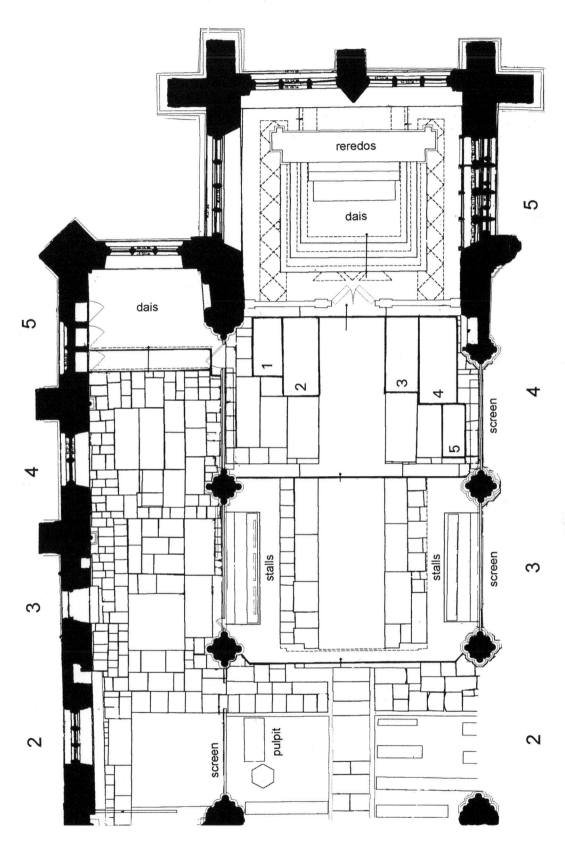

Figure 118. Chancel and north aisle: plan showing floor paving, 2001. The surviving medieval monuments are emphasized (M.1 to M.5). Scale 1:125. (adapted from Sterling Surveys)

medieval and later tomb-slabs; for details of the major monuments in the chancel, see p. 129.

A Yorkstone-paved central alley runs through bays 1 and 2, and continues into the eastern half of the nave. Cross-alleys run into the chancel aisles, and there is an expanded area of paving under the south arcade in bay 1, where the font formerly stood. Otherwise, bays 1 and 2 are floored with timber as a deck for pewing. Bay 3 has a wide central alley of 19th-century red and black ceramic tiling, interspersed with small squares of Yorkstone; this is edged with a black tile border containing the occasional Minton encaustic tile bearing a rosette. The alley is flanked by narrow strips of stone paving which incorporate tomb-slabs; those in turn are flanked by timber decks for the choir stalls. The tiled alley continues in bay 4, to either side of which is stone paving: this incorporates some important medieval slabs.

The sanctuary, bay 5, has two periods of tile flooring. Butterfield paved it with 6″ square Minton tiles, interspersed with diagonally-laid panels of Yorkstone paving; there was a small dais for the altar (Pl. 17). Partly on top of this, Scott constructed a substantial three-tiered dais with veined black marble steps and 4″ square encaustic tiles from the Godwin factory in Herefordshire, for the high altar and his proposed monumental reredos. Medieval tiles found on site were used as patterns for at least some of the designs.

The first step occurs at the bay 2/3 junction, where there has been a succession of screens, as evidenced by considerable damage to the inward-facing shafts of the north and south arcade piers. A step and possibly a screen are shown here in 1845 (Fig. 7).[13] The second step, at bay 3/4 junction, was created in the late 19th century, and the pier bases confirm that no step was intended here in the Middle Ages. The inward-facing shaft on the south side has been much repaired, as though there had been structural fixings here too. The third (sanctuary) step is now at the junction of bays 4 and 5 on the north but, owing to the lack of synchronization of the bay plan in this part of the church, on the south the step falls east of the double piscina. However, the level at which the piscina was constructed demands a step in front of it. There would have been an altar dais here in the early 14th century, before the chancel was extended to its present length. Also, the pier bases rise at this point, confirming that there was a medieval step close to the primary east wall. That arrangement must have been dispensed with at an early date, perhaps even in the 14th century. On 19th-century plans, the two sanctuary steps are shown 2 m further east, and they were surmounted by the altar rail. Buckler's drawing of 1812–13 shows the steps, but omits the rail.[14]

Roof

The chancel has a pointed waggon roof, constructed in two distinct sections with every rafter-couple having a curved underface and thus assuming the appearance of a rib (Fig. 102). The structure is complex and uses a prodigious quantity of timber. The eastern bays, which are Butterfield's work of 1847, have no tie-beams (they would interrupt the view of the east window), and are entirely constructed in oak. The roof is composed of rafter couples fitted with collars and arched braces. At intervals, a stubby king-post rises from the collar to the ridge-piece, and has four-way bracing. Although virtually invisible, even from scaffolding, these king-posts are carefully detailed with moulded octagonal capitals. Moreover, the collars are decorated with crenellations.

The western four roof bays (corresponding to bays 1 and 2 of the chancel structure) are Scott's work. They are of Baltic pine and are defined by five tie-beam trusses, the westernmost of which is placed against the chancel arch. The easternmost beam has a cartouche on its west face bearing the date '1863' in bas-relief. The wall-plates and tie-beams are well moulded, and the ends of the latter are partly supported by short wall-posts and curved braces. The posts, which are of reused oak, rise from stone corbels, semi-octagonal in plan and faceted to a point below (Fig. 102). The corbels are crudely made, with individual axe marks plainly visible, and they also exhibit considerable remains of white and ochre limewash. They are not Victorian, and a date in the 16th or 17th century seems likely.[15] Several have, however, been replaced with neater versions in the 19th century.

An elaborately detailed crown-post rises off each tie-beam to meet the apex of the waggon arch formed by the principals. The posts are octagonal and have moulded square bases and capitals, the latter embellished with chevron decoration. The waggon effect is obtained by attaching curved members (to form continuous, hollow-chamfered ribs) to the soffits of all the principal and common rafters, and the collars. In the apex of the roof, above the ribs, the principal rafters are scissor-braced; also, at intervals, there are short king-posts of square section rising from the collars to the ridge-piece.

The first truss, against the east face of the chancel arch has had the central section cut out of the tie-beam (and the crown-post removed) to prevent it from visually disrupting the apex of the arch. An iron plate has been introduced to tie the cut ends together, which have also been ornamentally carved. Presumably this modification dates from the late 19th century.

Old illustrations show a low-pitched, lead-covered roof on the chancel, with plain tie-beam trusses (in the easternmost bays) supporting king-posts with raking struts to the principals. When Buckler drew the sanctuary in 1812, there was no ceiling, although a decade later Britton and Skelton showed it ceiled (Figs 98 and 99). That roof structure must have been 18th century, potentially superseding a Tudor one. Stonesfield slates, introduced by Butterfield, now cover the chancel.

FITTINGS

Chancel furniture

The Tudor choir stalls, of which two survive, were given in the early 16th century by Abbot Richard Beauforest, whose name is still preserved on one of the original bench-ends (Figs 77 and 119). The inscription is carried on a scroll which winds around the shaft of a crozier.[16] Two further rows of stalls, on both north and south, were added in front of the Tudor ones by Butterfield and paid for by Macfarlane (Fig. 120).

The eastern bay is dominated by Scott's unfinished reredos and altar of 1874 (Pl. 16). The oak communion rail with turned balusters is early 18th century (Pls 5 and 18). The oak screens under the north and south arcades in bays 3 and 4 were installed by Butterfield, who removed the remains of their 14th-century predecessors. Only the cusped heads of the trefoil arches in bay 4 (south) are medieval, and they have been reframed (Figs 103 and 104). The matching screen with integral doorway in bay 2 (north) was originally

made to run across the north aisle, to enclose the organ. When the latter was moved, the screen was repositioned under the arcade (Fig. 105).

The pulpit, designed by Butterfield in 1852–53, is a relatively plain oak structure on a stone plinth (Fig. 105). It was criticised at the time by *The Ecclesiologist* as being 'not well designed constructionally'.[17] The pulpit has been moved several times, and when it was placed in its present position in 2000, an investigation revealed a wide masonry foundation for the north chancel wall of the Norman church. The predecessor pulpit lay on the edge of the chancel step, against the south arcade pier of bay 2/3 (plan, Fig. 7). That in turn had been relocated from the north side, where it was built against the pier of bay 1/2 (plan, Fig. 6).

One of the solidly constructed oak kneeling desks is probably by Butterfield: it has trefoil piercings in the front rail. Another, less weighty desk has two front rails with quatrefoil piercings. A plain X-framed oak table is also likely to be by Butterfield. A single, fussy and delicately carved *prie dieu* dates from the late 19th century.

A lightweight oak altar in the 'Churchwarden Gothick' style stands to one side of the quire, and is a rare survival from the 18th-century church (Fig. 121). It has a moulded top and a frame comprising four legs and stretchers, with two additional struts on each of the long sides, rising from the stretchers

FIGURE 119. *Chancel: inscribed Tudor quire stall and memorial brass to Abbot Beauforest (d. 1510). (Addington, 1845)*

FIGURE 120. *Chancel: decorated Tudor-style quire stall by Butterfield. (Warwick Rodwell)*

FIGURE 121. *Chancel: altar table in 'Churchwarden Gothick' style. (Warwick Rodwell)*

FIGURE 122. *Chancel: memorial brass to Abbot Richard Beauforest, d. 1510 (M.1). Scale 1:8. (Bertram, 2003)*

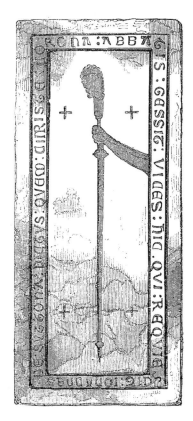

FIGURE 123. *Chancel: Purbeck marble indent for the brass of Abbot John de Sutton, d. 1349 (M.3). Scale 1:25. (Addington, 1845)*

to the top frame. The front is thus divided into three bays, and the top-rail is shaped to give each bay an ogival head.

An oak, X-framed sanctuary chair with a high, triangular back and profuse carving dates from the mid-19th century, and was perhaps designed by Butterfield (Pl. 17). Another, plainer 'Glastonbury-type' chair has a shield in the back carrying the dated initials 'CW 1867' (signifying 'churchwarden') and was probably designed by Scott.

The chancel was once lit by Victorian iron and brass candelabra of simple form, attached to the stalls: these were catalogue items, which were also used in the aisles and nave. The chancel also had iron and brass wall-brackets, mounted on the arcade piers, to hold oil lamps with glass reservoirs. Four of these brackets survive today, and have been restored; they are small but very elegant, and were surely made by Skidmore of Coventry in the early 1860s (Pl. 19).

Window glass

The chancel boasts some of the most magnificent 14th-century glass in Oxfordshire, which has been studied by several scholars.[18] The Jesse window contains sixteen figures in glass, most of which carry their name-labels (Pl. 9). The south window contains nine medieval armorial shields in the upper register of lights, and twelve in the lower. The four lights in the back of the sedilia and piscina contain roundels and a mixture of grisaille and other glass. Three of the roundels are figurative (Pl. 8).

Apart from the traceries at the tops of the main lights, the east window is filled with stained glass, a mixture of medieval and 19th century. The glazing for the newly restored rose was from the workshop of Michael O'Connor, 1847 (Pl. 11), but the east window was later partially reglazed by Clayton and Bell and embodies various memorial inscriptions, the latest being dated 1874 (Pl. 5).[19] The medieval glass is contained in the second register of main lights and in the reticulations immediately above them; there is also some in the third register. In the uppermost reticulation of the northernmost light is a quarry bearing the initials 'C.O', for Christopher O'Connor who was the brother and partner of Michael O'Connor.

Reused in the north window is a fragment of inscription: *BAPTIZAT CONVERSOS AD FIDEM*. This is probably part of the 13th-century Birinus window, of which an inscribed roundel survives in the north chancel aisle (Pl. 23).[20]

Monuments[21]

The three effigies that formerly lay in the chancel were removed to the south aisle in *c.* 1850 (p. 94).

The present arrangement of indents and inscribed slabs, to either side of the central alley in the quire, dates from the same period. These principally comprise the following:[22]

M.1 (Fig. 122). Purbeck marble indent containing the brass to Abbot Richard Beauforest (Bewfforeste, d. 1510), who stands above a separate inscribed panel. An inscribed scroll, now incomplete, issues from his mouth.[23] The indent is intact, but is crumbling around the edges: like all the other medieval slabs in the chancel and south-east chapel, it was set in Portland cement, which is at least partially responsible for accelerating the decay of the matrix. An attempt has been made to prise the abbot's brass out of the matrix, resulting in its being broken into two pieces (across the chest); the upper portion has been refixed. The lower one-third of the scroll has been lost. Some of the original black mastic filler survives in the lettering of the inscription plate.

M.2 (Pl. 20). Purbeck marble indent for brasses (all lost), comprising two kneeling figures with scrolls emerging from their mouths, and an oval cartouche above. One figure is clearly an angel, the other may have been either the deceased, or the Virgin Mary; if the latter, this represents an Annunciation. If the former, the Virgin may still have been depicted in brass in the mandorla.[24] This is a rare monument type without an exact parallel. No identification is possible, but the

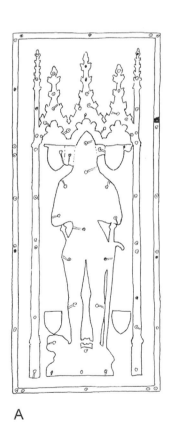 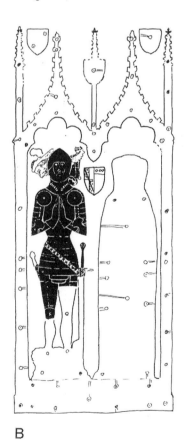 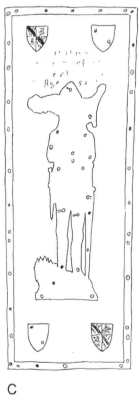

A   B   C

FIGURE 124. Civilian monuments: Purbeck marble indents and the remains of their brasses. A. Gilbert Wace, d. 1408 (M.4); B. John Drayton, d. 1417, and Isabel Drayton (M.11); C. William Drayton, d. 1398 (M.13). Drawn by Jerome Bertram. Scale 1:25. (Bertram, 2000)

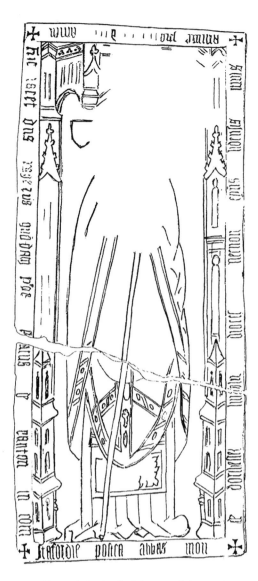

FIGURE 125. *Chancel: incised alabaster slab to Abbot Roger Smith, d. 1518 (M.5). Drawn by Jerome Bertram, after Carter. Scale 1:12. (Bertram, 2000)*

deceased must have been a canon who died c. 1420–40. John Clifton is a possible candidate (abbot, c. 1440–44) or his predecessor, John of Winchester.

M.3 (Fig. 123). Purbeck marble indent for a brass showing an arm appearing from the edge of the slab, with the hand grasping a crozier: the monument of Abbot John de Sutton, d. 1349. There were also individual brass letters forming an inscription around the margin of the stone, between a double-filleted border. The inscription is reconstructible.[25] There were also four individual inset crosses, towards the corners of the slab: no brass remaining. Abbots and bishops were sometimes commemorated by their croziers, rather than their effigies, and this example is often cited.[26] There was a second, almost identical slab to Abbot John de Cheltenham (d. 1333) formerly in the centre of the chancel, but now lost.[27]

M.4. (Fig. 124A). Purbeck marble indent for the brass of a knight standing under a triple canopy. There were also

four individual shields set into the field, and a filleted border (32 mm wide), of which a tiny fragment (25 mm long) remains in situ on the north side, where it is secured by an original rivet. Otherwise, no brass remains, although a good deal of mastic survives in the matrices. The shields were not secured by rivets, but relied on mastic alone. Since Leland's time, this has generally been identified as the monument to Sir Gilbert Wace of Ewelme (d. 1408).[28] In his will, Wace requested a chantry, but no further record of this has survived.

M.5 (Fig. 125). Incised effigial slab of white alabaster, now very worn and broken, but was drawn by Carter when it was legible.[29] It depicts the figure of an abbot, with a marginal inscription, the incisions all being filled with black mastic. The upper half of the stone is so worn that scarcely any of the incised lines survive, although a few letters of the inscription remain at the west end. The full text is known from antiquarian records. The lower part of the figure is legible, but still very worn. The inscription identifies this as the monument to Abbot Roger Smith, who later became a suffragan bishop (d. 1518).[30]

— Rectangular slab of black Tournai-type marble, very worn. An oval inset of white stone (probably alabaster) at the west end of the slab bears faint traces of an incised shield. There is nothing to suggest that the slab was ever inscribed. Date uncertain (18th century?).

NOTES

1　Even the chamfers on the plinth are diminished on the outer face of this buttress.
2　The central buttress is correctly represented in Fig. 82, but not in Fig. 101.
3　The lines of putlog holes are at vertical intervals of 1.0–1.2 m.
4　It is only the head that is weathered, not the shaft which is part of the 19th-century gable-coping. No cross is shown on this gable in antiquarian illustrations.
5　Is there a metal tying bar hidden in this transom?
6　Curiously, this gable fragment is c. 70 cm further west than would be expected if it represented the east wall of the chancel before bay 5 was added. Also, there is much brickwork (partly rendered) under the coping, which must raise questions about its age.
7　For an elevation drawing, see Simons, 2004, fig. 5.
8　Ballantyne, 2004, 39–42.
9　For the elevation, see Simons, 2004, fig. 6.
10　Ballantyne, 2004, 35–8.
11　*Ibid.*, 35.
12　*Ibid.*, 49–50.
13　The lines on the plan are ambiguous, and could represent two steps. Nothing is shown here on Freeman's plan (1852).
14　BL, Add. Ms 36,372, f. 249.
15　These corbels served no function in relation to the 18th-century roof, and must be relict from an earlier structure, possibly Tudor.

16 Illustrated *c.* 1780 by Grimm. Bertram, 2000, 30 (no. 27); 2003, 39, fig. 16.

17 Thompson, 1971, 479, pl. 362.

18 Newton, 1979; Ayers, 1991.

19 The persons commemorated are: Josh Wallis (d. 1854), James and Anne Macfarlane (d. 1849 and 1857), Mary Ann Chapple (d. 1866), Louisa Chapple (d. 1870), Amelia Watson (d. 1870) and Elizabeth Matson (d. 1874).

20 Newton, 1979, 48; Bertram, 2000, 17.

21 For extensive notes on the medieval floor slabs, see Bertram, 2000.

22 The notation for the major monuments follows that introduced by Paul in 1899. To avoid confusion with various other numberings, the letter 'M' has been prefixed. See also Perks and O'Connell, 1996.

23 For illustrations and descriptions, see: Addington, 1845, 15; Beaumont, 1913, 115; Bertram, 2000, 31 (no. 28); Bertram, 2003, 34–5, fig. 8.

24 Bertram, 2000, 26, 43 (no. 19). For a drawing of the matrix, showing fixings, see Bertram, 1976, 159, fig. 26.

25 Bertram, 2000, 22 (no. 12).

26 *E.g.* Addington, 1845, 14; Boutell, 1854, 54; Gough, 1789, **2**, pl. 6, fig. 5, p. cxvi; Haines, 1861, 57.

27 Bodl., MS Gough Maps, 26, f. 42b; Bertram, 2000, 21 (no. 11).

28 See *Oxf. Portfol. Mon. Brasses*, ser. 2, pt. iv (1954); Bertram, 2000, 24, 41 (no. 17). *Cf.* the similar triple-canopied brass to John Rede (d. 1404) at Checkendon (Oxon.).

29 Bodl., MS Don., b.220, f. 116; Don., c.90, f. 477. This monument was omitted from F.A. Greenhill's corpus, *Incised Effigial Slabs* (London, 1976).

30 Bertram, 2000, 32, 46 (no. 30).

CHAPTER 11

North Chancel Aisle (St Birinus's Chapel)

EXTERIOR (PLANS, FIGS 45 AND 118)

East wall

The wall is dominated by a large three-light window, with a string-course under the sill; below the window, the masonry is random rubble, including the plinth which is dressed with a plain chamfered course. Everything visibly abuts the Norman pilaster in the angle between the chancel and aisle. The east window has trefoiled heads to the outer main lights and a cinquefoiled head to the central one; above, are three circles containing cinquefoils in the tracery (Figs 126 and 127). All the cusping is pierced, and was renewed in the 19th century (Fig. 128).[1] Otherwise, the window is well preserved 13th-century work. The outer faces of the mullions and tracery are finished with roll mouldings. The two-centred head and jambs are well moulded, the latter having slender attached shafts

FIGURE 127. *North chancel aisle: east window. No cusping is shown in the main lights (cf. Figure 126). (Addington, 1845)*

FIGURE 126. *North chancel aisle: east window. (Warwick Rodwell)*

FIGURE 128. *North chancel aisle: detail of restored tracery in the east window. (Warwick Rodwell)*

FIGURE 129. North chancel aisle: exterior from the north. (Warwick Rodwell)

and capitals with rudimentary dogtooth ornament.[2] The hood-moulding terminates with a pair of medieval head-stops.

North wall

This reads externally as having five bays, each with a window, but these divisions do not correspond closely with the internal arrangements (Fig. 129). Several periods of work are represented here. It will be convenient to describe this aisle from east to west.

At the north-east angle is a squat and rather plain diagonal buttress of ashlar (Fig. 130). The chamfered plinth and string-course at sill level both continue around it from the east wall, and the construction is of random rubble throughout, except in the buttresses. A plain cavetto-moulded cornice of 19th-century date runs the whole length of the aisle.[3] The north-east buttress is capped with a transverse gablet with a simple moulded edge and a small floriated cross; the flanks carry matching half-gablets. The addition of the cross to a buttress gablet is unusual and could be related to the fact that it overlooked the monastic cemetery.

Bays 4 and 5 are defined by matching ashlar buttresses, similarly finished with gablets, and tied into the wall masonry with internal quoining (Fig. 133). The string-course at sill level is continuous. Moreover, there is another short length of similarly moulded string-course, at a higher level, between the

north-east buttress and the first window: neither of its ends now connects with anything, and superficially it appears to be a redundant feature. However, vestigial evidence remains to show that the string formerly ran into the chamfered weathering at the base of the buttress gablet, where it died away. There are hints that the same string-course also once existed in bay 4, but not in bay 3. The moulding has been hacked off, and was not continuous around the buttresses like the lower string. This series of short lengths of string-course in the present north wall relates to the first structural phase of the aisle, when the window openings were not as tall as they now are: the string linked their hood-mouldings (p. 78).

The two-light windows in bays 4 and 5 are identical: they have trefoil heads and a spherical triangle containing a trefoil in the tracery (Fig. 131); the mullions are roll-moulded and the jambs carry slender shafts, all *en suite* with the east window, although the rolls here have fillets while those in the east end do not. In bay 5 the capitals have dogtooth ornament, but not in bay 4 (Fig. 132). The two-centred window heads are well moulded, and have labels with short, returned ends and no head-stops. The hood-mouldings have largely been renewed, and it is unclear whether any head-stops could have been lost: Grimm's drawing indicates a head-stop on the east end of the label, in the late 18th century. Above the window in bay 4 is a reinforcing arch with voussoirs made of squared rubble, and a similar arch

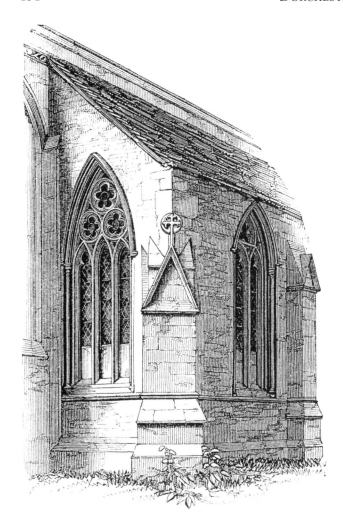

FIGURE 130 (above left). North chancel aisle: the north-east angle, with a floriated cross surmounting the buttress. This view predates the roof pitch being lowered. (Addington, 1845)

FIGURE 131 (above right). North chancel aisle: window in bay 5. (Addington, 1845)

FIGURE 132 (below). North chancel aisle: head of window in bay 5. (Warwick Rodwell)

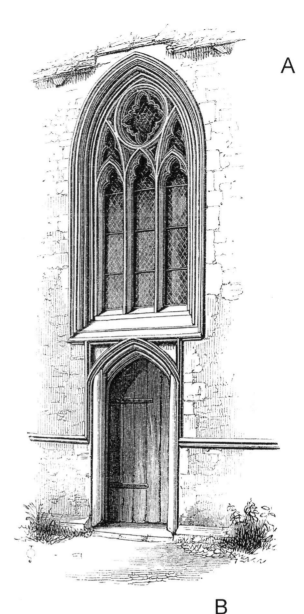

FIGURE 133 (above). North chancel aisle: doorway and window in bay 3. (Warwick Rodwell)

FIGURE 134. North chancel aisle. A (top right). Doorway and window in bay 3, before restoration. The wrong tracery is shown in the roundel and the door jambs and abutting string-course are incorrectly detailed. B (bottom right). Correct detail of the string-course and its disjuncture. (Addington, 1845)

is found above the western half *only* of bay 5; there is no comparable arch over the east window.[4]

Bay 3 contains a narrow doorway with a pointed head and, above, a three-light window with a re-inforcing arch of squared rubble (Fig. 133). The latter does not appear on Jewitt's pre-restoration drawing, and may therefore have been introduced when the wall-top was rebuilt (Fig. 134). The string-course is interrupted by the doorway, making an unusual detour to form both its hood-moulding and a square frame above, and that in turn carries the sill of the window. The doorway has heavy roll mouldings (one with a broad fillet), and the arch dies into the jambs. The simple medieval cross-boarded door with plain strap-hinges was replaced by Scott and fitted with oversized, florid hinges.

The centre light of the window is cinquefoiled, the others trefoiled; and the tracery is dominated by a large circle containing a heavily cusped, equal-armed cross. The mullions and jambs are moulded but, unlike the windows just described, they do not have flanking shafts with capitals and bases, nor a stopped hood-moulding: instead, the hood forms a continuous frame around the entire opening, connecting with that of the doorway below. The arch moulding is a flattened roll with a broad fillet. Finally, the moulding does not rise smoothly from the jambs to the apex of the arch: instead, the head gives the appearance of having settled and spread laterally during construction. The detailing of the doorway and window is coarse and inelegant, compared to the windows in bays 4 and 5. They are clearly not *en suite*.

Immediately west of the window, a vertical discontinuity in the rubble walling is apparent, and the chamfered plinth comes to an abrupt end, as does the moulded string-course (Fig. 135). The way in which the moulding is stopped shows that it once returned on to an abutting wall: that was the east end of the demolished transeptal chapel (for a reconstruction drawing, see Fig. 108).

The masonry of bay 2 is random rubble, without a plinth, and is post-Dissolution in date. This section of wall was erected to close an opening between the north aisle and a former chapel. There is a string-course which is set slightly higher than that in bay 3, and does not connect with it (Fig. 135). In section, the string is a half-roll, presumably of Norman date. It has been reused here, although set deeply into the rubble masonry so that its profile is partially masked. Also reset in bay 2 is a tall, three-light window (Figs 72 and 96). The tracery has much in common with that in bay 3, but not that in bays 4 and 5: the handling of the cusping, for example, is distinctly different. Overall, the window is considerably more elaborate. The rolls on the mullions are treated as shafts, being given tiny capitals and bases. The former have diminutive dogtooth ornament. There is also a recessed shaft with a foliate capital attached to the west jamb, while the east jamb is of plain, square-edged ashlar. The shaft is flanked by filleted rolls, and the foliage on the capital is well formed and deeply undercut; it is derived from 13th-century stiff-leaf types. The tracery contains a heavily cusped, six-pointed star-motif, which is intricately detailed; the centre is itself a sexfoil (*cf.* Fig. 72B). There is a hood-moulding with a short return on the west end only. The moulding on the east end of the hood simply dies out, as does that of the window arch itself where it runs into the unmoulded jamb.

This window has been relocated, and the anomalies present on its east side demonstrate that the jamb was once tucked into a tight corner where there was insufficient space to accord proper treatment to the mouldings. There can be little doubt that this was originally the east window of the north transept chapel: what is now its east jamb was previously the south jamb, abutting the chancel aisle. Relocation occurred in the later 16th or 17th century.

FIGURE 135. North chancel aisle: abutment scars of the demolished transeptal chapel at the junction of bays 2 and 3. Note also the non-aligned string-course: see Figure 134B. (Warwick Rodwell)

Between bays 1 and 2 is a post-medieval buttress of three stages, without a plinth, but around which the reused string-course runs.[5] The buttress marks a set-back in the line of the present north wall in bay 1. This thin wall was probably inserted in the 17th century to close off the truncated north transept. The masonry is again random rubble incorporating occasional ashlars and large blocks. Unlike the adjoining bay (no. 2) and the intervening buttress, it does not incorporate a reset string-course at sill level. Instead, it has two flat slabs of unmoulded limestone built in at string-course level, which appear to relate to a former sill. 18th-century illustrations show the window was formerly taller: the sill level must have been raised in the 19th century.

The window in bay 1 is an oddity of the Gothic Revival: it has four lights under a pointed head, and a crude attempt at Y-tracery (Fig. 97). The mullions all run full-height, and there is a transom at springer level. The design suggests a date in the 17th or even the early 18th century. The jambs and tracery have plain chamfers and there is a simple hood-moulding without label-stops. Around the apex of the arch is a short run of voussoirs and a wedge-shaped keystone, reminiscent of a reinforcing arch, although not performing the function of one.[6]

The north-west corner of the aisle is marked by a single, substantial, north-facing buttress of ashlar,

FIGURE 136. *North chancel aisle: cut-back and buttressed west wall of the former transept, retaining the string-course for weathering the lean-to cloister roof. (Warwick Rodwell)*

constructed in three stages without a plinth: it has been formed on the stump of the Norman west wall of the transept and roughly matches the buttress between bays 1 and 2 (Fig. 136). Again, it is probably 17th century.

West wall

Only a short length of what was once the west face of the Norman north transept survives. The mid-height string-course which formed a weathering for the lean-to cloister roof continues on to this wall from the nave (Fig. 136; Pl. 32). Lower down, and only found outside the new pentice building at its eaves level, is an offset of 10 cm, finished with a plain chamfer; the age and purpose of this feature is uncertain. It is more likely to be related to the erection of the buttress in the 17th century, than to be relict from the Norman period. It is not possible without archaeological investigation to establish the structural relationship between the west wall and the adjoining north wall of the nave (the latter being particularly complex: see below). Unlike the Norman nave, the transept wall displays little evidence of coursing, or for the use of squared rubble; also, flint nodules are present, and at least one piece of Roman brick: it is therefore likely to be relict from the Anglo-Saxon church (p. 31).

Tucked into the angle against the nave, is the fine late 12th-century doorway that gave access from the

FIGURE 137A *(left) and B (right). North chancel aisle: Transitional capitals of the nook-shafts flanking the doorway in the west wall of the former north transept. (Warwick Rodwell)*

cloister to the transept (Fig. 56); on balance, it seems likely that the immediately surrounding masonry is contemporary with the doorway, but the wall itself may be older (p. 31). The upper parts of the doorway are so well preserved, with crisp arrises, that it could easily be mistaken for a 19th-century reconstruction: however, 18th-century drawings confirm that it is basically authentic, although some elements are certainly restored.[7]

The arch, which comprises slightly more than a semicircle, encloses a tympanum bearing a lightly incised interlace design, and has a hood-moulding which descends on to moulded imposts. The doorhead is segmental and is flanked by a pair of nook-shafts with moulded bases and finely carved capitals that have been illustrated by several antiquaries.[8] The plain voussoirs are immaculately cut and finely jointed (c. 2–3 mm). The capitals are decorated with interlaced foliage of Transitional character, and around the base of each (on the neck-roll) are upright leaves (Fig. 137).

On Wood's plan the doorway is shown as functioning (Fig. 4), whereas all 18th- and early 19th-century illustrations depict it blocked with masonry, which included fragments of Birinus's shrine canopy. In 1858 this blocking was removed, but a rubble skin was reinstated externally, leaving a recess on the interior.[9] That in turn was removed in 1963, and the present oak doors fitted.[10] The date of the blocking which was removed by Scott is uncertain: if it was not inserted until the late 17th century, this would imply that the shrine fragments were still lying in or about the church, long after the Dissolution.

INTERIOR

Bay 1 is occupied by timber screens enclosing a new sacristy which was built in 2007, superseding an arrangement created in 1959. The entire space above the sacristy is filled with the rebuilt organ which is supported on a gallery. A timber staircase has been built at the interface between bays 1 and 2.

North wall

The wall is of two main periods: the west part (bays 1 and 2) is essentially post-Dissolution, and the remainder is 13th century. Between bays 1 and 2 can be seen part of a once-freestanding column with a moulded base and an impost formed by a cluster of stiff-leaf capitals. This was the central pier of a two-bay arcade between the north transept and its eastern chapels. The pier, which now serves as a respond, was completely embedded in later masonry until Scott exposed it in 1858, by creating a 'display' recess in the north wall. He installed the ashlar quoins to either side of the pier (Fig. 139). Owing to its having been embedded, a good deal of medieval dark red paint survives on the vertical mouldings of the pier.

The south respond, which falls between the Norman crossing arch and the north chancel arcade, is generally similar in style (Figs 140–142). The southern bay of the transept arcade is thus complete, with its richly moulded arch still spanning the aisle (Figs 64 and 138). The west-facing spandrels were embellished with blind trefoils (p. 74). The southern half-trefoil is intact, and only a fragment of what was originally

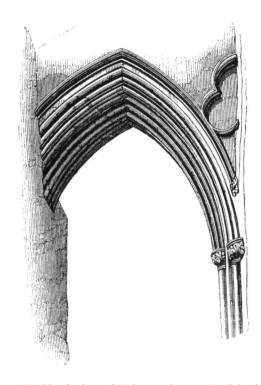

FIGURE 138. North chancel aisle: southern arch of the former east arcade of the north transept. This drawing was made before the pier on the northern flank (left) was exposed by Scott (cf. Figure 64). The half-spandrel on the right is decorated with a blind trefoil. (Addington, 1845)

FIGURE 139. North chancel aisle: stiff-leaf capitals forming the impost of the former arcade pier to the transept chapels. This feature now serves as a respond between bays 1 and 2. (Warwick Rodwell)

FIGURE 140. North chancel aisle: south respond and arch of the former transept arcade. The Norman crossing arch is on the right. (Warwick Rodwell)

the central trefoil in the spandrel above the arcade pier now remains (Figs 138 and 140).

The window in bay 1 has a plain, square-edged rear-arch made of reused ashlars; the mullions and transom have rolls on their internal faces; the sill has been raised, but no structural evidence is visible on account of cement rendering. In bay 2, a low, cement-rendered offset (30 cm wide) projects from the base of the wall. It is part of the post-Dissolution work, and of uncertain purpose: it could have had a timber top and served as a seat (*e.g.* in a private pew). From bay 3 to the east end is a moulded string-course at sill level; this is integral with a series of slender wall-shafts rising from ring-moulded bases to bell capitals with small-scale dogtooth ornament (Figs 67 and 68). The capitals, which now support nothing, are at mid-height in relation to the windows: they belong to an early phase when the aisle had a lower roof and a timber vault (p. 75). In the windows of bays 4 and 5, and in the east window, the reveals show clear evidence of having been heightened when the aisle roof was raised.

Subsidence towards the east end of the aisle is demonstrated by a slight dipping of the string-course below the windows in bays 4 and 5; a hump is also visible in the string below the east window. As with the chancel, the structural problem was doubtless caused by building on the very edge of the flood plain.

FIGURE 141. North chancel aisle: south respond and the richly moulded arch of the former arcade opening into the north transept chapels. The plain capitals of the chancel arcade are seen on the left. (Warwick Rodwell)

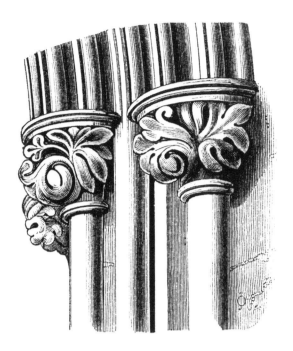

FIGURE 142. *North chancel aisle: detail of the stiff-leaf capitals to the former south respond of the east arcade. See also Figure 141. (Addington, 1845)*

FIGURE 143. *North chancel aisle: potential wafer-oven in the north wall of bay 3. (Warwick Rodwell)*

Three identical rectangular lockers occur in a row in bay 5 (Fig. 69). The oak doors and ferramenta date from Scott's restoration of 1858 (Fig. 70). Low down in bay 3, is a small, plain recess with a pointed and chamfered head, and a circular aperture in its back (now blocked). It is likely to be a wafer oven, perhaps

14th century rather than 13th (Fig. 143). An oddly shaped recess in bay 2 was contrived by Scott in order to display the fragment of an *in situ* 13th-century piscina, discovered during restoration (marked on plan, Fig. 9). The piscina, which was in the east wall of the transeptal chapels and intended to serve an altar in the northern cell, was apparently similar to that which still exists in bay 5 (see below).

The lower part of the wall in bays 3 and 4 was stripped of plaster up to string-course level, and recorded in 2004. The wall is of limestone rubble, and a change in construction was observed 90 cm above floor level. The lower masonry was coursed and the blocks more regular in shape; this raises the possibility that the 13th-century aisle incorporated even earlier fabric *in situ*.[11]

East and south walls

The east window is flanked by a pair of 13th-century capitals for timber vaulting, in the angles of the aisle (Fig. 68). High up in the south-east corner, and extending a short distance below the roof, is the arris of the plain Norman buttress that clasped the north-east corner of the chancel (the remainder of the buttress is visible externally). The level at which the buttress has been cut off indicates approximately where the 13th-century aisle roof initially abutted the chancel (Fig. 53).

In the south (arcade) wall, adjacent to the south-east corner, is a 13th-century trefoil-headed piscina which has lost its pierced tracery, but the basin is intact. There is no credence shelf, but an offset at the back of each reveal could have provided a lodging for a narrow wooden shelf.

West wall

This is cement rendered and the only visible features are the segmental rear-arch of the Norman doorway, with a chamfered hood-moulding above; and most of the southern jamb of a former high-level transept window similar to those in the nave. The reveals of the doorway are asymmetrical: the southern is splayed, while the northern is square, probably because the foot of the monastic night stair lay immediately inside. The window would have lit that stair.

There is no plinth along the base of this wall, nor any string-course at mid-height; there is however a distinct horizontal line and wave in the modern rendering, suggestive of a linear feature at the same level as the now-lost sill of the upper arch in the wall of the crossing .

Floor

The floor in bay 2 is timber decking, and in bays 3–4 it is a mixture of ledger slabs[12] and small pieces of plain paving (plan, Fig. 118). The latter, if *in situ*, represents the oldest area of flooring in the church.[13] In the area where the organ initially stood (bay 3) is Yorkstone paving, replacing a concrete slab. The altar dais in bay 5 is approached by two steps with limestone nosings. The top step is paved with plain red, black and yellow tiles (Minton?), laid diagonally (Fig. 69). This must be part of Scott's earliest work in the church. The bases of the vaulting-shafts in the eastern corners are engulfed by the steps, indicating that the upper one, at least, did not exist in the 13th century. However, if there had been no step, the piscina would have been rather high in the wall. Hence, there was probably one medieval step.

Roof

This is monopitched, lead covered, and abuts the chancel *c.* 70 cm below parapet level. There are coped parapets at the ends and a stone weathering-course on the chancel wall: all 19th century. Prior to the restoration, the pitch of the aisle roof was slightly steeper, and it abutted the chancel at parapet level. Internally, over bays 3–5, was a late medieval windbraced, purlin roof with the ends of the principals supported by hammerbeams (Figs 92 and 99). Scott's replacement roof is very plain (Fig. 64).

FITTINGS

Window glass

A medieval roundel reset in the central light of the east window is the earliest surviving glass in the church, dating from *c.* 1250 (Pl. 23).[14] It depicts St Birinus receiving a blessing from an archbishop, with a lay person in the background; the name 'Bernivs' [*sic*] appears at the bottom of the roundel. In the 18th century the name was prefixed by 'Sanctvs', which was lost during re-leading (Pl. 22). This roundel may represent the consecration of Birinus by the Archbishop of Milan, before he began his mission in Britain. It has been moved several times, its penultimate location being in one of the small 14th-century windows behind the sedilia in the south wall of the chancel.[15]

Organ

The Walker organ now stands on a modern gallery within what remains of the former north transept (north aisle, bay 1). It was originally installed in bay 3 in 1871 (Fig. 107), but was moved to bay 1 and restored by Walkers in 1959. In 2007 the gallery was redesigned and the organ rebuilt again.

Furniture

The 19th-century altar table is oak-framed with linenfold panelling filling the sides.

Plaques

There are several memorial plaques of 18th- to 20th-century date on the north wall, including one to Edith Stedman (d. 1978) who was the driving force behind the 1960s restoration.[16]

NOTES

1 While antiquarian views show cusping in the circles, they do not generally show it in the main lights (Fig. 127). Only one cusp in the southernmost light is original, as confirmed by Skelton (Fig. 99) and Jewitt (Fig. 129).

2 This, and other external ornament on the aisle, has the appearance of nail-head, but was presumably meant to be dogtooth (as on the capitals internally).

3 The cornice is older in bay 1, but whether it is reset medieval work, or 17th century, is uncertain.

4 The reinforcing arches may have been introduced during a Victorian rebuilding of the wall-top: see below, p. 173.

5 The string-course moulding on the west face of the buttress is not half-round in section, but more ovolo shaped. It may have been a length of pointed roll-moulding that was subsequently reworked. There is also a vertical chase, of unknown purpose, in the first stage of the west face.

6 See note 4.

7 *E.g.* Grimm's watercoloured sketch of *c.* 1780: BL, Add. Ms 15,545, f. 145.

8 *E.g.* by Buckler in 1813: BL, Add. Ms. 36,272, ff. 252, 255r, 256r. The nook-shafts are each of two pieces, secured with lead joints (and probably lead dowels that were poured *in situ*). See also Skelton, 1823, 7; Addington, 1845, 4.

9 The 1858 infill appears in a photograph by Taunt: COS, HT14016.

10 The faculty for reopening the doorway was obtained in 1962 (ORO, PAR87/11/L1/4.), and the work was carried out in 1963 (recorded on a plaque). Stedman (1971, 19) erroneously stated that the new doors had already been hung in 1960.

11 Few details are given in Simons, 2004, 14.

12 Perks and O'Connell, 1996.

13 For a differentiated plan, see Simons, 2004, fig. 12.

14 Newton, 1979. The roundel was included in 'The Age of Chivalry' exhibition at the Royal Academy of Arts in 1987: Alexander and Binski, 1987, 212, cat. 28.

15 The roundel was last conserved in 1969 by King and Sons of Norwich.

16 Dudley, 2005, 87–90.

CHAPTER 12

South Chancel Aisle (Lady Chapel, Requiem Chapel and Shrine Chapel)

EXTERIOR (PLANS, FIGS 45 AND 162)

South wall

Externally, there are only four bay divisions: the short fifth bay found internally at the east end is not separately expressed, but is contiguous with bay 4. The bays are defined by tall slender buttresses, the tops of which are steeply gabled (Figs 144 and 145). The four windows are identical and are of the same basic design as those in the nave aisle, but there are slight differences in their execution, in the mouldings and cusping (Figs 146 and 181).[1] The walls of this aisle are of rubble with a hint of squaring, laid to courses. Unlike the south nave aisle, there is no continuous moulded plinth, although the buttresses have individual chamfered plinths.

The wall is horizontally divided by two string-courses (beaked rolls), one at window sill level (contiguous with the nave aisle) and one at the springing of the window heads. The latter ends abruptly at the point where the nave aisle adjoins. The hood-mouldings are continuous with the string-

course, and the buttress gables are also linked to it. Except in bay 5, the lower string-course was wholly renewed in the 19th century and there is a suspicion that originally it too stopped short of linking up with the nave aisle, but the Victorian restorers succumbed to temptation and joined up the two components, even though their moulding profiles are different. Structural movement in bay 2 has resulted in a vertical split in the masonry below window sill level, and a deformity in the label-moulding above.

Notable variations occur in the masonry of this aisle, particularly in bay 1. Here, below the main string-course, three types of masonry are visible: at the bottom and in the centre are roughly squared blocks with wide joints, laid to courses (Norman work); under the window and to the right is a large patch of mixed small rubble without a hint of coursing; and against the west edge of the bay, adjacent to the first buttress of the nave aisle, is small squared rubble and some fine jointed ashlar (Fig. 147). Above the string-course is a vertical column of masonry which seems to be part of the nave aisle

FIGURE 144. South chancel aisle: exterior from the south-west. (Warwick Rodwell)

FIGURE 145. *South chancel aisle: stair-turret at the south-east corner. (Warwick Rodwell)*

FIGURE 147. *South chancel aisle: bay 1, incorporating remains of the Norman south transept wall below the string-course. (Warwick Rodwell)*

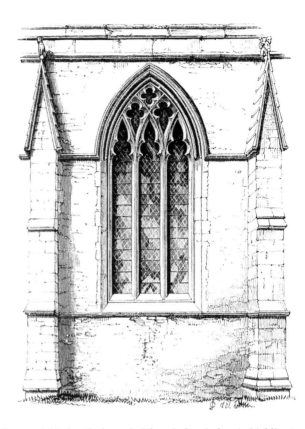

FIGURE 146. *South chancel aisle: window in bay 2. (Addington, 1845)*

FIGURE 148. *South chancel aisle: 'barrow door' in bay 3. (Warwick Rodwell)*

work. Separating it from the chancel aisle is a line of ashlars of various sizes having the appearance of being an internal quoin. The evidence would be consistent with the loss of either a pilaster-buttress from the south-west angle of the Norman transept, or the removal of the 13th-century diagonal buttress

that is now positioned at the south-west corner of the nave aisle (p. 173; Fig. 179).

The topmost *c.* 2 m of masonry below parapet level in bay 1 extends westwards over the scar just described. Together with the abruptly stopped string-course(s), this implies that the chancel aisle was constructed when the south-west corner of the Norman transept was still standing, and consequently that it antedates the addition of the nave aisle.

Below the main string-course in bay 3 is a blocked opening with a segmental arch, the whole formed entirely in squared rubble (Fig. 148). It does not have

FIGURE 149. *South chancel aisle: parapet and carved figures on the buttress copings. View north-east. (Warwick Rodwell)*

defined jambs, the masonry courses to either side appearing to be more-or-less continuous with the infill; the chamfered offset also continues undisturbed, although the ashlar course immediately above is interrupted. This was never a conventional doorway with dressings, but is another example of a 'barrow-hole', used during construction and then infilled (*cf.* Figs 111 and 148).

The south wall of the two chapel-bays (nos 4 and 5) is set slightly forward of the main line, and the buttress between bays 3 and 4 had to be made deeper in plan, to compensate. Two-thirds of the way towards the top of the wall there is a reduction in thickness, accompanied by a weathering, so that as it approaches parapet level the continuity of the external alignment of the face of the aisle is restored. The window in bay 4 has its glazing-line set further in than the others, with the result that both the sill and the external reveals were individually adapted to suit the anomalous circumstances. The level of the string-course below the window had to be adjusted too.

The buttresses are of ashlar, with internal quoins tying them to the rubble walling of the aisle. They also have a small chamfered offset at ground level, and this is continuous on the aisle wall too, except in bay 1 where much older masonry was incorporated. Above the offset is a single ashlar course, the purpose of which was to provide the masons with a clean line for laying the rubble-work. The buttress copings are particularly interesting for their human and animal carvings (Fig. 149).[2]

(i) The coping on bay 1/2 carries a griffin-like creature (Fig. 150). It has the body of a bird, with claws that grip the rolled top of the coping. The head is badly weathered, but it has a hooked beak and appears to turn slightly towards the south-west. It has swept-back

FIGURE 150. *South chancel aisle: winged creature on the buttress coping, bay 1/2. (Warwick Rodwell)*

wings (small pockets have been cut into the face of the parapet coping in order to accommodate the wing-tips),[3] and what looks like a tail hangs down the west face of the coping. The first part is thick, then there is

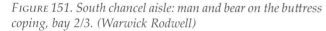

FIGURE 151. *South chancel aisle: man and bear on the buttress coping, bay 2/3. (Warwick Rodwell)*

FIGURE 152. *South chancel aisle: man and animal on the buttress coping, bay 3/4. (Warwick Rodwell)*

a bulge and the remainder is very thin. Superficially, this has the appearance of being a knotted tail, but it could perhaps be a fantastical beast with a second head (in place of a tail) which is biting a serpent. This is potentially significant since, according to legend, Birinus was killed by a snake bite.

(ii) The coping on bay 2/3 carries a very fine pair of figures, comprising a man and a bear (Fig. 151). The bear stands astride the rolled top of the buttress, his claws spread out to grip the sloping stone below. Although he has a benign expression, the bear is muzzled and is looking straight ahead and downwards. The man walks beside the bear on the east, his gaze turned towards the south-west. He appears to be wearing a Roman-style tunic, with a dagger hanging from his belt, and a cowl or Phrygian-style cap with a fastening under the chin.[4] His left arm is placed against the bear's left flank, and his hand is possibly holding something, but is too eroded to be certain; his right arm reaches over the hind quarters of the bear and his hand grips the top of a short staff-like object which has a looped attachment just above the mid-point. This is a stake to which the bear is chained. The figures on this buttress represent the well known medieval entertainment of a dancing bear and his dance-master.

Carved on the same block behind the man's right shoulder, is a short pilaster-like strip which is

incorporated in the parapet; its purpose is unclear.

(iii) The buttress coping of bay 3/4 is set at a slightly lower level than the others, for no apparent reason, and does not intrude upon the cornice moulding at the base of the parapet. The sculpture is the most weathered and difficult to interpret, but appears to comprise three figures (Fig. 152). The middle one is a man who sits astride the coping and looks towards the west, with his mouth open. He is very weathered, but may be wearing a tunic. His left arm is around the neck of a quadruped with a pointed face, which is looking to the south-west. The man's right leg hangs down over the roll-moulding on to the west side of the block below, while his left leg appears on the east side. The animal is sitting on its haunches: its right front paw rests on the roll moulding of the coping, and its left paw is lower down, on the side of the block. The man's left arm is missing but it was evidently outstretched towards the north, holding on to the third figure, another quadruped. The animal's head has been lost as a result of the stone splitting along its bed, which is in the vertical plane. The animal's front paws rest on the roll moulding, while its well preserved hind quarters appear on the eastern slope of the coping; it has a curling bushy tail, like a fox. The animals are both likely to be performing dogs or foxes, and the man between them would be their master.

(iv) The junction of bays 4/5 is articulated externally by a shallow buttress, the top of which projects less than the others from the wall-face, so that the coping is effectively recessed under the overhanging cornice and parapet. Crouching on the coping roll is a small beast which could not be accessed for close examination. It appears to have webbed feet and possibly a human head which is inclined towards the south-west.

The parapet masonry and plain cavetto cornice appear to be medieval (Fig. 149):[5] it is on a slightly larger scale than the 19th-century parapet to the south nave aisle, and there is a marked step at the junction between them. The alignment of the parapet is also instructive. First, it is not properly aligned with that of the south nave aisle; instead, in bays 1 and 2 it veers very slightly to the south, and then at the junction with bay 3 it noticeably turns north again. The survey of 2001 showed that the same deviations are present at ground level, although they cannot be detected there with the naked eye. This demonstrates that the chancel aisle was built not only upon the foundations of the south transept, but also on those of an attached chapel to its east (p. 75). It virtually proves that not only did the north transept have an eastern chapel in the 13th century, as was long ago deduced by Bond, but that a similar arrangement was replicated on the south.

The south-east corner of the aisle is marked by an octagonal stair-turret, the top of which was rebuilt in the 19th century, from one course below cornice level (Figs 100 and 145). The turret has shallow clasping buttresses facing south and east, with high-pointed gablets; it is capped by a spirelet with roll-mouldings on the angles. The east-facing buttress has a small head carved on the coping roll, possibly human.[6] The ground-level plinth and both string-courses follow around the turret, to the east end of the aisle.

The stair is lit by three windows, all in the south-east face. The first is chamfered and rebated and has a pointed head; the other two have flat heads. A small, square-headed doorway of uncertain age opens westwards out of the turret, into the south parapet gutter; the lower part of the south jamb appears to be medieval. The lightweight door is 19th century.

East wall

The architecture of the south wall continues around the east end, which is divided into two bays by a central buttress (Fig. 100). The string-courses and chamfered offset are present, although the latter is well above modern ground level here. The south-east angle-turret stands precipitously on the edge of the flood plain, the land falling away rapidly to the river. Consequently, *c*. 50 cm of rubble footing is exposed, which in its present form appears to be entirely 19th-century underpinning.

Either side of the buttress is a tall, three-light window with a tracery pattern that combines sub-

FIGURE 153. *South-east chapels: tracery of the east window, bay 5 (north). The remains of the Norman angle-buttress are glimpsed beside the hopper-head (see also Figure 54). (Warwick Rodwell)*

arching (*cf*. the west window of the nave aisle) with a central motif comprising a spherical triangle containing a trefoil with split cusps (Fig. 153). Instead of being plain chamfered, the mullions carry roll mouldings on their outer faces. The label-moulding on the northern window has medieval head-stops, but the southern window has one end of its moulding linked to the upper string-course on the stair-turret, while the other end has a short return which stops against the central buttress. The mullions were renewed in the 19th century, along with parts of the cusping; otherwise, these are well preserved 14th-century windows.

Beneath the more northerly window is another builders' door, similar to that in bay 3 on the south side (Fig. 154). Above the windows is a string-course (beaked roll with a fillet) which continues around the buttress, but not the corner turret. Two lancet windows

FIGURE 154. *South-east chapels: 'barrow door' in the east wall, bay 5 (north). (Warwick Rodwell)*

FIGURE 155. South-east chapels: restored gable and east window to the upper chamber, bay 5 (south). (Warwick Rodwell)

in the gable rest on this string-course, which marks the internal gallery level (Fig. 155). The window apertures are defined by two plain-chamfered orders, and there is a hood-moulding which is continuous with another string-course at eaves level. The top of the medial buttress is steeply gabled, like those on the south side of the chapel and the turret. The gable-end, buttress top and window heads are all 19th-century reconstructions.

As a result of Scott's underpinning, the east wall of the aisle and south side of the chancel appear to be of a single build at footing level, with the chamfered offset continuing from one to the other. The detailing of the buttresses is also closely similar. However,

there is no clear evidence higher up in the structure to confirm whether the chancel extension came first, or the south-east chapels.

Tucked into the angle between the east wall and south side of the chancel is a downpipe and outlet discharging from the valley gutter (Fig. 153), masking an important feature. It is a vertical length of Romanesque double-roll moulding rising from a weathered base, which projects from the east face of the chapel close to eaves level (Fig. 54).[7] This is a remnant of a Norman feature (p. 67). The rolls are abutted by the later chapel wall and its string-course. There are indications in the masonry below (in the form of a full vertical run of ashlar toothing) that the moulding and its base rested on top of an angle-buttress or corner-turret, which was cut back when the south-east chapels were added.

A few of the coping stones of the east gable are medieval, and are finished at the apex with a 19th-century cross mounted on a four-way gablet.

INTERIOR

East end

The east wall contains a pair of three-light windows with unusual traceries; these windows belong to two discrete, vaulted chapels. Both chapels have plain rectangular aumbries in the wall, just north of the altar; the oak doors are 19th century (Fig. 78). Bays 4 and 5 of the aisle were restored to their present form in 1872–74 by Scott, the arrangement comprising four quadripartite vaults, springing from wall-shafts and two free-standing piers on the axis of the chapel

FIGURE 156. South-east chapels: Scott's restored vaulting. View south-east with the central pier of bays 4/5 in the foreground. (Warwick Rodwell)

FIGURE 157. *South chancel aisle: intersection of the chapel vaulting (right) with the chancel arcade. View north-east in bay 4. (Warwick Rodwell)*

(Figs 106, 156 and 157). While the wall-shafts are 14th century, there were no piers remaining when Scott came to erect the vault (Fig. 99). It has sometimes been claimed that, although a vault was intended, none was built in the 14th century.[8] This is highly implausible, and it is most likely the vault became unsafe and was dismantled, or collapsed, on account of structural movement in the east end.

The 19th-century replacement vault abuts and seals plaster on the north, east and south walls. This plaster must post-date the destruction of the 14th-century vault, because the wall faces in the sides of the pockets would not originally have been plastered. Consequently, there is no clear evidence as to where the original floor over the vault lay: the pockets would have been infilled with rubble and a lime or gypsum floor-screed laid over that, or perhaps even a tile pavement. It seems likely that the loss of the original vault occurred in the 16th century, at the time when a new roof was constructed with moulded wall-plates. The wallplaster below may therefore be Tudor.[9]

The wall closing off the 19th-century vault pockets from the aisle to the west is of brick and stone rubble. It is finished flush with the gallery floor; a rectangular panel at the centre of the wall is pierced for ventilation. In bay 5, the north and south chapels are separated by a partly pierced screen wall, which is a 19th-century creation (Pl. 31). Solid masonry divides the northern chapel (Lady Chapel) from the chancel. The walls of the Lady Chapel were decorated in subtle tones by Clayton and Bell in 1893–94. There is a linear inscription, and repetitive use of a lily, dog-rose and the crowned Marian monogram 'MR' (Pl. 31). Above the string, on the north, is an Annunciation scene (Pls 28 and 29). The painter signed his name near the bottom of the archangel's cloak: 'W.T. Beane 1894'. The window reveal is decorated too, with a lily scroll and an inscription running around the soffit.[10] A trace of underlying medieval polychromy has been noted on the north wall, below the string-course.

The Lady Chapel decoration was in poor condition, and most of it had been obliterated by over-painting with emulsion. Investigation demonstrated that this once-fine scheme was salvageable and it was fully restored in 2006 (Pls 29 and 30).[11] The walls of the adjacent Requiem Chapel are not polychromed.

Stair-turret and gallery

The entrance to the stair-turret in the south-east corner is unusual: instead of the doorway being located diagonally across the corner, or in one wall, the opening itself is right-angled in plan, with two oak door leaves. These are 19th-century replacements for the 14th-century originals that appear in antiquarian illustrations (Fig. 158).

The doors open into a tiny lobby at the base of the stair, and the east wall is of squared rubble while the west wall is of ashlar. Ceiling the lobby is a segmental arch made of recycled Norman voussoirs with a small arris roll. The newel stair is constructed of ashlar and rises anticlockwise, and the stair-well is of two builds, the lower part being set back by 4 cm behind the upper. It is lit by simple rectangular slit windows, internally splayed. Again, recycled masonry is in evidence: *e.g.* some stones have a small roll moulding on one edge. After one complete turn of the stair, the ashlar lining gives way to unplastered squared rubble which contains the occasional reused ashlar including some with an arris roll.[12]

Also present are small pockets that have been roughly cut into the wall *in situ;*[13] at the top of the first turn four of these pockets occur, more or less at the same level. They must be associated with centring for the construction of the stair. Towards the top of the stair, the wall begins to corbel in, reducing its diameter, and the squared rubble gives way to rougher construction.

At the stair-head is a plain doorway with a two-centred arch, leading on to the gallery above the vault over bays 4 and 5. Originally, the door opened outwards from the stair, but was later reversed and now hangs in a secondary rebate within the stair-well. The door is oak, 19th century, with hinges that have split curls. A short, squinted passage, reconstructed

FIGURE 158. *South chancel aisle. A. Double piscina and angled doorway to the stair-turret at the south-east corner. B. Detail of the corbelled vaulting shaft in the angle above the doorway. (Addington, 1845)*

in the 19th century, leads from the doorway to the gallery over the vault. Here is a sizeable space under the aisle roof, with a pine boarded floor and balustrade along its western edge. The present floor is supported by the tie-beams of the roof trusses, and is clearly higher than the medieval level since it partly obstructs the embrasures of the two windows in the east wall.

The original use of the upper room is unknown: it could have been a chapel, watching-loft or treasury (p. 83). The two windows are widely-splayed with ashlar dressings and rough rubble jambs, and have lancet heads: the upper halves of both windows together, with the gable wall above, are 19th-century reconstructions (Fig. 159).

South wall

This is a generally plain wall; bays 1–4 are pierced by identical windows, the sills of which rest on a string-course.[14] Localized subsidence is evidenced by undulations in the string-course: it is noticeably humped under the windows in bays 1 and 2, and dips between bays 2 and 3. At eaves level in bays 4 and 5 the wall-plate is set back slightly, the junction

being masked by the wall-shaft supporting the vaulting at the east end of the aisle. The wallplaster is mostly medieval, and a large painting showing St Christopher carrying the Christ Child was exposed in 2006, between the windows of bays 1 and 2 (Pl. 26). An earlier painting of the same subject (but with a larger figure of the Christ Child) underlies it. Moreover, the first painting exhibits characteristics of true fresco work, which is rare in England after the early 12th century. Nevertheless, the paint here is on plaster that appears to run on to the jambs of 14th-century windows.[15] Traces of a third paint layer overlie the other two. Medieval polychromy has also been found between bays 2 and 3.

Under the window in bay 3 is a small recess with a pointed head. It is plain and has no mouldings on the face, but is weakly moulded (a wave and small bead) on the soffit edge of the arch. This is doubtless the head of a 14th-century piscina, which was found and reopened in the 19th century; the sides and base of the feature have presumably been destroyed, but the evidence is masked by wallplaster. The piscina must have served an altar placed against a screen at the entrance to the vaulted chapels.

FIGURE 159. South-east chapels: gallery with restored east windows and roof. (Warwick Rodwell)

In bay 5 is a fine double-bowled piscina with a narrow stone credence shelf (Fig. 158). The bowls are cinquefoiled internally.

West wall

The wall is divided into two registers by a string-course, above which the plaster appears to be 19th century; there are no visible features. Below the string, at the northern end of the wall, is the rear-arch of the small doorway leading into the chapels from the nave aisle (Fig. 57). It has a segmental head with a hollow moulding, and plain chamfered reveals with bar-stops.[16] Ephemeral traces of polychromy, possibly of three periods, survive just above the door.[17] These include green, which may be a border (17th century?).

Floor

The majority of the floor in bays 1 and 2 is of reclaimed Yorkstone, laid in 2001 to replace 1850s timber pew platforms; the plan (Fig. 162) shows the pre-2001 arrangement.[18] A squarish area of reused outdoor gravestones occurs on the north side of bay 2. Bays 3 and 4 are largely occupied by reset medieval tombs chests, indents and coffin lids, augmented by pieces of plain paving and some salvaged gravestones. The whole of this paving must have been relaid in the mid-19th century, many of the monuments having been removed from the chancel: these are described below (p. 153). At the centre of bay 4 is the 1964 reconstruction of the shrine of St Birinus (Fig. 76; Pl. 24). An excavation here revealed 2.8 m of archaeological deposits; fragmentary burials were encountered, and the side of a post-medieval brick-lined grave was also exposed (p. 13).

There are two stone steps up to the altar dais in each chapel in bay 5. The daises are covered with Godwin's encaustic and plain red tiles, arranged in lozenges with borders of black-glazed tiles, and green squares at the intersections.

Roof

This is 19th century and is constructed in two sections, a marked change of style occurring internally at the junction between bays 3 and 4; externally, it is covered with clay tiles throughout. An access dormer opens from the gallery into the valley gutter that runs the entire length of the church between the chancel/nave, and the two south aisles.

The first section comprises three bays of waggon roof of pointed form over aisle bays 1–3: it has tie-beams at either end.[19] The beams, which are cambered with roll-moulded arrises, support crown-posts with

FIGURE 160. South chancel aisle: junction of the roofs over the aisle (left) and vaulted chapels (right). (Warwick Rodwell)

moulded bases and capitals, rising to a heavy collar-purlin with beaded arrises (Fig. 160). The moulded wall-plates are of oak, and on the arcade wall the plate is partly supported on corbels. The easternmost corbel is decorated with crossed keys and a sword, and a St Andrew's cross with rosettes between the arms; below is the date 1872. The wall-plates are medieval and carry redundant mortices on the upper face at about 1.5 m intervals. All rafter-couples are collared and fitted with arched braces; rising from every fourth collar is a plain square king-post supporting the ridge-piece.

The second roof occurs over the vaulted south-east chapels (Fig. 159). After the easternmost truss of bay 3 there is a gap – of roughly one-quarter bay – before the first truss of the chapel roof. That roof is curiously constructed and comprises two full bays, followed by a half-bay, and then a quarter-bay against the east gable. This is a collared, tie-beam roof with arch-braced crown-posts, octagonal with moulded capitals and bases; there are four purlins per side, but no collar purlin. The timbers are unmoulded. The medieval moulded oak inner wall-plate on the south has redundant mortices in the top and inserted pieces in the lower roll, as though moulded posts had descended down the wall face at intervals. Part of the medieval oak wall-plate survives on the north too: it is set *c*. 30 cm higher than its southern counterpart, and its position was probably determined by the eaves level of a pre-existing chancel roof to which the aisle had necessarily to relate.

In the space between the vault and timber floor, scars on the walls indicate that there had previously been a flat ceiling just below the level of the present 19th-century floor. There is also evidence (at the bottoms of the rafters) to show that after the new roof was constructed in 1872, the spaces between the rafters were filled with lath-and-plaster (against the underside of the tiling), and limewash was then applied, covering the timberwork as well. This indicates that the underside of the new roof was initially exposed to view, the vault being rebuilt subsequently (*i.e.* the decision to reconstruct the missing vault was secondary): it was added in 1874.[20]

Towards the east end, in the last full and two part bays, most of the rafters are oak, hollow-chamfered (with neat stops) and have been reused from a late medieval or Tudor roof. One of the rafters in the final quarter-bay on the north preserves evidence of setting-out lines in red, which were drawn as a guide for the mouldings; scribing was not employed. The red material may be haematite, but there is no hint of decorative colouring on the timbers. It is uncertain whether these moulded timbers were originally rafters; occasional assembly marks are present.

In the half-bay towards the east the pine purlins have sections of old oak moulding attached to their inner faces, a purely decorative feature. The

FIGURE 161. *South-east chapels: moulded timber from a Tudor compartmented ceiling, reused as a purlin in the 19th-century roof. (Warwick Rodwell)*

mouldings, which comprise hollow chamfers flanked by rolls, are not from a roof but have the appearance of framing timbers from a 16th-century compartmented ceiling (Fig. 161). Notches cut into the mouldings suggest panelling members.

FITTINGS

Shrine of St Birinus

St Birinus was commemorated at Dorchester by a shrine which is recorded as having been erected in *c*. 1320: the exact site is not known, but it was probably located in the south transept or an adjoining chapel. The shrine was destroyed in the 1530s during the suppression of the abbey. It was made of fine-grained limestone and Purbeck marble.

The present structure, designed by F. Russell Cox, incorporates a few fragments of the 14th-century limestone shrine chest which were found in 1858, during Scott's restoration of the north chancel aisle (p. 138; Fig. 76 and Pl. 24). The shrine, erected in 1964, has been given a heavy mantle of paint and gilding, obscuring all evidence of the medieval polychromy. A trial investigation has demonstrated that the modern materials can be successfully removed, to reveal the original colours (Pl. 25).[21] The extant medieval stones are mostly from the vaulted canopy. While the approximate size and general form of the shrine – a two-tiered, canopied and rib-vaulted structure – is likely to be correct, there would have been much intricate detail, not represented here. Two sections of moulded cornice have been used as paving in the floor of the nave (see plan, Fig. 176). When reconstructed, the shrine pedestal was given a gabled timber roof, which has subsequently been removed.

Medieval Effigial Tombs

The aisle is home to four important medieval effigies, which have been noted by innumerable antiquaries.

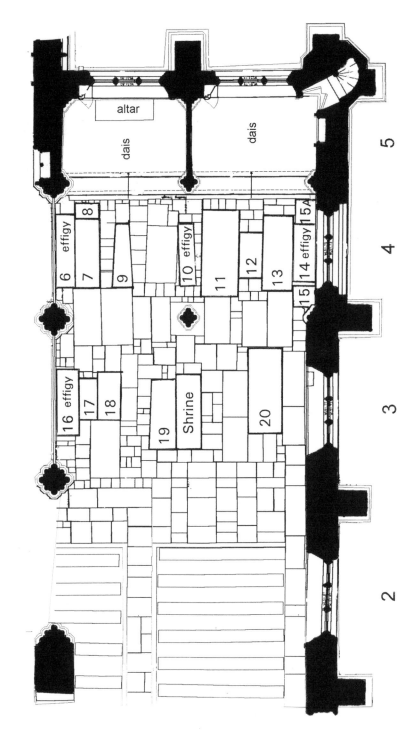

FIGURE 162. Plan of the south chancel aisle and chapels, showing floor paving, 2001. The surviving medieval monuments are emphasized (M.6 to M.20). Scale 1:125. (adapted from Sterling Surveys)

FIGURE 163. *South chancel aisle: tomb of Sir Hugh Segrave (M.6). (Warwick Rodwell)*

The figures were all moved to their present positions during the 19th century and it is not now possible to be certain of their original locations (plan, Fig. 162). The first three had not however been moved since the 16th century, and may thus have marked their respective burials. Despite neglect and abuse, traces of polychromy still remain, albeit much diminished since the mid-19th century. As recently as 1959, the effigies were attacked 'with soap and water and scrubbing brushes'.[22]

M.6 Sir Hugh Segrave (Figs 99 and 163) This late Gothic tomb-chest, surmounted with the alabaster effigy of a knight, formerly stood on the north side of the chancel, against the timber screen in arcade in bay 4 (plans, Figs 6 and 7). It was mentioned by Leland *et alia*, and has been illustrated on numerous occasions.[23] The identity of the knight as a member of the Segrave family is confirmed by painted arms that were formerly visible on the tomb chest (they also occur in window glass), but Parker's suggestion that the monument commemorated the first Lord Segrave is not sustainable.[24] Bertram identifies it with Sir Hugh Segrave, d. 1387;[25] this is compatible with the proposed stylistic date of *c*. 1400.[26]

The tomb-chest is made of clunch; the front and both ends are fully carved, but it has no back. The front and ends are covered with tabernacle work, fifteen bays in all: canopied niches containing statuettes on pedestals alternated with traceried panels containing painted shields. Scoring, to aid adhesion, in the backs of the niches indicates that the statuettes were affixed with plaster. The chest is badly battered and most of the canopy-work has been lost. However, one pinnacle at the north-east corner survives to provide evidence for

the pattern. Considerable traces of medieval polychromy survive too: red, sepia, pale bluish-green, dark green and a little gold.

The effigy has suffered damage, particularly at the corners. At the back, alongside the sinister leg, are the scars where four stoolings have been broken off: these doubtless supported a sword, of which nothing now remains. Scraps of red and ochre paint remain on the effigy; conservation was carried out in 1999 (p. 116). Both the chest and the effigy are heavily defaced with incised graffiti.

There is a problem in reconciling the effigy with the tomb chest: the former is too wide and lies uncomfortably on the latter. The effigy slab has smoothly finished edges on the front south (front) and west, but is very rough on the others. The only way of achieving an aesthetically acceptable union would be if the chest stood against a wall and the effigy was pushed back by *c*. 15 cm into a recess in the masonry behind. If that situation obtained, the tomb must have been moved from somewhere on a north wall: the most likely explanation is that the monument originally lay in the north transept chapel, and was moved into the quire when the chapel was demolished.

M.10 Cross-legged knight, potentially William de Valence the younger (Figs 99 and 164A) This is now centred in bay 4, between the two vaulting severies. On early plans it is shown on the south side of the chancel, against the arcade in bay 4, which tallies with Leland's description of its location in *c*. 1542 (plans, Figs 6 and 7).[27] Since Leland, the effigy has been noted by almost every writer on Dorchester, and has been illustrated by, *inter alia*, Grimm, Carter, Buckler, Skelton, Jewitt and Blore.[28]

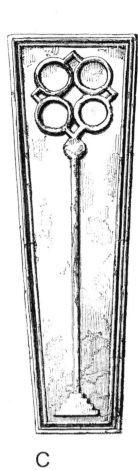

A   B   C

FIGURE 164. *South chancel aisle: three medieval monuments illustrated by Jewitt and Mackenzie. A. Cross-legged knight, potentially William de Valence the younger (M.10); B. Judge John Stonor (M.14); C. Cross-slab (M.9). The last has subsequently become seriously worn by foot-traffic. Not to scale. (Addington, 1845)*

The effigy is carved on fine-grained, cream limestone, and has been slightly defaced by graffiti, particularly on the shield.[29] The figure and its tomb-chest appear to be contemporary, and were designed to be seen in the round (*i.e.* not to be set against a wall). Considerable traces remain of turquoise blue paint; also some dark red in the dress folds. Apart from the missing sword, general wear, and some minor damage, the monument is in good condition. The sword blade must have been made of metal, and had a tang which was secured in a deep hole in the right hand (which clasps the hilt); a stooling on the knee provided support for the sword. The tomb chest was conserved in 1999 (p. 116).

Many views have been expressed on the effigy's date, as well as the potential identity of the knight commemorated. The latter has long been lost or, as Leland put it, 'whos name is there oute of remembrance'. A detailed study of the monument by Philip Lankester concluded that on stylistic grounds it was made *c.* 1280, and is plausibly identifiable with William de Valence the younger (d. 1282).[30]

M.14 Judge John Stonor (Fig. 164ʙ) This recumbent figure of a civilian in legal dress lies on a low chest, the sides of which bear shields of the arms of Stonor. The monument, which is carved on a slightly coarse, orange-yellow limestone, formerly lay against the south side of the chancel in bay 5, where it obstructed

access to the double piscina (Figs 77 and 98). Again, it was described in this location by Leland in *c.* 1542, and has been much illustrated since.[31] There is no reason to doubt the generally accepted view that the tomb commemorates John Stonor, Chief Justice of the Common Pleas, d. 1354, and that it was in its original location in the chancel (plans, Figs 6 and 7).[32]

The effigy slab has a moulded edge, which degenerates into a plain chamfer at the back, confirming that it was intended to lie against a south wall. The north and west sides carry shields with the arms of Stonor, while the foot (east) end of the chest does not bear a shield and has been partly made up with new stone, possibly indicating that the monument was built to overlap a sanctuary step.

The surface of the effigy appears to have been thoroughly scrubbed, but traces of limewash still remain under the canopy and in the folds of the clothes; no polychromy has been noted. Traces of fire-reddening are present on the effigy and canopy in several places; these are consistent with burning materials (*e.g.* from a roof) falling on to the monument. The tomb was conserved in 1999 (p. 116).

M.16 Bishop 'Aeschwine' (Fig. 165) Little is known about this somewhat battered limestone effigy of a bishop, dating from the late 13th or early 14th century. It was designed to be recumbent, as evidenced by the pillow

FIGURE 165. *South chancel aisle: effigy attributed to bishop* '*Aeschwine*' *(M.16). (Frank Blackwell, FRPS)*

under the bishop's head, but he also has a low pedestal beneath his feet, as befits a standing figure. This incongruous detail is not uncommon in recumbent effigies of the period.

The effigy now lies on a low, 19th-century plinth of ashlar, but prior to the restoration, it was displayed on the altar dais at the east end of the south nave aisle, where it had certainly lain since before 1768.[33] For many years it rested on two timber bearers, since these appear in several views. The effigy was said to have been 'dug up from under the floor some years since'.[34] The earliest of several illustrations seems to be by Grimm, *c*. 1780,[35] who identified the figure as 'Bishop Ashwyn', although upon what evidence is not recorded.

It may have been on the supposition that this was the figure referred to by Leland as 'the image of free stone that lay on the tumbe of Bisshop Aeschwine, as apperith by the inscription'.[36] There is no name on the effigy today and, most likely, its identity was incised on a chest which has since been lost.

The moulded edges of the integral slab on which the figure lies are badly broken away, a detail which is recorded in all antiquarian drawings. The moulding was probably continuous around three of the sides, terminating on the fourth (east) against the flanks of the pedestal on which the bishop notionally stands. The base of that pedestal is roughly tooled and was not meant to be seen. This can only imply that the effigy was placed with the pedestal hard against a structure such as an east wall, or a screen. The effigy still retains traces of painting: dark blue (lapis lazuli) occurs on the mitre, red on the chasuble, and pale blue on the dalmatic and tunic; pink and dark green are also present. The pale blue is not, however, primary, since it runs over areas where the surface of the masonry has been broken. A metal fixing in a lead plug occurs in the upper sinister corner of the pillow.[37]

It can hardly be coincidence that Leland described four effigies, and there are still four today. Moreover, only one represents a bishop. We should probably accept that the identifying inscription, reported by Leland, has somehow been lost. So who was Bishop Aeschwine? Lankester, *inter alia*, has suggested that he might be equated with the late Saxon prelate Aescwig (d. 1002).[38]

Addington rejected the identification of this effigy with Leland's Aeschwine (or Aescwig), basing his argument largely on the fact that the sculpture is not pre-Conquest. It was not, however, uncommon for religious communities to commission retrospective monuments to commemorate long-departed bishops, especially when there was a desire to proclaim the pedigree of the foundation. Thus, following the demotion of Wells from the status of cathedral to secular college, the canons commissioned retrospective effigies of seven of their Anglo-Saxon bishops: five of them date from *c*. 1200, and the other two from *c*. 1230.[39]

Floor slabs (plan, Fig. 162)[40]

M.7 Purbeck marble indent for a brass floriated cross with a filleted border and rosettes at the four corners. The last doubtless bore emblems of the Evangelists. The base of the cross has rounded steps, and the arms terminate in maple leaves: 14th century. The brass has been lost, and this has tentatively been identified as the monument to Gilbert Segrave.[41] A secondary inscription has been added at the west end, commemorating Anthony Pisley (d. 1707).

M.8 Part of a cut-down Purbeck marble indent, containing three shields in a row, each fixed with a single rivet. One shield remains (Idle or Ideley) and part of another (Drayton quartering Segrave); the third is missing.[42] This slab has been identified as belonging to Peter Idle (d. 1473/4), who had two wives, one a Drayton. The lost inscription is reconstructible from antiquarian records.[43]

M.9 (Fig. 164c). Purbeck marble grave cover, tapering in plan, with a roll-moulded edge and a deep groove around the inside.[44] The centre of the slab is recessed, so that the cross stands in bas-relief. The cross-head comprises four rings overlaid on a lozenge; there is a large knop on the shaft, and a four-stepped calvary base; uninscribed. This fine 14th-century coffin lid is in reasonably good condition.

M.11 (Fig. 124b). Very large Purbeck marble indent for brasses of two standing figures, a knight and a lady, framed under crocketed canopies; also four separate shields. Two-thirds of the brass of the knight survives; behind his head is a tilting helmet, formed in two separate pieces of brass (part of one is missing). Also remaining are tiny fragments at the tips of three of the five crockets of the canopy-work. All the rest of the brass is lost. This monument has generally been identified with Sir John Drayton (d. 1417) and his wife Isabel.[45] Much of the missing inscription is reconstructible from antiquarian sources.[46] The design is closely similar to the Felbrigg (Norf.) brass, dated 1416.[47]

M.12 Purbeck marble indent for brasses of two standing figures on a rectangular inscription panel; also a single child below and a shield above. All the brasses are lost, except the shield which bears a merchant's mark of c. 1500.[48] It is fixed with a single rivet. The slab has been identified as probably belonging to Robert Bedford (d. 1491) and Alice Bedford; an inscription was recorded in 1574.[49]

M.13 (Fig. 124c). Purbeck marble indent for a brass of a knight with his head resting on a tilting helmet; also four separate shields and a marginal inscription fillet fixed with rivets. All brasses lost, except two identical shields with the Drayton arms; traces of mastic remain in parts of the matrix. The former identification with Sir Richard Drayton (d. 1468) has been rejected in favour of Sir William Drayton (d. 1398).[50]

The slab has had a secondary use, with a roughly cut inscription being added at the west end. A deliberate attempt has been made to disguise the inscription by chiselling across it. Some of the lettering can be distinguished: it appears to be 17th or18th century.[51]

M.15 Part of a cut-down Purbeck marble indent containing three small, separate figures in a row. There was previously an inscription panel beneath them, but the slab has been truncated at this point.[52] Two brasses remain: a woman (now headless) in the middle, and a man to sinister. Of the dexter figure, only part of the outline of the matrix can be made out. This monument represents Margaret Beauforest (d. 1523)[53] and her two husbands: William Tanner and Richard Beauforest. The latter purchased the eastern arm of the abbey church at the Reformation and thus saved it for the parish (p. 40). The lost inscription is known from antiquarian records.[54]

M.15A Part of a cut-down Purbeck marble indent containing a single, small figure of a woman. The brass remains, but is headless. The slab has been cut off at the level of the feet: the figure presumably stood on an inscription panel. The slab has been identified as belonging to Janet Sherrey (d. c. 1490–1500). Apparently, there was a loose brass representing a group of five daughters, which was in the vestry in 1892, but later lost; it was recovered in 1979 and put in the Abbey Museum, but is now lost again. The inscription is known from antiquarian records.[55]

M.17 Purbeck marble indent for the brass of a kneeling figure, probably an abbot, with a scroll issuing from his mouth, and a small figure above; brasses all lost. The indent has been neatly cut into three pieces – probably to make floor slabs – and later reassembled again. Identification as an abbot is implied by the rounded projection behind the figure's shoulder, that being the head of a pastoral staff (cf. the Beauforest brass, M.1). Bertram has suggested identification with Abbot Thomas, c. 1480.[56]

M.18 Purbeck marble indent for brasses of two standing figures above a rectangular inscription panel, with two separate children below that; brasses all lost, but rivets remaining. Bertram has suggested identification with William Young (d. 1530/1) and Alice Young.[57]

M.19 (Fig. 166a). Tapered Purbeck marble indent for brasses of a large floriated cross with a separate panel for a veiled female head above, a double-lined border and marginal inscription. Brasses all lost, but traces of the fixing mastic remain. Only a few letters of the inscription can now be made out. Bertram has identified the inscription with a female member of the de Lovell family, and dated it to c. 1325–30.[58]

M.20 (Fig. 166b). Very large Purbeck marble indent for brasses of two floriated crosses, with two demi-figures above; also a marginal inscription comprising individual letters set between a double border. The matrices for occasional letters can be distinguished on all four borders. The brasses are lost, none being fixed with rivets. Bertram has identified this as the monument to John de Leuknor and his wife, c. 1325.[59]

Also of importance:

– Black marble indent containing an enamelled brass fillet with the Evangelists' symbols at the corners (Pl. 21). Commemorates Mary Sewell (d. 1850) and her son Henry (d. 1843).[60] Some of the brass remains, but is loose in part (much of St John is missing, as is half of St Luke), and the enamelling is deteriorating seriously. The enamel colours are red, blue, dark green and black.

– A small, heavily worn limestone slab with the remains of a largely illegible inscription dated 1714; it also carries evidence of six fixings for a rectangular brass plate, now missing.[61]

Window glass

The two east windows contain brilliantly coloured glass, and are erroneously said to have been commissioned by Butterfield from the Hardman workshop, in 1853–54.[62] They commemorate members

A

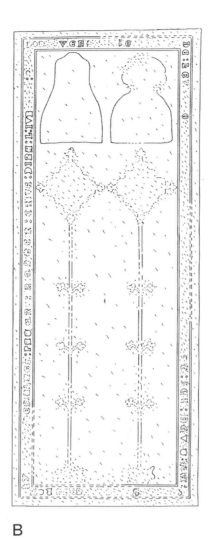

B

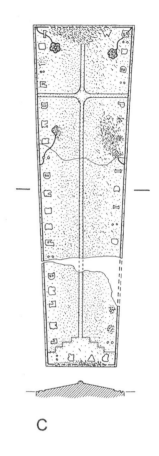

C

FIGURE 166. *Three medieval Purbeck marble indents for brasses with marginal inscriptions formed by individual letters. A. South chancel aisle (M.19); B. South chancel aisle (M.20); C. Nave (M.21). Scale 1:25. Drawn by John Blair. (Bertram, 2000)*

of the Cripps family, who died some years earlier. The northern window (Ascension), is a memorial to John and Mary Cripps; the southern (Resurrection) commemorates James Cripps (d. 1838) and Mary Cripps (d. 1842). The glass is by Hardman and although the general design and composition of both windows is similar, but there are many differences in the execution. The lettering of the inscriptions, for example, is in different fonts, although both are on the same yellow ground.

The two stained glass windows on the south (bays 4 and 5) are a memorial to John Gill Godwin and contain glass made by Mayer of Munich, 1899. Their workshops were in London.[63]

Various

The carved timber retable, painted and gilded, in the Lady Chapel was designed by F.E. Howard and came from Dorchester Missionary College, where it had been a memorial to students killed in the Great War, 1914–18. The stone altar upon which it stands is dated

1873, a memorial to Bishop Samuel Wilberforce. The front is carved with triangular, cusped motifs based on the windows in the back of the chancel sedilia.

The oak lectern embodies a combination of pseudo-Romanesque and early Gothic details (Fig. 167). The base bears the joiner's name, which has been applied with a metal stamp: 'J.R. TURRILL, 1863'; although this places the lectern in Scott's period, it is doubtful whether he had a personal hand in its design. Turrill was a local joiner, who was evidently employed by Scott.[64]

Finally, the chapel houses an oak bier with hinged carrying-handles. It is modestly ornamented with scratch-mouldings and is dated 1685: a fine example of its type.

Miscellanea on the Gallery

Attached to the east wall is a white marble monument in the form of a cartouche, in memory of Jefferey Cripps (d. 1761); it was presumably relocated here in the 1870s. Also stored on the gallery are many

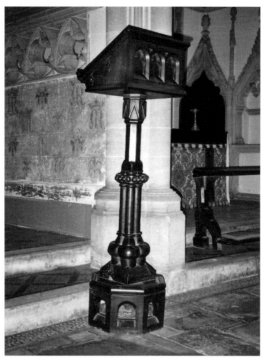

FIGURE 167. *South chancel aisle: oak lectern by J.R. Turrill, 1863. (Warwick Rodwell)*

pieces of timber from 19th-century furnishings. These include: low benches of small scale, with crenellated ends, presumably for children (Butterfield); sections of a low screen and matching door with quatrefoil and trefoil piercings in the panels, having a crenellated top rail (Butterfield's chancel screen);[65] and sections of the internal oak lobby by   Scott that formerly enclosed the main south doorway, dismantled 2002.

NOTES

1   The nave aisle windows have continuous wave mouldings between arch and jamb, whereas the chancel aisle has roll-mouldings on the arch that die into chamfered jambs. The quatrefoils in the tracery are more rounded in the chancel aisle than in the nave aisle, which are distinctly pointed.

2   The figures were first illustrated by Buckler in 1813: BL, Add. Ms. 36,372, f. 254v.

3   The figure is rather flat on the east, with less relief to the carving: this may be due to weathering and a loss of stone. The stone is edge-bedded and a substantial flake may have become detached.

4   The carver of this figure may be the same as the cowled male heads in the south nave aisle (p. 167).

5   A single block from a large cavetto cornice embellished with grotesque figures survives in the lapidarium: the extant figure has the body of a lion with a quasi-human face. The scale is too large for the block to have come from the aisle parapet, and it is more likely from a tower.

6   The head has not been inspected at close quarters.

7   It appears that the rolls are of different diameters,

possibly because there was a triplet of rolls at the angle of the buttress.

8   *E.g.* Freeman, 1852, 164–5, 168.

9   The wall is covered with cream coloured hair plaster containing an aggregate of small river pebbles. It is closely similar to the construction mortar used in the south wall. The wallplaster is Tudor or later, but the masonry should be 14th century, unless partial rebuilding occurred when the vault was destroyed. The plaster carries multiple layers of limewash, but no polychromy is in evidence.

10   The first phase of painting was complete and reported upon in the *Parish Magazine* in Oct. 1893. The Annunciation was added in the following year.

11   Ballantyne, 2004, 25–34; 2006.

12   Putlog holes, averaging 10 x 15 cm, are present and formed with ashlars.

13   They vary in size from *c.* 5 cm square to *c.* 7 x 10 cm.

14   For an elevation of bays 1–3, see Simons, 2004, fig. 7.

15   Ballantyne, 2004, 18; 2006.

16   For an elevation of the wall, see Simons, 2004, fig. 8.

17   Ballantyne, 2004, 45–6.

18   The plan by Sterling Surveys (2001) shows the old pew arrangement.

19   The western truss is shown in bare outline in Simons, 2004, fig. 8.

20   *Proc. Oxford Archit. Hist. Soc.*, n.s. **4** (1882), 76.

21   By Nimbus Conservation: report by M. O'Connor (January 2000).

22   Stedman, 1971, 7.

23   *E.g.* BL, Add. Mss 36,372, f. 263; 42,009, f.52; 15,545, f. 155; Bodl., Gough Maps, 27, f. 38.

24   Parker, 1882, xiii; Lankester, 1987, 154–5.

25   Bertram, 2000, 36.

26   Sherwood and Pevsner (1974, 581) suggest that the effigy and tomb-chest do not belong together.

27   Smith, 1964, 117.

28   *E.g.* BL, Add. Mss 36,372, f. 262; 15,545, f. 159.

29   The graffiti are mostly initials (some quite ancient), but also includes one motif comprising a series of concentric circles.

30   Lankester, 1987. This paper contains full references to source-material. See also Bertram, 2000, 35.

31   *E.g.* BL, Add. Mss 36,372, f. 261; 42,009, f. 52; 15,545, f. 156–7.

32   Lankester, 1987, 154; Bertram, 2000, 35–6.

33   Bodl., Gough Maps, 26, f. 42B(f).

34   Addington, 1845, 35.

35   BL, Add. Mss 36,372, f. 260; 15,545, f. 158.

36   Smith, 1964, 117.

37   This is likely to be for an original fixing. A hole drilled diagonally through the front of the pedestal, containing a wooden plug is, on the other hand, certainly more modern: purpose unknown.

38   Lankester, 1987, 154; Bertram, 2000, 35.

39   Robinson, 1914; Rodwell, 1982.

40   For extensive notes on the medieval slabs, see Bertram, 2000.

41   Bertram, 2000, 23, 40 (no. 15).

42   The third shield is in the British Museum: Stephenson, 1926, 404, (no. III), confirmed by Bertram.

43   Bertram, 2000, 27–8 (no. 22).

44 Gough, 1786–96, **1**, cix, pl. 3.5; Addington, 1845, 31; Bertram, 2000, 48.

45 For a reconstruction of the knight's brass, see Beaumont, 1913, 28. See also: *The Builder*, **78**, 13; *Gents. Mag.* 1796, i, 105, fig. 1; Hewitt, 1855, **3**, 420; Boutell, 1847 and 1849, 134.

46 For a detailed discussion, see Bertram, 2000, 25–6 (no. 18).

47 Beaumont, 1913, 24.

48 This was not recorded in F.A. Girling, *English Merchants' Marks* (London, 1964). However, it is close to one on a brass in Thame church, belonging to Geoffrey Domer (d. 1502); *ibid.*, p. 42. See also: *The Builder*, **78**, 13; *Proc. Soc. Antiq. Lond.*, ser. 2, **12** (1887), 8.

49 Bertram, 2000, 29–30 (no. 25).

50 *The Builder*, **78**, 13. For discussion, see Bertram, 2000, 23–4, 41 (no. 16).

51 The inscription begins: 'In memory of ... wife of ...' A possible reading of the date is 1691. The initial '1' has a cross-bar. This inscription was overlooked by Perks and O'Connell (1996).

52 Stephenson, 1926, 404, no. VI seems to imply that the inscription was then extant; but Stephenson, 1938, 789 records it as 'now completely lost'.

53 There is confusion over her date of death: some writers quote 1513, *e.g.* Stephenson, 1926, 404, no. VI.

54 Bertram, 2000, 33, 47 (no. 32); 2003, 31, fig. 4.

55 *Ibid.*, 29, 45 (no. 24).

56 *Ibid.*, 29, 43 (no. 23).

57 *Ibid.*, 2000, 33–4 (no. 33).

58 *Ibid.*, 2000, 20, 38 (no. 8).

59 *Ibid.*, 2000, 20, 38 (no. 9).

60 Perks and O'Connell, 1996, no. 157.

61 *Ibid.*, no. 163. The evidence for this post-medieval brass seems to have been overlooked by all previous commentators.

62 Sherwood and Pevsner (1974, 583) assigned the windows to 1830 and 1842, respectively, but Tyack (2005, 58) correctly dated them to *c.* 1874. For the inscriptions, see Perks and O'Connell, 1996.

63 The receipt for making and installing these windows (£300) is in the ORO: Mss Oxf. Dioc. pps. c.1796/2.

64 The PCC has a quotation from G. Wheeler and J.R. Turrill of Dorchester, dated 20 Dec. [1860/61?], for making screens (probably for the chancel). The letter was sent to the vicar, and signed 'We remain Sir G. Scott's and Your Obed.ᵗ Servants'.

65 For this screen in its original and reduced forms, see Tyack, 2005, fig. 39 and fig. 44, respectively. See also Fig. 102.

CHAPTER 13

Crossing and Transepts

EXTERIOR (PLANS, FIGS. 45 AND 168)

Nothing is externally visible of the crossing, and there is no evidence to show whether it was ever surmounted by a tower. Parts of the transept walls survive (south and west) and these are described along with the aisles into which they have subsequently been integrated.

(i) About one-third of the west wall of the north transept, including the Norman doorway, incorporated in the north chancel aisle, bay 1 (p. 137; Figs 56 and 136; Pl. 32).

(ii) The complete west wall of the south transept, now preserved inside the 14th-century south nave aisle (p. 175; Pl. 38).

(iii) The lower part of the south wall of the south transept, subsequently incorporated in the south chancel aisle, bay 1 (p. 142; Fig. 147).

INTERIOR

The site of the former crossing has long been absorbed into the chancel, and is therefore numbered as bay 1 of the chancel (Fig. 168). However, the crossing is still structurally distinguishable by its tall, plain arches to north and south (Figs 57, 58 and 102). Of the east and west arches, only the latter survives, and that has in effect become the chancel arch. The original chancel arch, on the east side of the crossing, has been entirely lost (see further below).[1]

Chancel arch

The surviving western arch is two centred, and of two orders with a hood-moulding. The inner order is square, the outer roll-moulded. The arch springs from contemporary responds, each comprising a square-section pilaster flanked by nook-shafts (Figs 50 and 56).[2] These have moulded bases and chamfered plinths. The chamfer returns on the east face of the northern plinth (*i.e.* facing into the nave), but has been hacked off the southern plinth, leaving a residual scar. The superbly preserved capitals are of late Norman style decorated with upright leaves; the carving is crisp and well undercut (Figs 51 and 169). Although the chancel arch and responds are symmetrically moulded to east and west, the capitals

and their polygonal abaci are oddly asymmetrical in plan and have a greater projection towards the east. The reason for this is not apparent. The plinths stand rather high in relation to the present floor and they have evidently been underbuilt, demonstrating that floor level in the nave and crossing has been lowered by *c.* 25 cm; that took place in the 14th century.

The mid-height string-course of the nave (p. 165) continues around the chancel arch and along the north and south walls of the crossing, until it is truncated by the Gothic arcades to the chancel aisles (bay 2). Within the crossing, on both sides, the string is crudely breached by the tall arches that formerly opened into the transepts but which are clearly not in their original form (Figs 58 and 170).

North and south crossing arches (north and south aisles, bay 1)

The tall, round-headed north and south arches comprise an incompatible mixture of elements, and have variously been described as Anglo-Saxon and 17th century (p. 31). They are demonstrably neither: the west responds of both north and south arches have ashlar dressings and chamfered plinths which connect with those of the chancel arch.[3] The masonry is entirely 12th-century work, which rises to a height of 2.5 m; above that is a section of rough walling with rounded and plastered arrises.[4] This is clearly rubble masonry which has been cut back to align with the Norman ashlar reveals below: almost certainly, the head of a low arch opening into each transept has been removed. Above the arch, the Norman string-course doubtless continued uninterrupted.

Below string-course level, both eastern responds are very clumsily formed and entirely devoid of dressings. Again, what we see today is cut-back rubble walling disguised with an irregular plaster finish. Essentially, the eastern flanks of the former crossing are now merely rectangular piers of masonry between bays 1 and 2 of the chancel arcades. However, on both north and south, a narrow ledge (25–28 cm) topped with blocks of limestone has been created as the setting for a side-altar (Figs 59, 93, and 102). In the case of the southern arch, the wallplaster above the ledge is medieval and bears ephemeral traces of

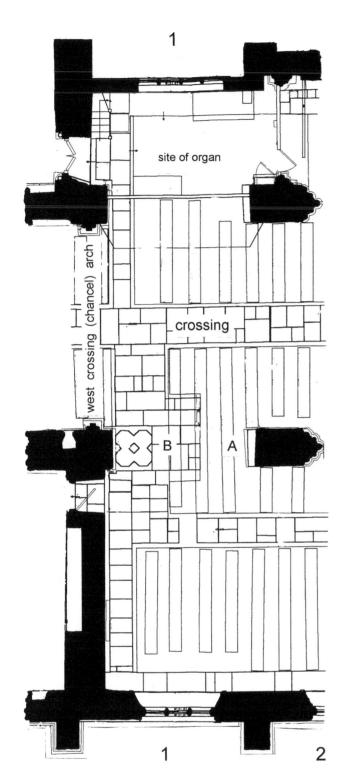

FIGURE 168 (left). Plan of the area formerly comprising the crossing and transepts, 2001. Two successive positions occupied by the font are marked 'A' and 'B'. Scale 1:125. (adapted from Sterling Surveys)

FIGURE 169. Chancel arch: asymmetrical south (top right) and north (bottom right) imposts (cf. Figure 51). (Warwick Rodwell)

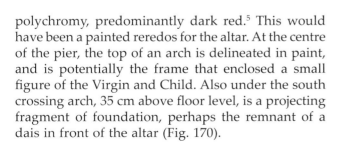

polychromy, predominantly dark red.[5] This would have been a painted reredos for the altar. At the centre of the pier, the top of an arch is delineated in paint, and is potentially the frame that enclosed a small figure of the Virgin and Child. Also under the south crossing arch, 35 cm above floor level, is a projecting fragment of foundation, perhaps the remnant of a dais in front of the altar (Fig. 170).

Above the string-course, and clearly founded on it, is a large semicircular arch on both north and south. These arches are well built with plain ashlar dressings, although secondary chamfers have been cut on them, *in situ*.[6] The arches are undoubtedly original Norman work and they represent the plain outer orders from which either inner moulded orders, or groups of sub-arches, have been removed (Fig. 59).

In sum, the evidence points to the Norman crossing being two-storied, with an upper and lower register of openings: in the late medieval period, these were joined together to create the present anomalous arches; for discussion, see p. 70.

Within the crossing, just above the crown of the southern arch, is an area of preserved medieval wallplaster bearing traces of a pseudo-ashlar pattern painted in red; the decoration also extends slightly eastwards from the arch. Double lines were used for both the horizontal and vertical components, suggesting that this decoration is late 12th or 13th century. The horizontal lines are somewhat wavy, not having been applied with much care. Possible traces of a red painted frieze occur just below a horizontal bulge in the plaster near the top of the south wall; this was probably the line of a former wallplate which was continuous from the crossing to the chancel. However, that wallplate would have been lower than the top of the present 14th-century chancel arcade (bays 2–4) and hence must have belonged to a 13th-century chancel. Although a search was made, no trace of the pseudo-ashlar painting was found on wallplaster in the vicinity of the 14th-century arcade. Nor could any polychromy be found on the north wall of the crossing, where the plaster may have been renewed.

Floor

This is partly composed of timber pew platforms of the 1850s, and partly paved with Yorkstone; there are no visible memorial slabs. For a short period between 1845 and *c*. 1855, the font stood under the south crossing arch: at first it lay towards the east (Figs 7 and 102), and was later moved westwards (Fig. 184). A discrete area of mid-19th-century paving consisting of four octagons of Yorkstone, surrounded by plain red and black Minton tiles, adjoins the later site (Fig. 168, positions 'A' and 'B', respectively).[7]

NOTES

1   If the crossing was square in plan, the eastern arch must have been at about the point where the Gothic arcade has its respond in bay 2 of the chancel. On the other hand, one might have expected the east side of the crossing to align with that of the transepts, which would imply a rectangular central space. While rectangular Norman crossings are not unknown (Thurlby, 2003), that cannot have obtained at Dorchester since the mid-height string-course survives unbroken on the north and south wall faces in the crossing, past the transept position.

FIGURE 170. *Crossing arches: view north from the south chancel aisle. The rebuilt organ (2007) occupies the site of the former north transept. (Warwick Rodwell)*

2   Two deeply incised compass-drawn circles occur on the face of the square moulding, on both north and south, at *c*. 1.2. m above floor level. They seem too regular to be casual graffiti.

3   Some of this masonry exhibits fine diagonal tooling typical of late Norman work. The plinth chamfer once returned inside the south transept, stopping against its west wall; like the return into the nave, that chamfer has been hacked off leaving only a slight bulge in the plaster at the base of the wall.

4   The arrises of the ashlar work have been given secondary chamfers with simple bevelled stops: late medieval or Tudor.

5   Ballantyne, 2004, 43–4; 2006.

6   The chamfers have been coarsely chiselled onto the north and south faces of both transept arches, but the positions of their simple, bevelled chamfer-stops vary. The date of this slight embellishment is uncertain.

7   The position of the font under the crossing arch is incorrectly marked on Addington's plan (Fig. 7): it was further west.

CHAPTER 14

Nave

EXTERIOR (PLANS, FIGS 45 AND 176)

The lower half of the north wall is now entirely enclosed within an oak-framed pentice (Cloister Gallery) which was erected in 2001 on the site of the former south cloister walk (Fig. 171). The new construction is in eight bays, with folding shutters along the north side and a door opening into the cloister garden from bay 1. The monopitched roof is stone tiled, and eaves level is likely to be close to that of the medieval cloister. The floor is paved with Yorkstone. The frames defining the bays stand slightly away from the nave wall, so that its masonry can be inspected. Bays 1 to 6 house a lapidary display (Pl. 46), bay 7 contains a toilet, and there is a boiler-house with a sunken floor in bay 8. That area alone was archaeologically excavated in advance of construction.[1]

North wall

This is divided at mid-height by a moulded string-course, and the nature of the masonry above is distinctly different from that below; it is topped with a plain parapet and cavetto-moulded cornice. The wall has excited much interest amongst antiquaries, and contains important archaeological evidence (p. 29).

A. Below the string-course (Fig. 16; Pl. 33)

The lower half of the wall is of two distinctly separate builds, and periods, there being a more-or-less vertical break in construction four metres from the east end. West of this the wall dates from the late 11th century and is constructed of neatly coursed, squared blocks of limestone rubble; the average course depth is 15 cm, while some are as little as 12

FIGURE 171. Nave and pentice (Cloister Gallery), from the north. (Warwick Rodwell)

cm, and just a few are up to 20 cm. Slight undulations occur in the coursing, and the joints are relatively wide (averaging 3 cm), necessitating the use of a prodigious quantity of lime mortar. The mortar is soft, pale buff in colour and contains much gravel as aggregate;[2] occasionally, a small piece of flint occurs as packing in the joints. In the late 19th century there was a superficial application of struck-pointing in Portland cement.

A plain offset (10 cm wide) occurs 40 cm above modern floor level, and this potentially represents an original plinth: it has the same masonry facing as the nave wall, indicating that it was intended to be visible and is not exposed foundation work. It corresponds to the top of the chamfered plinth of the 12th-century doorway leading into the transept; the present floor level appears to be *c*. 10 cm below the original threshold. Filled putlog holes are discernible, as is a clear building-lift (a temporary break in construction) 2.05 m above the offset.[3]

The easternmost 4 m of wall is differently constructed, using uncoursed rubble laid in a darker, buff-coloured mortar, with a greater range of coarse aggregate.[4] Three periods of work are discernible here. The latest is at the east end of the wall where a small 14th-century doorway with a pointed head has been tucked into the angle with the former north transept.[5] It has a wave-moulded arch and jamb on the west, but none on the east. The decayed remains of a hood-moulding include a short return at the west end; over the apex of the arch are a few rubble

voussoirs arranged as a reinforcing arch (*cf*. windows in the north chancel aisle).

The 14th-century doorway is partly cut through a blocked semicircular-headed opening in the wall. This feature represents the scar left after the stone lining of a major arch was removed (p. 30).[6] The blocking occurred either when the western part of the nave wall was constructed in the late 11th century, or when it was heightened.[7] The materials used are more similar to those in the upper part of the nave, but the mortar is virtually indistinguishable from that in the lower wall.[8] The arch and the masonry in which it was set were of Anglo-Saxon date.

Just below the string-course, and where the pentice roof now abuts, are various infilled pockets, at least three of which contain the decayed ends of rafters from a previous lean-to structure here. That was not the medieval cloister roof, but the pentice shown on Wood's plan (Fig. 4).

B. Above the string-course (Figs 171 and 172)
The upper half of the north wall is of rubble laid to courses with wide joints. The masons sorted the rubble by thickness, to ensure regularity within individual courses, although some are twice the depth of others.[9] The three-light reticulated windows in bays 1 and 2 are of plain construction, the only elaboration being brooch stops on the chamfers of the mullions (but not the jambs). The limestone blocks comprising the jambs are meanly sized, so that there is hardly anything to key into the surrounding rubble masonry.

Nothing remains of the former window in bay 3, its dressings having been wholly removed; however,

FIGURE 172. *Nave: upper part of the north wall, with a restored Norman window, bay 4. (Warwick Rodwell)*

FIGURE 173. *Nave: Tudor window in the north wall, bay 5. To the left (east) is coursed Norman masonry; above and to the right is later random rubble. (Warwick Rodwell)*

the rubble infilling is visibly smoother in finish and paler in colour. The uppermost 1.5 m of walling between the windows in bays 3 and 4 has also been rebuilt, and immediately east of the infilling in bay 3 is a vertical panel of small flat pieces of stone. This has the appearance of masonry stitching, but there is no apparent reason for it. Bay 4 contains a tall round-headed window of Norman style, rising from the string-course. Its dressings were wholly renewed in 1882 (Fig. 172). Pre-restoration illustrations do not show a window here, which probably indicates that not only had the original opening been blocked but that the dressings had also been removed, as in bay 3 (Pl. 3).[10]

A narrow and shorter window in bay 5 also uses the string-course as its sill. With its four-centred head and plain jambs made of upright blocks, this is entirely Tudor (Fig. 173). The head is cut in a slim block, over which is a relieving arch of rubble. All the rubble masonry above and to the west of this window, as far as the tower, has been rebuilt, partly in the 16th century and partly in 1602 when the tower was erected. This later walling does not imitate the coursing of the Norman work.

INTERIOR

There is a string-course around the walls at mid-height:[11] visually, it appears square in section with a large roll on the lower arris, but the top is slightly bevelled. On the north, the string is continuous, although sections have been renewed and in the

FIGURE 174. Nave: lintelled recess and Tudor window at the north-west corner, bay 5. (Warwick Rodwell)

westernmost bay it appears to be bedded on pieces of clay tile of indeterminate age (Fig. 174). On the south wall, the string has mostly been destroyed by the 14th-century arcade: however, a length survives at the west end (where it is a 19th-century replacement), and a short section at the east end, adjacent to the chancel arch (Fig. 50). On both north and south, the string-course is continuous across the responds of the chancel arch, and into the former crossing. The Norman string is not present on the rebuilt west wall.

North wall

The lower part of the wall is almost featureless. At the east end is a small, plain 14th-century doorway that led out to the cloister: it was blocked with masonry in the 18th century, but was reopened in 2002 to provide access to the Cloister Gallery. The passage through the wall is squinted, reflecting the desire to insert the door as far towards the east as possible, doubtless necessitated by its relationship to the rood screen. The pointed rear-arch is finished with plain 19th-century plaster, but there is medieval wallplaster on the reveals; that on the east bears graffiti, including a single word in medieval Gothic lettering. The threshold is of worn limestone paving, incorporating a few 14th-century glazed tiles with stencilled designs.[12] Evidently, the threshold was fully tiled, and as these wore out they were replaced by paving, except at the margins where the survivors are almost unworn.[13]

West of the doorway, in bay 2, is a sizeable wall-cupboard, or locker, with a rectangular opening, rebated to receive a pair of doors (traces of hinge pintles remain). The interior is neatly plastered and has a flat lintelled roof (unlike the smaller locker in the south wall). It is too far west to have been an aumbry associated with an altar in front of the rood screen. It could have lain within a separately screened chapel. When plaster was stripped from restricted areas on the lower part of the north wall structural details were exposed, including a line of putlog holes.[14] Between the locker and the cloister doorway, a rectangular patch of infilling suggested that a feature has been lost from here, possibly another cupboard. That could have been an aumbry in front of the rood screen.

The nave has an assortment of windows of the 12th, 14th and 16th centuries. Elements of the five-aside Norman openings survive: they were tall and round headed. In the north wall there are 14th century, three-light reticulated windows in bays 1 and 2 (Fig. 171). The plain reveals with unmoulded arrises rise from the string-course; they have dropped rear-arches of chamfered, segmental form. The sills are steeply downward-splayed. The mullions are chamfered and, as on the exterior, have tall brooch-stops. The dressings of the rear-arches seem to be Norman, but rebuilt to suit the widened apertures.[15]

There is now no window in bay 3, but most of the Norman east jamb is exposed in the wallplaster, and the lowest block of the west jamb is still *in situ* above the string-course.[16] A small section of a segmental rear-arch is also exposed in a gap which has been left in the wallplaster. In bay 4 a tall window preserves the Norman form, but little fabric: as noted above, the semicircular outer aperture is a replacement of 1882, complete with a glazing groove. The rear-arch has been renewed: it has a segmental head with a moulded arris. The lower part of the east splay has largely been rebuilt, but the west splay is primary. The dressings of the latter have fine diagonal tooling and exhibit numerous masons' marks. The steeply sloping sill is plastered.

Bay 5 contains another tall window, asymmetrically placed within a large recess that occupies the full width of the bay above string-course level. The head of the recess is bridged by two oak lintels carried on stone corbels set into the reveals (Fig. 174).[17] Both timbers are recycled, having once been medieval principal rafters. They were only installed in their present positions in the 19th century, when chamfers with hollow stops were added.[18] The recess, which has a plastered flat back, must date in part from 1602 because its western splay is formed by one facet of the polygonal buttress at the north-east corner of the tower. The eastern splay is dressed with Norman ashlar (with some masons' marks visible) and descends to string-course level: it appears to be a primary window reveal, subsequently adapted to serve the recess. The external window head is three-centred, while the rear-arch is more markedly four-centred. The head is also rebated to receive a timber sub-frame or shutter inside the ferramenta.

South wall

On the south side are the blocked remains of two Norman windows, in bays 1 and 5, respectively. In bay 1, only the east jamb of the rear-arch survives. In bay 5, part of the chamfered west jamb of the external aperture is preserved in the arcade wall.[19] The unmoulded jamb of the rear-arch is likewise visible in the nave, but the arch itself is missing on account of the top of the wall having been rebuilt. The dressings of the window are finished with fine diagonal tooling.

A simple rectangular opening that formerly gave access on to the rood loft (from the south nave aisle) lies just west of the chancel arch (Figs 50 and 183). Its threshold is 30 cm above the string-course, indicating that the beams carrying the loft were seated on the latter. Cut into the wall below the loft is a locker or cupboard with a plain rectangular opening, rebated to receive a door.[20] Internally, the locker is sub-circular in plan and is roughly plastered. It may have been an aumbry associated with an altar placed in front of the rood screen.

South nave arcade

The bulk of the south wall is taken up by the 14th-century arcade of three bays (occupying bays 2–4: Pl. 34). Its impost level coincides with the Norman string-course, and the arcade is substantially in original condition. The piers are compound, quatrefoiled in plan with attached shafts; on each diagonal face, midway between the four principal shafts, are lesser shafts flanked by hollow mouldings (Fig. 115c). The capitals are undecorated, bell-moulded with double abaci. The bell-shaped bases rest on diagonally-set, chamfered square plinths.

The arches are of two chamfered orders, separated by a wide sunk-chamfer, slightly hollowed. All three orders are assembled from a large number of voussoirs. Indeed, there are so many small blocks that we may suspect they are reused stone.[21] The hood-moulding, which is present on the south side of the arcade only, has a sunk-chamfer. There are no label-stops at the two extremities, only short returns. The label-stop between bays 2 and 3 is an unworked square block, 19th century; the stop between bays 3 and 4 is similar, but chamfered on the top face, and may be older. These blocks were presumably inserted into pockets that originally held carved label-stops: possibly they were explicitly popish and succumbed to destruction at the Reformation. Parts of the arcade were not thoroughly scraped in the 19th century and patches of limewash remain. No masons' marks have been observed.

Built into the west face of the first pier, 2 m above the floor, is a heavy stone bracket of semi-octagonal plan (Figs 175 and 191A; Pl. 34).[22] It is primary to the construction of the arcade and is embedded in the pier as far as its mid-point. The bracket is somewhat

FIGURE 175. *Nave arcade: carved bracket on the arcade pier of bay 2/3. (Frank Blackwell, FRPS)*

wider than the pier and its ends project wing-like to north and south, although part of the northern wing has been broken off.[23] The principal faces of the bracket (north, west and south) are sculpted, but the back (east) face of the wings is plain. The sculpture depicts five hooded monks in woodland, the trees being represented by large knobbly leaves and stems. Additionally, at the extremity of the south face is a small naked male figure – probably the devil – holding a horn-like object to his mouth. A sketch of the 1790s reveals that foliage has been lost from the damaged northern end, as has the head of the first monk.[24]

The purpose of the bracket is uncertain, and there may have been other architectural elements once associated with it. For example, the plain backs to the wings might argue for timber screens running north and south from the pier.[25] There is a step in the floor of the nave aligned on this pier, which may reflect a liturgical division between the nave and chancel of the parochial component of the abbey church. Various interpretations of the bracket's function have been offered, but it is difficult to suggest what it might have supported in this marginal location. It is excessively large for a lamp bracket, and it is more likely that it held devotional objects, perhaps associated with a chapel in the nave. A wayward interpretation offered in the 18th century saw the carving as depicting 'the five foolish virgins' crouching in a posture of humiliation, 'and an angel sounding a trumpet': Addington rightly dismissed this as 'very doubtful'.[26] The figures are clearly male, and a more plausible explanation is that they are sleeping monks who are being awakened by the devil blowing his horn: a satirical reflection of the effects of the long hours spent in services.

The uppermost blocks in both the east- and west-facing shafts of the first pier (bay 2/3) display a vertical joint resulting from a medieval repair of the stone. A new front to the shaft has been shaped and fitted using hot resin mastic: both sides of the joint display the characteristic pink colouration resulting from heating the stone before applying the resin.[27] This repair was probably carried out during the construction of the arcade, and other medieval repairs using hot mastic are present here too (Pl. 35).[28]

The arcade piers exhibit various post-medieval repairs, and the west respond had a small horizontal slot cut in its inner roll (and later infilled with mortar) near to the top. This must have been for a fixture, but it is not typical of a screen fixing. Some columnar sections have badly chipped arrises which are noticeable in the bed-joints. Either these moulded stones were recycled in the 14th century, or they suffered rough handling between cutting and erection.

West wall

The west wall of the nave is difficult to interpret. Much of it comprises the rebuilt tower of 1602, but earlier work is incorporated, especially in the southern one-third, where the medieval staircase survives. In an attempt to gain more information about what lies under the wallplaster, a remote-sensing survey was carried out in 2001 by Dr Christopher Brooke. Although this revealed several anomalous patches and breaks in the masonry construction, it failed to shed significant light on the archaeology of the west wall.[29]

The string-course between the first and second stages on the exterior of the tower continues around the polygonal buttress at the north-east angle of the tower (a small part of which is exposed within the nave) and, curiously, the moulding visible within the nave has the appearance of being weathered. Above the string, the tower masonry includes finely jointed ashlar and a few pieces of knapped flint. The tower string does not continue across the west wall. However, c. 80 cm above tie-beam level in the nave roof is a second string-course, square in section and quadrant-moulded on the upper arris: it is unrelated to any detail visible elsewhere on the exterior of the tower.[30] This could have been intended as a weathering for the flashing to a flat lead roof or a transverse gutter. A third string-course with a cavetto moulding on the lower arris is only 1.2 m above the second. This moulding, which been substantially hacked to accommodate the present roof structure, probably equates with the string-course around the exterior of the tower at the junction between the second and third structural stages.[31]

Floor

The floor is on two levels, separated by a limestone step running across the nave at the junction between bays 2 and 3 (plan, Fig. 176). A similar step also returns under the arcade in bay 2. This was necessitated by the two eastern bays of the nave being 18 cm lower than the remainder and the adjoining south aisle. It is clear from the arcade bases and other features that the lower level obtained throughout the nave in the 14th century. When the floor was repaved in 1747 the level may have been raised. There is an infilled Victorian boiler-chamber beneath the paving at the north-west corner.[32]

In bays 1 and 2 the floor is entirely late 19th century, comprising a central alley, paved with Yorkstone and flanked by softwood decking upon which pews are mounted. No ledgers are apparent. By contrast, the floor in bays 3–5 is a palimpsest of reused materials, including ledger slabs and gravestones (Pl. 34). The majority of these are 17th and 18th century, and some are headstones brought in from the churchyard.[33] There are also plain paving slabs, a few 14th-century decorated floor tiles, some

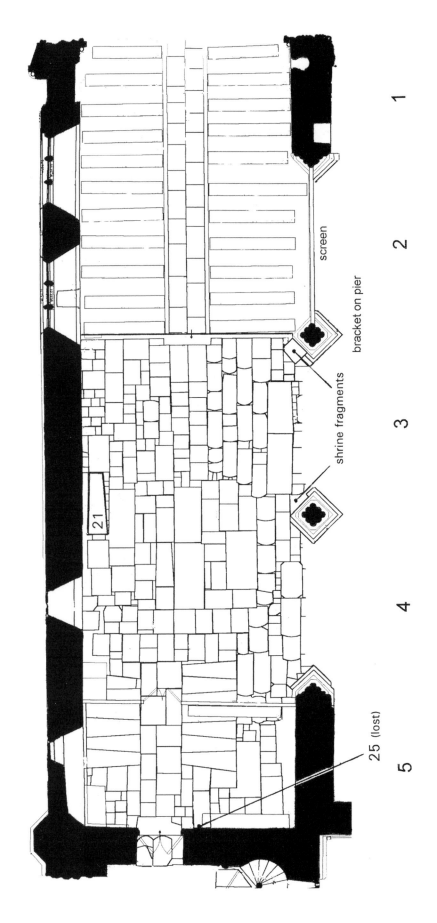

Figure 176. Plan of the nave, showing floor paving, 2001. The surviving medieval monument (M.21) and shrine fragments are emphasized; a second medieval monument (M.25) has been lost from the west end. (adapted from Sterling Surveys)

later tiles, and several small areas of Roman cement screed. Some of the plain slabs are limestone, old and well worn; others are Yorkstone, and were introduced in the mid-19th century. Amongst the latter is a group of eleven identical, tapered slabs in bay 5, having the appearance of medieval coffin lids. However, they have clearly never been used for that purpose, and are Victorian.

Many slabs in the nave are fractured, and some exhibit star-cracking, which is the result of violent impact occurring at a single point. This can only have been caused by a heavy object falling from above (Fig. 177). The most likely time for this to have occurred is when the nave was reroofed in 1862, although it is difficult to envisage Scott tolerating such blatant damage.

Notable amongst the flooring materials are:

(i)   A medieval coped coffin lid (M.21: Fig. 166c; see p. 170), set against the north wall in bay 3, where it was first recorded on plan in 1899 (Fig. 9).

(ii) Two moulded cornice blocks in Purbeck marble from a major 14th-century monument. They have hollow-chamfered mouldings bearing individual, knobbly leaves. One block is against the north-west face of the arcade pier to bay 2/3; the other against the north-east face of pier 3/4. These are important pieces, almost certainly from the cornice of St Birinus's shrine.

(iii) A small, tapered limestone coffin lid, south-west of M.21. This is likely to be medieval, but is featureless.

(iv) Two pieces of a black marble wall monument, dated 1638, bearing a lengthy Latin inscription. One is flat, the other segmental in section; now laid in the floor against the north wall, west of M.21. These are the remnants of the elaborate wall-mounted memorial to Edward Clarke that adorned the chancel.

(v)   Next to the last, a rectangular white marble panel also from a once-fine wall monument, bearing a Latin inscription to Francis Dandridge, d. 1714.

(vi) In several places where limestone slabs have decayed, a bed of dark brown 'Roman cement' was laid down in the 18th or early 19th century, and scored around the edges to imitate joints between paving stones. Most unusually, the mason then impressed his hobnailed boot in the wet cement, and several impressions have survived (Fig. 178). They mirror the practice of plumbers, who often left their foot or hand 'prints' on lead roofs (by scoring the outlines with a sharp instrument).

Roof

The roof was entirely reconstructed by Scott, in 1862. It is of crown-post type, with six-canted, scissor-braced rafter-couples and a central purlin, but no collars. The structure is arranged in eight bays with trusses at both ends, and does not correlate meaningfully with the five architectural bays below.[34] The roof is of Baltic pine but is not as ornately detailed as that over the south aisle. The tie-beams have filleted rolls on their lower arrises, and the arch-braced

FIGURE 177. *Nave: floor slab with star-fracturing caused by violent impact. (Warwick Rodwell)*

FIGURE 178. *Nave: boot-nail impressions in a patch of Roman cement in the floor, probably early 19th century. (Warwick Rodwell)*

principals are without collars; the crown-posts have moulded capitals and bases with four-way bracing directly on to the principals and the central purlin. The oak wallplates, which are double-stacked and moulded, are partly 19th century and partly medieval. Also in oak are the short wall-posts and plain braces beneath the tie-beams: they are made from ancient timbers (possibly principal rafters) and exhibit redundant mortices and peg-holes. Examination of two of these braces by dendrochronology in 2003 showed that they had belonged to a structure dating from the second quarter of the 17th century.[35] A date in the 1630s is most likely, and this is reconcilable with the churchwardens' statement in 1623 that the timber work of the nave roof was out of repair. Hence, the nave may have been reroofed at about the same time as the south aisle in 1633. Alternatively, the 17th-century timbers in the nave might have been 'imported' by Scott in 1862, he having reroofed the aisle in the previous year (p. 111).

An inconspicuously carved date (1854) occurs on one of the timbers at the north-east corner of the nave, which places it in Butterfield's period. The wall-posts rest on quadrant-shaped stone corbels most of which appear to be 19th century, although at least four are potentially late medieval in date and may be presumed to be *in situ*. That being so, the window in bay 3 must have been blocked when the tie-beam roof was first constructed, because one of the corbels is set into its filling. The corbel at the west end of the south wall carrying the thin end-truss alongside the tower is medieval, and old wallplaster survives in the gap between the truss and the west wall. This plaster has partly been trapped by raising the south wall of the nave, which occurred in two phases: first, a late medieval addition of *c.* 60 cm of rubble masonry and, second, 30 cm of 19th-century brickwork to carry the valley gutter between nave and aisle. The late medieval masonry must represent a rebuilding of the wall-top, rather than heightening *per se*: the rear-arch of the Norman window in bay 5 was lost in that rebuild. No comparable evidence exists for raising or rebuilding the top of the north wall, and the level of the window heads implies that it has always been at its present height. A possible explanation for the medieval reduction of the south wall might be that a narrow aisle with a monopitched roof was added sometime prior to the erection of the present 14th-century aisle (*cf.* p. 80).

The nave roof is covered with red clay tiles. The east wall (now chancel arch, originally part of the crossing) is expressed above the roof-line with a parapet-coping. It is on the same axis as the wall separating the two southern aisles.

FITTINGS

Screen

Under the arcade in bay 2 is a low timber screen, partly of 14th-century date but heavily restored in the 19th century. The screen itself is of oak, framed in five bays, and currently stands one metre high on the stone step between nave and aisle. The sill and three of the four chamfered muntins are 19th century; the one original muntin has a bar-stop at the top of the chamfer but nothing at the lower end, perhaps implying that it has been shortened. The pseudo-crenellated top rail is essentially medieval although it has had a new facing strip applied on the north

side. The frame is filled with plain oak panels: each has a groove on one long edge and a bevelled tongue on the other, to allow them to interlock as an early form of tongue-and-groove boarding. Since the top-rail is formed in one piece and has stopped mouldings at both ends, it was unquestionably made for its present position, and has never been part of the rood screen as some antiquaries claimed.

Screwed to the top of the rail are several 19th-century iron plates of sexfoil pattern that formerly held metal stanchions supporting a rail and curtain, as seen in old photographs. There are no mortices or other evidence of medieval fixings which indicates that this was the top-rail, and not the mid-rail, of a screen, although its current low level would lead to the latter supposition. What survives today could be the rebuilt upper section of a once much taller side-screen with solid panels. In this connection, it may be noted that there are infilled vertical chases in both stone responds extending for a metre above the present position of the rail: hence, there was formerly a 2 m high screen here.

Glass

Windows in bays 1 and 2 contain reset medieval armorial glass representing the shields of England, and the Earls of Cornwall and Lancaster, respectively.

The stained glass window in bay 4 was given the parishioners in 1887 in memory of the William Charles Macfarlane, Vicar of Dorchester, 1856–85. The leaded glazing in bay 5 is ancient and includes some good crown glass. At the top of the window is a cut-down quarry incised with a cursive inscription, reading *Wilkins 1834 Glazier*.[36] The internal ferramenta appear to be Tudor.

Floor slabs

M.21 (Fig. 166c). Set into the floor against the north wall is an interesting and unusual medieval Purbeck marble coffin lid; it is coped and tapering, with a small bead-moulding around the edge.[37] It has a plain, raised cross running down the full length, and a stepped base; the arms do not have decorated terminals, but continue to the edges of the slab. In the two western corners are incised five-petalled rosettes attached to stems, and there are vestiges of two more below the arms of the cross. An inscription in Lombardic characters ran around all four sides of the cover; the indents for the letters are boldly and deeply cut, but the brass has all gone. The remains of the inscription read:

[+] W | S: KE: P[AR]: ICI: P[ASSEZ]: | PVR: | LALME: FRERE: RAVF: [P]R | I[EZ]

'You who pass by here, pray for the soul of Brother Ralph'. Nothing further is known of Ralph, but his monument dates from *c.* 1300–30.

[M.25] There was another medieval limestone coffin lid, standing upright against the west wall, but is now lost.

It was a small coped and tapered slab which bore a cross fleury.[38]

Furniture

The plain oak benches were designed by Butterfield, c. 1853. There is an early 18th-century oak-framed table with turned legs and stretchers, and a modern top. This was presumably used as the sole altar, and may originally have been fitted with a marble top, as was sometimes the case in the 18th century.[39]

NOTES

1   Keevill, 2003.
2   The gravel aggregate is very mixed, the average being 3–4 mm across, but with some pebbles up to 10 mm across, and occasionally larger.
3   The break is emphasized by a wide bed-joint in the masonry containing many small fragments of clunch, used as packing material. These appear to be masons' waste derived from the preparation of ashlars or other dressed blocks. Clunch waste is also found as an occasional filling material in joints above the building-lift, but not below it.
4   The mortar is soft and the aggregate ranges in size from 2 mm to 20 mm, and occasionally up to 30 mm. The walling is entirely of rubble and lacks even roughly squared blocks. Pieces of flint are also incorporated.
5   The cut for inserting this doorway is clear; buff coloured mortar was used, with oyster shells packing the joints.
6   The ghosted outline of the arch is clear, and Grimm marked it on one of his sketches, c. 1780: BL, Add. Ms 15,545, f. 144. It is indicated on only one published plan (Anon., 1910, 233).
7   The filling contains at least one blocked putlog hole for a timber 20 cm square. The plinth at the base of the wall is now continuous, but there is a slight difference in the character of the masonry between the eastern and western sections. The eastern part of the plinth has probably been created to match the western, although whether this was done in the Norman period, or as part of the 19th-century restoration, could only be determined archaeologically.
8   The masonry includes flattish pieces of limestone, which are not characteristic of the lower western part, and the mortar in the blocked opening is slightly yellower. The sequence could be established archaeologically.
9   It has not been possible to examine this wall at close quarters, or to inspect the mortar.
10   E.g. see Buckler's sketches of 1802: BL, Add. Ms 36,405, f. 48r.
11   On the north side, the internal string-course is c. 60 cm lower than the external. None of the external string survives on the south, but its position is marked towards the east end by a distinct shouldering in the wallplaster. This also continues on to the east wall of the nave aisle, which was formerly the exterior of the Norman south transept. Hence the string-course coincided with a slight setback (less than 5 cm) in the Norman external wall faces.
12   The designs have not been studied, but appear to originate from the tilery at Penn, Bucks. Two sizes are present: 10.5 cm and 12.5 cm square.
13   For a plan of the threshold, see Keevill, 2003, fig. 14. Some of the medieval tiles were stolen in 2003.
14   Simons, 2004, 10, fig. 3.
15   In bay 5 the east jamb is almost certainly primary, and only the west jamb has been repositioned, while in bay 4 the spacing suggests that neither jamb is Norman work in situ.
16   A second, somewhat similar block has confusingly been placed alongside the sole survivor of the west jamb (probably in the 19th century), so that together their splays form a V-shaped feature in the wall. This is a purely antiquarian display.
17   The head projects above the level of the stone corbels supporting wall-posts for the roof; the east corbel is medieval, the west is later.
18   The front timber, having partly decayed, was removed in 2003, repaired and reinstated. An attempt to date it by dendrochronology was unsuccessful. Archaeological recording of this and other work on the nave roof was carried out by Oxford Archaeology.
19   This provides the only primary evidence for the external detail of the Norman windows. Vertical scarring in the medieval wallplaster below the surviving fragment of west jamb hints at a 19th-century antiquarian exploration to search for more evidence, but evidently none was preserved.
20   The lintel is made from a length of Norman string-course with a 10 cm diameter roll (only visible from inside the cupboard). The roof of the cupboard comprises exposed Norman wall-core, with coarse pebbly mortar.
21   The innermost order is made of stones varying between 25 cm and 75 cm long; the blocks of the middle order are 20–30 cm; and of the outer order 18–32 cm. The sections of hood-moulding measure 50–60 cm.
22   Although the artist shows the bracket projecting from the wall of the south chancel aisle in Fig. 191A, it has never been in this location, as Skelton (1823, 6) confirms.
23   The fracture here suggests multiple blows, not a simple accident.
24   BL, Add. Ms. 29,931, ff. 185–6.
25   On the south side of the pier, is a small square pocket to anchor a metal fixing into the shaft, and there is repaired damage to its base. No evidence of attachment occurs on the north face of the pier. Cut into the top of the bracket, against the west shaft of the pier, is another pocket.
26   Gough, 1789, 1, 307; Skelton, 1823, 6; Addington, 1845, 36.
27   There is now a thin line of mortar in the joint on the west face, indicating that the resin bond failed and the repair was re-adhered using lime mortar.
28   E.g. there are two separate repairs to the west-facing shaft directly above the carved bracket attached to bay 2/3 pier.

29 Brooke also examined the west end of the north wall, with similarly inconclusive results. His report is summarized in Keevill, 2003, 319–22.

30 The moulding being on the upper arris suggests that the string is inverted, and is perhaps a reused feature: it could be Norman. The string-course does not extend across the full width of the west wall, having possibly never been present on the southernmost one-third (*i.e.* it is absent where the masonry encasing the medieval tower stair survives).

31 Like the second string, this does not extend across the full width of the nave, and is again absent towards the southern end.

32 Keevill, 2003, fig. 18.

33 The different materials are highlighted on plan: Simons, 2004, figs 11 and 12.

34 The easternmost section, against the chancel arch, is only a half-bay. One truss has been drawn: Simons, 2004, fig. 4.

35 Sapwood did not survive, but the heartwood-sapwood boundary occurred at 1612; the maximum date-range for felling is therefore 1621 to 1653. *Vernacular Archit.*, **35** (2004), 99.

36 Since the lead cames slightly overlap the inscription, the quarry must have been repositioned. It was presumably salvaged from another window.

37 Coales, 1987, 167, fig. 212. Badham and Norris, 1999, 149; Bertram, 2000, 17, 37 (no. 2).

38 Gough, 1786–96, **2**, intro., cxvi, pl. 6.4; Bertram, 2000, 35, 48 (uninscr. 3).

39 It is possibly the draped altar shown by Britton in 1821 (Fig. 98).

CHAPTER 15

South Nave Aisle and Porch (People's Chapel)

West wall

The archaeology of the west wall is problematic, apart from the gable which is a 19th-century rebuild (Fig. 75). The masonry comprises flattish pieces of neatly squared rubble, laid to courses, and a few pieces of medieval roof tile are incorporated. Also, immediately above the plinth are some small, neatly squared blocks of a pale coloured limestone which are visually distinct from the remainder of the masonry. They are obviously reused, and are reminiscent of Roman *opus quadratum* masonry (Fig. 19).

The wall contains a modest doorway and above it, but not quite axially aligned, is a large window, the sill of which rests on a hollow-moulded string-course that continues around the south side and includes the buttresses. The doorway has a pointed head, and the outer of the two orders of mouldings contains florets. The jambs have attached shafts with octagonal bases and plain capitals. Outside the hood-moulding, which was renewed in the 19th century, is a reinforcing arch of reasonably well cut voussoirs. The hood-moulding has returned ends but no label-stops and, oddly, does not connect with a string-course at capital level on the doorway. This low-level string, which is badly weathered, runs northwards from the doorway to the corner of the nave, but only a single block continues southwards. Beyond this is an irregular patch of rough rubblework, indicating that something was keyed in it this point, and later removed. This scar is likely to be the result of a post-medieval structural attachment. It would appear that the string-course originally stopped against the diagonal buttress at the south-west corner of the aisle. Below string level, at the north end of the wall, is a second area of rough rubble, which appears to be another attachment scar.

The major question concerns the originality of the doorway in relation to the surrounding masonry of the wall. On the one hand, there is no evidence that the jambs of the doorway were cut into an older wall, and the arch is definitely contemporary with the masonry above it, yet on the other hand there is such blatant discontinuity in the moulded detail that two periods of work seem to be implied. Thus, the moulded ashlar plinth stops abruptly at the door jambs, as though it had been cut through; and the same applies to the low-level string-course.[1] That moulding does not even have stopped ends, and its relationship to the hood-moulding is bizarre. In short, the string-course connects with nothing and serves no purpose: it recurs in bay 1 (only) on the south side, where again it is difficult to explain. It is also noticeable that the bases of the attached shafts to the doorway are set very low in relation to the chamfered component of the plinth.

The west wall is dominated by a large window with intersecting tracery and high-pointed trefoil heads to the main lights and trefoiled sub-arches. The hood-moulding and the ring of neat voussoirs reinforcing it are 19th century (associated with the rebuilding of the gable), and the jambs are substantially renewed too. Although the string-course below sill level continues around the south-west buttress, there is a disjuncture which is disguised by the presence of a modern carved head representing Edith Stedman, founder of the American Friends of Dorchester Abbey (Fig. 179).[2] This replaces a weathered medieval head, which ended its days as a garden ornament.[3] The string-courses to either side have different moulding profiles.

The south-west corner of the aisle is marked by a diagonally placed buttress of large proportions, having been designed to incorporate statue niches in two registers (Figs 74 and 179). The buttress was removed from the corner of the south transept and rebuilt here in the 14th century (p. 78). The lower register is built entirely of ashlar and has a single flat-backed niche in its south-west face. Capable of holding a life-sized statue, the opening is lined with attached shafts carrying rather crude stiff-leaf capitals[4] and a moulded arch with filleted rolls (Fig. 180). The bases are too eroded to describe. Flanking the niche are two square-section, pilaster-like mouldings which rise from the chamfered plinth and die back into the face of the buttress just above capital level.

The string-course dividing the two stages is a beaked roll, renewed in the 19th century, and above this are statue niches on the west and south-west faces of the buttress; the south-east face in plain. These

FIGURE 179. *South nave aisle: repositioned diagonal buttress at the south-west angle, with statue niches. (Warwick Rodwell)*

FIGURE 180. *South nave aisle: detail of the capitals of the lower niche on the south-west face of the angle-buttress. (Warwick Rodwell)*

FIGURE 181. *South nave aisle: window in bay 1. The plinth is pierced by the head of the small window to the crypt below the aisle. (Addington, 1845)*

niches are not only shallower than the lower one, but have splayed reveals and rubble backs. Again, the heads of the niches are moulded and the reveals have attached shafts with capitals that are very worn but appear to carry stiff-leaf decoration. The salient angles are clasped by pairs of square-section mouldings rising from chamfered bases; they terminate in small heads which form the stops for the gablets that crown the niches.

The buttress is capped by a solid turret of polygonal form, which was rebuilt in the 19th century. The poppy-head terminals to the gablets have also been renewed, together with the crocketed pinnacles occupying the salient angles.

Both the window and the west door must be 14th century, as are the crocketed pinnacles on the corner buttress, but the niches are certainly older and the stiff-leaf capitals date from the mid-13th century. The door and its ornate ironwork are 19th century.

South wall

The three-light windows in bays 1–4 have cusped intersecting Y-tracery, *en suite* with the slightly more elaborate tracery of the west window (Figs 5 and 181). The windows are superficially similar to those of the south chancel aisle, but there are significant differences in detail (p. 142). Some replacement of stones in the jambs and the hood-mouldings has taken place, and the label-stops are 19th century, but otherwise the 14th-century work is mostly intact. An original stop

– a female head – is preserved on the west side of bay 3. The window in bay 4 is shorter than the others, its sill resting on the same string-course as the west window; the string then drops to run beneath the sills of the taller windows in bays 1–3, at the same time embracing the buttresses. At the point where the string drops, in the west angle of the bay 3/4 buttress, is a medieval carved head. This originally overlooked the south doorway, but is now immediately above the porch roof and consequently is all but invisible from the churchyard.

The string-course was renewed in the 19th century, as was much of the moulded plinth. All the weatherings and the faces of some of the buttresses have also been thoroughly restored in the 19th and 20th centuries. Where the bases of the buttresses can be seen in drainage gulleys, they display evidence of an offset (c. 5 cm) below the plinth, marking 14th-century ground level. By contrast, the aisle wall lacks any offset, perhaps indicating that the two elements are not contemporaneous. It may also be noted that there are no ashlars forming internal quoins between the aisle wall and its buttresses, which contrasts with the situation in the south chancel aisle. The possibility that the present aisle incorporates earlier foundations and fabric has been considered (p. 80).

Below the window in bay 4 is the south doorway, which is similar in style to that in the west wall (Fig. 182). There are two steps down to floor level inside the church. The doorway has a two-centred arch, with florets in the hollow-moulded outer order. The hood-moulding has short returns and no label-stops. Unlike the west door, these returns align with the lower string-course but are not physically linked. An outer ring of plain ashlar voussoirs springs from the string. The jambs of the doorway carry attached shafts with capitals and bases similar to those of the west door, and once again no attempt has been made to relate the deep bolection-moulded plinth to the doorway. The 19th-century oak door has ornate ironwork; it superseded a plain boarded door which may have been medieval, but more likely it was 17th century.

The plain parapet and cornice were renewed in the 19th century. The cornice moulding is not the same as that on the chapel to the east, and nor are the parapets exactly aligned. The former transept wall, separating this aisle from the chancel aisle, is finished above roof level with a coping, the lower end of which terminates in a four-way gablet.

INTERIOR
North wall

The spur of solid wall at the east end (bay 1) is pierced at a high level by a plain rectangular doorway with a flat lintel and chamfered arris with tall brooch-stops (Fig. 183).[5] This doorway gave access on to the rood loft (p. 94). There is dark red paint on the eastern

FIGURE 182. South nave aisle: doorway in the south wall, bay 4. (Addington, 1845)

jamb. At a low level in the same bay is a locker with a chamfered and rebated surround; tell-tale marks relating to former hinge pintles show that there were two doors. Internally, the cupboard is rectangular and plastered. It is too large to have been an aumbry for the altar at the east end of the aisle, and is in any case on the wrong side of the passage leading through to the shrine chapel. More likely, the locker contained a devotional object, or was a place for pilgrims visiting the shrine to deposit gifts of money before passing through the door into the chancel aisle.

Bays 2–4 are occupied by the nave arcade (p. 166). Traces of the external chamfered opening of a Norman window are exposed in bay 5 (p. 166).

East wall

This wall is remarkable for its two registers of medieval painting, which were largely concealed from view until 1862, when the limewash was scraped off and the paintings over-restored by Clayton and Bell.[6] Conservation and the retouching of missing areas was carried out in 2005 by Ann Ballantyne. The elevation of the wall demonstrates the relationships between the major elements (Pl. 38).[7] At the northern end is a small, pointed doorway inserted in the 14th century (Figs 183 and 184). It opens into the south chancel aisle (now the Shrine Chapel). The arch and jambs are wave-moulded, and there is a hood-moulding with returned ends, both of which are oddly tilted instead of being horizontal. The hood-moulding was made for a larger doorway, and some stones were omitted during reassembly here. It is suggested that this was originally an external door

FIGURE 183. *South nave aisle: features at the north-east corner, including a locker adjacent to the nave arcade, the doorway opening eastwards into the chancel aisle, and the high-level doorway to the rood loft. (Warwick Rodwell)*

FIGURE 184. *South nave aisle: doorway in the east wall, opening into the south chancel aisle. The returns on the label-moulding are not accurately rendered. The font is glimpsed on the left, beyond the panelled end of a box pew. (Addington, 1845)*

in the south chancel aisle (p. 83). A 15 cm step (down) in the doorway was not originally intended and has been created by lowering the floor in the chancel aisle. The present door is 19th century, painted.

Wallpainting: lower register
The lower tier of wallpainting represents a Crucifixion framed within a rectangular panel, with a red diapered background (Pl. 40). Unfortunately, a great deal of the plaster in the lower register was renewed in the 19th century, and accompanied by substantial repainting: to what extent this was based on secure evidence is now impossible to tell.[8] Two periods of medieval work are represented here, the diapered 'brocade' pattern having been added in the early 15th century.[9] To either side of the Crucifixion are flanking panels filled with stencilled leaves and small pentagonal motifs.

This was clearly the reredos to an altar which stood against the east wall. The whole composition is markedly asymmetrical in its layout, and the left-hand border of the northern panel (entirely 19th century) was probably fabricated to align with the top step of the Victorian altar dais below. The original border is likely to have been further north, perhaps coinciding with the edge of the second step. Thus, the Crucifixion would have been better centred within the overall composition, and more aesthetically placed in relation to the medieval dais. Below the

main panels is a plain red dado with a decorative border and a wavy-line band at mid-height.

Wallpainting: upper register
High up in the wall is a wide, arched recess 55 cm deep with a flat back (Pl. 39). The head is pointed and the arris has a continuous, slightly hollow chamfer with pyramidal stops at the base but no imposts. The sill is of rubble with a mortared finish. A change of plane occurs in the back of the recess at the springing level of the arch, forming a marked shoulder. Another change in the plane of the east wall is present to the north of the arch.[10] The masonry is entirely concealed by lime plaster which is uneven in texture and exhibits much evidence of patching. Past claims that this arch originally belonged to a window in the transept are surely erroneous: the feature was more likely constructed as an altar recess.

The recess bears at least two painted schemes of decoration. As seen today, the back of the recess is occupied by a large cross, painted in dark red on an ochre background. It is very plain, the arms are thin, and they have unadorned, squarish terminals.[11] The foot of the cross may have been intended to be a square block, the base of which is 85 cm above the sill of the recess. At the same level, distinct changes are observable in the exposed polychromy on the flanks and chamfers of the recess. Here, an earlier scheme is partially exposed. Painting in the lower region comprises free-flowing scrollwork drawn in red, which is assignable to the late 13th century. Higher up, this has been obliterated by the 14th-century scheme which includes the cross. Associated with, or later than, that is a formal interlace pattern drawn in red on an ochre ground; the design is Renaissance-influenced and may be 16th century. In addition to these schemes, there is chevron decoration, in black, running around the chamfer of the arch: it is difficult to see how this can be later than the early 13th century.[12]

Running down the central axis of the cross is a scored line in the plaster, which relates to its setting out; that line passes over the shoulder in the masonry. The upper arm of the cross was evidently quite short, and its terminal has been lost where a plaster repair 60 cm across has taken place.[13] Some 35 cm beneath the north-pointing arm of the cross is a small 19th-century repair in the plaster, set within a much larger, older patch. This is matched by another old repair beneath the south-pointing arm.[14] These patches suggest the former presence of a symmetrical pair of corbels or other fixings set into the back of the recess. However, Ballantyne reports these patches as being earlier than the painted cross: she suggests that a timber rood may have been fixed here initially.

The earliest scheme certainly antedates the mid-14th century, confirming that there was a structure on this site before the present aisle was erected (see further, p. 80). There must have been a gallery or upper room, with its floor corresponding to the base of the painted recess. If the floor abutted the south wall it must have cut across the window in bay 1: while there is no evidence for that being so, it would not have been an uncommon occurrence. It is likely that the rood loft stair was also contrived within this aisle, rather than in the nave.[15]

South wall

This is lime plastered, partly ancient and partly Victorian. Removal of the cementitious area below sill level revealed the fabric of the south wall.[16] It is composed of rectangular blocks of limestone, fairly well squared but varying in size, laid roughly to courses. A line of putlog holes was noted, and a small, round-arched feature which is blocked. Although at the right level, the latter seems to be both too small and too far from the south door for a stoup, and its purpose is therefore enigmatic.

Extending up to 30 cm above modern floor level is evidence of a former offset which has been cut back flush with the wall face above. This is not consistent with the loss of a medieval stone wall-bench, the top slabs of which would have left tell-tale evidence in the fabric. It represents a former foundation offset at the original floor level for the aisle (see further, p. 179).

The wall is divided into two registers by a moulded string-course which is coincident with window-sill level in bays 1 to 3. The string then rises vertically alongside the doorway, before returning at sill level under the window above; it continues on to the west wall where, again, it separates the head of the doorway from the window above. The string-course in bay 4 is a 19th-century renewal, perhaps indicating that there had been a post-medieval feature constructed in the south-west corner of the aisle which had necessitated hacking off the projecting moulding.

There are four windows. The reveals are mostly of ashlar with plastered soffits,[17] slightly dropped rear-arches and label-mouldings. The angles are embellished with a double-hollow moulding with a slender roll between; the latter is topped by a small bell capital with a double moulded abacus (cf. the capitals of the nave arcade). The mouldings rise from oddly proportioned bases, octagonal in plan and surmounted by a mushroom-shaped moulding carrying the stooling for a roll which serves as a diminutive shaft. The rear-arch mouldings have a flattened roll, filleted and keeled.

Just above arch-springing level, on either side of every window reveal, a small pocket (averaging 5 cm square) has been cut into the first voussoir. The pockets have been infilled with medieval mortar, but their purpose was to hold a horizontal timber spanning the aperture and carrying the centring necessary for the construction of the rear-arch. In bay 1 only, two vertical chases have also been cut into the first pair of voussoirs, showing that a timber was subsequently slotted into the aperture; its date and purpose are unknown but it could possibly have been associated with a gallery at this end of the aisle.

There has been some 19th-century restoration to the tracery, but the windows are largely original. In bay 1 the east label-stop bears a heavily scraped, male head with the mouth slightly open, and a garment wrapped around it; traces of dark red paint occur. The west stop depicts a female with headdress. Bay 2 has a male head on the east stop, with a cap from under which emerges flowing hair; and the west stop also has a male head with a scarf wound around it.[18] The east stop in bay 3 is similar, while the west stop has a male head with large, pointed ears, scroll-like hair and a prominent chin.[19] In bay 4 the sill is much higher, owing to the presence of the doorway below. The east label-stop is another male with a scarf, and the west stop has been lost. The mouldings of the capitals and the clumsy bases in this bay differ slightly from those of the other windows.

The south doorway has a plain chamfered rear-arch with stops, and a segmental head which is hollow moulded. Blocked draw-bar sockets in the reveals show that the door could be secured from inside the church. A semi-octagonal oak draught-

FIGURE 185. South nave aisle: piscina and sedilium or tomb-recess in the south wall, bay 1. (Warwick Rodwell)

lobby was constructed within the aisle by Scott. This was dismantled in 2002 and replaced with a new structure of engraved glass.[20]

In the south-east corner of the aisle, 75 cm below the wall-plate, are the cut-back remains of a medieval stone corbel with red paint on its west side. It could have supported a wall-post associated with the original roof; if so, there are likely to have been other corbels along the south wall which have been hacked off and concealed by plaster. Also in the south-east corner, just below the corbel and forming part of the south transept wall, is a vertical series of ashlars bearing a crude chamfer. This feature, damaged and largely obscured by the abutment of the aisle, is not easily explained except as the scar remaining after the removal of the buttress from the south-west corner of the transept: it was repositioned when the aisle was built (p. 78; Fig. 179).

Finally, in the south wall of bay 1 is an original piscina and a low-level recess: the former is integrated with the string-course, and the latter is incorporated within the window sill, where it interrupts the string (Figs 185 and 186). The piscina has a pointed trefoil head and a shallow moulding running across the back of the recess: as a credence shelf it was extremely narrow. The bowl projects slightly from the wall-face and has a moulded rim, drain-hole and central sinking in the form of a quatrefoil. The hood-moulding is linked with the string-course on the west but, being close to the corner of the aisle, no attempt was made to continue the string eastwards.

The recess beneath the window is generally supposed to have been a sedilium, but it is unusual in comprising a single, broad seat without a canopy or subdivisions. It could seat two persons, but not the usual three. The arrises of the jambs have wave-mouldings and bull-nosed stops. Two other possible

FIGURE 186. South nave aisle: piscina during repairs to the wallplaster. (Martin Ashley Architects)

uses may be considered. First, this could be a tomb-recess that contained an effigy relating to a burial in the crypt below. A potential objection is the fact that the recess is rather short (1.5 m) to contain an adult-sized effigy, and the reveals are slightly splayed in relation to the back. It is not typical of a tomb-recess, but that function cannot be ruled out. Secondly, the ledge could have been designed as the setting for an Easter sepulchre, which was a popular liturgical feature in the 14th century. The proportions of the recess would suit such a use, but Easter Sepulchres were nearly always on the north side of the altar. In this instance, however, such a position would have been logistically impossible. A tomb recess often doubled as an Easter sepulchre. The lower part of the west jamb of the feature has been damaged, where a pocket was cut into the wall to receive a timber; this was probably a fixing for a low screen or altar rail.

West wall

Central to the end of the aisle is the west doorway, the rear-arch of which has a segmental head with hollow moulding and plain chamfered jambs with stops (*cf.* the rear-arch of the small doorway in the east end). The reveals are lined with ashlar and there are infilled sockets that were intended to receive a draw-bar for securing the door from inside the church.

The upper part of the wall is filled with a great window, rising into the gable. Much of the intersecting tracery is original although patched in places, but the mullions are 19th-century renewals. The reveals are flanked by two orders of attached shafts, the outer a plain roll, the inner filleted. The outer capitals have upright naturalistic (oak?) leaves, while the inner capitals are bell-shaped and surmounted by a double abacus. The shafts rise from water-holding bases on square plinths. The mullions have convex chamfers and a roll-moulded inner face; by contrast, the south windows have hollow-chamfered mullions without roll mouldings.

The rear-arch has a complex moulding of 13th-century type, composed of many voussoirs.[21] The bed-joints are wide and filled with cement, and the arrises are badly damaged: this arch must have been rebuilt from recovered fragments in the 19th century, when the original form of the west gable was reinstated. The label has a stop on the north representing a pope with a pointed cap rising through a crown; there was no stop on the south, only a short return on the moulding. Yellow ochre and white limewash survive extensively in the mouldings, more so here than anywhere else in the church.

The handling of the two reveals is not identical, and the inner capital on the south is a 19th-century restoration. The bases to the shafts are of a type common in the mid-13th century, not the 14th century. The detailing of the west window bears no stylistic resemblance to that of the south windows: all the mouldings are different. The west window is plainly earlier than the rest, and reset (p. 79).

Floor

The present paving is 19th century, incorporating materials of various ages (plan, Fig. 187). The medieval functional logistics in this aisle are perplexing: it would clearly have been unworkable as it now is, and serious changes must have been wrought. Three different levels are indicated by 14th-century features:

(i) The thresholds of the west and south doorways: two steps lead down from these to the general floor level.
(ii) The altar dais above the crypt at the east end: four steps rise up to this from the present aisle floor.
(iii) The bases of the nave arcade and threshold of the

doorway leading to the chancel aisle: these are all one step below present floor level.

When plaster was removed from the south wall, evidence of a cut-back foundation offset was revealed, pointing to an original floor level along the whole length of the aisle corresponding to the door thresholds. That would reduce the elevation of the dais to two steps, which would be more plausible. However, at the same time it would increase the differential with the nave floor to three steps. It is clear from the arcade bases that there never were steps along this east–west line, and that is also confirmed by the threshold level of the small doorway in the east wall (Fig. 184). The only viable option is to envisage the aisle as being divided longitudinally by a screen which stood on an abrupt change of level equivalent to three steps. In other words, the present wide aisle was initially conceived as a narrower aisle and, running separately alongside it at a lower level, a passage. Three steps were probably provided at the west end, for access from the aisle down to the passage level.[22] It is not difficult to envisage why a passage was required here, it being the only way that pilgrims could gain access to the shrine chapel without passing through the monastic quire.

Although there was a raised medieval floor at the end of the aisle, above the crypt, the present compromise of levels and the tiered dais is partly a post-Dissolution creation (Pl. 38). However, when the aisle was repaved in the 19th century, the levels and steps do not seem to have been changed. The main area is paved with a mixture of ledgers and other materials, including plain limestone slabs laid in rows; a strip of relaid medieval decorative tiles was created as an antiquarian display against the timber screen under the arcade (bay 2; Pl. 36). This was typical of Scott's approach to preserving evidence of former flooring materials.[23] Also reset in the floor are two matrices for 15th-century brasses near the font, the very worn remains of a medieval coped coffin lid in front of the altar steps,[24] and various later memorials.[25] The tiered dais at the east end has slender stone nosings to the steps but is otherwise entirely covered with Victorian glazed encaustic tiles from the Godwin factory at Lugwardine, Herefordshire (Pl. 37). These are mostly brown with cream-slipped designs, and there are some black border-tiles. These were standard Godwin designs and, unlike those in the sanctuary, were not copies of medieval tiles actually found at Dorchester.[26] Previously, the dais was 'chiefly of brick, with a few figured tiles'.[27]

Roof

This is of four bays with tie-beams supporting arch-braced crown-posts and collars; the rafter-couples are canted and scissor-braced (Fig. 188). It is well constructed in Baltic pine and is more ornately

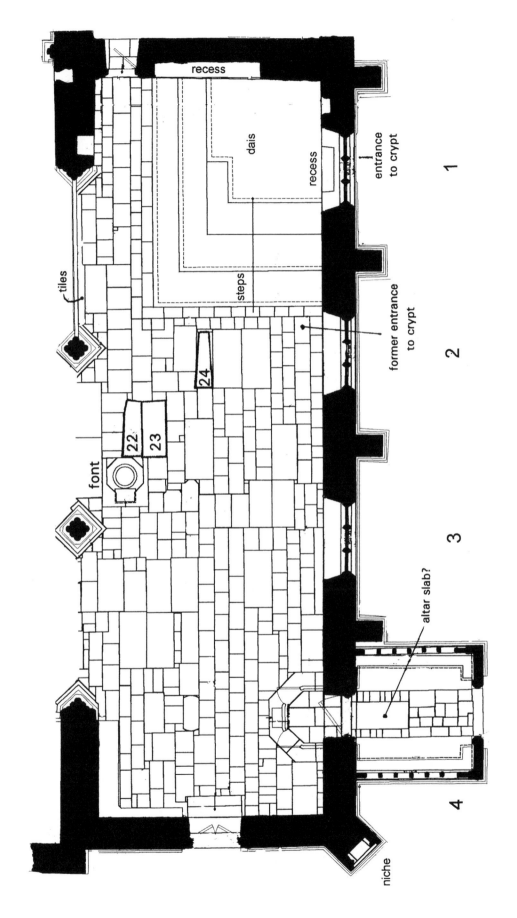

FIGURE 187. *Plan of the south nave aisle and porch, showing floor paving, 2001. The medieval monuments are emphasized (M.22 to M.24). (adapted from Sterling Surveys)*

FIGURE 188. *South nave aisle: Scott's roof of 1861. (Warwick Rodwell)*

FIGURE 189. *South nave aisle: cartouche with the date '1861' carved on a tie-beam. (Warwick Rodwell)*

FIGURE 190. *South nave aisle: Norman lead font bowl on Butterfield's plain stone base. View looking north. (Warwick Rodwell)*

detailed than the nave roof. The tie-beams have filleted rolls on their lower arrises, the principal rafters are straight, and without collars; the crown-posts have moulded capitals and bases with four-way bracing (moulded) directly on to the principals and the central purlin. The roof is dated on the easternmost tie-beam by a bas-relief inscription in a cartouche: '1861' (Fig. 189). The double wallplates are of oak, the inner being moulded and carrying pine crenellations; the merlons are pierced with encircled quatrefoils. On the arcade wall the plate is carried on 19th-century moulded stone corbels which are relatively plain, except for a more elaborately detailed one at the east end. It does not appear that any medieval oak plates have survived in this aisle.

The top of the arcade wall was rebuilt in brick in the 19th century, to support the valley gutter. The roof is covered with red clay tiles.

FITTINGS

Font

The font stands in bay 3, close to the arcade, which is its fifth recorded location (Fig. 190; Pl. 38). It was positioned here in *c.* 1855–58, having previously stood on two successive sites under the south crossing arch since 1844/45 (Figs 102 and 184); before that it was on the dais at the east end of the south chancel aisle

(Figs 99 and 191), having been removed in 1809 from the middle of the nave (Fig. 6). The Norman bowl attracted the attention of early antiquaries, and has been illustrated many times, the first being Stukeley in 1736,[28] followed by Grimm in *c.* 1780.[29] Gough reported the belief that it was 'of Birinus' time ... the most antient and perhaps only one of its kind in the world'.[30] It is currently assigned to *c.* 1170–80 on art-historical grounds.

The bowl is circular, measuring 66 cm in diameter and 35.5 cm deep; it is of cast lead, decorated in high relief with an arcade of eleven round arches, separated by pilasters with cubical capitals, chevron-decorated shafts and moulded bases. The spandrels between the arches contain small leaf motifs, and there are continuous borders of acanthus leaves and other elements on projecting mouldings around the top and bottom of the bowl. Beneath every alternate pilaster is a small roundel. Each arch contains a nimbed male figure seated on a bench: they all carry a book in one hand, while two of them hold an instrument in the other. One of those is a key (Fig. 192), the other is unidentified. There are six poses, five of which are repeated once. The figures have been assumed to represent the Apostles (minus Judas), the one brandishing a key being safely identifiable as St Peter.[31] The bowl is likely to be of local manufacture, and one of the figures, with his right hand raised in blessing, has been compared to the Christ in Majesty depicted on the Norman seal of Wallingford priory, c. 1170.[32]

In the 19th century, the bowl was provided with a new lead base which was soldered internally around the edge. Holes in the rim and broken-off iron nails demonstrate that a hasp or other locking device was once fitted, as with most fonts. The bowl has unfortunately been treated with black paint, presumably in the late 19th century. Some thirty lead fonts of various dates survive in England, and while they have attracted a good deal of attention as curiosities, they have not been subjected to rigorous study.[33] Romanesque bowls have survived in sixteen churches, of which Dorchester is the only one with monastic origins. Later examples include a fine 13th-century bowl at nearby Long Wittenham.

Generally, lead font bowls were cast flat, and often in several pieces, but one or two may have been produced as cylinders, with the base being added separately. The method of manufacture of Dorchester's font is puzzling: the thick wall, high-relief decoration, and moulded bands at the top and bottom would make it difficult to bend a flat casting into a cylinder. However, the bowl has a soldered vertical seam internally, suggesting that it was indeed a flat casting which was then wrapped round to form a cylinder. Externally, the seam is not visible, and its position is obscured by one of the pilasters between the decorative arcading. That pilaster exhibits signs of 'lead disease', which may be the result of the soldered joint breaking down. Furthermore, it should be noted that the flat top of the rim has been added as a separate piece: a horizontal soldering-line is visible internally and, in some places externally, it can be seen where the added rim has overlapped cast elements of the decorative band.

For the most part, neither the figures nor the decoration are crisp, and that is not owing solely to wear and tear. Blurring is mainly the result of poor casting, using a wooden pattern and clay mould, rather than the 'lost wax' process. Cursory examination did not reveal any evidence of the details having been enhanced by chiselling, after casting. However, there are various letters, lines and other marks that have been secondarily applied to the fields under the arches. Some are merely graffiti that have been scratched on, but others have been applied using punches and engraving tools. They are probably all post-medieval in date, and some of the letters have a 17th-century appearance. The initials include, 'IB', 'EB' and 'IC'.[34] There are also many random scratchings and some deeply scored lines inside the bowl; the latter appear to have been made with deliberation.

The bowl now rests on an inelegant limestone drum with a quadrant moulding around the base, the whole being raised on an octagonal plinth of Yorkstone with a footpace to the west. The floor immediately around the font contains a border of late 19th-century inlaid tiles; this work dates from the mid or late 1850s, when the font was moved, but the stone drum is slightly earlier.[35] The bowl is covered with a flat oak lid decorated with iron straps and trefoils: it is a catalogue item and probably dates from the 1870s. Prior to Butterfield's restoration of the chancel, the bowl stood on an octagonal stone base, the sides of which were decorated with blind trefoil panels, and the top was moulded and crenellated (cf. the top rail of the oak screen under the nave arcade). This base was late 14th or 15th century (Fig. 191). Standing on the bowl was a plain, high-pointed cover (presumably oak), polygonal in plan and having a turned finial. That was possibly 17th century, rather than medieval.[36]

Floor slabs[37]

The following are of interest:[38] for locations, see plan, Fig. 187.

M.22 Immediately east of the font. Purbeck marble indent for brasses of a standing figure with an inscription plate below. Identifiable as the monument to Agnes Bedford (d. 1518/19); the inscription was recorded before it was lost.[39]

M.23 Adjacent to the last, on the south. Purbeck marble indent for brasses of a standing figure and an inscription plate below. Identifiable as the monument to William Bedford (d. 1516); the inscription was recorded before it was lost.[40]

M.24 Adjacent to the steps leading up to altar. Medieval limestone coffin lid; slightly coped, and tapered. Badly eroded, but a small area of polished surface still remains towards the south edge; no decoration now visible, but there was once a raised cross. This is almost certainly the late 13th-century floriated cross-slab that was illustrated by several antiquaries in the 18th and early 19th centuries.[41]

– West of the last is a rectangular limestone slab bearing traces of burning on the surface. No hint of decoration or inscription, and rough axe-marks suggest this may be the underside of a slab that has been inverted. It is potentially a late medieval ledger.

– Black marble slab with a Latin inscription to Francis Dandridge (d. 1714). This is a fine slab, one of very few in good condition.

– Slab commemorating Michael Desvaupons, Archdeacon of Dol in Brittany (d. 1798). He was a Roman Catholic refugee from the French Revolution who lived at Overy with the Davey family (p. 105, n. 32).[42]

B

A

FIGURE 191. Font. A. Mackenzie's view of the south-east chapels, showing the font on the dais. Confusingly, he has employed artistic licence in attaching to the south wall the carved bracket that is integral with one of the arcade piers in the nave (Figure 175). B. Jewitt's drawing of the font in the same location, shortly before its medieval stone base was destroyed. (Skelton, 1823; Addington, 1845)

FIGURE 192. Font: detail of the figure of St Peter, holding a book and a key. (Addington, 1845)

– The slab commemorating 29-year old Sarah Fletcher (d. 1799) contains a fulsome and emotional inscription, describing her 'artless Beauty, innocence of Mind and gentle Manners', but her 'Nerves were too delicately Spun to bear the rude Shakes and Jostlings … in this transitory World … the Sunk and died a Martyr to Excessive Sensibility'.

Altar

Oak-framed altar with six legs and moulded top: presumably by Scott, c. 1861 (Fig. 193).

Oak chest

A substantially restored oak chest of medieval type stands against the south wall (Fig. 194). The chest is of joined construction and of 'clamped front' type: four vertical boards (stiles) form the corners, their lower ends being carved as bracket feet.[43] The side and end panels are horizontal boards, chase-tenoned into the corners. The only decoration comprises a short run of nail-head ornament on the curved bracket of the restored front right foot; although 19th century, this presumably copies what was there. The front left foot is original but too decayed to be certain of the decoration.

FIGURE 193. *South nave aisle: oak altar and tiled dais by Scott, c. 1861. This view antedates the restoration of the wallpainting in 2005. (Warwick Rodwell)*

FIGURE 194. *South nave aisle: medieval iron-bound oak chest, heavily restored. (Warwick Rodwell)*

FIGURE 195. *South nave aisle: cast iron plaque on the south wall, 1858. (Warwick Rodwell)*

FIGURE 196. *Crypt: external entrance (formerly a window) in the south nave aisle, bay 1. (Warwick Rodwell*

The lid is made from two boards, strengthened with battens at the ends, and attached by eight T-hinges of the type used on doors in the 17th and 18th centuries. There are three locks with long hasps and back-straps; the central lock-plate has concave sides and is medieval, the others probably later. On each end of the chest is a centrally fixed iron ring-handle. The exterior is laced with thin iron straps, all seemingly of 19th-century date, fixed with a mixture of nails and woodscrews. The chest was, however, originally iron-bound, and the residual rust scars are visible. Various graffiti occur on the lid, including: 'IB 1655', 'RH', and 'AB'. The interior was originally fitted with tills at both ends, but they have gone, leaving the tell-tale chases in the front and back and the pivot-holes for the lids. The floor was been replaced with modern deal boards.

It is difficult to date the chest. The concave lock-plate is likely to be 15th century, but the stiles with mouldings on their inner edges point to an earlier origin, as does the replica nail-head ornament. This chest may well date from the early 13th century.

Plaque

Affixed to the south wall, adjacent to the west corner, is a later 19th-century cast iron plaque with an inscription which interestingly reveals the technology of its production (Fig. 195). The plaque has a border and lettering in relief, which reads:

> A Grant of { £170 } towards the { Rebuilding } of this Church was made by the Incorporated Society for Promoting the Enlargement, Building, and Repairing of Churches and Chapels, on the express and acknowledged condition that { 528 } seats should be reserved for the use of the poorer inhabitants of this Parish forever, such seats being distinguished by the numbers { 1 to 21 24 to 51 54 to 77 and 79 to 94 all } inclusive.

The plaque was cast in a sand mould, from a wooden pattern which embodied all the non-specific wording. Long slots were left in the pattern, into which individual letters and numbers were fitted, to record the details specific to this church; blanks were also used to fill excessive spaces in the slots. The insertions are indicated here by brackets { }. The seat numbers recorded do not approach the required total of 528.

CRYPT

Beneath part of bay 1 of the aisle is a small stone-vaulted crypt, dating from the 14th century (Pl. 41). Access was originally from within the aisle, but since the 17th century the crypt could only be entered externally via a former window at ground level in the south wall (Figs 4, 181 and 196). The opening has been blocked with stone to deter vandalism, but local residents recall playing in the crypt as children. Victorian reflooring in the aisle has obliterated all

evidence of the former access point, which was probably capped by a large slab.

The chamber is 3.5 m (11½ ft) square in plan and occupies an area which equates closely with the top of the tiled dais in the south-east corner of the aisle (plan, Fig. 91). The crypt was formed by excavating a pit and lining its walls with masonry, which is 30–40 cm thick at maximum. Three of the crypt's walls are built of coursed rubble and were finished with lime rendering of coarse gritty texture and brownish colour, although the surface has largely been lost and only the base material now survives. Fragments of medieval clay roofing tile occur in both the walls and the vault. Limewash was subsequently applied over the render and stone mouldings. The north wall is featureless, as is the east wall apart from a small pocket at the very centre: this is likely to have held a block of timber which served as a ground for attaching something (perhaps a crucifix?). The original entrance to the crypt was in the west side, adjacent to the southern corner, showing that there must have been a flight of steps leading down from the junction of bays 1 and 2 within the aisle, against the south wall. The narrow opening has been damaged, but its segmental arch comprised two reused pieces of elaborate 13th-century arch-moulding resting on plain-chamfered ashlar jambs; only one moulded stone survives *in situ*, the other having been dislodged when a hole was broken through, seemingly as part of an attempt to explore the original entrance (Fig. 197).[44]

The crypt was subjected to a keyhole archaeological investigation in 1938, when a 3 ft square pit was excavated in the floor at the north-east corner, and was not backfilled.[45] The purpose of the excavation is not recorded, but it was most likely to search for possible Roman remains under the church. The original floor of the crypt is exposed here: it is of lime mortar, *c.* 5 cm thick. Below is the natural brickearth, which was excavated to a depth of 40 cm.; presumably

FIGURE 197. Crypt: vault-rib springing from the south-west corner. To the right is the former internal entrance with its damaged arch and earth filling. (Warwick Rodwell)

nothing was found, any earlier remains having been removed when the crypt was constructed. There do not appear to be any archaeologically significant deposits overlying the crypt floor.

Breaking through the blocked entrance in the west wall probably occurred sometime after the 'excavation', and was accompanied by a tunnelling operation under the Victorian stone steps in the aisle. The tunnelled area is now a chaotic mess of soil and rubble and, without clearance, it is not possible to rediscover the original form of the entrance passage and steps to the crypt.[46] They seem to have been infilled in the 19th century, when brick foundations were laid to carry the tiled dais and steps in the chapel. It seems likely that the entrance to the crypt comprised a narrow passage, with steps, alongside the south wall.

The south wall, containing the window, is markedly different from the other three. The eastern part, below vault-springing level, consists of large squared chalk blocks set in brown mortar (not very gritty), and is not bonded to the adjoining east wall (Fig. 198). Traces of white lime plaster remain. One of the chalk blocks has been removed,[47] exposing soil behind it; this seems to show that the wall is very thin here. Below the window, however, the wall is of coursed rubble laid in very gritty brown mortar. There is also a small, unexplained offset in the masonry at internal sill level (which is one course above vault-springing level). It seems clear that the south wall incorporates older fabric than the crypt itself. The window opening is at ground level, where the chamfered plinth of the aisle is modified to accommodate it (Fig. 196). The aperture is rectangular and plain chamfered externally, and the soffit slopes downwards through the thickness of the wall. This was done to direct more light into the crypt. The external height of the window opening is uncertain since the original sill has gone and a modern slab has been inserted at a higher level. Sockets for ferramenta remain in the outer frame.[48] Internally, the reveal is widely splayed and has a low segmental rear-arch which is chamfered; the construction of the vault just clips the arch. The sill to the reveal has been broken away, but was either sloping or stepped and was probably finished with plaster. Various graffiti occur on the ashlar masonry around the window: the earliest is dated 1807.

The quadripartite vault has plain chamfered ribs which intersect on a keystone at the centre: there is no boss, although a small drilled hole occurs at the intersection. The webs are formed of thin flat pieces of ashlar and were probably not plastered but flush-pointed (*pierre perdue* style) and heavily limewashed. Holes have been broken through the vault in three places, and subsequently repaired from above. The ribs rise from springer-capitals in the four corners, 1.38 m above floor level. The mouldings on the bell-capitals are all different and there are no wall-shafts.

FIGURE 198. Crypt: large ashlar masonry in the south wall (right) and rubble in the east wall (left). (Warwick Rodwell)

They are consistent with a date in the early or mid-14th century. No masons' marks were noticed, with the possible exception of one on the rear-arch of the window.

SOUTH PORCH

Exterior

The porch is a squat structure with a plain, low-angled gable, a deep, bolection-moulded plinth, and oak-framed sides containing open tracery (Fig. 199). The deep plinth, which is largely a 19th-century renewal, does not connect with the masonry of the south aisle, but merely abuts it. During the restoration, the roof was lowered to its present (*i.e.* original) angle: sometime in the 17th or 18th century a more steeply pitched structure covered with tiles had been erected over it, partly obstructing the aisle window (Figs 5 and 74; Pl. 1).[49] The masonry on the south face has largely been renewed, but what remains of the original work has been heavily pecked for keying rendering. The entrance arch is four-centred and carries Tudor wave mouldings both externally and internally; they have plain, run-out chamfer-stops. The shallow, trefoil-headed niche over the door is a 19th-century renewal of a previous feature that is shown in early illustrations.

The timber-framed upper parts of the east and west sides each contain six unglazed, cinquefoil-

Figure 199. Porch: viewed from the south-east. (Warwick Rodwell)

Figure 200. Porch: cinquefoiled lights in the sides, now reconstructed. (Addington, 1845)

headed lights. The wallplates, end-posts and substantial parts of the tracery are original, but the sills and mullions are 19th century (Fig. 200).[50] There is no evidence for an earlier porch abutting the south doorway, and none was intended.

Interior

The low-pitched lead roof is laid on closely-spaced, plain chamfered rafters with boards running

Figure 201. Porch: restored oak roof. (Warwick Rodwell)

longitudinally between them, and rebated into their upper edges (Fig. 201). Some of the rafters and many of the boards have been renewed. A cambered and chamfered tie-beam at either end carries the ridge-piece, and is in turn supported by posts with moulded jowls.

Stone benches flank the east and west sides, with short returns at their southern ends. The slabbed bench-top, which has a plain chamfer on its lower arris, bears sundry graffiti. The floor paving is historic and of interest: the central area comprises limestone paving slabs, flanked by rows of stone sets (Fig. 202; plan, Fig. 187). The slabs include one which originated as either the top of a tomb-chest, or the *mensa* of a medieval altar; the slab measures 1.7 m by 0.9 m. Adjacent cobbles were lifted in 1999, when it was established that the slab has a square edge, basal

FIGURE 202. *Porch: floor paving, including a large altar or tomb slab placed directly in front of the church door. (Warwick Rodwell)*

FIGURE 203. *Porch: two rectangular patches of mortar, filling neatly cut pockets in the altar or tomb slab. (Warwick Rodwell)*

chamfer and rough underside.[51] The upper surface is well worn and no trace of consecration crosses can be seen, but the presence of two small, mortar-filled, rectangular pockets in the upper surface raises the possibility of relic containment within an altar (Fig. 203). However, only one pocket would be expected for such a purpose.

NOTES

1 Confirmation that the plinth is original to the west wall, and not a later insertion, is provided by the presence of a single ashlar course directly above it, before the squared rubblework begins.

2 *Country Life*, **157** (16 Jun. 1975), 1632; Bloxham, 2002, 13; Dudley, 2005, fig. 65.

3 Stedman, 1971, 77.

4 These are the plain type of leaf with a prominent central rib, or 'finger'.

5 The doorway measures 1.75 m high by 61 cm wide. It is rebated on the south face, while the arrises on the north face have been crudely chamfered *in situ*. The

arcade wall is battered on its south face, and thus the jambs to the opening are flush with the wall-face at the top, but inset by 8–9 cm at the bottom.

6 Addington (1845, 36) mentions only the head of a female saint, by which he presumably meant the Virgin in the lower register. See also: *The Ecclesiologist*, **24** (1863); Keyser, 1883, 87; Poyntz, 1891, 223; Hunt, 1956, pl. 30; Bertram, 2000, 21. The painting is well illustrated in Rosewell, 2008, fig. 185, where it is assigned to the early 14th century.

7 For a drawing, see Simons, 2004, fig. 9.

8 Ballantyne, 2003, 7; 2006. These reports record the extent of the surviving medieval work.

9 Ballantyne, 2006.

10 The latter relates to the loss of the Norman string-course that formerly ran around the exterior of the transept (p. 69).

11 The vertical arm is 12.5 cm wide, and the horizontal 10 cm wide. The block-like terminals have rounded corners.

12 Illustrated in Ballantyne, 2004, 14 (upper); 2006.

13 The upper arm of the cross, including its terminal, cannot have been more than 65 cm high, since there is no sign of red paint continuing above the repair patch.

14 These repairs average 45–50 cm across.

15 The stair was doubtless of timber. There cannot have been an internal stone stair-turret as at Cirencester (Glos.), or Sedgeford (Norf.): the latter was offered as a potential analogue by Ballantyne (2003, 9).

16 For the elevation, see Simons, 2004, fig. 10.

17 In bay 4 the reveals are plastered.

18 This bears a passing resemblance to the Phrygian cap often depicted in Roman sculpture.

19 The latter is clearly by the same hand as the sculptor of the east label-stop in bay 1 and west stop in bay 2.

20 Dudley, 2005, fig. 71.

21 Addington (1845, 37) was the first to note that the mouldings of the then-blocked west window were earlier than the main fabric of the aisle.

22 While it was common for medieval church floors to slope in sympathy with the lie of the land, clearly a different situation obtained here and deliberate changes of level were embraced. The difference between the door thresholds and the arcade base is at least 45 cm: that could not realistically be accommodated by sloping the floor across the width of the aisle. It was not uncommon for aisles and side-chapels with crypts below to have their floors raised above the general level by several steps (*e.g.* Burford). Screens guarded the change of level.

23 At Lichfield Cathedral, for example, Scott created a 'museum display' of salvaged floor tiles in one corner of the sacristy.

24 The indents are shown on Paul's plan (1900, nos 22 and 23), but the coffin lid is not: it has been added to the series as M.24.

25 For the memorial inscriptions, see Perks and O'Connell, 1996.

26 *Contra* Bloxham, 1990, 3.

27 Addington, 1845, 35.

28 Bodl., MS Top. Eccles. d.6, f. 11r.

29 BL, Add. Ms 15,545, ff. 148–53. Grimm drew the entire decorative scheme, but very inaccurately.

30 Gough, 1786–96, **1**, 307. He was quoting from Stukeley's over-enthusiastic assessment of the font. See also Skelton, 1823, 3–4.

31 Zarnecki, 1957, *passim*, and pls 45–52, 54 and 55. Zarnecki suggested that the second figure holding an instrument was possibly St Andrew.

32 Zarnecki, 1957, pls 52 and 53.

33 See, generally, Fryer, 1900; Bond, 1908a, 77–87; Clapham, 1934; Druce, 1934; Zarnecki, 1957.

34 'IB' may be the same person who left his mark very prominently on the lid of the oak chest: 'IB 1655' (see p. 185).

35 Butterfield's stone base, glimpsed in Fig. 102, dates from the late 1840s or early 1850s.

36 The only illustration of it is by Grimm, *c.* 1780: BL, Add. Ms 15,545, f. 149. The cover may have been discarded when the font was moved in 1809.

37 For notes on the medieval slabs, see Bertram, 2000.

38 Not listed by Perks and O'Connell, 1996.

39 Bertram, 2000, 32, 47 (no. 31).

40 *Ibid.*, 31, 47 (no. 29).

41 Gough, 1786–96, **2**, intro., cxvi, pl. 6.3; Bertram, 2000, 35, 48 (uninscr. no. 2).

42 Skelton, 1823, 8.

43 For chest construction, see Chinnery, 1979, 110–12; Sherlock, 2008, 16, fig. 20.

44 The missing piece of arch moulding may well be amongst the rubble and soil on the floor of the crypt.

45 Information from the Hon. Georgina Stonor. The exploration was carried out by a party from Oxford, which included (Sir) Mortimer Wheeler. The party then went on to excavate in the cellars at Stonor Park; that investigation was also abandoned, leaving the tools and buckets still on site (2004).

46 The tunnel is *c.* 2 m long: exposed in it, and forming the roof, is the underside of three of the stone steps associated with the altar dais above the crypt. The spoil from the tunnel forms a scree slope spreading out from the south-west corner of the crypt, where it descends from vault-springing level. Miss Stonor recalled seeing steps in this corner in the 1940s or '50s, but none are visible now. The débris has been augmented by modern rubbish thrown in from the churchyard.

47 The block lies loose in the rubble on the floor of the crypt.

48 One socket survives in each jamb, and there was probably a second, since lost.

49 See also: BL, Add. Ms 36,405, f. 49v.

50 Further fragments of the original oak tracery were lying loose and unlabelled in the storage area in the ground stage of the tower (2004).

51 Oxford Archaeology, 'Dorchester Abbey Church: Archaeological Watching Brief Report' (September 2003). The slab is shown on Jewitt's drawing of the doorway in 1845 (Fig. 182).

CHAPTER 16

Tower

EXTERIOR

The west tower is square in plan and of three structural stages, plus a plinth and crenellated parapet (Figs 38, 45 and 204; Pls 1–3). The top of the tower bears the dated initials 'I.W. 1602'.[1]

General construction, buttresses and staircase

Three of the corners are clasped by octagonal buttresses which rise to the full height without offsets, and they are not crowned by turrets or pinnacles. The string-courses which define the stages are continuous around the buttresses, and there is a slight set-back in the face at each level.

The south-east corner is different: it is square and unbuttressed and houses the newel stair which provides access to the upper levels. Although internally the stair is contained in a turret-like structure, it lacks the clearcut external definition usually associated with stair-turrets; nor does it rise

to the full height of the tower, but ends two-thirds of the way up the top stage. This block of masonry housing the stair is earlier than the rest of the tower, and has usually been assigned to the 14th century. That is probably its date, although the masoncraft here is unlike anything seen elsewhere in the 14th-century church: it is of random rubble without any hint of coursing. The rubble itself is mostly small and of mixed origin: much is limestone, but there are also unworked flint nodules and the occasional piece of tufa.[2] Today, the staircase is mildly expressed externally on the south face of the tower (Fig. 74), but not on the east (Fig. 205), by a vertical disjuncture at the second and third stages. The anomalous relationship of the turret is further emphasized by the fact that the string-courses of 1602 do not cross it.

FIGURE 205. *Tower: east face rising above the nave roof, showing the pseudo-long-and-short quoining of the stair-turret. (Warwick Rodwell)*

FIGURE 204. *Tower: south elevation. (Warwick Rodwell)*

FIGURE 206. Tower: north-west buttress with uncompleted flushwork. (Warwick Rodwell)

FIGURE 207. Tower: south-west buttress with uncompleted flushwork. (Warwick Rodwell)

The main body of the tower is constructed largely of limestone rubble, laid to neat courses. There are also occasional courses of recycled ashlar. The octagonal corner buttresses are faced with angled ashlar quoins, between which are variously-sized, rectangular panels of flint flushwork, all laid in regular courses. The buttresses thus have a chequered appearance almost from top to bottom. Curiously, the lowest 1.25 m to 1.85 m of the first stage does not contain flushwork, except in the case of the north-west buttress where there are a couple of panels (Fig. 206); otherwise, the infilling between the ashlars comprises either squared blocks of rough limestone, or a mixture of small rubble (Fig. 207).[3] Two explanations may be offered. First, the idea of incorporating panels of flint flushwork may have been adopted only after the construction of the buttresses had begun.[4] Secondly, it may have been envisaged that the lowest parts of the buttresses would be partly obscured by abutting structures, and it was therefore pointless to decorate them with flushwork. In this connection, it may be noted that Wood's plan shows a cloister-like passage running across the north face of the tower; and two of the antiquarian views of the church depict a wall (on the line of the precinct gateway abutting the south-west buttress (for abutments, see p. 55).

Considerable renewal of both the ashlar and the flint flushwork has taken place in modern times: the replacement knapped flints are of poor quality compared to the original work. With the exception of the buttresses, the masonry of the tower was intended to be covered with a thin lime render which would have disguised the mixture of materials. Extensive traces of the substrate of the render still remain.

At the ground stage, the south face of the tower is contiguous with that of the earlier stair-turret, and the two have been well bonded. However, the junction is discernible largely by the fact that the turret was constructed of random rubble, unlike the coursed work of the tower. Above the first string-course the tower walls are slightly set back, while the stair-turret continues to rise vertically. Consequently, there is a step of *c*. 8 cm in the south wall face from hereon up, and a crude quoin had to be formed on this salient angle of the turret. For the first metre, the quoin is of ashlar with a good arris, but for about the next four metres no attempt seems to have been made to form an arris; instead, roughly squared pieces of limestone, and even the occasional flint nodule, had to suffice.[5]

Above the level of the second string-course the face of the tower sets back again, thereby causing the masonry of the turret to project by *c*. 15 cm in the third stage (Fig. 94). On the east face of the tower, above the nave roof, there are no string-courses or offsets, and thus the turret does not project. The two periods of masonry have been smoothly bonded, but the junction between them is nevertheless still discernible by the lack of regular coursing in the older work.

The south-east corner of the tower is not visible at a low level, being abutted by the south aisle. However, the corner emerges into the open above wall-top level. Here, the quoin is formed of limestone ashlars laid more-or-less alternately in upright and flat positions. As early as 1845 it was noted that this is strikingly reminiscent of Anglo-Saxon or Saxo-Norman 'long-and-short' work (Figs 94 and 205).[6] The observed structural sequence confirms that the south-east corner of the tower is older than the west wall of the south aisle, which itself is 14th century. The abutment of the south wall of the nave against the tower stands *c.* 70 cm higher than that of the aisle. Moreover, scarring on the east face of the tower hints at the possibility of the nave wall having risen even higher than it does today.[7]

Stage 1

The entire tower, including the stair-turret, is unified at ground level by a plinth which is topped with a chamfer and bolection moulding (Figs 207 and 208). The walling above the plinth begins with a neat ashlar course, except where the staircase is: this omission confirms that while the plinth is primary to the majority of the tower, it had to be inserted into the base of the pre-existing stair-turret. The plain slit window which at first sight appears to have been cut through the plinth, to light the lowest level of the staircase, is in reality an older feature and the plinth has simply clasped it (Fig. 208). The unmoulded aperture is cut into a single slab of yellow shelly limestone. Higher up is a second rectangular window, the aperture having an external rebate. It is composed of separate blocks of yellow limestone.

In the north and south walls are two-light windows with four-centred heads, under a moulded square label. In the masonry directly above is a semi-elliptical relieving arch of crude ashlar work. On the south side of the tower, the mullion and sill have been renewed, following the removal of a doorway which had been created in the opening in the 18th century, accessed by a short flight of steps (Figs 5 and 7).[8] In the late 19th century, a new doorway was cut through the north wall, to provide the vicar with a private entry convenient for the vicarage (Fig. 206). The doorway has a pointed head and heavy mouldings, including a hood-moulding with coarse foliate label-stops.

Stage 2

The masonry is well coursed and composed of a mixture of carefully squared rubble and flattish slabs that may have been cut from former ashlars.

There is a round-headed window on each of the three exposed faces, and their arrises have a thirty-degree chamfer. The southern window was examined from scaffolding in 2003. The head is cut as a complete arch from a single block of limestone, over which is neatly fitted a second arch made of tightly jointed voussoirs; that too is a complete semicircle resting on shoulders formed by the jamb-stones of the opening. Above again is a relieving arch of segmental

form made from squared rubble. Between the outer two arches pieces of clay roof tile are used as packing.[9] Elsewhere in this stage tile fragments occur as levelling material. Although superficially Romanesque in appearance, these windows do not appear to incorporate any reused elements.[10] The stair is lit by a plain rectangular slit-window with a chamfered arris. It is formed from four blocks of limestone: the head and sill are recent replacements. The eastern upright has a pocket cut into it, indicating that it is a reused block.

Stage 3

The masonry is similar to that of the middle stage, but there is a greater preponderance of good ashlars, especially towards the top of the belfry. On the east face it is noticeable how the masonry alongside the belfry opening, up to springer level, is different from both the staircase corner and the ashlar-work towards the top (Fig. 205). This intermediate masonry is of thin flat pieces of limestone and roughly squared rubble laid to courses. Furthermore, it could be argued that the belfry opening has been inserted into that rubble, rather than being of contemporary build.

Belfry openings are present on all four faces, although the eastern one is partially obstructed by the nave roof. The opening must be off-centre since the ridge of the nave roof aligns with its southern jamb, not with the mullion. The openings are of two pointed lights fitted with simple Y-tracery; the arrises carry a small chamfer, but otherwise there are no mouldings, nor is there a label (Fig. 94). Although presumed to date from 1602, the general appearance is of 13th-century plate-tracery: could they be recycled? Each opening has an outer ring of ashlar voussoirs of varying sizes. The openings are filled with wooden louvres, slotted into channels cut in the jambs and mullions.

FIGURE 208. Tower: plinth on the south side, encapsulating an early window in the base of the stair-turret. (Warwick Rodwell)

Fixed over the upper part of the tracery in the west face is a skeleton clock dial, decorated in black and gold, and presumably of the same date as the clock movement (1868). Early 19th-century illustrations show a diagonally-set square dial (probably of timber) in the same position.[11]

The crenellated parapet, which rests on a hollow-moulded string-course, has been substantially reconstructed in recent years, with many new merlons. The tower is finished by a low pyramidal roof covered with red clay tiles, recessed behind the parapet. Rising from the apex is a 19th-century weather-vane in the form of a cockerel. Early 19th-century drawings show a plainer vane of the 17th or 18th century.[12]

INTERIOR

Stair-turret

Hexagonal in plan, this projects substantially into the south-east corner of the tower throughout its height, and houses a stone newel stair. The construction is coursed rubble with limestone ashlar quoins, giving the impression of being designed as indoor work rather than external: before it became part of the present tower in 1602, this stair was inside a previous building (p. 55). The entrance to the stair is in the north face, where the threshold of the doorway is 26 cm lower than the present floor of the tower. There is a small 'well' formed in front of the door, and in it is revealed a narrow foundation offset to the west wall of the nave, probably dating from the Norman period. The doorway has a pointed head, is chamfered with wave mouldings on its outer face, and has brooch-stops at the base. The surround is rebated to carry a door which opens on to the stair. There is no hood-moulding, only an outer reinforcing arch of rubble voussoirs over the doorway.

The staircase rises clockwise and the treads are fairly well worn. With a radius of 95 cm (3 ft), the stair is generous for a belfry. The interior is constructed of neat courses of squared rubble[13] and was previously rendered with cream lime-mortar tempered with coarse gravel; most of this has been stripped but small areas still remain just below the vault supporting the treads. The stair is not of the usual late medieval construction, where each tread is made from a large block of limestone, with an integral newel section at one end. Instead, the newel section (17 cm diameter) and a short part of each tread is cut from one block, and the remainder of the tread is composed of either one or several further blocks. Not being self-supporting, the whole is carried on a helical rubble-built vault. Cut into the lining of the stair-well, on average c. 1.5 m above tread level, are numerous small pockets, 7–10 cm square; they are shallow and have not been infilled. The pockets, which tend to occur in groups of three, on the same horizontal plane (at about 95 cm intervals), were associated with supporting temporary platforms and the formwork necessary for the construction of the helical vault. Similar pockets are commonly seen in other stairwells.

The soffit of the helix contains long pieces of stone that mostly run with the direction of the stair:[14] the stones are bedded in lime-mortar, with oyster shells used as packing in the joints; the soffit of the vault has been carefully shaped to provide a smooth curve to the helix. Final shaping must have taken place, using a bolster or axe, after the vault had been constructed and the formwork dismantled. It appears that open joints were then pointed and lime mortar smeared over any irregularities, to achieve a reasonably smooth finish to the soffit.

Close to the base of the stair is a rectangular slit window facing south; it has splayed reveals and a flat stone lintel. The window is at step level. Towards the top of the ground stage, the stair is lit by another similar window.

The first doorway opens from the west face of the stair into the ringing chamber, and is original (Fig. 95). It has a pointed head and a broad, unstopped chamfer; the surround is rebated and in it hangs a 19th-century oak door. Alongside, was possibly a tall, narrow secondary opening in the north-west face of the turret. This feature, now blocked, appears as a slight recess inside the ringing chamber, edged with squared rubble: it remains enigmatic.

The second doorway, with its pointed head and plain chamfers, is similar to the first. It opens off the north face of the stair-turret into the clock chamber. The surround is rebated and in it hangs a 19th-century oak door. At the second stage the stair is lit by a simple slit window facing south, with a corbel forming a shoulder to the lintel on one side only. This window is at step level, and its splayed jambs are formed with ashlar. At about belfry floor level is an infilled feature on the north-west face of the turret, which may have been a window or small doorway: it seems to be secondary.

The stair emerges into the belfry at the south-east corner, where there is no stair-cap structure, just a low, coped balustrade around the well. The latter is lined with flat pieces of limestone rubble, laid in buff-coloured mortar tempered with mixed gravel. It would appear from scars in the wall that the stair once rose a little higher (probably two steps). Several pieces of thick red brick (6 cm) incorporated in the primary structure of the stair-well, close to the top, are Roman. In the vicinity of four-to-five steps from the top there is evidence of burning on the treads and on the masonry of the stair-well, indicating that the tower roof was burnt at some time.

Stage 1 (Ground Stage)

The tower is entered from the nave through a four-centred, Tudor-style arch with broad and ungainly

FIGURE 209. Tower: interior of the north window of the second stage, seen in the ringing-chamber. (Warwick Rodwell)

chamfers. This is set into a round-headed opening which forms the rear-arch; its jambs are unmoulded and pass squarely through the thickness of the wall. The doorway, which is not aligned on the axis of the nave, is 17th century. Until 2006, this tall first stage was divided into two levels by a modern timber and plasterboard ceiling. At ground level was a makeshift kitchen, and above was a cavernous space used for light storage. The interior has now been refitted on three levels with a connecting timber staircase: kitchen, choir vestry and storage. The walls are mostly lined with cupboards and modern materials, with the result that little of the historic fabric can be examined. Until 2006, featureless limewashed rubble was exposed.

There are two-light windows in the north and south walls, but nothing in the west. The rear-arches are semicircular, composed of large ashlar voussoirs with an outer reinforcing ring of rubble voussoirs; the reveals are splayed, and the sills are angled steeply downwards. The possibility that the rear-arches are recycled Norman masonry has been considered, but the rough axing on the voussoirs militates against such an interpretation: the arches must be accepted as early 17th century.

The faces of the stair-turret have a small offset at window-sill level, presumably indicating that there had previously been a floor or gallery approximately where the modern ceiling now is. However, that must relate not to the present tower but to its 14th-century

predecessor. The offset is an original feature, and is not the site of a string-course or other lost decorative feature. In the north wall is an external doorway, adjacent to the west corner: no opening is shown here on plans of the mid-19th century and this entrance must have been newly created during the Victorian restorations. A flight of six steps connects it to tower floor level. The pointed rear-arch of the doorway has ashlar-lined reveals and a reinforcing arch of squared rubble.

The underside of the ringing-chamber floor is visible: it is carried on massive pine beams resting on stone corbels. The beams are additionally strengthened with timber struts and iron straps, all 19th century; some old timbers have been reused for common joists.

Stage 2a (Ringing Chamber)

The present floor is *c.* 50 cm lower than it was originally. There is an offset on the east wall, and shallow horizontal channels in the north and west walls, where floor beams were built in as the tower was constructed. Three plain, round-headed windows open through the north, west and south walls (Fig. 209). The reveals and soffits are of rubble, dressed with limestone ashlar, and the glazing is mounted in an oak frame set into a rebate behind the lining of the arch on the outer face of the tower. The frames are 19th-century replacements: they are well made and have chamfered arrises. The windows have a Romanesque appearance, but are apparently entirely 17th-century work.

The north face of the stair-turret has been cut back to provide clearance for one of the two great oak beams running east–west across the chamber, carrying the floor of the clock chamber above. The bearing-ends of these beams have been strengthened by pine supports, iron straps and stone corbels let into the wall. The floor joists are also supported on beams placed flat against the north and south walls of the tower, again resting on corbels. The major timbers may be suitable for dating by dendrochronology. A 19th-century brick chimney rises in the north-east corner, carrying the modern stainless steel flue from the boiler.

Stage 2b (Clock Chamber)

This chamber has no windows and is not separately expressed in the external architecture of the tower. The floor has been entirely reconstructed with reused timber, and there is a bell manhole in the centre. Holes in the joists indicate the previous positions of bell-ropes. There is an original set-back in the north face of the stair-turret, evidently to accommodate an east–west floor beam.

A massive pine frame supporting the floor of the belfry above rests on posts rising from stone corbels set into the tower walls. There are two beams running east–west and two running north–south. The posts are strutted, and the corbels are 19th-century renewals: were the originals of stone or timber? There is a slight offset at this level around all four walls of the tower.[15] The offset suggests that the original floor frame for the belfry was *c.* 30 cm lower than the present one, and that it was built-in as the walls were constructed.

A recess in the east wall, beside the turret, receives the opening door.

Stage 3 (Belfry)

The walls, which are unplastered and of coursed rubble, contain occasional pieces of reused (sometimes moulded) ashlar and sparse fragments of clay roofing tile. Several blocks carry a flattened roll moulding and residual scarring where something has been hacked off the face of the stone.

The pointed belfry openings are internally splayed, and unmoulded. The arches all have double rings of voussoirs, the outer being composed of recycled blocks; 19th-century graffiti, mostly initials, are present on some of the ashlars around the openings. The mullions are plain chamfered, being essentially octagonal in section.

The oak bell-frame rests on four beams which run north–south; it has eight compartments, reflecting the number of bells accommodated. That confirms the date of the frame as 1867, although the carpentry might suggest that it was much older. Prior to 1867, there were only six bells. The construction comprises an upper and a lower frame without any vertical posts between them: instead there is a lattice of angled struts connecting the two (Fig. 210). The upper and lower frames have subsequently been tied together with iron rods, and angle-irons have been bolted to many of the carpentry joints in order to provide rigidity where slackness has occurred through age.

FIGURE 210. *Tower: detail of the construction of the bell-frame.* (*Warwick Rodwell*)

The five oldest bells still hang by their cannons. Refurbishment in 1987 involved fitting new bearings, iron headstocks and timber wheels. Some of the headstocks were previously timber.

Floor

The ground floor was paved with stone, probably in the mid-1860s, and includes many gravestones which were once in the churchyard; there is also an area of 20th-century concrete.

Roof

The pyramidal roof is a 19th-century construction in pine, by Scott. It consists of two pairs of cross-frames, one above the other.[16] Each tie-beam supports not only the two principals and a pair of queen-posts with four-way diagonal strutting, but also an additional post at the centre of the beam. Consequently, a cluster of eight posts rises, like a compound column, under the apex of the roof. The principals of the upper cross-frame, being set diagonally across the tower, form the hip-rafters. There are two lines of purlins per side. The roof has been repaired in the 20th century, and the bearing-ends of the tie-beams are supported by timber corbels strapped to them with U-shaped iron bolts. Access to the parapet gutter is via an iron ladder and hatch from the belfry.

FITTINGS

Sundial

On the south face of the south-west buttress is an engraved and gilded stone sundial, inscribed *lux dei umbra*. Installed in 2000, it replaces an older one, which was probably 18th century.[17]

Painted boards

In the ringing chamber are various painted boards:

(i)   Over the north window (Fig. 209) is a long narrow board, painted dark red and bearing the text:
      + *THIS IS NONE OTHER THAN*
      THE HOUSE OF GOD +
      Mid-19th century in date, the origin of this item has not been traced.

(ii) On the east wall is a board carrying, 'Rules for the Dorchester Company of Ringers, January 1868'.

(iii) Painted peal board commemorating ringing 728 changes in 1861.

(iv) Peal board commemorating a complete peal of 5,040 changes by the Appleton Society of Change Ringers in 1868.

(v)   Board commemorating the restoration of the bells in 1987. It records that the work was carried out by Whites of Appleton, and the bells were retuned by the Whitechapel Bellfoundry.

Turret-Clock

The turret-clock is a fine specimen, and is now electrically wound. It has a three-train movement in a wrought iron frame, although originally it had only two trains (Pl. 43). The mechanism is complete and has not suffered the kind of damage often witnessed as a result of fitting automatic winders. The setting-dial carries an inscription recording that the clock was *Made by John Moore and Sons, Clerkenwell, London. 1868.*

The frame was extended on the south to receive the chiming train in 1900, as recorded by a second plate: *To the Greater Glory of God and in Honour of St Birinus the Chimes were added to this clock by bequest of John Gill Godwin, A.D. MDCCCC. On whose soul will sweet Jesus have mercy. Vicar – N.C.S. Poyntz.* The clock chimes on four bells and strikes the hours on the tenor.

Bells

The bellframe supports eight bells of various ages.[18] They were hung in their present frame in 1867, rehung in 1936, and rehung again in 1987.

TREBLE
Founder	Mears and Stainbank, Founders, London
Inscription	*In honorem S.S. Trinitas. D.D. Dorcensi Ecclesiae incolae A.D. 1867*
	'In honour of the most Holy Trinity, donated to the church of Dorchester by the inhabitants A.D. 1867'
Date	1867

SECOND
Founder	Mears and Stainbank, Founders, London
Inscription	*In honorem S.S. Trinitas D.D. Dorcensi Ecclesiae I.A. Macfarlane A.D. 1867*
	'In honour of the most Holy Trinity, I.A. Macfarlane donated to the church of Dorchester A.D. 1867'
Date	1867

THIRD
Founder	– [Reading]
Inscription	*Love God*
Date	1651

FOURTH
Founder	Henry Knight I [Reading]
Inscription	*Henri Knight Made Mee*
Date	1603

FIFTH
Founder	– [Henry Knight I, Reading]
Inscription	*Sancta Toma Ora Pro Nobis*
	'Saint Thomas, pray for us'
Date	1606

SIXTH
Founder	– [Henry Knight I, Reading]
Inscription	*Virginiis Egregie dicar Campana Maria*
	'I shall be called the bell of the famous Virgin Mary'
Date	1591

SEVENTH
Founder	– [Exeter]
Inscription	*PETRE: TUIS: APERI: DA: PAULE: TUIS: MISERERI*
	'Peter, open to thine own. Grant mercy, Paul, to thine'
Date	*c.* 1370–80

TENOR
Founder	– [Wokingham foundry marks]
Inscription	*PROTEGE BIRINE QUOS CONVOCO TU SINE FINE RAF RASTWOLD*
	'Do thou Birinus, protect for ever those whom I summon. Ralph Rastwold'
Date	*c.* 1370–80 (Rastwold died 1383)

The seventh and tenor bells are of exceptional importance, especially the latter on account of its florid inscription, which follows the style of manuscript illumination.[19] The dates of these two bells are disputed, it having been suggested that they could be as early as the mid-14th century.[20]

Notes

1. The initials 'I.W.' are cut in the masonry of the west-facing quoin of the south-west buttress, five courses below the parapet string-course; and the date '1602' occurs on the second course.
2. Unlike the remainder of the tower, there is no brick or tile present, except where post-medieval repairs have occurred. The tufa could be reused Roman building material.
3. In the north-east buttress flushwork begins at 1.25 m above the moulded plinth, but several of the panels contain only a few pieces of flint set amongst rubble. In the south-west buttress there is no flushwork until 1.85 m above plinth level.
4. In which case, the appearance of a single panel of flushwork low down in the north-west buttress, and the very narrow strip of flushwork incorporated in the tower plinth near the north-east corner, are unexplained.
5. Unfortunately, some of this less regular material has been removed in modern times and ashlars inserted instead, thus creating an impression of neat quoining.
6. Addington, 1845, 40.
7. The scar takes the form of projecting rubblework associated with the nave wall-core.
8. BL, Add. Ms 36,405, f. 48v.
9. The roof tiles, which are 10–15 mm thick, may be peg-tiles or possibly medieval lug-tiles; no defining features can be seen.
10. *Contra* Freeman, 1852, 279–80 and Bloxham, 1990.
11. BL, Add. Ms 36,405, f. 48v.

12 *Ibid*.

13 The rubble includes some pieces of limestone that had previously suffered burning.

14 Changes in the direction of placing the long stones define the lifts in which the stair vault was constructed. These changes equate with the lines of pockets in the outer wall.

15 The offset measures *c.* 10 cm on the south, but is only 5–7 cm on the other three sides. It does not occur on the stair-turret.

16 The beams of the lower cross-frame follow the cardinal points, whereas those of the upper frame run from corner to corner in the tower.

17 Dudley, 2005, fig. 69. For a photograph of the old sundial, see Bloxham, 1990, 13.

18 For full details and discussion, see Sharpe, 1950. The inscriptions were inaccurately copied by Addington (1845, 40).

19 Illustrated in Tiller, 2005, fig. 4.

20 Sharpe, 1950, 117–21.

CHAPTER 17

Churchyard and Abbey Guest House

CHURCHYARD

The substantial churchyard lies entirely to the south of the church, where it sweeps round in a curvilinear plan and is largely defined by a low wall, except on the east where a wire fence and intermittent hedge follow the scarp of the floodplain of the river Thame.[1] There are two entrances: the lychgate on High Street to the west, and a small gate in the southern boundary opposite the church porch. The lychgate is a massively framed, oak structure with a tiled roof. Although 15th-century in style, the gate was designed by Scott and erected in 1867.[2] The inner and outer arches both carry inscriptions.[3] The framing stands on a buttressed stone plinth. The original design did not include gates, which were added subsequently, hinged on separate posts set into the ground. Before the lychgate was erected, there was a simple barred gate.

The ground within the churchyard falls gently towards the south, and very slightly to the west. It was closed for burial in 1893, and has been partly cleared of tombstones. There are a few trees, both here and in the cloister garden, including several yews, but none is of great age. Late Victorian photographs show the churchyard without any major trees, although several of modest size lay close to the porch.[4] The present yews were planted in the mid-19th century and the one standing just south of the churchyard cross is in approximately the same position as a yew that was illustrated in 1823.[5]

Buildings adjoining the churchyard

Several buildings and gardens adjoin the boundaries of the southern churchyard and some, at least, may represent encroachments (plan, Fig. 3). On the north-west, adjacent to the lychgate (on its north side), is the garden wall of 'The Priory', which runs up to the west end of the guest house (Pl. 44). This 18th-century brick wall, built on an older rubble foundation, marks the division between the outer and inner monastic courts (Fig. 31; p. 51).

A. South of the main entrance to the churchyard is 'Lychgate Cottage' (Figs 29 and 211; Pl. 44), its east side coincident with the churchyard boundary. Outwardly, this appears to be an early 18th-century stone-built house with red brick quoins, now stripped of its intended rendering. This has revealed a construction of neatly coursed limestone rubble in thin

FIGURE 211. *Churchyard: Lychgate Cottage, from the south-east. (Warwick Rodwell)*

FIGURE 212 (top left). Churchyard: ruined cottage, looking south-east. (Warwick Rodwell)

FIGURE 213 (left). Churchyard: Thatched Cottage, from the west. (Warwick Rodwell)

FIGURE 214 (above). Churchyard: Toll Cottage, from the south-east. (Warwick Rodwell)

FIGURE 215 (below). Dorchester Vicarage (now Rectory): south front. (Warwick Rodwell)

pieces. There are brick dressings to all openings (block-bonded in courses of three), and a plat-band of three brick courses on the west (unusually, the uppermost course is chamfered), with glazed headers.

The cottage has gable-end stacks, dormers, and mullioned-and-transomed windows in oak on the front; also, it formerly had them to the rear. These features indicate a date in the late 17th century, or very early years of the 18th century. There is nothing older in evidence, either externally or internally, despite casual claims of an earlier origin.[6] The tithe map shows another building, of equal size, just to the south, where there is now only garden. The presence of a yew tree just inside the boundary at the southern tip of the garden suggests that there has been an encroachment on the churchyard.

B.   Close to the south-east corner of the church is the ruined shell of a tiny one-roomed cottage (frontispiece; Figs 100 and 212; Pl. 1), built on the floodplain

FIGURE 216. *The Manor House, Dorchester: the Gothick west façade has been added to a much earlier building. The three-storied block to the left was formerly part of the same property. (Warwick Rodwell)*

adjoining the churchyard boundary. Photographs and early drawings show that it was constructed partly of brick and stone rubble, upon which stood timber framing, and it had a thatched roof; there was a clapboarded extension on the north.[7] Dating is difficult, based on the surviving ruins, which have been much rebuilt: three of its walls now stand to a height of *c.* 1.2 m, but the west side has entirely gone. The remains of the fireplace appear to be no older than the late 18th century. However, the cottage probably originated in the 17th century, if not the late 16th. It fell into demise in the 1960s and suffered a terminal mishap whilst repairs were in progress in 1964: the chimney fell, bringing the floors with it.[8] Soon afterwards, the cottage was burnt out. There is a small garden stretching across the floodplain, which is church property; otherwise the floodplain belongs to the Manor House.

C. Further south, and also built on the floodplain adjacent to the churchyard boundary, is a timber-framed and thatched building, known as 'The Thatched Cottage' (frontispiece; Fig. 213), which dates from the 17th century. At the time of the tithe award (1846) this comprised two cottages, each with its own garden. It is not now church property.

One of these cottages was presumably the sexton's house, to which reference is made in the 19th century. Both lay outside the churchyard and were owned by the Earl of Abingdon in the mid-19th century, but later acquired personally by Poyntz, the vicar. In 1930, his widow donated the cottages to the PCC. The southern cottage was sold in 1962.

D. Outside the south entrance is Toll Cottage (Fig. 214), a small, single-storey red brick building with a stone plinth and half-octagonal bay facing onto the turnpike road. The cottage, which is of late 18th-century date, was built on the highway verge, close to the churchyard wall. Later, a modest extension was added to the north, and that was built directly upon the churchyard wall. Cut on the plinth at the south-east corner of Toll Cottage are two lines marking flood levels, dated 1 November 1828 and 15 November 1894.

Although it has never been used as churchyard *per se*, the lawn and shrubbery (Cloister Garden) occupying the site of the claustral ranges to the north, form part of the church property. Two buildings abut this area.

E. On the west is the vicarage (now 'The Rectory') and its walled garden (Fig. 215). The house was designed in the Gothic style by the London-based architect David Brandon and built in 1856–57.[9]

F. On the north is the Manor House and its grounds (Fig. 216). Behind its Gothick façade, the house incorporates 16th-century fabric which is likely to be of monastic origin (p. 49).

Boundaries

A low, curvilinear wall defines the churchyard on the south and south-west, beginning at the edge of the floodplain, close to Thatched Cottage. The wall swings around the south side of the churchyard and then continues its curving course north-westwards, beyond the present south-west corner, and embracing Lychgate Cottage and its garden (Fig. 217). Topographically, it would appear that the cottage and its garden have been cut out of the historic churchyard. The boundary wall is of three different

FIGURE 217. Churchyard: boundary wall on the south-west, constructed of reused ashlar. Towards the left-hand end is an infilled opening. (Warwick Rodwell)

FIGURE 218. Churchyard: boundary wall on the south-west, showing reused limestone ashlars and an infilled opening. (Warwick Rodwell)

builds: the southern sector is of particular interest, being constructed from very large limestone ashlar blocks which have clearly been salvaged from an earlier structure.[10] The wall, which stands between 0.9 m and 1.5 m high, has a brick coping.[11] The southern entrance to the churchyard is integral. The position of a narrow third entrance, on the south-west side of the churchyard, is clearly visible in the wall; the opening was infilled with ashlar sometime in the 19th century (Fig. 218).

The garden wall of Lychgate Cottage, fronting on to High Street, is of rough limestone rubble, containing the occasional fragment of post-medieval brick, set in a matrix of yellow sandy mortar; its average height is one metre. On the west, the wall is capped with red brick, while on the south-west it has a pitched

stone coping. The boundary between the churchyard and Lychgate Cottage is also an early 19th-century garden wall of stone with a pitched coping.

On the south, there is little differential (0.3 m) between the level of the churchyard inside and the road outside the wall, but towards the west the churchyard rises a metre above external footpath level, and the southern end of the garden of Lychgate Cottage stands *c.* 0.7 m above street level. The walls to the churchyard and cottage, which date from the late 18th or early 19th century, do not appear to perpetuate ancient boundaries, and consequently have no relevance in defining the medieval monastic precinct. They are, rather, the product of 18th-century turnpiking and road realignment in the early 19th century.

However, the date and origin of the large ashlar blocks is of interest. Their scale is not commensurate with any extant masonry in the abbey. More likely, they derive from the late medieval bridge over the Thame which was demolished in 1816, having been replaced by the present Dorchester Bridge (plan, Fig. 2). The former was first described as 'a very faire bridge of stone' in *c.* 1542 by Leland, when it was relatively new, and a drawing was made of it prior to demolition (Fig. 219).[12] The bridge was a substantial structure comprising five arches and a long, stone-revetted causeway, all faced with ashlar.

Memorials

A generous scattering of memorials now remains in the churchyard, and these are mostly headstones of the 18th and 19th centuries, although a few older stones survive: one is dated 1671, another 1699. A

FIGURE 219. Tudor bridge of limestone ashlar over the Thame, demolished 1816. (Gentleman's Magazine, 1818)

major clearance operation must have taken place around 1870, when many 17th- and 18th-century headstones were taken into the church and used as floor paving (Pl. 34). Another phase of clearance occurred in the mid-20th century. Weathering has taken a severe toll on the inscriptions and decorative elements, and most of the extant stones are partly or even wholly illegible. Like the memorials inside the church, a brief record of the inscriptions in the churchyard was made in the 1990s.[13] The headstone to John Davey (d. 1863) is of particular interest because he was a Roman Catholic and major benefactor of the St Birinus's Catholic church in Dorchester.[14]

In addition to the headstones, there are several chest-tombs and two iron-railed enclosures. One of the latter is a delicate gothick structure, dated 1865 (Fig. 220). However, the archaeologically most important monument in the churchyard is a Tudor-Gothic altar-tomb close to the south nave aisle (Fig. 221). It has a plain, chamfered top slab and side panels with blind trefoil arcading; except on the west end, where there is an inscription in a rectangular frame. There is no evidence to indicate that the inscription is secondary, and it dates the monument to 1634. In style, however, the tomb-chest has the appearance of being early 16th century. The robust nature of the monument indicates that it was not an indoor tomb which has been ejected; moreover, it was in the churchyard when Buckler drew it in c. 1812–13.[15] This tomb provides another example of the continuation of the Gothic style well into the post-medieval era (p. 100).

Churchyard Cross

A few metres south-west of the church porch stands the medieval churchyard cross of limestone, now in an advanced state of decay. It is most likely to date

FIGURE 220. Churchyard: iron-railed, Gothic-style tomb dating from 1865, south of the guest house. (Warwick Rodwell)

from the late 14th or 15th century.[16] There is no reason to suspect that the cross is not in its original position, and the earliest view of it there dates from c. 1720 (Fig. 5). Two detailed sketches made by Buckler in 1812–13 provide the best record of the cross,[17] which is raised on two steps, both octagonal in plan (Fig. 34).

The stone base-block is square, with the four corners stop-chamfered to produce an octagonal upper face.[18] The stops appear to have been large concave-sided bevels with bars above, but they are now unrecognizable. The cross-shaft, which is leaded into a socket in the base-block, is octagonal in section and tapers slightly; it emerges from a square base and has brooch stops. The base-block has decayed significantly since Buckler drew it. The shaft is also fissured and weak, and there is now no head to the cross. Early 19th-century illustrations show it surmounted by a block with a basal moulding which was seemingly the stump of the original cross-head, later fitted with a gnomon and serving as a sundial. In c. 1872, the cross suffered drastic 'restoration',

Figure 221. Churchyard: Tudor-style tomb-chest with an inscription dated 1634. (Warwick Rodwell)

Figure 222. Late 12th-century respond capital in the lapidary collection. (David Kendrick)

when an elaborately carved aedicular head (designed by Scott) replaced the remaining fragment on top of the shaft (Pl. 45); that was considered unstable and was removed in the 1990s.[19] It is now displayed inside the church.[20] There was an unrecorded inscription of several lines, cut on the south face of the base-block, presumably to commemorate Scott's restoration. The inscription is visible in photographs of the early 20th century, but no trace of it remains today.

Immediately south of the cross was formerly an ancient yew tree, illustrated and commented upon by Skelton.[21] It had been superseded before the end of the 19th century.

Abbey Guest House (Dorchester Abbey Museum)

This interesting survival from Dorchester's monastic era stands to the west of the tower (Figs 34, 41 and 42; Pl. 1), and the medieval origins of the building have been discussed on p. 59.

In 1652 the building was converted into a free grammar school, and that is probably when the outshut containing a staircase at the east end was built (Figs 32 and 34). Further structural changes occurred in the 18th and 19th centuries, especially to windows and doorways. Buckler published a view of the building in his series of engravings of grammar schools.[22] In 1858, reorganization turned this into the boys' National School, and it was finally closed in 1959. A Victorian engraving shows a timber-framed belfry of skeletal form perched on the west end of the roof.[23] It also appears in early photographs.[24] In the 1960s the building was refitted as the Abbey Museum and Tea Room.

A brief report on the building was prepared in 1991,[25] but a detailed study of this interesting structure awaits the undertaking.

Notes

1   The height of the scarp averages 1.5 m.
2   Correspondence concerning the cost of the work survives, including a letter from Scott's office to Bignell, dated 14 Feb. 1867 (in the possession of the PCC).
3   On the inner face of the west arch:
    ++ERECTED+ BY + GEORGE +

+ *AND + ESTHER + MAY + 1867.*+
On the inner face of the east arch:
++IN + MEMORY + OF + JOSEPH +
+ G +
+ LATHAM + OF + BISHOPSCOURT.+
On the outer face of the east arch:
Restored in 1981 by American Friends in Memory
of Edith Gratia Stedman, OBE.

4   *E.g.* Taunt, 1906, frontispiece (photograph taken 1890).
    See also a view of 1872: COS, HT01327.

5   Skelton, 1823, 5. The same tree, artistically repositioned
    to reveal the churchyard cross, is shown in a view of
    1842 (frontispiece). The present tree, which has two
    stems, is not old enough to be the one illustrated, and
    must be a replacement. Another yew of similar age
    stands in the south-east part of the churchyard; a third
    occurs at the southern tip of the garden of Lychgate
    Cottage; and a fourth is found in the cloister
    garden.

6   Inf. from Prof. Malcolm Airs.

7   Photographs dating from the late 19th century exist in
    the Taunt Collection in COS and NMR (see esp. nos.
    1337, 3043, 8479).

8   Stedman, 1971, 42.

9   See also Tiller, 2005, 72, fig. 42. For Bandon, see RIBA,
    Directory of British Architects, 1834–1914, **1** (2001),
    242–3.

10 At least one block bears a mason's mark in the form
    of a 'X'. The joints are very wide.

11 In the south-eastern part, the ashlar is only two or

three courses high (*c.* 0.6 m), with brickwork above.

12 Cook and Rowley, 1985, 54; Smith, 1964, 118; *Gents.
    Mag.*, 1818.

13 Perks and O'Connell, 1996.

14 Tiller, 2005, fig. 52.

15 BL, Add. Ms 36,372, f. 254v. The tomb also appears on
    Harris's view of *c.* 1720 (Fig. 5).

16 Curiously, Dorchester is not included in an early 18th-
    century list of churchyard crosses in Oxfordshire:
    Oxoniensia, **63** (1998), 250.

17 BL, Add. Mss 36,372, f. 265r; 36,432, f. 1485. The
    published view dates from 1827.

18 For brief notes on the cross and its Oxfordshire context,
    see Marples, 1973, 306.

19 For a drawing which purports to show the cross before
    restoration, see Vallance, 1920, 44, fig. 65. This seems
    to be an enhanced version of Buckler's drawing, and
    the detail is probably not accurate. For a view of the
    'restored' cross, see Bloxham, 1990, 12.

20 Kendrick, 2002.

21 The cross was described as being 'shadowed by an
    yew-tree of considerable age' (Skelton, 1823, 6, illus.
    p. 5).

22 Bodl., MS Top. Gen. c.103. Reproduced in Anon.,
    1976.

23 The engraving is unsigned and undated, but must be
    after *c.* 1870. Copy shown to me by John Metcalfe.

24 By Taunt in COS and NMR (especially no. 10631).

25 RCHME, 'Historic Building Report: The Abbey Guest
    House, Dorchester-on-Thames' (unpubl. ms, 1991).

CHAPTER 18

Architectural Fragments

Many architectural fragments were formerly displayed on timber racking in the south chancel aisle, and on one rack were four bays of the canopy vaulting belonging to the shrine of St Birinus.[1] When the shrine was reconstructed in 1964, the canopy fragments were built into it, and the other lapidary material was dispersed. In 2005, the abbey's collection of loose architectural fragments was assembled in a lapidarium in the new Cloister Gallery (Pl. 46). An inventory of the stones has been compiled by David Kendrick.[2]

Little is known about the origins and discovery of this material, except that the shrine canopy fragments were recovered in 1858 from the blocking of the doorway in the west end of the north aisle (p. 138). Other items were doubtless also found during the course of the Victorian restorations. Apparently, some of the fragments (including capitals and moulded ribs) were discovered in 1878 'in an old farm house in this village'.[3]

The collection contains an interesting selection of capitals and voussoirs ranging in date from the mid-12th century to the mid-13th (Fig. 222). Nothing earlier has been noted, although there is a miscellany of undistinguished later medieval material. There are capitals with Transitional leaves akin to those on the imposts of the chancel arch, as well as examples with waterleaf and stiff-leaf decoration. Several sections of string-courses, voussoirs and vaulting ribs have dog-toothing. One capital, dating from the mid-12th century, carries an uncommon motif in the form of an inverted pyramid with stepped sides; this detail occurs on St Augustine's Abbey gatehouse, Bristol.

The two monolithic limestone coffins[4] were formerly displayed in the north aisle, where they appear on several early plans of the church: one is of plain rectangular form, the other has a shaped head-recess. They are medieval, but not closely datable (13th–15th century). Vague records mention the discovery of at least four stone coffins at various times during repairs to floors:[5]

1. A coffin containing the remains of a corpse, said to be wrapped in 'gilt scollopt leather' and accompanied by a pewter chalice, was uncovered in the chancel in *c.* 1750.[6] It was left *in situ*.

2. A second coffin was found nearby at the same time. It was 'full of mould'.[7]
3. A coffin was found in the south aisle, at a later date (but before 1813).
4. A coffin with a head-recess was found in 1813.

A stone coffin was observed in the south chancel aisle in 2001, against the arcade, when the floor was being renewed; it was not investigated.[8] Another coffin, with a shaped head-recess, containing an intact burial, was found at the same time during excavations in the south cloister. It was recorded and left *in situ*.[9]

The medieval assemblage ranges in date from the mid-12th to the late 14th century, and there is nothing diagnostically Anglo-Saxon or early Norman. Some of the later medieval pieces are derived from small-scale architecture, indicative of monumental tombs, or a shrine. The collection also includes fragments of post-medieval memorials.

Lapidary items noted elsewhere, in and around the church, during the present study are as follows:

(i) The ornately carved 19th-century replacement head for the churchyard cross (Pl. 45) is mounted on a window sill in the south nave aisle, and the cross that surmounted the head is displayed in the medieval locker in the north wall of the nave. Designed by G.G. Scott, *c.* 1872.[10]
(ii) In the shrubbery against the north boundary of the cloister garden are various pieces of rough building stone, several tombstones, and a few other items of archaeological interest. At least one ashlar block carries a roll moulding, and there is a damaged but substantially complete medieval stone mortar. Octagonal in plan with four projecting lugs, this is a particularly large example of the type. Medieval mortars of large size were sometimes pressed into use as post-medieval fonts and fountains. There is also a small, complete mortar in the lapidary collection.[11]

In addition to the loose items, a small number of moulded stones have been casually built into the fabric of the church, most notably in the wall of the staircase in the south-east turret (p. 148), and inside the belfry of the tower. Some at least are Norman in origin. There is surprisingly little decoratively worked stone visible in local buildings.

Notes

1　The display, protected by a wire cage, can be seen in photographs of the late 19th and early 20th century: *e.g.* NMR, CC73/01055. Also, see Poyntz, 1891, 224.

2　Kendrick, 2002. A copy of the inventory is held by the PCC.

3　Noted in J.M. Bignell's letter to the vicar, 17 Jul. 1879: transcript in Ashley, 2000.

4　Kendrick, 2002, cat. T.001 and T.002.

5　Brewer, 1813, 378.

6　Also reported by Gough (1789, **1**, 307).

7　*Ibid.*, 307.

8　Keevill, 2003, 348.

9　*Ibid.*, 348, figs 17 and 23; 2005, fig. 15.

10　Kendrick, 2002, cat. T.147. For a photograph of the complete head *in situ* on the churchyard cross, see Bloxham, 1990, 12.

11　*Ibid.*, cat. T.148.

Appendix

Handlist of Archival Sources for Dorchester Abbey

Four major archives hold unpublished material relating to Dorchester-on-Thames, including numerous illustrations by J. and J.C. Buckler, J. Carter, S.H. Grimm and W. Stukeley. Unfortunately, the Buckler and Carter collections are divided between the British and Bodleian Libraries: thus, one may hold the field sketches of a particular view or feature, while the other holds the completed drawings of the same.[1]

BRITISH LIBRARY, LONDON (MANUSCRIPTS DEPT.)

Drawings by Edward Blore

Add. Ms 42,001, f. 59; 42,009, ff. 7, 52, 67; 42,030, f. 112; 42,031, f. 101.

Drawings by John Buckler

Add. Ms 27,766; 36,372, ff. 249–265; 36,405, ff. 44–51; 36,432, f. 1485.

Drawings by John Carter

Add. Ms 29,931, ff. 179–199, 210–220; 29,932, f. 29; 29,943, f. 106.

Drawings by Samuel Henry Grimm

Add. Ms 15,545, ff. 135–164.

Miscellaneous notes and drawings

Earthworks
Add. Ms 38,776.
Notes by W.H.D. Sweeting
Add. Ms 37,180, f. 13.
Monuments, Inscriptions, Heraldry, etc.
Sl. Ms 3,836, f. 14.
Lans. Ms 874, f. 144.
Harl. Ms 261, 17; 965, pp. 48–64; 6365.
Add. Ms 37,608, f. 575; 41,598, f. 49.
Sepulchral Brasses
Add. Ms 32,478, f. 64; 32,489, cc. 3, 4; 32,490, O.6, N.42, AA.29, KK.16; 34,894, S.7.
Stained Glass
Add. Ms 34,866, ff. 158, 160; 34,867, f. 83; 34,872, f. 212; 35,211, R.4–7.

School Statutes

Add. Ms 25,426.

Charters

Woll. xi. 25.
Harl. S8 I.29.
Harl. 44 F.30.
Add. Ch. 20,361.

BODLEIAN LIBRARY, OXFORD

MS Top. Gen.

a.5, ff. 52–53; a.11, f. 123; a.15, f. 52 (Buckler); a.19, f. 80.
b.53, f. 20 (Stukeley).
c.103, f. 20 (Buckler); c.112, f. 106.
e.23.

MS Top. Eccles.

b.42, ff. 20–23.
d.6, ff. 9–11, 59 (Stukeley).
e.4, ff. 586–591.

MS Top. Oxon.

a.24, ff. 100, 102–104; a.38, ff. 72–91; a.64, nos. 10–11 (Buckler); a.66, nos. 217–219 (Buckler).
b.24, f. 124 (Buckler); b.42, f. 123 (Buckler); b.63, ff. 4, 13, 55, 64, 120, 129; b.75; b.89, f. 166; b.90, no. 83; b.165, ff. 179, 182, 184, 205, 207, 418 (Buckler, *et al.*); b.220, ff. 110–121; b.282, f. 2 (J.P. Neale); b.283, ff. 10–13 (J.P. Neale).
c.38, f. 28; c.60, f. 189; c.103, ff. 382, 384–386; c.158, ff. 10, 17, 26, 41, 47, 71, 90, 203, 210; c.160, f. 312; c.166, pp. 39–50; c.167, p. 361; c.371; c.447, f. 117; c.470, ff. 5–6 (C. Barry); c.522f. 2; c.532, ff. 22, 29–36, 44–45 (Buckler, *et al.*); c.688, ff. 42–43; c.852, f. 28.
d.90; d.195, ff. 305–70; d.514, f. 21; d.795, ff. 210–211.
e.263, f. 60; e.286, ff. 122–125.
Box No. 3.

MS Rawl.

B.397.

MS Wood

d.14.
e.1.

---

[1] For detailed descriptions of the holdings, see Rodwell, 2005a, app. 2.

MS Oxf. Dioc. pps.
b.70, ff. 269, 273, 277–280.

MS Dep.
a.26, ff. 73–78.
b.204, ff. 85–86.
d.540.

MS Don.
b.220, f. 116.
c.90, pp. 477, 484, 489; c.92, ff. 125–127.
d.140, ff. 14–26; d.141, ff. 15–16; d.149, f. 287.

MS Drawings Gen.
c.9, f. 18.

G.A. Oxon.
a.117, pp. 104, 240.

Gough Maps
26, f. 42B (Stukeley and Gough); 221, f. cviii; 222, f. 101; 223a, f. cxvi; 224, ff. 246 bis, 319; 225, f. 261 (Carter), f. 367; 227, ff. 26–48 (Carter); 228, ff. 7, 32, 318, 391.

Gough Gen. Topog.
33, f. 192.

OXFORDSHIRE RECORD OFFICE, OXFORD

(i) Parochial Papers
Registers
PAR87/1/R1–R6.
Vestry Minutes
PAR87/2/A1/1–5.
Churchwardens' Accounts
PAR87/4/F1–2, 7.
Correspondence regarding Dilapidations
PAR87/10/C1/1.
Terriers and Inventories
PAR87/10/E1, 3–6.
Newspapers
PAR87/10/N1/1.
Parsonage Matters
PAR87/10/Y1, 10–11.
Church Fabric
PAR87/11/A1/1.
PAR87/11/C2/1.
PAR87/11/F1/1–2.
Faculties
PAR87/11/L1/1–2, 4, 5.
Heating Plans
PAR87/11/Y1/1.
Plans and Drawings of Church
PAR87/11/Y2/1/1–6.
Y2/2/1–3, 5–44, 46–60.
Drawings by Jewitt
PAR87/11/Y2/3/1–34.
School
PAR87/14/1/A2.

(ii) Oxford Diocesan Papers
MSS Oxf. Archd. Oxon. pps. c.159.
MSS Oxf. dioc. pps. b.70, ff. 269, 273, 277–280.
MSS Oxf. Dioc. pps. c.748, ff. 61–62.
MSS Oxf. Dioc. pps. c.1796.
MSS Oxf. Dioc. pps. c.1797/2/2–3.

(iii) Maps
A Map of the County of Oxford.
    Surveyed by Richard Davis, 1793–94; published 1797.
PC/087/H/1
    A Plan of the Parish of Dorchester in the County of Oxford.
    Surveyed and drawn by John Neighbour, St Clements, Oxford. 1837 and 1838.
Tithe Map and Award, No. 132.
    A Plan of the Parish of Dorchester.
    Surveyed by Neighbour and Son, Oxford. 1845. Accompanying tithe award roll, 1846.

CENTRE FOR OXFORDSHIRE STUDIES, OXFORD

The centre holds various material, mostly published rather than archival. This includes:

(i)   Most of the photographic collection of H.W. Taunt of Oxford. See also NMR (below).
(ii) Sundry photographs by Packer, and others.
(iii) Illustrations taken from various published antiquarian works, including the scarce plan and view by J. Harris, *c.* 1720 (from Stevens, 1722).
(iv) Pamphlets, offprints and ephemeral publications relating to Dorchester.

NATIONAL MONUMENTS RECORD, ENGLISH HERITAGE, SWINDON

Church
Buildings File
BF 058224
Measured Drawings File
56/00035–40 and 00107–109.
93/09770–76.
94/02162–63.
CVMA (Corpus Vitrearum Medii Aevi) Archive
Photographs of stained glass.
Photograph Box
A large collection of views, ranging in date from pre-1875 to the 1960s. The collection includes some outstanding shots by H.F. Taunt, both internal and external.

Abbey Guest House
Buildings File
BF086871
Photograph Box
Includes good shots by H.F. Taunt, and later views.

Other Structures: Churchyard, Cross, Cottages, Tollhouse, Abbey Barns, etc.

Photograph Box
Numerous photographs.

ARCHIVAL MATERIAL HELD BY OTHER INSTITUTIONS

Miscellaneous collections are held by the following.

Dorchester Parochial Church Council
Museum, Abbey Guest House, Dorchester-on-Thames.

Society of Antiquaries of London
Burlington House, Piccadilly, London.

Royal Institute of British Architects
Drawings Collection, Victoria and Albert Museum, London.

Incorporated Church Building Society
Lambeth Palace Library, London.

BIBLIOGRAPHY

ABBREVIATIONS

BAR	British Archaeological Reports (British series)
Bodl.	Bodleian Library, Oxford
BL	British Library, London
CBA	Council for British Archaeology
COS	Centre for Oxfordshire Studies, Westgate, Oxford
Hist. Eccles.	Bede, *Historia Ecclesiastica* (Sherley-Price, 1965)
ICBS	Incorporated Church Building Society
LPL	Lambeth Palace Library, London
NMR	National Monuments Record, English Heritage, Swindon
OAS	Oxford Architectural Society (predecessor of OAHS)
OAHS	Oxfordshire Architectural and Historical Society
OHS	Oxford Historical Society
OS	Ordnance Survey
ORO	Oxfordshire Record Office, Oxford
ORS	Oxfordshire Record Society
OUDES	Oxford University Department for External Studies
PCC	Parochial Church Council, Dorchester-on-Thames
RCHME	Royal Commission on the Historical Monuments of England
VCH	Victoria County History of England

BIBLIOGRAPHY

Abrams, L., and Carley, J.P., (eds.), 1991. *The Archaeology and History of Glastonbury Abbey*. Boydell, Woodbridge.

Addington, H., 1845. *Some Account of the Abbey Church of St Peter and St Paul, at Dorchester, Oxfordshire*. Oxford. Reissued 1848 in, *Memoirs of Gothic Churches*. Parker, Oxford.

Addington, H., and Macfarlane, W.C., 1860/1882. *Some Account of the Abbey Church of St Peter and St Paul, at Dorchester, Oxfordshire*. Oxford. New edn. of Addington, 1845, with additional notes; also publ. as an appendix to Parker, 1882.

Alexander, J., and Binski, P. (eds.), *Age of Chivalry. Art in Plantagenet England, 1200–1400*. British Academy, London.

Allen, G.W.G., 1938. 'Marks seen from the Air in the Crops near Dorchester, Oxon.', *Oxoniensia*, **3**, 169–71.

Andrews, F.B., 1901. *The Benedictine Abbey of SS Mary, Peter and Paul, at Pershore, Worcestershire*. Birmingham.

Anon. [W.H. St. J. Hope], 1910. 'Dorchester Abbey Church', *Archaeol. J.*, **67**, 333–5.

Anon., n.d. [*c.* 1925]. *A Short History and Brief Description of Dorchester Abbey, Oxfordshire*. Privately printed.

Anon. [1964]. *The Shrine of St Birinus, Dorchester Abbey*. Privately printed, Abingdon.

Anon., 1976. *Dorchester-on-Thames Grammar School*. Privately printed, Dorchester.

Arnold-Forster, F., 1899. *Studies in Church Dedications*. 3 vols. London.

Ashley, M., 2000. *Dorchester Abbey, Dorchester-on-Thames, Oxfordshire. Conservation Plan*. Desktop report, Martin Ashley Architects, Richmond. [copy held by PCC]

Aston, M., 1974. 'The Roman Town Defences at Dorchester, Oxon. An Interim Assessment', *CBA Group 9, Newsletter*, **4**, 3–4.

Atkinson, R.J.C., Piggott, C.M., and Sanders, N.K., 1951. *Excavations at Dorchester, Oxon. First Report*. Ashmolean Mus., Oxford.

Ayers, T., 1991. 'The Sanctuary of Dorchester Abbey, Oxfordshire: Its Design and Iconography'. Unpubl. M.A. Dissertation, Courtauld Institute of Art, University of London.

Ayers, T., 2002. 'Vitraux, Retables et *English Decorated Style* la Verrière Orientale de l'Eglise Abbatiale de Dorchester, Comte d'Oxford', *Représentations Architecturales dans les Vitraux*, 105–11. Dossier de la Commission Royale des Monuments, Sites et Fouilles, **9**. Brussels.

Ayre, K., 2002. *Medieval English Figurative Roundels*. Corpus Vitrearum Medii Aevi, Summary Cat. **6**. British Academy, Oxford.

Babington, C., (ed.), 1865. *Polychronicon Ranulphi Higden Monachi Cestrensis*, vol. II. Rolls Ser., **41**. HMSO, London.

Badham, S., and Norris, M., 1999. *Early Incised Slabs and Brasses from the London Marblers*. Soc. Antiq. London, Res. Rep., **60**. London.

Ballantyne, A., 2003. *The Abbey Church of Saint Peter & Saint Paul, Dorchester, Oxfordshire*. Unpubl. report on wallpaintings. [copy held by PCC]

Ballantyne, A., 2004. *The Abbey Church of Saint Peter & Saint Paul, Dorchester, Oxfordshire*. Unpubl. report on wallpaintings. [copy held by PCC]

Ballantyne, A., 2006. *The Abbey Church of Saint Peter & Saint Paul, Dorchester, Oxfordshire. Conservation Reports on work carried out in the People's Chapel, Lady Chapel and Shrine Chapel, 2005–6*. Unpubl. report on wallpaintings. [copy held by PCC]

Barker, P.P., and Brookes, C.F., 1999. *Report on a Ground Probing Radar Survey at Dorchester Abbey Church*. Desktop report, Stratascan. [copy held by PCC]

Barker, P.P., and Brookes, C.F., 2000. *Report on a Ground Probing Radar Survey at Dorchester Abbey Church*. Desktop report, Stratascan. [copy held by PCC]

Barns, T., 1881. 'Dorchester in British and Roman Times', *Proc. Oxford Archit. Hist. Soc.*, new ser. **4**, 33–4.

Beaumont, E.T., 1913. *Ancient Memorial Brasses*. OUP, London.

Beeson, C.F.C., 1989. *Clockmaking in Oxfordshire, 1400–1850*. Mus. of Science, Oxford.

Benson, D., and Miles, D., 1974. *The Upper Thames Valley: An Archaeological Survey of the River Gravels*. Oxford Archaeol. Unit, Survey no. **2**.

Bertram, J., 1976. *Lost Brasses*. Newton Abbot.

Bertram, J., 2000. *A Catalogue of Medieval Inscriptions in the Abbey Church of Dorchester, Oxfordshire*. Privately printed, Oxford.

Bertram, J., 2003. 'Medieval Inscriptions in Oxfordshire', *Oxoniensia*, **68**, 27–53.

Bertram, J., 2004. *Gough's Sepulchral Monuments ... in the Gough Manuscripts of the Bodleian Library*. Privately printed, Oxford.

Best, H., 1967. *A Pilgrimage to Dorchester Abbey: A Guide to the Ecclesiastical and Architectural History*. New edn., 1969. Privately printed, Abingdon.

Best, H., 1970. *The Abbey Church of St Peter and St Paul, Dorchester, Oxon.: A Guide to the Ecclesiastical and Architectural History*. Photo-Precision, St Ives. [Guide book]

Blair, J., 1992. 'Anglo-Saxon Minsters: A Topographical Review', in J. Blair and R. Sharpe (eds.), *Pastoral Care before the Parish*, 226–66. Leicester UP.

Blair, J., 1994. *Anglo-Saxon Oxfordshire*. Stroud.

Blair, J., 1996. 'Churches in the Early English Landscape: Social and Cultural Contexts', in J. Blair and C. Pyrah (eds.), *Church Archaeology. Research Directions for the Future*, 6–18. CBA, Res. Rep. **104**.

Blair, J., 2005. *The Church in Anglo-Saxon Society*. OUP, Oxford.

Blatch, M., 1997. *The Churches of Surrey*. Chichester.

Bloxham, R., 1990. *Dorchester Abbey, Oxfordshire*. Watford. [Guide book]

Bloxham, R., 2002. *Dorchester Abbey, Oxfordshire*. Dorchester. [Guide book]

Bond, F., 1908a. *Fonts and Font Covers*. OUP, London.

Bond, F., 1908b. *Screens and Galleries in English Churches*. OUP, London.

Bond, F., 1913. *An Introduction to English Church Architecture*, **1**. (Dorchester, pp. 254–69). OUP.

Bond, F., 1916. *The Chancel of English Churches*. OUP, London.

Bond, J., and Tiller, K., 2005. 'Cathedral and Abbey, 635–1536', in Tiller, 2005, 24–38.

Bouchier, E.S., 1918. *Notes on the Stained Glass of the Oxford District*. Oxford.

Boutell, C., 1847. *Monumental Brasses and Slabs*. London.

Boutell, C., 1849. *The Monumental Brasses of England; A Series of Engravings upon Wood*. London.

Boutell, C., 1854. *Christian Monuments in England and Wales*. London.

Bradley, R., 1978. 'Rescue Excavation in Dorchester-on-Thames, 1972', *Oxoniensia*, **43**, 17–39.

Bradley, R., 1990. *The Passage of Arms: An Archaeological Analysis of Prehistoric Hoards and Votive Deposits*. CUP, Cambridge.

Brakspear, H., 1900a. 'Lacock Abbey, Wilts.', *Archaeologia*, **57**, 125–58.

Brakspear, H., 1900b. 'Lacock Abbey Church', *Archaeol. J.*, **57**, 1–9.

Brakspear, H., 1923. 'Excavations at some Wiltshire Monasteries', *Archaeologia*, **73**, 225–52.

Brewer, J.N., 1813. *The Beauties of England and Wales*, **12**, pt. 2. (Dorchester, pp. 369–80). London.

Briggs, G., Cook, J., and Rowley, T., (eds), 1986. *The Archaeology of the Oxford Region*. OUDES, Oxford.

Britton, J., 1835. *Chronological History of Christian Architecture in England*. 5 vols. London.

Britton, J., 1836. *Cathedral Antiquities: Historical and Descriptive Accounts of English Cathedrals*. 5 vols. London.

Brooke, C.J., 2001. *Dorchester Abbey, Oxfordshire: A Ground-Based Remote Sensing Survey of the West Wall*. Unpubl. report.

Broomhead, F., 1995. *The Book Illustrations of Orlando Jewitt*. Private Libraries Assn., Pinner.

Broomhead, F., 1996. 'Orlando Jewitt: Wood Engraver to the Oxford Society for Promoting the Study of Gothic Architecture', *Oxoniensia*, **61**, 369–78.

Burnham, B.C., and Wacher, J., 1990. *The 'Small Towns' of Roman Britain*. London.

Caley, J., Ellis, H., and Bandinel, B., (eds.), [W. Dugdale], 1846. *Monasticon Anglicanum. A History of the Abbies and other Monasteries ... in England and Wales*. London. (Dorchester, vol. **6**, 323–4.)

Camden, W. See Gibson, 1695; Gough, 1789.

Carter, J., and Britton, J., 1837. *The Ancient Architecture of England*. New edn., London. First edn., by Carter, 1795.

Carter, H., 1962. *Orlando Jewitt*. OUP, London.

Chambers, R.A., 1987. 'The Late- and Sub-Roman Cemetery at Queenford Farm, Dorchester-on-Thames, Oxon.' *Oxoniensia*, **52**, 35–69.

Chinnery, V., 1979. *Oak Furniture: The British Tradition*. Woodbridge.

Church, W.A., 1845. *Patterns of Inlaid Tiles from Churches in the Diocese of Oxford*. London.

Clapham, A.W., 1934. *English Romanesque Architecture after the Conquest*. Oxford. Repr. 1964.

Clark, A., (ed.), 1891. *The Life and Times of Anthony Wood, Antiquary, of Oxford, 1632–1695, described by Himself. Vol I: 1632–1663*. OHS, **19**.

Coales, J., (ed.), 1987. *The Earliest English Brasses*. Monumental Brass Soc., London.

Coldstream, N., 1976. 'English Decorated Shrine Bases', *J. Brit. Archaeol. Ass.*, **129**, 15–34.

Collingwood, R.G., and Wright, R.P., 1965. *The Roman Inscriptions of Britain. I Inscriptions on Stone*. Oxford.

Cook, J., and Rowley, T., (eds.), 1985. *Dorchester through the Ages*. OUDES, Oxford.

Cordeaux, E.H., and Merry, D.H., 1955. *A Bibliography of Printed Works relating to Oxfordshire*. OHS, new ser. **12**. Oxford.

Cordeaux, E.H., and Merry, D.H., 1981. *A Bibliography of Printed Works relating to Oxfordshire. Supplementary Volume*. OHS, new ser. **28**. Oxford.

Crawford, O.G.S., 1927. 'Air Photographs near Dorchester', *Antiquity*, **1**, 469–74.

Crick, J., 1991. 'The Marshalling of Antiquity: Glastonbury's

Historical Dossier', in Abrams and Carley, 1991, 217–43.

Crook, J., 2000. *The Architectural Setting of the Cult of Saints in the Early Christian West, c. 300–1200*. Oxford.

Cunningham, C.J.K., and Banks, J.W., 1972. 'Excavations at Dorchester Abbey, Oxon.', *Oxoniensia*, **37**, 158–64.

Davey, E.C., 1897. *Memoirs of an Oxfordshire Old Catholic Family and its Connections, from 1566 to 1897*. London.

Davis, F.N., (ed.), 1922. *Parochial Collections made by Anthony à Wood and Richard Rawlinson. Pt. 2*. ORS, **4**. Oxford. (Dorchester, pp. 114–23).

Dean. M., 1986. 'The Angel Choir and its Local Influence', in *Medieval Art and Architecture at Lincoln Cathedral*, 90–101. Brit. Archaeol. Ass., Conference Trans., **8**.

Dickinson, T.M., 1974. *Cuddesdon and Dorchester-on-Thames: Two Early Saxon 'Princely' Sites in Wessex*, BAR, **1**. Oxford.

Doggett, N., 1986. 'The Anglo-Saxon See and Cathedral of Dorchester-on-Thames: the Evidence Reconsidered', *Oxoniensia*, **51**, 49–61.

Doggett, N., 2005. 'The Dissolution and After: Dorchester Abbey, 1536–c.1800', in Tiller, 2005, 39–48.

Drake, C.S., 2002. *The Romanesque Fonts of Northern Europe and Scandinavia*. Boydell, Woodbridge.

Druce, G.C., 1934. 'Lead Fonts in England, with some Reference to French Examples', *Archaeol. J.*, new ser. **39**, 289–329.

Dudley, N., 2005. 'Dorchester and its Abbey Recollected, 1920–2005', in Tiller, 2005, 84–99.

Dugdale, W. See Caley, Ellis and Bandinel, 1846; also Stevens, 1722.

Durham, B., and Rowley, T., 1972. 'A Cemetery Site at Queensford Mill, Dorchester', *Oxoniensia*, **37**, 32–7.

Eames, E.S., 1980. *Catalogue of Medieval Lead-Glazed Earthenware Tiles*. 2 vols. British Museum Publications, London.

Evans, J.T., 1928. *The Church Plate of Oxfordshire*. Oxford.

Fernie, E., 1983, *The Architecture of the Anglo-Saxons*. London.

Field, J.E., 1909. 'Abbot Beauforest of Dorchester', *Berkshire, Buckinghamshire, Oxfordshire Archaeol. J.*, **15**, 61–2.

Fisher, G., Stamp, G., et al., 1981. *Catalogue of the Drawings Collection of the Royal Institute of British Architects: The Scott Family*. RIBA, London.

Ford, E.B., and Haywood, J.S., 1984. *Church Treasures in the Oxford District*. Gloucester.

France, N.E., and Gobel, B.M., 1985. *The Romano-British Temple at Harlow, Essex*. West Essex Archaeol. Group.

Freeman, E.A., 1851. *The Origin and Development of Window Tracery in England*. Oxford.

Freeman, E.A., 1852. 'On the Architecture of the Abbey Church of Dorchester', *Archaeol. J.*, **9**, 158–69; 262–80; 329–35. Republ. in Parker, 1882.

Frere, S.S., 1962. 'Excavations at Dorchester-on-Thames, 1962', *Archaeol. J.*, **119**, 114–49.

Frere, S.S., 1984. 'Excavations at Dorchester-on-Thames, 1963', *Archaeol. J.*, **141**, 91–174.

Fryer, A.C., 1900. 'Leaden Fonts', *Archaeol. J.*, **57**, 40–51.

Gelling, M., 1953. *The Place-Names of Oxfordshire*. Eng. Place-Name Soc., **23**. Cambridge.

Gibson, E., [W. Camden], 1695. *Camden's Britannia, with Additions and Improvements*. London.

Gomme, G.L. (ed. F.A. Milne), 1897. *The Gentleman's Magazine Library. English Topography, Part IX*. London.

Gough, R., 1786–96. *Sepulchral Monuments in Great Britain*. 2 vols. in 5. London.

Gough, R., [W. Camden], 1789. *Camden's Britannia*, **1**. London. 2nd edn., 1806.

Graham, M., 1973. *Henry Taunt of Oxford. A Victorian Photographer*. Oxford Illustrated Press.

Graham, R., (ed.), 1919. *The Chantry Certificates and the Edwardian Inventories of Church Goods*. ORS, **1**. Oxford.

Gransden, A., 1982. *Historical Writing in England*, **2**. London.

Gray, M., 1977. 'Northfield Farm, Long Wittenham', *Oxoniensia*, **42**, 1–29.

Haberly, L., 1937. *Medieval English Pavingtiles*. Oxford.

Haines, H., 1861. *A Manual of Monumental Brasses*. Oxford.

Halsey, R., 1988. 'The 12th-Century Church of St. Frideswide's Priory', *Oxoniensia*, **53**, 115–67.

Hamilton, N.E.S.A., (ed.) [William of Malmesbury], 1870. *Chronicles and Memorials of Great Britain and Ireland: De Gestis Pontificum Anglorum, Lib. IV*. Rolls Ser., **52**, 312. HMSO, London.

Harman, M., Lambrick, G., Miles, D., and Rowley, T., 1978. 'Roman Burials around Dorchester-on-Thames', *Oxoniensia*, **43**, 1–16.

Harvey, J.H. (ed.), 1969. *William Worcestre: Itineraries*. Oxford.

Hassall, T., 1986. 'The Oxford Region from the Conversion to the Conquest', in Briggs, *et al.*, 1986, 109–14.

Hawkes, S.C., and Dunning, G.C., 1961. 'Soldiers and Settlers in Britain, Fourth to Fifth Century', *Medieval Archaeol.*, **5**, 1–70.

Hearn, M.F., and Thurlby, M., 1997. 'Previously Undetected Wooden Ribbed Vaults in Medieval Britain', *J. Brit. Archaeol. Ass.*, **150**, 48–58.

Hearne, T., 1889–1915. *Remarks and Collections of Thomas Hearne, Vols. II, IV, V, VII, VIII, X*. OHS, **7**, **34**, **42**, **48**, **50** and **67**. Oxford.

Heighway, C., and Bryant, R., 1999. *The Golden Minster. The Anglo-Saxon Minster and Later Medieval Priory of St Oswald at Gloucester*. CBA, Res. Rep. **117**.

Henig, M., and Booth, P., 2000. *Roman Oxfordshire*. Stroud.

Hewitt, J., 1855. *Ancient Armour and Weapons in Europe*. 3 vols. (publ. 1855–60).

Hill, F., 1965. *Medieval Lincoln*. CUP.

Hill, R.M.T., (ed.), 1954. *The Rolls and Register of Bishop Oliver Sutton, 1280–1299. Vol. III*. Lincoln Rec. Soc., **48**.

Hodges, C.C., 1888. *The Abbey of St Andrew, Hexham*. Privately printed.

Hoey, L., 1994. 'Stone Vaults in English Parish Churches in the Early Gothic and Decorated Periods', *J. Brit. Archaeol. Ass.*, **147**, 36–51.

Hogg, A.H.A., and Stevens, C.E., 1937. 'The Defences of Roman Dorchester', *Oxoniensia*, **2**, 41–73.

Horsley, J., 1732. *Britannia Romana*. London.

Howard, F.E., 1910. 'Screens and Rood-Lofts in the Parish Churches of Oxfordshire', *Archaeol. J.*, **67**, 151–201.

Huggins, P.J., Rodwell, W.J., and Rodwell, K.A., 1982. 'Anglo-Saxon and Scandinavian Building Measurements', in P.J. Drury (ed.), 1982. *Structural Reconstruction: Approaches to the Interpretation of Excavated Remains of Buildings*, 21–65. BAR, **110**. Oxford.

Hunt, J.E., 1956. *English and Welsh Crucifixes, 670–1550*. SPCK, London.

Impey, E., ed., 2008. *The White Tower*. Yale UP and Historic Royal Palaces, London.

James, M.R., 1926. *Abbeys*. Great Western Railway, London.

Jessel, P., and Stedman, E., n.d. [*c*. 1970]. '*These Notable Things': 800 Years of Dorchester Abbey*. Privately printed.

Johns, C.M., and Potter, T.W., 1983. *The Thetford Treasure: Roman Jewellery and Silver*. British Museum, London.

Johns, C.M., and Potter, T.W., 1985. 'The Canterbury Late Roman Treasure', *Antiq. J.*, **65**, 312–52.

Keevill, G.D., 2003. 'Archaeological Investigations in 2001 at the Abbey Church of St Peter and St Paul, Dorchester-on-Thames, Oxfordshire', *Oxoniensia*, **68**, 313–62.

Keevill, G., 2005. 'The Archaeology of Dorchester Abbey', in Tiller, 2005, 10–23.

Kendrick, D.J., 2002. *Dorchester Abbey, Dorchester-on-Thames, Oxfordshire: Worked Stones*. 4 vols. Unpubl. report. [copy held by PCC]

Keyser, C.E., 1883. *A List of Buildings having Mural and Other Painted Decorations*. London.

Keyser, C.E., 1911. 'The Norman Architecture of Berkshire', *Trans. Newbury Dist. Field Club*, **5**.

King, D., 1672. *Cathedral and Conventual Churches of England and Wales*. Second edn. London. Reissued, 1969, ed. H. Colvin.

Kirk, J.R., and Leeds, E.T., 1952–53. 'Three Early Saxon Graves from Dorchester, Oxon.', *Oxoniensia*, **17/18**, 63–76.

Kirkpatrick, H.F., n.d. [1927], *Dorchester-on-Thame* [sic] *and the Abbey Church of Saint Peter and Saint Paul*. Famous Churches and Abbeys, No. 38, SPCK, London. Second. edn., 1930. Other edns., n.d. [1955; 1959].

Lambourn, E.A.G., 1949. *The Armorial Glass of the Oxford Diocese, 1250–1850*. OUP, London.

Lane-Fox, A. [Gen. Pitt-Rivers], 1870. 'On the Threatened Destruction of the British Earthworks near Dorchester', *J. Ethnolog. Soc. London*, new ser. **2**, 412–15.

Lankester, P.J., 1987. 'A Military Effigy in Dorchester Abbey, Oxon.', *Oxoniensia*, **52**, 145–72.

Lewis, M.J.T., 1966. *Temples in Roman Britain*. CUP, Cambridge.

Long, E.T., 1972. 'Medieval Wall Paintings in Oxfordshire Churches', *Oxoniensia*, **37**, 86–108.

Macfarlane, W.C., 1881. *A Short Account of Dorchester, Oxfordshire, Past and Present*. J. Parker, Oxford. Other edns, 1884, 1892; also published in Parker, 1882, 13–30.

Marples, B.J., 1973. 'The Medieval Crosses of Oxfordshire', *Oxoniensia*, **38**, 299–311.

May, J., 1977. 'Romano-British and Saxon Sites near Dorchester-on-Thames, Oxfordshire', *Oxoniensia*, **42**, 42–79.

Miles, D., 1978. 'Iron Age and Roman Dorchester', *Archaeol. J.*, **135**, 288–9.

Miller, P., and Saxby, D., 2007. *The Augustinian Priory of St Mary Merton, Surrey: Excavations 1976–90*. Museum of London, Monogr. **34**.

Montague, J., 2006. 'The Cloister and Bishop's Palace at Old Sarum with some thoughts on the Origins and Meaning of Secular Cathedral Cloisters', *J. Brit. Archaeol. Ass.*, **159**, 48–70.

Moorman, J.R.H., 1994. *Lanercost Priory*. 3rd edn. Privately printed.

Morant, R.W., 1995. *The Monastic Gatehouse*. Lewes.

Morris, R., 1989. *Churches in the Landscape*. London.

Neal, D.S., 1967. 'The Roman Mosaic in the Church of St Oswald, Widford', *Antiq. J.*, **47**, 110–11.

Newton, P.A., 1979. *The County of Oxford: A Catalogue of Medieval Stained Glass* (Dorchester, pp. 77–88). Corpus Vitrearum Medii Aevi, British Academy. OUP, London.

Pantin, W.A., 1939. 'The Oxford Architectural and Historical Society, 1839–1939', *Oxoniensia*, **4**, 174–8.

Parker, J.H., 1845. *Dorchester Church*. Privately printed.

Parker, J.H., 1868. 'On the Roman Occupation of Dorchester', *Proc. Oxford Archit. Hist. Soc.*, new ser. **2**, 90–9.

Parker, J.H., 1881/1907. *A B C of Gothic Architecture*. 1st edn. 1881; 13th edn. 1907. London.

Parker, J.H., 1882. *The History of Dorchester, Oxfordshire*. London.

Paul, R.W., 1900. 'The Abbeys of Great Britain, No. 32: Dorchester Abbey', *The Builder*, **78** (6 Jan. 1900), 11–14.

Paul, R.W., 1912. 'The Plan of the Church and Monastery of St Augustine, Bristol', *Archaeologia*, **63**, 231–50.

Pearce, S.S. (ed.), 1918. *The Clergy of the Deaneries of Henley and Aston and of the Peculiar of Dorchester during the Settlement of 1559 and afterwards*. OAS, Oxford.

Perks, G.D., and O'Connell, P., 1996. 'Transcriptions of Gravestones in Dorchester Abbey Church, Oxon.' Unpubl. ms. [copy held by PCC]

Petts, D., 2003. *Christianity in Roman Britain*. Stroud.

Pevsner, N., and Metcalf, P., 1985a. *The Cathedrals of England: Southern England*. Harmondsworth.

Pevsner, N., and Metcalf, P., 1985b. *The Cathedrals of England: Midland, Eastern and Northern England*. Harmondsworth.

Peyton, S.A., (ed.), 1928. *The Churchwardens' Presentments in the Oxfordshire Peculiars of Dorchester, Thame and Banbury*. ORS, **10**. Oxford.

Poyntz, N.C.S., 1891. 'Notes on the Abbey Church of Dorchester, Oxon.', *J. Brit. Archaeol. Ass.*, **47**, 222–4.

Pugin, A.C., and Walker, T.L., 1836. *History and Antiquities of the Vicars' Close, Wells*. Pugin's Examples of Gothic Architecture, ser. 3, **1**. London.

RCHME, 1922. *An Inventory of the Historical Monuments in Essex: Vol. III*. HMSO, London.

RCHME, 1924. *An Inventory of the Historical Monuments in London: Vol. I, Westminster Abbey*. HMSO, London

RCHME, 1987. *Churches of South-East Wiltshire*. HMSO, London.

Rickman, T. (ed. J.H. Parker), 1817/1848/1862. *An Attempt to Discriminate the Styles of Architecture in England from the Conquest to the Reformation*. First edn., 1817; fifth edn., 1848; sixth edn. 1862. Oxford and London.

Rivet, A.L.F., and Smith, C., 1979. *The Place-Names of Roman Britain*. London.

Roberts, E., 1993a. *The Hill of the Martyr: An Architectural History of St Albans Abbey*. Privately printed, Dunstable.

Roberts, E., 1993b. *The Wall Paintings of Saint Albans Abbey*. Friends of St Albans Abbey.

Roberts, H.V.M., 1930. 'Dorchester on Thame [sic], Oxfordshire', *The Builder*, **139**, (5 Sep. 1930), 378–9.

Robinson, D.M., 1980. *The Geography of Augustinian Settlement*. BAR, **80**. Oxford.

Robinson, J.A., 1914. 'Effigies of Saxon Bishops at Wells', *Archaeologia*, **65**, 95–112.

Rodwell, K.A., (ed.), 1975. *Historic Towns in Oxfordshire: A Survey of the New County*. Oxford Archaeol. Unit, Survey no. **3**.

Rodwell, W., 1981/1989/2005. *The Archaeology of the English Church*. London. Second edn., 1989; third edn., 2005.

Rodwell, W., 1982. 'The Anglo-Saxon and Norman Churches at Wells', in L.S. Colchester (ed.), *Wells Cathedral: A History*, 1–23. Shepton Mallet.

Rodwell, W., 1984. 'Churches in the Landscape: Aspects of Topography and Planning', in M.L. Faull (ed.), *Studies in Late Saxon Settlement*, 1–25. OUDES, Oxford.

Rodwell, W., 1993. 'The Development of the Quire of Lichfield Cathedral: Romanesque and Early English', in J. Maddison (ed.), *Medieval Art and Architecture at Lichfield Cathedral*, 17–35. Brit. Archaeol. Ass., Conference Trans. **13**.

Rodwell, W., 2001. *Wells Cathedral: Excavations and Structural Studies, 1978–93*. 2 vols. English Heritage, Archaeol. Rep. **21**. London.

Rodwell, W., 2004. 'Revealing the History of the Cathedral: 4. Archaeology of the Nave Sanctuary', *Friends of Lichfield Cathedral: Sixty-Seventh Ann. Rep.*, 18–35. Lichfield.

Rodwell, W., 2005a. *The Abbey Church of St Peter and St Paul, Dorchester-on-Thames, Oxfordshire: An Archaeological and Historical Survey, with Notes on the Fabric and Fittings of the Church*. 3 vols. Desktop report, privately printed for Dorchester PCC.

Rodwell, W., 2005b. 'Begun while the Black Death Raged: The Vicars' Close at Wells', in R. Hall and D. Stocker (eds), *Vicars Choral at English Cathedrals: History, Architecture and Archaeology*, 112–37. Oxbow, Oxford.

Rodwell, W., Hawkes, J., Howe, E., and Cramp, R., 2008. 'The Lichfield Angel: A Spectacular Anglo-Saxon Painted Sculpture', *Antiq. J.*, **88**, 48–108.

Rodwell, W., forthcoming [2010]. *St Peter's, Barton-upon-Humber. A Parish Church and its Community*, vol. 1. English Heritage and Oxbow, Oxford.

Rogan, J. (ed.), 2000. *Bristol Cathedral: History and Architecture*. Tempus, Stroud.

Rollason, D.W., 1978. 'Lists of Saints' Resting-Places in Anglo-Saxon England', *Anglo-Saxon England*, **7**, 61–93. CUP, Cambridge.

Rosewell, R., 2008. *Medieval Wall Paintings in English and Welsh Churches*. Boydell, Woodbridge.

Rowley, T., 1974. 'Early Saxon Settlements in Dorchester-on-Thames', in T. Rowley (ed.), *Anglo-Saxon Settlement and Landscape*, 42–50. BAR, **6**. Oxford.

Rowley, T., 1975. 'The Roman Towns of Oxfordshire', in W. Rodwell and T. Rowley (eds.), *The 'Small Towns' of Roman Britain*, 115–24. BAR, **15**. Oxford.

Rowley, T., and Brown, L., 1981. 'Excavations at Beech House Hotel, Dorchester-on-Thames, 1972', *Oxoniensia*, **46**, 1–61.

Rush, M., 2004. *A Geophysical Investigation into the Monastic Buildings at Dorchester-on-Thames Abbey, Oxfordshire*. Unpubl. M.Sc. Dissertation, University of Reading.

St Joseph, J.K.S., 1966. *The Uses of Air Photography*. Cambridge.

Scott, G.G., 1879. *Lectures on the Rise and Development of Medieval Architecture*. London.

Sharpe, E., 1849. *A Treatise ... on Decorated Window Tracery in England*. London.

Sharpe, E., 1871. *An Account of the Churches Visited during the Lincoln Excursion of The Architectural Association, 1870*. London.

Sharpe, F., 1950. *The Church Bells of Oxfordshire. Volume II*. ORS, **30**. Oxford.

Sharpe, R., 1991. 'Eadmer's Letter to the Monks of Glastonbury concerning St Dunstan's Disputed Remains', in Abrams and Carley, 1991, 205–15.

Sherley-Price, L. (transl.), 1965. *A History of the English Church and People*. Harmondsworth.

Sherlock, D., 2008. *Suffolk Church Chests*. Suff. Inst. Archaeol. and Hist.

Sherwood, J., 1989. *A Guide to the Churches of Oxfordshire*. Oxfordshire Historic Churches Trust.

Sherwood, J., and Pevsner, N., 1974. *Buildings of England. Oxfordshire*. (Dorchester, pp. 576–83). Penguin, Harmondsworth.

Simons, E., 2004. *Dorchester Abbey. Historic Building Analysis*. Oxford Archaeology, unpubl. report. [copy held by PCC]

Skelton, J., 1823. *Antiquities of Oxfordshire: Dorchester Hundred*. Oxford.

Smith, L.T. (ed.), 1964. *The Itinerary of John Leland*, **1**, 116–18. London. Repr. of 1907 edn.

Smith, V., 2004. *The Romano-British Religious Centre of Vagniacis, at Springhead, Kent*. Gravesend Hist. Soc.

Stamp, G., (ed.), 1995. *G.G. Scott, Personal and Professional Recollections*. Stamford.

Stedman, E.G., 1971. *A Yankee in an English Village*. Privately printed for Dorchester Abbey Museum.

Stenton, F., 1947. *Anglo-Saxon England*. Oxford.

Stephenson, M., 1926. *A List of Monumental Brasses in the British Isles*. London.

Stephenson, M., 1938. *Appendix to a List of Monumental Brasses in the British Isles*. Privately printed, London.

Stevens, C.E., and Keeney, G.S., 1935. 'Ramparts of Dorchester', *Antiquity*, **9**, 217–19.

Stevens, J., [Dugdale] 1722. *The History of the Ancient Abbeys, Monasteries, Hospitals, Cathedral and Collegiate Churches .... *London.

Stonor, R.J., 1952. *Stonor. A Catholic Sanctuary in the Chilterns from the Fifth Century till Today*. 2nd edn. Privately printed: R.H. Johns, Newport, Mon.

Taunt, H.W., 1906. *Dorchester (Oxon.) and its Abbey Church*. Taunt and Co., Oxford.

Taylor, H.M., and Taylor, J., 1965. *Anglo-Saxon Architecture*. 2 vols. Cambridge.

Thomas, C., 1981. *Christianity in Roman Britain to A.D. 500*. London.

Thompson, A.H., 1919. 'The Priory of St Mary of Newstead', *Trans. Thoroton Soc. Nottinghamshire*, **23**, 33–141.

Thompson, M., 2001. *Cloister, Abbot and Precinct in Medieval Monasteries*. Tempus, Stroud.

Thompson, P., 1971. *William Butterfield*. Cambridge, Mass., USA.

Thurlby, M., 2002. 'Minor Cruciform Churches in Norman England and Wales', *Anglo-Norman Stud.*, **24**, 239–59.

Thurlby, M., 2003. 'Anglo-Saxon Architecture beyond the Millennium: Its Continuity into Norman Building', in N. Hiscock (ed.), *The White Mantle of Churches: Archi-*

tecture, Liturgy and Art around the Millennium, 119–37. Brepols.

Tiller, K. (ed.), 2005. *Dorchester Abbey: Church and People, 635–2005.* Oxford.

Tracy, C., 1987. *English Gothic Choir-Stalls, 1200–1400.* Woodbridge.

Tristram, E.W., 1955. *English Wall Painting of the Fourteenth Century.* London.

Tyack, G., 2005. 'The Abbey Restored, *c.* 1800–1920', in Tiller, 2005, 49–60.

Turner, W.H. (ed.), 1871. *The Visitations of the County of Oxford taken in the Years 1566, 1574 and 1634.* Harleian Soc., **5**.

Vallance, A., 1920. *Old Crosses and Lychgates.* London.

Vallance, A., 1947. *Greater English Church Screens.* London.

VCH (ed. W. Page), 1907. *Oxfordshire, Vol. II.* London.

VCH (ed. L.F. Saltzman), 1939. *Oxfordshire, Vol. I.* London.

VCH (ed. M.D. Lobel), 1962. *Oxfordshire, Vol. VII: Dorchester and Thame Hundreds.* (Dorchester, principally pp. 39–64). OUP, London.

Watts, D., 1991. *Christians and Pagans in Late Roman Britain.* London.

Webster, C., and Elliott, J. (eds.), 2000. '*A Church as it should be*': *The Cambridge Camden Society and its Influence.* Stamford.

Whitelock, D., (ed.), 1961. *The Anglo-Saxon Chronicle.* London.

Wickenden, N., 1992. *The Temple and Other Sites in the North-Eastern Sector of Caesaromagus.* CBA, Res. Rep. **75**.

Wood, L., 1982. 'The Dorchester Peculiar, 1536–1837', *Oxfordshire Local Hist.*, **1**(5), 2–15.

Zarnecki, G., 1957. *English Romanesque Lead Sculpture.* Tiranti, London.

Index

Pages in bold are those on which illustrations appear.

South west view of the church at Dorchester. Oxfordshire, taken 1792. east.

Pl. 1. Dorchester Abbey and guest house from the south-west. Watercoloured drawing by John Carter, 1792. (Bodleian Library, University of Oxford, Gough Maps, 227, fol. 33)

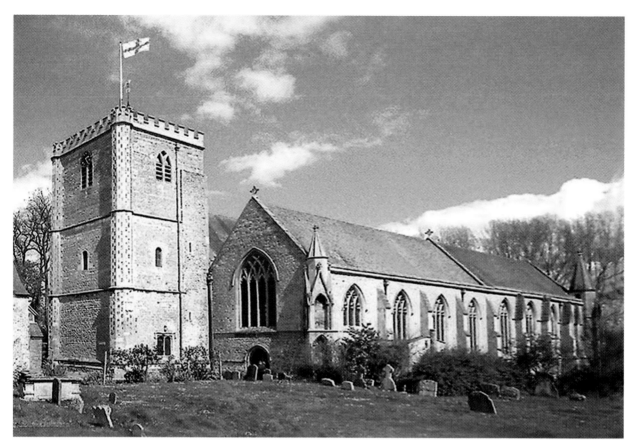

PL. 2. *The church from the south-west. (Frank Blackwell, FRPS)*

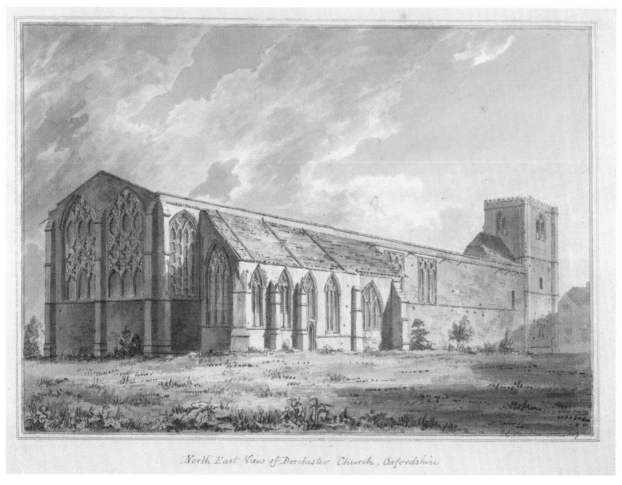

North East View of Dorchester Church, Oxfordshire

PL. 3. *The church from the north-east. Watercoloured drawing by John Chessell Buckler, 1809. (Bodleian Library, University of Oxford, MS Top. Oxon. d.66, fol. 218)*

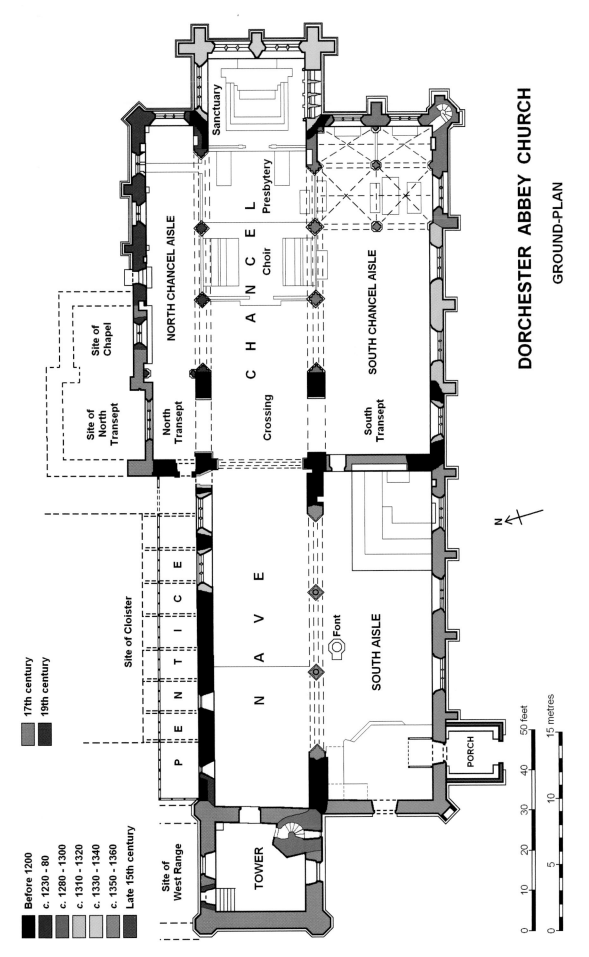

Site of West Range

TOWER

P E N T I C E

Site of Cloister

Site of North Transept

Site of Chapel

North Transept

NORTH CHANCEL AISLE

Sanctuary

N A V E

Font

SOUTH AISLE

PORCH

Crossing

C H A N C E L

Choir

Presbytery

South Transept

SOUTH CHANCEL AISLE

N

0   10   20   30   40   50 feet

0   5   10   15 metres

DORCHESTER ABBEY CHURCH

GROUND-PLAN

Pl. 4. Plan of the church, showing structural phasing. Drawn by James Bond. (Tiller, 2005)

Pl. 6. North chancel aisle: interior, looking east. (Warwick Rodwell)

Pl. 5. Chancel: interior, looking east. (Frank Blackwell, FRPS)

PL. 7. Chancel: piscina and sedilia in the south wall of the sanctuary. (Frank Blackwell, FRPS)

PL. 8 Chancel: 14th-century stained glass roundel in the sedilia, depicting the Eucharist. (John Metcalfe)

PL. 9. Chancel: 14th-century figures in stained glass and stone in the Jesse window. (Frank Blackwell, FRPS)

PL. 10. Chancel: Butterfield's restored circle in the apex of the east window, 1848. (John Metcalfe)

PL. 11. Chancel: detail of one of the angels by Michael O'Connor in the east window, 1848. (John Metcalfe)

PL. 12. *Chancel: semi-grotesque head on the central pier in the east window. (John Metcalfe)*

PL. 13. *Chancel, south arcade: head-stop representing a bishop. (John Metcalfe)*

PL. 14. *Chancel, south arcade: head-stop representing a tonsured monk. (John Metcalfe)*

PL. 15. *Chancel, south arcade: head-stop representing a hooded monk. (John Metcalfe)*

PL. 16. *Chancel: Butterfield's polychromatic tiling on the east wall, largely concealed behind the base of Scott's unfinished reredos.* (*Warwick Rodwell*)

PL. 17 (top left). Chancel: Butterfield's polychromatic stone and tile floor, and oak sanctuary chair. Scott's polychromatic dais for the high altar (lower right) overlies the earlier floor. (Warwick Rodwell)

PL. 18 (left). Chancel furnishings: double piscina in the south wall, reconstructed screen in bay 4 and Georgian altar rails. (Warwick Rodwell)

PL. 19 (above). Chancel: painted wrought iron and brass wall-bracket for holding an oil lamp, 1860s. (John Metcalfe)

PL. 20. Chancel: Purbeck marble indent for a brass of unusual form, c. 1420–40 (monument M.2). (Warwick Rodwell)

PL. 21. South chancel aisle: black marble slab containing the enamelled brass to Mary Sewell, d. 1850. (Warwick Rodwell)

Painting in the south window of the chancel, half the size of the original [from a tracing of the glass] and without the leadwork.

PL. 22. *Stained glass roundel depicting St Birinus. Watercoloured drawing by John Carter, 1792–93; made from a tracing, omitting the leading. (Bodleian Library, University of Oxford, Gough Maps, 227, fol. 47)*

PL. 23. *North chancel aisle: stained glass roundel of c. 1250, depicting the blessing of Birinus ('Bernivs') by an enthroned archbishop. (Frank Blackwell, FRPS)*

PL. 24. *South chancel aisle (Shrine Chapel):*
shrine of St Birinus, reconstructed 1964. The
gabled roof has since been removed. (Frank
Blackwell, FRPS)

PL. 25. *South chancel aisle*
(Shrine Chapel): detail of one of
the vaulted canopies of the shrine,
as restored in 1964. (Warwick
Rodwell)

PL. 26. South chancel aisle: wallpainting depicting St Christopher and the Christ Child. (Frank Blackwell, FRPS)

PL. 27. South chancel aisle: St Christopher wall painting. Detail of the Christ Child. Watercolour by Rebecca Hind. (Private collection)

PL. 28. South chancel aisle (Lady Chapel): wallpainting of the Annunciation by Clayton and Bell, 1894. View before conservation, when the wall below the dado was concealed by emulsion paint. (Warwick Rodwell)

PL. 29. Lady Chapel: the Annunciation, after conservation and retouching. (John Metcalfe)

PL. 30. *Lady Chapel: head of the archangel Gabriel, after conservation. (Ann Ballantyne)*

PL. 31. *Lady Chapel: low stone screen between the north and south chapels, 1872–73, with decoration added in 1894. Seen here after the removal of emulsion paint. (John Metcalfe)*

PL. 32. *North transept: west wall and Romanesque doorway. Rectified photograph taken in 2001, before the cloister pentice was erected. (The Downland Partnership)*

PL. 33. *Nave: eastern part of the north wall, showing the outline of an infilled Anglo-Saxon arch, pierced by a small 14th-century doorway. Rectified photograph taken in 2001, before the doorway was unblocked and the new cloister pentice erected. (The Downland Partnership)*

Pʟ. 34. *Nave: south arcade and floor of reset tombstones. View south-east. (Warwick Rodwell)*

PL. 35. *Nave: medieval mastic repair to a fractured moulding on an arcade pier. (Warwick Rodwell)*

PL. 36. *South nave aisle: medieval floor tiles reset by Scott beside the screen in bay 2. (Warwick Rodwell)*

PL. 37. *South nave aisle: glazed tiles from the Godwin factory on the altar dais. (Warwick Rodwell)*

PL. 38.   *South nave aisle: general view looking east, before conservation of the wallpainting above the altar dais. (Frank Blackwell, FRPS)*

Pʟ. 39. South nave aisle: painted altar recess associated with an upper chapel. (Warwick Rodwell)

Pʟ. 40. South nave aisle: painted reredos of the lower chapel, after conservation. (John Metcalfe)

PL. 41. *Crypt: south-west corner, showing the original window (left) and entrance (right), now blocked with soil and rubble. (Frank Blackwell, FRPS)*

PL. 42. *St John the Baptist, Burford. North-east bay of the crypt. (Warwick Rodwell)*

PL. 43. *Tower: detail of clock mechanism, 1868. (Warwick Rodwell)*

PL. 44. *Churchyard entrance: mid-20th-century watercolour of the lychgate, flanked by The Priory (left) and Lychgate Cottage (right). (Private collection)*

PL. 45. *Churchyard cross: detail showing St Peter on the restored head by Sir George Gilbert Scott, c. 1872. (Frank Blackwell, FRPS)*

PL. 46. *Cloister Gallery and lapidary display. (Frank Blackwell, FRPS)*

PL. 47. *Romanesque voussoir with beak-head ornament. Watercolour by Rebecca Hind. (Private collection)*